משה‏ ס‏[
ויבוא על משה‏[
ואשר יעקב לוא‏[
]‏ אל אהרון‏[
]ל‏ ואש והו‏[ ]אשר‏[
]לפני‏[ ]ועל כיא‏[ ]אל‏[
]אל‏ ויהי אל‏[ ]בא‏[
]ואש‏[
]אל עדת ישראל‏[

Jonah

**Hermeneia
—A Critical
and Historical
Commentary
on the Bible**

Old Testament Editorial Board

Sidnie White Crawford, University of Nebraska, chair
Paul D. Hanson, Harvard University, emeritus
Thomas Krüger, University of Zurich
Peter Machinist, Harvard University
S. Dean McBride Jr., Union Theological Seminary
   in Virginia, emeritus
Andreas Schuele, University of Leipzig
David Vanderhooft, Boston College
Molly Zahn, University of Kansas

New Testament Editorial Board

Harold W. Attridge, Yale University, chair
Adela Yarbro Collins, Yale University
Eldon Jay Epp, Case Western Reserve University
Hans-Josef Klauck, University of Chicago
AnneMarie Luijendijk, Princeton University
Laura S. Nasrallah, Harvard University

Jonah

A Commentary

by Susan Niditch

Edited by
David Vanderhooft

Fortress Press Minneapolis

**Jonah
A Commentary**

Copyright © 2023 Fortress Press, an imprint of 1517 Media

All rights reserved. Except for brief quotations in critical articles or reviews, no part of this book may be reproduced in any manner without prior written permission from the publisher. Email copyright@1517.media or write to Permissions, Fortress Press, PO Box 1209, Minneapolis, MN 55440-1209.

Scripture quotations from the New Revised Standard Version of the Bible are copyright © 1989 by the Division of Christian Education of the National Council of the Churches of Christ in the U.S.A. and are used by permission.

Cover and interior design by Kenneth Hiebert
Typesetting and page composition by
The HK Scriptorium

Print ISBN: 978-0-8006-9903-1

eISBN: 978-1-5064-8683-3

Manufactured in the U.S.A.

To Rebecca and Elizabeth

About the Author

Susan Niditch is the Samuel Green Professor of Religion at Amherst College. She was educated at Harvard University, where her teachers, Albert Bates Lord, Frank Moore Cross, Paul D. Hanson, and Isadore Twersky, deeply influenced her scholarly interests and approaches. Her areas of research and teaching include ancient Israelite literature from the perspectives of the comparative and interdisciplinary fields of folklore and oral studies; biblical ethics with special interests in war, gender, and the body; the reception history of the Bible; and the rich symbolic media of biblical ritual texts. Her most recent book is *The Responsive Self: Personal Religion in Biblical Literature of the Neo-Babylonian and Persian Periods* (AYBRL; New Haven, CT: Yale University Press, 2015). She is currently completing a new book, *Ethics in the Hebrew Bible and Beyond* (Oxford University Press, forthcoming 2023).

Endpapers

The endpapers of this Hermeneia volume show fragments 82–87 of 4QXII^g (=4Q82), originally published on Plate LIX of DJD XV. The fragments depict material from Jonah 2:3–3:3. Used with permission of the Israel Antiquities Authority. Photographer: Najib Anton Albina.

Contents
Jonah

Foreword to Hermeneia	ix
Acknowledgments	xi
Reference Codes	xiii
1. Abbreviations	xiii
2. Short Titles	xv

Introduction — 1
- Narrative Structure — 2
- Text — 4
- Linguistic Register — 5
- Jonah and the Twelve — 9
- Jonah as Holy Man and Narrative Character — 12
- Matters of Context and Authorship — 15
- Religion as Lived and Personal — 19
- Worldview and Genre — 20

■ Commentary

1:1–3 Charge and Avoidance — 27
- Translation — 27
- Textual Notes — 27
- Commentary — 27
- Overview of Jonah 1:1–3, Comparative Folklore, and Reception — 35

1:4–16 Group Punishment and Mollification — 38
- Translation — 38
- Textual Notes — 39
- Commentary — 40
- Overview of Jonah 1:4–16, Comparative Folklore, and Reception — 50

2:1–11 Individual Punishment, Petition, and Forgiveness — 53
- Translation — 53
- Textual Notes — 53
- Commentary — 54
- Overview of Jonah 2:1–11, Comparative Folklore, and Reception — 65
  - Comparative Folklore — 66
  - Appropriations — 69
  - Artistic Representations — 74
    - *Jewish Mosaics of Late Antiquity and Jonah* — 76

3:1–4 Charge and Fulfillment — 86
- Translation — 86
- Textual Notes — 86
- Commentary — 86
- Jonah 3:1–4 and Comparative Folklore — 89

3:5–10	Repentance and Forgiveness	**91**
	Translation	91
	Textual Notes	91
	Commentary	92
	Overview of Jonah 3:5–10, Rabbinic Reception, and Comparative Folklore	98
	Rabbinic Reception	98
	Animal Folklore and Jonah 3:5–10	100

4:1–5	Anger, Accusation, and Departure	**102**
	Translation	102
	Textual Notes	102
	Commentary	102
	Overview and Folk Motif	110

4:6–11	Mollification, Destruction, Anger, and Stasis	**111**
	Translation	111
	Textual Notes	111
	Commentary	112
	Overview of Jonah 4:6–11: Message and Meaning in the Narrative of Jonah	118
	Jonah beneath the Vine: Appropriation in Late Antiquity	120
	Jonah and Judaism: Yom Kippur	122

■ Back Matter

Bibliography
  1. Commentaries   125
  2. Text Editions   127
  3. General Studies   127

Indexes
  1. Passages   147
  2. Authors   152
  3. Subjects   158

Designer's Notes   161

Foreword

The name *Hermeneia,* Greek ἑρμενεία, has been chosen as the title of the commentary series to which this volume belongs. The word *Hermeneia* has a rich background in the history of biblical interpretation as a term used in the ancient Greek-speaking world for the detailed, systematic exposition of a scriptural work. It is hoped that the series, like its name, will carry forward this old and venerable tradition. A second, entirely practical reason for selecting the name lies in the desire to avoid a long descriptive title and its inevitable acronym, or worse, an unpronounceable abbreviation.

The series is designed to be a critical and historical commentary to the Bible without arbitrary limits in size or scope. It will utilize the full range of philological and historical tools, including textual criticism (often slighted in modern commentaries), the methods of the history of tradition (including genre and prosodic analysis), and the history of religion.

Hermeneia is designed for the serious student of the Bible. It will make full use of ancient Semitic and classical languages; at the same time, English translations of all comparative materials—Greek, Latin, Canaanite, or Akkadian—will be supplied alongside the citation of the source in its original language. Insofar as possible, the aim is to provide the student or scholar with full critical discussion of each problem of interpretation and with the primary data upon which the discussion is based.

Hermeneia is designed to be international and interconfessional in the selection of authors; its editorial boards were formed with this end in view. Occasionally the series will offer translations of distinguished commentaries which originally appeared in languages other than English. Published volumes of the series will be revised continually, and eventually, new commentaries will replace older works in order to preserve the currency of the series. Commentaries are also being assigned for important literary works in the categories of apocryphal and pseudepigraphical works relating to the Old and New Testaments, including some of Essene or Gnostic authorship.

The editors of *Hermeneia* impose no systematic-theological perspective upon the series (directly, or indirectly by selection of authors). It is expected that authors will struggle to lay bare the ancient meaning of a biblical work or pericope. In this way the text's human relevance should become transparent, as is always the case in competent historical discourse. However, the series eschews for itself homiletical translation of the Bible.

The editors are heavily indebted to Fortress Press for its energy and courage in taking up an expensive, long-term project, the rewards of which will accrue chiefly to the field of biblical scholarship.

The editor responsible for this volume is David Vanderhooft of Boston College.

Sidnie White Crawford *Harold W. Attridge*
For the Old Testament   For the New Testament
Editorial Board   Editorial Board

Acknowledgments

This commentary was made possible by the generous support of the Trustees of Amherst College, who provided me with two sabbatical leaves and an additional grant from the Faculty Research Award Program. I am also grateful to my students who explored Jonah with me from a variety of perspectives in courses on biblical ethics, late biblical literature, rabbinic literature, and lived religion. Their questions and comments always spur me to look at the ancient literature from new and challenging directions and I appreciate their thoughtful creativity and capacity to learn. Deepest thanks go to my dear husband of forty-six years, Robert Doran, who patiently listened to me as I would read him various paragraphs of commentary and for whom no question about the nuances of the Greek text was too dull-witted or distracting. I thank him as always for his patience, his attention to detail, and his erudition. Luiz Gustavo Assis carefully and expertly assisted in the final preparation of the manuscript for the press and my volume editor, David Vanderhooft, read the penultimate draft with sensitivity and extraordinary erudition, offering thoughtful suggestions both at the end of the process and throughout. I thank him for his friendship and support.

I dedicate this volume to our daughters, Rebecca and Elizabeth, beautiful and brilliant women of whom we are so proud.

December 20, 2020

Reference Codes

1. Abbreviations

ABG	Arbeiten zur Bibel und ihrer Geschichte	BIOSCS	*Bulletin of the International Organization for Septuagint and Cognate Studies*
ABR	*Australian Biblical Review*	BJS	Brown Judaic Studies
AGAJU	Arbeiten zur Geschichte des antiken Judentums und des Urchristentums	*BN*	*Biblische Notizen*
		BRev	*Bible Review*
		BSC	Bible Study Commentary
AIL	Ancient Israel and Its Literature	*BT*	*The Bible Translator*
AJA	*American Journal of Archaeology*	BTB	*Biblical Theology Bulletin*
AJBI	*Annual of the Japanese Biblical Institute*	*BZ*	*Biblische Zeitschrift*
		BZAW	Beihefte zur Zeitschrift für die alttestamentliche Wissenschaft
AJSR	*Association for Jewish Studies Review*	CAD	*The Assyrian Dictionary of the Oriental Institute of the University of Chicago* (21 vols.; Chicago: Oriental Institute of the University of Chicago, 1956–2011)
ANEM	Ancient Near East Monographs		
ANETS	Ancient Near Eastern Texts and Studies		
AOTC	Abingdon Old Testament Commentaries	CBC	Cambridge Bible Commentary, New English Bible
ArBib	The Aramaic Bible	*CBQ*	*Catholic Biblical Quarterly*
ATD	Das Alte Testament Deutsch	CBQMS	Catholic Biblical Quarterly Monograph Series
ATSAT	Arbeiten zu Text und Sprache im Alten Testament	CBSC	Cambridge Bible for Schools and Colleges
AUSS	*Andrews University Seminary Studies*	CHANE	Culture and History of the Ancient Near East
AYB	Anchor Yale Bible	*CJ*	*Conservative Judaism*
AYBRL	Anchor Yale Bible Reference Library	ConBOT	Coniectanea Biblica: Old Testament Series
BA	*Biblical Archaeologist*	CRC	ChiRho Commentary
BASOR	*Bulletin of the American Schools of Oriental Research*	*CritInq*	*Critical Inquiry*
BBR	*Bulletin for Biblical Research*	*CTJ*	*Calvin Theological Journal*
BCOT	Biblical Commentary on the Old Testament	DCH	David J. A. Clines, ed., *Dictionary of Classical Hebrew* (9 vols.; Sheffield: Sheffield Phoenix, 1993–2016)
BDB	Francis Brown, S. R. Driver, and Charles A. Briggs, *A Hebrew and English Lexicon of the Old Testament* (Oxford: Clarendon, 1907)		
		DD	*Dor le Dor*
BEATAJ	Beiträge zur Erforschung des Alten Testaments und des Antiken Judentums	DJD	Discoveries in the Judaean Desert
		DSB	Daily Study Bible
		EB	Expositor's Bible
BETL	*Bibliotheca ephemeridum theologicarum lovaniensium*	EBib	Etudes bibliques
		ErIsr	*Eretz-Israel*
BetM	*Bet Mikra*	*ExpTim*	*Expository Times*
BG	Biblische Gestalten	FAT	Forschungen zum Alten Testament
BHQ	Adrian Schenker et al., eds., *Biblia Hebraica Quinta* (Stuttgart: Deutsche Bibelgesellschaft, 2004–).	FFC	Folklore Fellows Communications
		GHAT	Göttinger Handkommentar zum Alten Testament
BHS	Karl Elliger and Wilhelm Rudolph, eds., *Biblia Hebraica Stuttgartensia* (Stuttgart: Deutsche Bibelgesellschaft, 1983)	GKC	Wilhelm Gesenius, *Gesenius' Hebrew Grammar* (ed. Emil Kautzsch; trans. Arthur E. Cowley; 2nd ed.; Oxford: Clarendon, 1910)
Bib	*Biblica*		
BibInt	*Biblical Interpretation*	GS	Göttingen Septuaginta
BibInt	Biblical Interpretation Series		
BibSac	*Bibliotheca Sacra*		

HALOT	Ludwig Koehler, Walter Baumgartner, and Johann J. Stamm, *The Hebrew and Aramaic Lexicon of the Old Testament* (trans. and ed. under the supervision of Mervyn E. J. Richardson; 4 vols.; Leiden: Brill, 1994–1999)	*JNSL*	*Journal of Northwest Semitic Languages*
		JOTT	*Journal of Translation and Text-linguistics*
		Joüon	Paul Joüon, *A Grammar of Biblical Hebrew* (trans. and rev. T. Muraoka; 2 vols.; Rome: Pontifical Biblical Institute, 1991)
HAR	*Hebrew Annual Review*		
HAT	Handbuch zum Alten Testament	*JPOS*	*Journal of the Palestine Oriental Society*
HBT	*Horizons in Biblical Theology*		
HS	*Hebrew Studies*	JPSBC	Jewish Publication Society Bible Commentary
HSCL	Harvard Studies in Comparative Literature	*JQR*	*Jewish Quarterly Review*
HSM	Harvard Semitic Monographs	JSJSup	Supplements to the Journal for the Study of Judaism
HSS	Harvard Semitic Studies		
HThKAT	Herders Theologischer Kommentar zum Alten Testament	*JSOT*	*Journal for the Study of the Old Testament*
HTR	*Harvard Theological Review*	JSOTSup	Journal for the Study of the Old Testament: Supplement Series
HUCA	Hebrew Union College Annual		
IB	George A. Buttrick, et al., eds., *The Interpreter's Bible* (12 vols.; New York: Abingdon, 1951–1957)	*JTS*	*Journal of Theological Studies*
		KAT	Kommentar zum alten Testament
		KHC	Kurzer Hand-Commentar zum Alten Testament
IBHS	Bruce K. Waltke and M. O'Connor, *An Introduction to Biblical Hebrew Syntax* (Winona Lake, IN: Eisenbrauns, 1990)	*LASBF*	*Liber Annus Studii Biblici Franciscani*
		LBC	Layman's Bible Commentary
ICC	International Critical Commentary	LHBOTS	Library of Hebrew Bible/Old Testament Studies
IDB	George A. Buttrick, ed., *The Interpreter's Dictionary of the Bible* (4 vols.; New York: Abingdon, 1962)	LSJ	Henry George Liddell and Robert Scott, *An Intermediate Greek-English Lexicon: Founded upon the Seventh Edition of Liddell and Scott's Greek-English Lexicon* (New York: Harper & Brothers, 1889)
IJT	*Indian Journal of Theology*		
Int	Interpretation		
ITC	International Theological Commentary	LSTS	Library of Second Temple Studies
		LitTheo	*Literature and Theology*
ITS	Indian Theological Studies	MIP	Medieval Institute Publications
IUFS	Indiana University Folklore Series	NCBC	New Collegeville Bible Commentary
JAF	*Journal of American Folklore*		
JANER	*Journal of Ancient Near Eastern Religions*	NEBAT	Die Neue Echter-Bible: Kommentar zum Alten Testament
JAOS	*Journal of the American Oriental Society*	NIB	Leander E. Keck, ed., *The New Interpreter's Bible* (12 vols.; Nashville: Abingdon, 1994–2004)
Jastrow	Marcus Jastrow, *A Dictionary of the Targumim, the Talmud Babli and Yerushalmi, and the Midrashic Literature, with an Index of Scriptural Quotations* (2 vols.; New York: Pardes, 1950)	NIBC	New International Biblical Commentary
		NICOT	New International Commentary on the Old Testament
		NIVAC	New International Version Application Commentary
JBL	*Journal of Biblical Literature*		
JBQ	*Jewish Bible Quarterly*	*NovT*	*Novum Testamentum*
JBTh	*Jahrbuch für biblische Theologie*	NSKAT	Neuer Stuttgarter Kommentar: Altes Testament
JCSMS	*Journal of the Canadian Society of Mesopotamian Studies*		
JETS	*Journal of the Evangelical Theological Society*	*NYFQ*	*New York Folklore Quarterly*
		OTE	Old Testament Essays
JHebS	*Journal of Hebrew Scriptures*	OTG	Old Testament Guides
JHS	*Journal of Hebrew Studies*	OTL	Old Testament Library
JJA	*Journal of Jewish Art*	OTM	Old Testament Message
JJS	*Journal of Jewish Studies*	*OTS*	*Old Testament Studies*
JNES	*Journal of Near Eastern Studies*	OtSt	Oudtestamentische Studiën

PAFSBSS	Publications of the American Folklore Society, Bibliographical and Special Series
PAPHS	*Proceedings of the American Philosophical Society*
PIBA	*Proceedings of the Irish Biblical Association*
PMLA	Publications of the Modern Language Association of America
PRSt	*Perspectives in Religious Studies*
PTR	*Princeton Theological Review*
RB	*Revue Biblique*
RHPR	*Revue d'histoire et de philosophie religieuses*
RRJ	*Review of Rabbinic Judaism*
SBLStBL	Society of Biblical Literature Studies in Biblical Literature
SBLSymS	Society of Biblical Literature Symposium Series
SBLTCS	Society of Biblical Literature Text-Critical Studies
SBS	Stuttgarter Bibelstudien
ScEs	*Science et Esprit*
Scrip	*Scriptura*
SCS	Septuagint Commentary Series (Brill)
SEÅ	*Svensk exegetisk årsbok*
SHBC	Smyth & Helwys Bible Commentary
SJLA	Studies in Judaism in Late Antiquity
SJOT	*Scandinavian Journal of the Old Testament*
SR	*Studies in Religion/Sciences Religieuses*
SSU	Studia Semitica Upsaliensia
SV	Skizzen und Vorarbeiten
SVC	*Studies in Visual Communication*
TDOT	G. Johannes Botterweck, Helmer Ringgren, and Heinz-Josef Fabry, eds., *Theological Dictionary of the Old Testament* (trans. John T. Willis et al.; 17 vols.; Grand Rapids: Eerdmans, 1974–2018)
TLJS	Taubman Lectures in Jewish Studies
Tradition	*Tradition: A Journal of Orthodox Jewish Thought*
TOTC	Tyndale Old Testament Commentaries
TynBul	*Tyndale Bulletin*
TZ	Theologische Zeitschrift
VT	Vetus Testamentum
VTSup	Supplements to Vetus Testamentum
WBC	Word Biblical Commentary
WeBC	Westminster Bible Companion
WUNT	Wissenschaftliche Untersuchungen zum Neuen Testament
WW	*Word and World*
ZAW	*Zeitschrift für die alttestamentliche Wissenschaft*
ZS	*Zeitschrift für Semitistik und verwandte Gebiete*

Rabbinic Writings

m.	Mishnah
m. Taʿan.	Mishnah, Tractate Taʿanit
b.	Babylonian Talmud
b. B. Bat.	Babylonian Talmud, Tractate Baba Batra
b. Ber.	Babylonian Talmud, Tractate Berakot
b. Ned.	Babylonian Talmud, Tractate Nedarim
b. Sanh.	Babylonian Talmud, Tractate Sanhendrin
b. Šabb.	Babylonian Talmud, Tractate Šabbat
b. Taʿan.	Babylonian Talmud, Tractate Taʿanit
Midrash	
Exod. Rab.	Exodus Rabbah
Gen. Rab.	Genesis Rabbah
Mek.	Mekilta

2. Short Titles

Abusch, "Jonah and God"
  Tzvi Abusch, "Jonah and God: Plants, Beasts, and Humans in the Book of Jonah (An Essay in Interpretation)," *JANER* 13 (2013) 146–52.

Achtemeier, *Minor Prophets 1*
  Elizabeth Achtemeier, *Minor Prophets 1* (NIBC; Peabody, MA: Hendrickson, 1996).

Ackerman, "Jonah"
  James S. Ackerman, "Jonah," in Robert Alter and Frank Kermode, eds., *The Literary Guide to the Bible* (Cambridge, MA: Belknap Press of Harvard University Press, 1987) 234–43.

Ackerman, "Satire and Symbolism"
  James S. Ackerman, "Satire and Symbolism in the Song of Jonah," in Baruch Halpern and Jon D. Levenson, eds., *Traditions in Transformation: Turning Points in Biblical Faith; A Festschrift Honoring Frank Moore Cross* (Winona Lake, IN: Eisenbrauns, 1982) 213–46.

Adelman, "Through the Looking Glass"
  Rachel Adelman, "Through the Looking Glass: Pirqe de-Rabbi Eliezer's Portrait of an Apocalyptic Prophet," *Journal of the Faculty of Religious Studies, McGill University* 39 (2011) 79–92.

Albertz et al., *Formation of the Book of the Twelve*
  Rainer Albertz, James D. Nogalski, and Jakob Wöhrle, eds., *Perspectives on the Formation of the Book of the Twelve: Methodological Foundations–Redactional Processes–Historical Insights* (BZAW 433; Berlin: de Gruyter, 2012).

Alexander, "Jonah: An Introduction"
: T. Desmond Alexander, "Jonah: An Introduction and Commentary," in David W. Baker, T. Desmond Alexander, and Bruce K. Waltke, *Obadiah, Jonah and Micah: An Introduction and Commentary* (TOTC 26; Downers Grove, IL: InterVarsity Press, 1988) 49–144.

Alexander, "Jonah and Genre"
: T. Desmond Alexander, "Jonah and Genre," *TynBul* 36 (1985) 35–59.

Allen, *Joel, Obadiah, Jonah, and Micah*
: Leslie C. Allen, *The Books of Joel, Obadiah, Jonah and Micah* (NICOT; Grand Rapids: Eerdmans, 1976).

Almbladh, *Studies in the Book of Jonah*
: Karin Almbladh, *Studies in the Book of Jonah* (SSU 7; Uppsala: Coronet Books, 1986).

Alter, *Strong as Death*
: Robert Alter, *Strong as Death Is Love: The Song of Songs, Ruth, Esther, Jonah, and Daniel; A Translation with Commentary* (New York: Norton, 2015).

Anderson, "Jonah's Peculiar Re-Creation"
: Joel Edmund Anderson, "Jonah's Peculiar Re-Creation," *BTB* 41 (2011) 179–88.

Antwi, *Book of Jonah*
: Emmanuel Kojo Ennin Antwi, *The Book of Jonah in the Context of Post-Exilic Theology of Israel: An Exegetical Study* (ATSAT 95; St. Ottilien: Eos, 2013).

Ballard, Stager, et al., "Iron Age Shipwrecks"
: Robert Ballard, Lawrence Stager, et al., "Iron Age Shipwrecks in Deep Water off Ashkelon, Israel," *AJA* 106 (2002) 151–68.

Barré, "Jonah 2, 9"
: Michael Barré, "Jonah 2, 9 and the Structure of Jonah's Prayer," *Bib* 72 (1991) 237–48.

Ben Zvi, *Signs of Jonah*
: Ehud Ben Zvi, *Signs of Jonah: Reading and Rereading in Ancient Yehud* (JSOTSup 367; London: Sheffield Academic Press 2003).

Berger, *Jonah in the Shadows of Eden*
: Yitzhak Berger, *Jonah in the Shadows of Eden* (Indiana Studies in Biblical Literature; Bloomington: Indiana University Press, 2016).

Bewer, "Jonah"
: Julius A. Bewer, "Jonah," in Hinckley G. T. Mitchell, John Merlin Powis Smith, and Julius A. Bewer, *A Critical and Exegetical Commentary on Haggai, Zechariah, Malachi and Jonah* (ICC 23; New York: Scribner, 1912).

Bickerman, "Les deux erreurs"
: Elias Bickerman, "Les deux erreurs du prophète Jonas," *RHPR* 45 (1965) 232–64.

Bickerman, *Four Strange Books*
: Elias Bickerman, *Four Strange Books of the Bible: Jonah, Daniel, Koheleth, Esther* (New York: Schocken, 1967).

Bolin, *Freedom beyond Forgiveness*
: Thomas M. Bolin, *Freedom beyond Forgiveness: The Book of Jonah Re-Examined* (JSOTSup 236; Sheffield: Sheffield Academic Press, 1997).

Bolin, "'Should I Not Also Pity Nineveh?'"
: Thomas M. Bolin, "'Should I Not Also Pity Nineveh?' Divine Freedom in the Book of Jonah," *JSOT* 67 (1995) 109–20.

Brenner, "Jonah's Poem"
: Athalya Brenner, "Jonah's Poem out and within Its Context," in Philip R. Davies and David J. A. Clines, eds., *Among the Prophets: Language, Image and Structure in the Prophetic Writings* (JSOTSup 144; Sheffield: Sheffield Academic Press, 1993) 183–92.

Brenner, "Linguistic Criteria"
: Athalya Brenner, "Linguistic Criteria for Dating the Book of Jonah" [in Hebrew], *BetM* 79 (1979) 395–405.

Brody, "Each Man Cried Out to His God"
: Aaron J. Brody, *"Each Man Cried Out to His God": The Specialized Religion of Canaanite and Phoenician Seafarers* (HSM 58; Atlanta: Scholars Press, 1998).

Brown, *Jonah: The Reluctant Prophet*
: Erica Brown, *Jonah: The Reluctant Prophet* (New Milford, CT: Maggid Books, 2017).

Brown, *Obadiah through Malachi*
: William P. Brown, *Obadiah through Malachi* (WeBC; Louisville: Westminster John Knox, 1996).

Bruckner, *Jonah, Nahum*
: James K. Bruckner, *Jonah, Nahum, Habakkuk, Zephaniah* (NIVAC; Grand Rapids: Zondervan, 2004).

Casson, *Ships and Seamanship*
: Lionel Casson, *Ships and Seamanship in the Ancient World* (Princeton, NJ: Princeton University Press, 1971).

Cathcart and Gordon, *Targum of the Minor Prophets*
: Kevin J. Cathcart and Robert P. Gordon, *The Targum of the Minor Prophets: Translated with a Critical Introduction, Apparatus, and Notes* (ArBib 14; Wilmington, DE: Glazier, 1989).

Christensen, "Jonah and the Sabbath Rest"
: Duane L. Christensen, "Jonah and the Sabbath Rest in the Pentateuch," in Georg Braulik, Walter Gross, and Sean McEvenue, eds., *Biblische Theologie und gesellschaftlicher Wandel: Für Norbert Lohfink SJ* (Freiburg: Herder, 1993) 48–60.

Christensen, "Narrative Poetics"
: Duane L. Christensen, "Narrative Poetics and the Interpretation of the Book of Jonah," in Elaine R. Follis, ed., *Directions in Biblical Hebrew Poetry* (JSOTSup 40; Sheffield: JSOT Press, 1987) 29–48.

Conroy, "Jonah and Nahum"
: Charles Conroy, "Jonah and Nahum in the Book of the Twelve: Who Has the Last Word?," *PIBA* I32 (2009) 1–23.

Cook and Winter, *On the Way to Nineveh*
: Stephen L. Cook and S. C. Winter, eds., *On the Way to Nineveh: Studies in Honor of George M. Landes* (ASOR Books 4; Atlanta: Scholars Press, 1999).

Cooper, "In Praise of Divine Caprice"
: Alan Cooper, "In Praise of Divine Caprice: The

Significance of the Book of Jonah," in Philip R. Davies and David J. A. Clines, eds., *Among the Prophets: Language, Image and Structure in the Prophetic Writings* (JSOTSup 144; Sheffield: JSOT Press, 1993) 144–63.

Craghan, *Esther, Judith, Tobit, Jonah, Ruth*
John F. Craghan, *Esther, Judith, Tobit, Jonah, Ruth* (OTM 16; Wilmington, DE: Glazier, 1982).

Craig, *Poetics of Jonah*
Kenneth M. Craig Jr., *A Poetics of Jonah: Art in Service of Ideology* (2nd ed.; Macon, GA: Mercer University Press, 1999).

Craigie, *Twelve Prophets*
Peter C. Craigie, *Twelve Prophets*, vol. 1: *Hosea, Joel, Amos, Obadiah, and Jonah* (DSB; Philadelphia: Westminster, 1984).

Cross, "Studies in the Structure"
Frank Moore Cross, "Studies in the Structure of Hebrew Verse: The Prosody of the Psalm in Jonah," in H. B. Huffmon, F. A. Spina, and A. R. W. Green, eds., *The Quest for the Kingdom of God: Studies in Honor of George E. Mendenhall* (Winona Lake, IN: Eisenbrauns, 1983) 159–67.

Crouch, "To Question an End"
Walter B. Crouch, "To Question an End, to End a Question: Opening the Closure of the Book of Jonah," *JSOT* 62 (1994) 101–12.

Cryer, *Divination*
Frederick H. Cryer, *Divination in Ancient Israel and Its Near Eastern Environment: A Socio-Historical Investigation* (JSOTSup 142; Sheffield: JSOT Press, 1994).

Davies and Clines, *Among the Prophets*
Philip R. Davies and David J. A. Clines, eds., *Among the Prophets: Language, Image and Structure in the Prophetic Writings* (JSOTSup 144; Sheffield: JSOT Press, 1993).

Day, "Interpretation of the Book of Jonah"
John Day, "Problems in the Interpretation of the Book of Jonah," in A. S. van der Woude, ed., *In Quest of the Past: Studies on Israelite Religion, Literature and Prophetism; Papers Read at the Joint British-Dutch Old Testament Conference, Held at Elspeet, 1988* (OtSt 26; Leiden: Brill, 1990) 32–47.

Drazin, *Unusual Bible Interpretations*
Israel Drazin, *Unusual Bible Interpretations: Jonah and Amos* (Jerusalem: Gefen, 2016).

Dreier, "JHWHs Grenzenlose Liebe"
Vjatscheslav Dreier, "JHWHs Grenzenlose Liebe: JHWH und seine Schöpfung im Jonabuch," in Manfred Oeming, ed., *Ahavah: Die Liebe Gottes im Alten Testament* (ABG 55; Leipzig: Evangelische Verlagsanstalt, 2018) 233–56.

Eynikel, "One Day"
Erik Eynikel, "One Day, Three Days, and Forty Days in the Book of Jonah," in Patrick Chatelion Counet and Ulrich Berges, eds., *One Text, A Thousand Methods: Studies in Memory of Sjef van Tilborg* (BibInt 71; Leiden: Brill, 2005) 65–76.

Ferreira, "Note on Jonah 2:8"
Johan Ferreira, "A Note on Jonah 2:8: Idolatry and Inhumanity in Israel," *BT* 63 (2012) 28–38.

Foley, *Immanent Art*
John Miles Foley, *Immanent Art: From Structure to Meaning in Traditional Oral Epic* (Bloomington: Indiana University Press, 1991).

Freedman, "Did God Play a Dirty Trick?"
David Noel Freedman, "Did God Play a Dirty Trick on Jonah at the End?," *BRev* 6 (1990) 26–31.

Fretheim, *Message of Jonah*
Terence E. Fretheim, *The Message of Jonah: A Theological Commentary* (Minneapolis: Augsburg, 1977).

Friedlander, *Pirke de Rabbi Eliezer*
Gerald Friedlander, *Pirke de Rabbi Eliezer (The Chapters of Rabbi Eliezer the Great) according to the Text of the Manuscript Belonging to Abraham Epstein of Vienna: Translated and Annotated with Introduction and Indices* (New York: Benjamin Blom, 1971).

Gaines, *Forgiveness in a Wounded World*
Janet Howe Gaines, *Forgiveness in a Wounded World: Jonah's Dilemma* (SBLStBL 5; Atlanta: Society of Biblical Literature, 2003).

Gaster, *Myth, Legend, and Custom*
Theodor H. Gaster, *Myth, Legend, and Custom in the Old Testament: A Comparative Study with Chapters from Sir James G. Frazer's Folklore in the Old Testament* (2 vols.; 1969; repr., Gloucester, MA: Peter Smith, 1981).

Gitay, "Jonah: The Prophecy of Antirhetoric"
Yehoshua Gitay, "Jonah: The Prophecy of Antirhetoric," in Astrid B. Beck et al., eds., *Fortunate the Eyes That See: Essays in Honor of David Noel Freedman in Celebration of His Seventieth Birthday* (Grand Rapids: Eerdmans, 1995) 197–206.

Golka, "Jonah"
Friedemann W. Golka, "Jonah," in George A. F. Knight and Friedemann W. Golka, eds., *Revelation of God: A Commentary on the Books of the Song of Songs and Jonah* (ITC; Grand Rapids: Eerdmans, 1988).

Good, *Irony in the Old Testament*
Edwin M. Good, *Irony in the Old Testament* (Sheffield: Almond, 1981).

Greenberg, *Biblical Prose Prayer*
Moshe Greenberg, *Biblical Prose Prayer as a Window to the Popular Religion of Ancient Israel* (TLJS 6; Berkeley: University of California Press, 1983).

Gregg, *Shared Stories*
Robert C. Gregg, *Shared Stories, Rival Tellings: Early Encounters of Jews, Christians, and Muslims* (Oxford: Oxford University Press, 2015).

Guillaume, "End of Jonah"
Philippe Guillaume, "The End of Jonah Is the Beginning of Wisdom," *Bib* 87 (2006) 243–50.

Gunn and Fewell, *Narrative in the Hebrew Bible*
David M. Gunn and Danna Nolan Fewell, *Narrative in the Hebrew Bible* (Oxford: Oxford University Press, 1993).

Hachlili, *Ancient Mosaic Pavements*
  Rachel Hachlili, *Ancient Mosaic Pavements: Themes, Issues, and Trends; Selected Studies* (Leiden: Brill, 2009).

Halpern and Friedman, "Composition and Paronomasia"
  Baruch Halpern and Richard E. Friedman, "Composition and Paronomasia in the Book of Jonah," *HAR* 4 (1980) 79-92.

Hamel, "Taking the Argo"
  Gildas Hamel, "Taking the Argo to Nineveh: Jonah and Jason in a Mediterranean Context," *Judaism* 44 (1995) 341-59.

Handy, *Jonah's World*
  Lowell K. Handy, *Jonah's World: Social Science and the Reading of Prophetic Story* (London: Equinox, 2007).

Harris, "Contextual Reading"
  Robert A. Harris, "Contextual Reading: Rabbi Eliezer of Beaugency's Commentary on Jonah," in Kathryn F. Kravitz and Diane M. Sharon, eds., *Bringing the Hidden to Light: The Process of Interpretation; Studies in Honor of Stephen A. Geller* (Winona Lake, IN: Eisenbrauns, 2007) 79-101.

Hesse and Kikawada, "Jonah and Genesis 1-11"
  E. W. Hesse and I. M. Kikawada, "Jonah and Genesis 1-11," *AJBI* 10 (1984) 3-19.

Jellinek, *Bet ha-Midrasch*
  Adolf Jellinek, ed., *Bet ha-Midrasch: Sammlung kleiner Midraschim und vermischter Abhandlungen aus der ältern jüdischen Literatur* (6 vols.; Leipzig, 1853-1877; repr., Jerusalem: Bamberger & Wahrmann, 1938).

Jensen, *Understanding Early Christian Art*
  Robin Margaret Jensen, *Understanding Early Christian Art* (London: Routledge, 2000).

Jenson, "Interpreting Jonah's God"
  Philip Peter Jenson, "Interpreting Jonah's God: Canon and Criticism," in Robert P. Gordon, ed., *The God of Israel* (Cambridge: Cambridge University Press, 2007) 229-45.

Jenson, *Obadiah, Jonah, Micah*
  Philip Peter Jenson, *Obadiah, Jonah, Micah: A Theological Commentary* (LHBOTS 496; London: T&T Clark, 2008).

Johnson, "Jonah II. 3-10"
  A. R. Jonhson, "Jonah II. 3-10: A Study in Cultic Phantasy," in H. H. Rowley, ed., *Studies in Old Testament Prophecy Presented to Theodore H. Robinson by the Society for Old Testament Study on His Sixty-fifth Birthday, August 9th, 1946* (Edinburgh: T&T Clark, 1957) 82-102.

Kadari, "Aggadic Motifs"
  Tamar Kadari, "Aggadic Motifs in the Story of Jonah: A Study of Interaction between Religions," in Alberdina Houtman et al., eds., *Religious Stories in Transformation: Conflict, Revision and Reception* (Jewish and Christian Perspectives 31; Leiden: Brill, 2016) 107-25.

Kaplan, "Archaeology and History"
  Jacob Kaplan, "The Archaeology and History of Tel Aviv-Jaffa," *BA* 35 (1972) 66-95.

Kaplan, "Jonah and Moral Agency"
  Jonathan Kaplan, "Jonah and Moral Agency," *JSOT* 43 (2019) 146-62.

Keil and Delitzsch, *Twelve Minor Prophets*
  C. F. Keil and F. Delitzsch, *The Twelve Minor Prophets* (trans. James Martin; BCOT 1; Edinburgh: T&T Clark, 1874).

Keller, "Jonas"
  Carl A. Keller, "Jonas, le portrait d'un prophète," *TZ* 21 (1965) 329-40.

Kim, "Jonah Read Intertextually"
  Hyun Chul Paul Kim, "Jonah Read Intertextually," *VT* 126 (2007) 497-528.

Knight, *Ruth and Jonah*
  George A. F. Knight, *Ruth and Jonah: Introduction and Commentary* (Torch Bible Commentaries; London: SCM Press, 1950).

Komlós, "Jonah Legends"
  Ottó Komlós, "Jonah Legends," in O. Komlós, ed., *Etudes orientales à la mémoire de Paul Hirschler* (Budapest: Allamositott, 1950) 41-61.

Kraeling, "Evolution of the Story of Jonah"
  Emil G. Kraeling, "The Evolution of the Story of Jonah," in *Hommages à André Dupont-Sommer* (Paris: Adrien-Maisonneuve, 1971) 305-18.

Kravitz and Sharon, *Bringing the Hidden to Light*
  Kathryn F. Kravitz and Diane M. Sharon, eds., *Bringing the Hidden to Light: The Process of Interpretation: Studies in Honor of Stephen A. Geller* (Winona Lake, IN: Eisenbrauns, 2007).

Kugel, *How to Read the Bible*
  James L. Kugel, *How to Read the Bible: A Guide to Scripture, Then and Now* (New York: Free Press, 2007).

LaCocque and LaCocque, *Jonah*
  André LaCocque and Pierre-Emmanuel LaCocque, *Jonah: A Psycho-Religious Approach to the Prophet* (Studies on Personalities of the Old Testament; Columbia: University of South Carolina Press, 1990).

Lanchester, *Obadiah and Jonah*
  H. C. O. Lanchester, *Obadiah and Jonah* (CBSC; Cambridge: Cambridge University Press, 1918).

Landes, "Case for the Sixth-Century"
  George M. Landes, "A Case for the Sixth-Century BCE Dating of the Book of Jonah," in Prescott H. Williams Jr. and Theodore Hiebert, eds., *Realia Dei: Essays in Archaeology and Biblical Interpretation in Honor of Edward F. Campbell, Jr. at His Retirement* (Scholars Press Homage Series 23; Atlanta: Scholars Press, 1999) 100-116.

Landes, "Kerygma"
  George M. Landes, "The Kerygma of the Book of Jonah: The Contextual Interpretation of the Jonah Psalm," *Int* 12 (1967) 3-31.

Lasine, "Jonah's Complexes"
  Stuart Lasine, "Jonah's Complexes and Our Own: Psychology and the Interpretation of Jonah," *JSOT* 41 (2017) 237–60.

Lauterbach, *Mekilta de-Rabbi Ishmael*
  Jacob Z. Lauterbach, *Mekilta de-Rabbi Ishmael* (3 vols.; 1933–1935; repr., Philadelphia: Jewish Publication Society of America, 1976).

Levine, "Place of Jonah"
  Baruch A. Levine, "The Place of Jonah in the History of Biblical Ideas," in Stephen L. Cook and S. C. Winter, eds., *On the Way to Nineveh: Studies in Honor of George M. Landes* (ASOR Books 4; Atlanta: Scholars Press, 1999) 201–17.

Limburg, *Jonah*
  James Limburg, *Jonah: A Commentary* (OTL; Louisville: Westminster John Knox, 1993).

Ling, *Ancient Mosaics*
  Roger Ling, *Ancient Mosaics* (Princeton, NJ: Princeton University Press, 1998).

Lord, *Singer of Tales*
  Albert B. Lord, *The Singer of Tales* (HSCL 24; Cambridge, MA: Harvard University Press, 1960; repr., 1988).

Magness et al., "Huqoq Excavation"
  Jodi Magness et al., "The Huqoq Excavation Project: 2014–2017 Interim Report," *BASOR* 380 (2018) 61–131.

Magonet, *Form and Meaning*
  Jonathan Magonet, *Form and Meaning: Studies in Literary Techniques in the Book of Jonah* (Bible and Literature 8; Sheffield: Almond, 1983).

de Moor, *Elusive Prophet*
  Johannes C. de Moor, ed., *The Elusive Prophet: The Prophet as a Historical Person, Literary Character and Anonymous Artist* (OtSt 45; Leiden: Brill, 2001).

Muldoon, *In Defense of Divine Justice*
  Catherine L. Muldoon, *In Defense of Divine Justice: An Intertextual Approach to the Book of Jonah* (CBQMS 47; Washington, DC: Catholic Biblical Association of America, 2010).

Mulzer, "Satzgrenzen im Jonabuch"
  Martin Mulzer, "Satzgrenzen im Jonabuch im Vergleich von hebräischer und griechischer Texttradition," *BN* 113 (2002) 61–68.

Myers, *Book of Jonah*
  Jacob M. Myers, *The Book of Hosea, the Book of Joel, the Book of Amos, the Book of Jonah* (LBC 14; Richmond, VA: John Knox, 1959).

Narkiss, "Sign of Jonah"
  Bezalel Narkiss, "The Sign of Jonah," *Gesta* 18 (1979) 63–76.

Nel, "Symbolism and Function"
  Philip J. Nel, "The Symbolism and Function of Epic Space in Jonah," *JNSL* 25 (1999) 215–24.

Neusner, *Eliezer ben Hyrcanus*
  Jacob Neusner, *Eliezer ben Hyrcanus: The Tradition and the Man* (2 vols.; SJLA 3–4; Leiden: Brill, 1973).

Niditch, *Responsive Self*
  Susan Niditch, *The Responsive Self: Personal Religion in Biblical Literature of the Neo-Babylonian and Persian Periods* (AYBRL; New Haven: Yale University Press, 2015).

Nogalski, *Book of the Twelve*
  James D. Nogalski, *The Book of the Twelve: Hosea–Jonah* (SHBC; Macon, GA: Smyth & Helwys, 2011).

Nogalski, "Intertextuality and the Twelve"
  James D. Nogalski, "Intertextuality and the Twelve," in James W. Watts and Paul R. House, eds., *Forming Prophetic Literature: Essays on Isaiah and the Twelve in Honor of John D. W. Watts* (JSOTSup 235; Sheffield: Sheffield Academic Press, 1996) 102–24.

Nowack, *Die kleinen Propheten*
  Wilhelm Nowack, *Die kleinen Propheten* (GHAT; Göttingen: Vandenhoeck & Ruprecht, 1922).

Pelli, "Literary Art of Jonah"
  Moshe Pelli, "The Literary Art of Jonah," *HS* 20/21 (1979–1980) 18–28.

Perry, "Changing God's Mind"
  T. A. Perry, "Changing God's Mind: Abraham versus Jonah," in Diana Lipton, ed., *Universalism and Particularism at Sodom and Gomorrah: Essays in Memory of Ron Pirson* (AIL 11; Atlanta: Society of Biblical Literature, 2012) 43–52.

Person, *In Conversation with Jonah*
  Raymond F. Person Jr., *In Conversation with Jonah: Conversation Analysis, Literary Criticism, and the Book of Jonah* (JSOTSup 220; Sheffield: Sheffield Academic Press, 1996).

Procksch, *Die kleinen prophetischen Schriften*
  Otto Procksch, *Die kleinen prophetischen Schriften nach dem Exil* (Stuttgart: Verlag der Vereinsbuchhandlung, 1916).

Redditt and Schart, *Thematic Threads*
  Paul L. Redditt and Aaron Schart, eds., *Thematic Threads in the Book of the Twelve* (BZAW 325; Berlin: de Gruyter, 2003).

Robinson, *Die zwölf kleinen Propheten*
  Theodore H. Robinson, *Die zwölf kleinen Propheten: Hosea bis Micha* (HAT 1/14; Tübingen: Mohr Siebeck, 1954).

Rofé, *Prophetical Stories*
  Alexander Rofé, *The Prophetical Stories: The Narratives about the Prophets in the Hebrew Bible, Their Literary Types and Their History* (Publications of the Perry Foundation for Biblical Research in the Hebrew University of Jerusalem; Jerusalem: Magnes Press, Hebrew University, 1988).

Rosenberg, "Jonah and the Prophetic Vocation"
  Joel Rosenberg, "Jonah and the Prophetic Vocation," *Response* 22 (1974) 23–26.

Russell, "Sennacherib's Lachish Narratives"
  John Malcolm Russell, "Sennacherib's Lachish Narratives," in Peter J. Holliday, ed., *Narrative and Event in Ancient Art* (Cambridge Studies in New Art History and Criticism; Cambridge: Cambridge University Press, 1993) 55–73.

Salters, *Jonah and Lamentations*
R. B. Salters, *Jonah and Lamentations* (OTG; Sheffield: JSOT Press, 1994).

Sasson, Jack M.
Jonah: A New Translation with Introduction, Commentary, and Interpretations (AB 24B; Garden City, NY: Doubleday, 1990; repr., AYB 24B; New Haven: Yale University Press, 2010).

Schart, "Jonah-Narrative"
Aaron Schart, "The Jonah-Narrative within the Book of the Twelve," in Rainer Albertz, James D. Nogalski, and Jakob Wörle, eds., *Perspectives on the Formation of the Book of the Twelve: Methodological Foundations–Redactional Processes–Historical Insights* (BZAW 433; Berlin: de Gruyter, 2012) 109–28.

Schellenberg, "Anti-Prophet among the Prophets?"
Annette Schellenberg, "An Anti-Prophet among the Prophets? On the Relationship of Jonah to Prophecy," *JSOT* 39 (2015) 353–71.

Schmidt, *Jona*
Hans Schmidt, *Jona: Eine Untersuchung zur vergleichenden Religionsgeschichte* (FRLANT 9; Göttingen: Vandenhoeck & Ruprecht, 1907).

Scholem and Schwab, "On Jonah"
Gershom Scholem and Eric J. Schwab, "On Jonah and the Concept of Justice," *CritInq* 25 (1999) 353–61.

Schöpflin, "Notschrei, Dank und Disput"
Karin Schöpflin, "Notschrei, Dank und Disput: Beten im Jonasbuch," *Bib* 78 (1997) 389–404.

Scott, "Sign of Jonah"
R. B. Y. Scott, "The Sign of Jonah," *Int* 19 (1965) 16–25.

Seidler, "'Fasting,' 'Sackcloth'"
Ayelet Seidler, "'Fasting,' 'Sackcloth,' and 'Ashes': From Nineveh to Shushan," *VT* 69 (2019) 117–34.

Shemesh, "'And Many Beasts'"
Yael Shemesh, "'And Many Beasts' (Jonah 4:11): The Function and Status of Animals in the Book of Jonah," *JHebS* 10 (2010) 2–26.

Sherwood, *Biblical Text and Its Afterlives*
Yvonne Sherwood, *A Biblical Text and Its Afterlives: The Survival of Jonah in Western Culture* (Cambridge: Cambridge University Press, 2000).

Sherwood, "Cross-Currents"
Yvonne Sherwood, "Cross-Currents in the Book of Jonah: Some Jewish and Cultural Midrashim on a Traditional Text," *BibInt* 6 (1998) 49–79.

Simon, *Jonah*
Uriel Simon, *Jonah* יונה: *The Traditional Hebrew Text with the New JPS Translation* (JPSBC; Philadelphia: Jewish Publication Society of America, 1999).

Smart, "Book of Jonah"
James D. Smart, "The Book of Jonah," *IB* 6:875–94.

Spier, *Picturing the Bible*
Jeffrey Spier, ed., *Picturing the Bible: The Earliest Christian Art* (Fort Worth, TX: Kimbell Art Museum, 2007).

Strack and Stemberger, *Introduction to the Talmud and Midrash*
H. L. Strack and Günter Stemberger, *Introduction to the Talmud and Midrash* (trans. and ed. Markus Bockmuehl; Minneapolis: Fortress Press, 1992).

Strawn, "Jonah's Sailors"
Brent A. Strawn, "Jonah's Sailors and Their Lot Casting: A Rhetorical-Critical Observation," *Bib* 91 (2010) 66–76.

Strawn, "On Vomiting"
Brent A. Strawn, "On Vomiting: Leviticus, Jonah, Ea(a)rth," *CBQ* 74 (2012) 445–64.

Struppe, *Die Bücher Obadja, Jona*
Ursula Struppe, *Die Bücher Obadja, Jona* (NSKAT 24.1; Stuttgart: Katholisches Bibelwerk, 1996).

Stuart, *Hosea–Jonah*
Douglas Stuart, *Hosea–Jonah* (WBC 31; Waco, TX: Word Books, 1987).

Sweeney, "Synchronic and Diachronic"
Marvin A. Sweeney, "Synchronic and Diachronic Concerns in Reading the Book of the Twelve Prophets," in Rainer Albertz, James D. Nogalski, and Jakob Wöhrle, eds., *Perspectives on the Formation of the Book of the Twelve: Methodological Foundations–Redactional Processes–Historical Insights* (BZAW 433; Berlin: de Gruyter, 2012) 21–34.

Sweeney, *Twelve Prophets*
Marvin A. Sweeney, *The Twelve Prophets* (2 vols.; Berit Olam; Collegeville, MN: Liturgical Press, 2000).

Thompson, *Motif Index*
The Motif-Index of Folk Literature (6 vols.; Bloomington: Indiana University Press, 1955–1958).

Tigay, "Days of Awe"
Jeffrey Tigay, "The Book of Jonah and the Days of Awe," *CJ* 38 (1985–1986) 67–76.

Trépanier, "Story of Jonas"
Benoit Trépanier, "The Story of Jonas," *CBQ* 13 (1951) 8–16.

Trible, "Book of Jonah"
Phyllis Trible, "The Book of Jonah: Introduction, Commentary, and Reflections," *NIB* 7:463–529.

Trible, *Rhetorical Criticism*
Phyllis Trible, *Rhetorical Criticism: Context, Method, and the Book of Jonah* (Guides to Biblical Scholarship: Old Testament; Minneapolis: Fortress Press, 1994).

Trible, "Studies in the Book of Jonah"
Phyllis Lou Trible, "Studies in the Book of Jonah" (PhD diss., Columbia University, 1963).

Tucker, *Jonah*
W. Dennis Tucker Jr., *Jonah: A Handbook on the Hebrew Text* (rev. and expanded ed.; Waco, TX: Baylor University Press, 2017).

Van Hoonacker, *Les douze Petits Prophètes*
A. Van Hoonacker, *Les douze Petits Prophètes* (EBib; Paris: Gabalda, 1908).

Vawter, *Job & Jonah*
  Bruce Vawter, *Job & Jonah: Questioning the Hidden God* (New York: Paulist Press, 1983).

Wade, *Books of the Prophets*
  G. W. Wade, *The Books of the Prophets Micah, Obadiah, Joel and Jonah* (London: Methuen, 1925).

Walsh, "Between Text and Sermon"
  Carey Walsh, "Between Text and Sermon: Jonah 3," *Int* 69 (2015) 338–40.

Walton, "Jonah"
  John H. Walton, "Jonah," in Bryan Beyer and John H. Walton, *Obadiah, Jonah* (BSC; Grand Rapids: Zondervan, 1982) 11–81.

Walton, "Object Lesson"
  John H. Walton, "The Object Lesson of Jonah 4:5–7 and the Purpose of the Book of Jonah," *BBR* 2 (1992) 47–57.

Watts, *Books*
  John D. W. Watts, *The Books of Joel, Obadiah, Jonah, Nahum, Habakkuk, and Zephaniah* (Cambridge: Cambridge University Press, 1975).

Watts and House, *Forming Prophetic Literature*
  James W. Watts and Paul R. House, eds., *Forming Prophetic Literature: Essays on Isaiah and the Twelve in Honor of John D. W. Watts* (JSOTSup 235; Sheffield: Sheffield Academic Press, 1996).

Weber, *Jona*
  Beat Weber, *Jona: Der widerspenstige Prophet und der gnädige Gott* (BG; Leipzig: Evangelische Verlagsanstalt, 2016).

Weimar, *Jona*
  Peter Weimar, *Jona* (HThKAT; Freiburg im Breisgau: Herder, 1917).

Van Wijk-Bos, "No Small Thing"
  Johanna W. H. van Wijk-Bos, "No Small Thing: 'The Overturning' of Nineveh in the Third Chapter of Jonah," in Stephen L. Cook and S. C. Winter, *On the Way to Nineveh: Studies in Honor of George M. Landes* (ASOR Books 4; Atlanta: Scholars Press, 1999) 218–38.

van Wijk-Bos, *Ruth, Esther, Jonah*
  Johanna W. H. van Wijk-Bos, *Ruth, Esther, Jonah* (Knox Preaching Guides; Atlanta: John Knox Press, 1986).

Wilson, "Jonah in the Biblical Tradition"
  Robert R. Wilson, "Jonah in the Biblical Tradition," *Reflection* 76 (1978) 6–8.

Wöhrle, "So Many Cross-References!"
  Jacob Wöhrle, "So Many Cross-References! Methodological Reflections on the Problem of Intertextual Relationships and Their Significance for Redactional Analysis," in Rainer Albertz, James D. Nogalski, and Jakob Wöhrle, eds., *Perspectives on the Formation of the Book of the Twelve: Methodological Foundations–Redactional Processes–Historical Insights* (BZAW 433; Berlin: de Gruyter, 2012) 3–20.

Wolff, *Obadiah and Jonah*
  Hans Walter Wolff, *Obadiah and Jonah: A Commentary* (trans. Margaret Kohl; Minneapolis: Augsburg, 1986).

Wolff, *Studien zum Jonabuch*
  Hans Walter Wolff, *Studien zum Jonabuch: Mit einem Anhang von Jörg Jeremias*. Neukirchen-Vluyn: Neukirchener Verlag, 2003.

Zimmermann, "Problems and Solutions"
  Frank Zimmermann, "Problems and Solutions in the Book of Jonah," *Judaism* 40 (1991) 580–89.

Zlotowitz and Scherman, *Sefer Yonah/Jonah*
  Meir Zlotowitz and Nosson Scherman, *Sefer Yonah/Jonah: A New Translation with a Commentary Anthologized from Talmudic, Midrashic and Rabbinic Sources* (Brooklyn, NY: Mesorah, 1978).

Introduction

The book of Jonah is an unusual and intriguing composition, preserved in the corpus of the so-called Minor Prophets. The book contains only one brief oracle at 1:2, repeated at 3:2, a directive from the deity Yahweh to Jonah concerning Nineveh. Moreover, Jonah himself is an unexpected sort of prophetic figure who runs away immediately after receiving his first commission. Jonah is a petulant prophet who openly expresses frustration with and anger toward God. He is pouting and acerbic. Those he is charged to warn are not only foreigners but, more specifically, Assyrians of Nineveh. On the one hand, Nineveh is a quintessentially magnificent ancient metropolis whose status and power rise in one century and fall in the next. The Assyrians, however, are also Israel's archetypal enemies and oppressors, those who conquered the northern kingdom in 721 BCE, exiling its elites. This traumatic event in the history of Israel becomes a symbol of utter defeat and devastation in the biblical corpus and in the wider ancient Levant, as seen, for example, in the Assyrians' own iconic representation of the Judeans' experience of military and political ruin in the propagandistic reliefs that adorned Sennacherib's palace in Nineveh. Judeans, the residents of Lachish, defeated during the Assyrian campaigns of the late eighth century BCE, are shown subjected to forced marches into exile; some kneel in subservience about to be slaughtered by Assyrian weapons, and others have been flayed.[1] These are the enemies whom Jonah must warn about a coming cataclysm and save. The story of Jonah, moreover, is rich in folk motifs—the gigantic fish who swallows Jonah, the magical plant that suddenly sprouts to provide shade, and the attribution of human characteristics to animals. At the same time, much in this little four-chapter work looks familiar to the reader of biblical literature, for example, the call to the prophet; the power of the deity manifested in sea and storm; the lament from the watery Deep; the prophet's intimacy with the deity, and even his despondency; the concern with sin and repentance; and divine punishment and forgiveness.

The present volume provides a new translation of Jonah and a detailed commentary, line by line and section by section, that seeks to explore the nature of this work, its texture, content, meaning, messages, and contexts, both literary and sociohistorical. I will ask what is unique and what is conventional about this work within the anthology of the Hebrew Bible but will also explore within certain parameters the rich afterlife of Jonah, for this work has been cherished and recontextualized in Jewish and Christian verbal and nonverbal traditions.

The introductory discussion that precedes and prepares for the close work treats the following interrelated topics, which will inform the analysis throughout: the story, its structure and key scenes with attention to the traditional motifs that an author employs to build a story; the textual and manuscript traditions in which are preserved variations and continuities in content and expression; the language in which this story is expressed, its register and related questions concerning genre, tone, date, and links with the wider biblical tradition; the literary context of Jonah in biblical tradition, its place among the Twelve, and questions concerning intertextuality; comparisons between Jonah and other biblical prophets, with an emphasis on characterization and the nature of prophetic literature; the religious dimension, ways in which Jonah exemplifies qualities of personal religion; questions concerning sociohistorical context and worldview of the writer and intended audience, meaning and message; and Jonah and its reception history, case studies in the afterlife of Jonah.[2]

---

1   See David Ussishkin, *The Conquest of Lachish by Sennacherib* (Publications of the Institute of Archaeology 6; Tel Aviv: Tel Aviv University, Institute of Archaeology, 1982); John Malcolm Russell, "Sennacherib's Lachish Narratives," in Peter J. Holliday, ed., *Narrative and Event in Ancient Art* (Cambridge Studies in New Art History and Criticism; Cambridge: Cambridge University Press, 1993) 55–73.

2   For overviews of major directions in Jonah scholarship in the twentieth century, see two essays by Claude Lichtert: "Un siècle de recherche à propos de 'Jonas': (1re partie)," *RB* 112 (2005) 192–214; and "Un siècle de recherche à propos de 'Jonas': (2e partie)," *RB* 112 (2005) 330–54; and Jörg Jeremias, "Das Jonabuch in der Forschung seit Hans Walter Wolff," in Hans Walter Wolff, *Studien zum Jonabuch: Mit einem Anhang von Jörg Jeremias*, by Hans Walter Wolff (Neukirchen-Vluyn: Neukirchener Verlag, 2003; original without appendix by Jeremias, 1965) 93–128.

Narrative Structure

A first challenge is to outline the structure of the book of Jonah, the better to gain a sense of the storyteller's craft, his sense of story, and in turn to understand ways in which subsequent writers in the tradition have chosen to develop key scenes in various media. Attention to narrative structure also contributes to the framework of this commentary, its layout and analysis.

In contrast to each of the other "Twelve Minor Prophets," the biblical collection to which Jonah has been assigned by ancient collators, Jonah reads as a story composed of a series of interlocking sets of motifs that constitute key segments of plot. The Russian formalist Vladimir Propp employs the term "moves" to delineate such narrative segments, each of which is a whole that leads to the next move.[3] Each move in Jonah involves an action and a reaction or reactions, and often the reaction functions as a new action to which a character or characters respond, and so the story proceeds until its enigmatic conclusion.[4]

---

[3] Vladimir Propp, *Morphology of the Folktale* (2nd ed.; rev. and ed. Louis A. Wagner; Publications of the American Folklore Society, Bibliographical and Special Series 9; Austin: University of Texas Press, 1968; Russian original, 1928).

[4] For seven-part structural maps of Jonah, see Uriel Simon, *Jonah* יונה: *The Traditional Hebrew Text with the New JPS Translation* (JPSBC; Philadelphia: Jewish Publication Society, 1999) xxv; James Limburg, *Jonah: A Commentary* (OTL; Louisville: Westminster John Knox, 1993) 38; Peter Weimar, *Jona* (HThKAT; Freiburg im Breisgau: Herder, 1917); Beat Weber, *Jona: Der widerspenstige Prophet und der gnädige Gott* (BG 27; Leipzig: Evangelische Verlagsanstalt, 2016) 38. Weber also points to a two-part structure in Jonah 1–2 and Jonah 3–4 contrasting "sea" with "land." On the significance of a seven-part structure, see also Vjatscheslav Dreier, "JHWHs Grenzenlose Liebe: JHWH und seine Schöpfung im Jonabuch," in Manfred Oeming, ed., *Ahavah: Die Liebe Gottes im Alten Testament* (ABG 55; Leipzig: Evangelische Verlagsanstalt, 2018) 233–56, here 241–42; and David A. Dorsey, who also emphasizes chiasms and repetitions as they relate to key messages of Jonah ("Literary Architecture and Meaning in the Book of Jonah," in David Merling, ed., *To Understand the Scriptures: Essays in Honor of William H. Shea* (Berrien Springs, MI: Institute of Archaeology, Siegfried H. Horn Archaeological Museum, Andrews University, 1997) 57–69.

For an approach to the structure of Jonah in acts and scenes, see John D. W. Watts, *The Books of Joel, Obadiah, Jonah, Nahum, Habakkuk, and Zephaniah* (CBC; Cambridge: Cambridge University Press, 1975) 75–97; for the delineation of five scenes rather than seven, see Carl A. Keller, "Jonas, le portrait d'un prophète," *TZ* 21 (1965): 330–34; Janet Howe Gaines, *Forgiveness in a Wounded World: Jonah's Dilemma* (SBLStBL 5; Atlanta: Society of Biblical Literature, 2003) 27, 29; and Wolff, *Studien zum Jonabuch*, 84–89.

Concerning the structure of content in Jonah and its implications, see also Jack M. Sasson, *Jonah: A New Translation with Introduction, Commentary, and Interpretations* (AB 24B; Garden City, NY: Doubleday, 1990; repr., AYB 24B; New Haven: Yale University Press, 2010) 16–20; Walter B. Crouch, "To Question an End, to End a Question: Opening the Closure of the Book of Jonah," *JSOT* 62 (1994) 102–12; Steven L. McKenzie, "The Genre of Jonah," in Mark A. O'Brien and Howard N. Wallace, eds., *Seeing Signals, Reading Signs: The Art of Exegesis; Studies in Honour of Antony F. Campbell, SJ for His Seventieth Birthday* (JSOTSup 415; London: T&T Clark, 2004) 159–71, here 160; and T. Desmond Alexander, "Jonah: An Introduction and Commentary," in David W. Baker, T. Desmond Alexander, and Bruce K. Waltke, *Obadiah, Jonah and Micah: An Introduction and Commentary* (TOTC 26; Downers Grove, IL: InterVarsity Press, 1988) 68–75.

For an application of conversation analysis as an exegetical technique with implications for an understanding of the structure of Jonah and the thematic orientation of its author, see Raymond F. Person Jr., *Conversation with Jonah: Conversation Analysis, Literary Criticism, and the Book of Jonah* (JSOTSup 220; Sheffield: Sheffield Academic Press, 1996); on structure and dialogue, see Terence E. Fretheim, *The Message of Jonah: A Theological Commentary* (Minneapolis: Augsburg, 1977) 55, 117–18. For a recent commentary, see Kevin J. Youngblood, *Jonah: God's Scandalous Mercy* (Grand Rapids: Zondervan, 2013). Also attuned to matters of structure and varieties of discourse, John W. Roffey attempts to identify the roles of "prophetic, narrative, and wisdom discourse" in Jonah ("God's Truth, Jonah's Fish: Structure and Existence in the Book of Jonah," *ABR* 36 [1988] 1–18). See also Brent A. Strawn ("Jonah's Sailors and Their Lot Casting: A Rhetorical-Critical Observation," *Bib* 91 [2010] 66–76, here 67), who builds on Phyllis Trible's work on the structure of Jonah (Trible,

1. Charge and Avoidance
An opening call to Jonah by Yhwh (action) evokes Jonah's response of fleeing to the sea (reaction). The prophet takes passage on a ship bound for Tarshish to escape rather than cry out against Nineveh in accordance with the deity's wishes (1:1–3).[5]

2. Group Punishment and Mollification
God responds with a storm (action), and the sailors are persuaded by their passenger Jonah to throw him, the recalcitrant prophet, overboard lest they all die (reaction) (1:4–16).

3. Individual Punishment, Petition, and Forgiveness
Jonah is swallowed by a fish (action) and responds with a prayer (reaction). This reaction serves as a new action that motivates the deity to have the fish vomit Jonah up onto the shore (reaction) (2:1–11).

4. Charge and Fulfillment
A second time God orders Jonah to Nineveh (action) and this time the prophet goes as ordered and warns the Ninevites of their city's impending doom (reaction) (3:1–4).

5. Repentance and Forgiveness
The Ninevites respond with repentance, an action that is also a reaction, and the deity responds by rescinding the judgment he had planned against them (3:5–10).

6. Anger, Accusation, and Departure
Jonah responds with anger (action/reaction) and asks to die, exiting the city and sitting in a hut he has built, waiting to see what will happen to the city (action/reaction) (4:1–5).

7. Mollification, Destruction, Anger, and Stasis
God creates a bush to shade the prophet from the sun (action), and Jonah responds with relief (reaction). The deity, however, causes a worm to kill the bush and intensifies the sun's heat (action), Jonah becomes angry, again wishing to die (reaction), and the deity responds to Jonah, emphasizing the importance of saving life. Here the story ends; there is no subsequent action or reaction (4:6–11).

Critical pieces in this tale of Jonah thus include the divine charge and Jonah's fleeing; Jonah's punishment by storm and being cast into the sea; being swallowed by a fish, lamenting, being vomited up; Jonah's second charge and journey to Nineveh; repentance of Ninevites, relenting by deity, and prophet's anger with a second flight to the outskirts of city; growth of the shade plant and Jonah's relief; the plant's death and Jonah's anger; response of deity.[6] One can already anticipate the scenes and imagery that will engage later artists. How might one illustrate the angry sea? What does the fish look like? What sort of plant shades the prophet?

Some of these motifs are typical of plots in traditional literature: emphasis on journeys;[7] confrontation with a life-threatening situation or character; rescue by a helper who is also an antagonist. Versions of these components are found in a wide array of folk traditions, in which they contribute to various plots and media: the runaway

---

Rhetorical Criticism, Appendix, 237–44). Building on the work of E. W. Hesse and I. M. Kikawada ("Jonah and Genesis 1–11," *AJBI* 10 [1984] 3–19), Duane L. Christensen draws connections between patterns of content in Jonah and those of Genesis 1–11 ("Jonah and the Sabbath Rest in the Pentateuch," in Georg Braulik, Walter Gross, and Sean McEvenue, eds., *Biblische Theologie und gesellschaftlicher Wandel: Für Norbert Lohfink SJ* [Freiburg: Herder, 1993] 48–60, here 49–50).

5 David J. Downs treats Jonah's flight as the first in a series of additional exiles (in the sea; in the fish; in Nineveh; and east of the city) that capture the tone and message of the narrative and point to its postexilic author's engagement with themes of banishment and return ("The Specter of Exile in the Story of Jonah," *HBT* 31 [2009] 27–44).

6 For insightful comments on a number of these recurring motifs in ancient Mediterranean literature, see Wolff, *Studien zum Jonabuch*, 21–28.

7 Janet Howe Gaines describes Jonah as "journey literature" and points to themes of quest and initiation while drawing interesting comparisons with classic novels including *Huckleberry Finn* and *Moby Dick* (*Forgiveness in a Wounded World*, 11, 65).

servant; death takes a holiday; the sea-monster; the journey to the land of the dead and return.[8]

The specification of these motifs in Jonah reflects particular prophetic and Israelite orientations:

- the antagonist and rescuer is the deity Yahweh
- the journey is motivated by a divine call to the prophet, which the prophet either avoids or complies with
- the call is associated with the related message about obedience and disobedience, sin and forgiveness, that frames the narrative as a whole
- the power of the deity emerges in the storm, the sea, and the wider divine capacity to kill and revivify
- when threatened with death, the hero engages in a lament
- the deity performs a kind of parable involving the plant to make a point about choosing life over death.

Like other biblical characters, Jonah actually seeks to die at some points and engages in intimate and emotional verbal exchanges with the deity.[9] Some of the motifs are striking in their evocation of contemporary concerns, for example, the interest in the well-being of animal and plant life as integral and parallel to human well-being.

All of the motifs and patterns discussed above, their connections with worldwide folk literature, their links to the Israelite-specific literary tradition, and their continuing relevance to contemporary readers will be treated in the detailed commentary sections to follow that reflect Jonah's structural narrative building blocks. First it is critical to ask more basic questions about the very words and language in which content is conveyed.

Text

Scholars working on biblical literature and other classical Jewish texts have available to them various manuscript traditions that often reflect textual differences. Such variations may result from scribal or copying errors that enter a shared tradition, or they may reflect additions or deletions of a more compositional nature. Textual variants may reflect different versions of narratives, oracles, other biblical passages, or versions of larger books that coexisted. Such variant traditions may have circulated in different ancient Jewish communities or been preserved by the same community. For example, the Qumran covenanters composed and preserved ancient religious texts at the turn of the eras and accepted and appreciated multiplicity and variation within the received tradition. Variant readings may be the result of or be reflected in the translation process, for some textual variants can be detected only in ancient translations of Hebrew texts that are now lost. What is interesting about Jonah, however, is the continuity of manuscript traditions, that is, the absence of extensive variation between the Hebrew version and other manuscript traditions, in contrast to the versions of many other biblical works.[10] There is relatively little difference among the ancient Hebrew manuscripts. Those preserved in the Middle Ages are largely the same as the second-century CE texts found at Wadi Murabbaʿât (Mur) about fifteen kilometers south of Khirbet Qumran.[11] These versions diverge in only minor ways from the portions of Jonah found among manuscripts of the Dead Sea Scrolls stored at Qumran and predating the Common Era (4QXII^a [4Q76], ca. 150–125 BCE; 4QXII^f [4Q81], ca. 50 BCE; 4QXII^g [4Q82], ca. last third of the first century BCE).[12] Similarly, the Greek witnesses to the text (G and

---

8   For observations concerning traditional motifs in connection with a comparative study of Jonah and the Argonautica, see Gildas Hamel, "Taking the Argo to Nineveh: Jonah and Jason in a Mediterranean Context," *Judaism* 44 (1995) 341–59, here 343–44.

9   With an interest in Jonah's genre as short story, Lowell K. Handy offers a list of typical characteristics of the genre as understood by him and a subset of elements that characterize biblical short stories (*Jonah's World: Social Science and the Reading of Prophetic Story* [Bible World; London: Equinox, 2007] 113–14).

10 For a nice case study exploring the possible significance for meaning and message of some variations that are evidenced in the Septuagint and Masoretic traditions, see Larry Perkins, "The Septuagint of Jonah: Aspects of Literary Analysis Applied to Biblical Translation," *BIOSCS* 20 (1987) 43–53.

11 P. Benoit, J. T. Milik, and R. de Vaux, *Les Grottes de Murabbaʿât* (2 vols.; DJD 2; Oxford: Clarendon, 1961) 1:190–92.

12 Eugene Ulrich, Frank Moore Cross, and Russell E. Fuller, *Qumran Cave 4.X: The Prophets* (DJD 15; Oxford: Clarendon, 1997) 229–32, 268–70, 309–13. The manuscripts of the Twelve were edited by Russell E. Fuller.

the first-century Greek text from Naḥal Ḥever)[13] display continuity with the Hebrew (MT, Mur), rather than the transmission of variant versions. The same applies to the Vulgate (Vg) and earlier Old Latin (OL). Therefore, while the notes that precede each commentary section do take stock of differences, nuances, translation choices, and their implications, the impression that emerges is not one of strongly variant traditions. The text-critical notes that accompany each portion of Jonah frequently reveal the translators' aesthetics or the theological choices of ancient translators rather than work with a different text and variant readings. Nor do these textual traditions reveal an effort to make sense of textual problems that obscure meaning.

In contrast to Greek and Latin manuscript traditions, the Syriac and Aramaic versions of Jonah partake in a genre of translation and transmission in which framing, interpretation, and elaboration are expected and transformative, reflecting the worldview of early precursors to midrashists.[14] These examples of Aramaic refashioning of the text will be discussed where relevant in the text-critical notes, as a preliminary way of exploring reception history in brief, for they reflect the worldviews of their authors more than textual variations, reception rather than recension.

The work on textual variation in Jonah that follows rests on the shoulders of several colleagues: Phyllis Trible's careful study of the text of Jonah; Jack Sasson's Anchor Bible commentary, in which he acknowledges Trible's contribution while thoughtfully indicating the ways that textual variation influences his own translation; the studies of Karin Almbladh; and the useful notes to the Book of the Twelve Prophets prepared by Anthony Gelston for the Quinta edition of the Biblica Hebraica (BHQ).[15] Gelston's text is based on the Masoretic Hebrew manuscript of the Twelve Prophets held in the National Library at St. Petersberg and includes additional references to the Tiberian manuscripts, the Aleppo Codex, and the Cairo Codex. A pre-Masoretic tradition of Jonah is also included in the notes of BHQ (Mur 88). The Old Greek witness to Jonah (G) as well as other ancient readings preserved in Greek are found in the Göttingen edition,[16] consulted by Gelston and this commentary. An additional manuscript to consider is the Greek translation of a version of Jonah found at Naḥal Ḥever and dating to no later than the second century CE, a text that generally agrees with the MT. The Old Latin (OL) and the Vulgate (Vg.) are also referenced in BHQ and in the notes in this volume when interesting textual variations or nuances are in evidence. An edition of the Old Latin as compiled from available OL sources is provided in a study by W. O. E. Oesterley, which has also been consulted.[17] The targumic text (Tg.) employed is that of Alexander Sperber,[18] supplemented by the excellent apparatus and notes in Kevin Cathcart and Robert Gordon's translation and the study by Étan Levine.[19] The Peshitta (S) is the text prepared by George A. Kiraz and Joseph Bali.[20]

Linguistic Register

The lack of variation among the textual traditions may well be due to the textural nature of the piece of litera-

---

13 Emanuel Tov, *The Greek Minor Prophets Scroll from Naḥal Ḥever (8ḤevXIIgr)* (Seiyâl Collection 1; DJD 8; Oxford: Clarendon, 1990).

14 See the discussion by Étan Levine, *The Aramaic Version of Jonah* (Jerusalem: Jerusalem Academic Press, 1975) 12–17.

15 Phyllis Lou Trible, "Studies in the Book of Jonah" (PhD diss., Columbia University, 1963) 30–33; Sasson, *Jonah*; Karin Almbladh, *Studies in the Book of Jonah* (SSU 7; Uppsala: Coronet Books, 1986); Anthony Gelston, ed., *The Twelve Minor Prophets* (BHQ 13; Stuttgart: Deutsche Bibelgesellschaft, 2010).

16 Joseph Ziegler, ed., *Duodecim prophetae* (GS 13; Göttingen: Vandenhoeck & Ruprecht, 1967).

17 W. O. E. Oesterley, "The Old Latin Texts of the Minor Prophets. III," *JTS* 5 (1904) 378–86.

18 Alexander Sperber, ed., *The Bible in Aramaic: Based on Old Manuscripts and Printed Texts,* vol. 3: *The Latter Prophets according to Targum Jonathan* (Leiden: Brill, 1992).

19 Kevin J. Cathcart and Robert P. Gordon, *The Targum of the Minor Prophets: Translated with a Critical Introduction, Apparatus, and Notes* (ArBib 14; Wilmington, DE: Glazier, 1989); Étan Levine, *The Aramaic Version of the Bible: Contents and Context* (BZAW 174; Berlin: de Gruyter, 1988).

20 George A. Kiraz and Joseph Bali, eds., and Donald M. Walter, trans., *The Syriac Peshitta Bible with English Translation: The Twelve Prophets* (Piscataway, NJ: Gorgias Press, 2012).

ture that is Jonah, its author's very language and style of expression. This is a work of carefully chosen but restricted vocabulary, a work characterized by simplicity, repetition, and participation in a traditional-style Israelite medium that employs formulaic expressions and ways to describe certain pieces of content within a narrative context.[21] These choices in expression alert the receiver of this tale, ancient or modern, to the narrative's vital concerns and major themes.

A key root found throughout Jonah, for example, is the Hebrew root "to be bad" or in a noun form "badness" (רעע), often translated, depending on context, as "calamity" or "wrongdoing." To be faithful to the Hebrew, I consistently employ "evil" as my translation of the words related to this root. One can argue, in fact, that even seemingly chance experiences of disaster in the ancient world were perceived not as random occurrences but as payback from the gods, recrimination for insults to the deity or deities, divine wrath in response to actions about which one might even be unaware. Death itself is not a random occurrence. In any event, calamity is also experienced as evil to the sufferer himself or herself. The translation "evil" thus seems apt on many levels.[22]

Other significant recurring terms include: "to go down" (ירד), "to go" (בוא), "to fear" (ירא), "to hurl" (טול), "deep sleep" (תרדמה), "sea" (ים), "to be angry" (חרה), "great" (גדול), "to appoint" (מנה).[23] Longer formulas are found describing the deity's compassion (3:9; 4:2), the prophet's depression (4:3, 8), and the sea's stormy condition (1:11; 13). Variants concerning divine compassion (Exod 34:6; Joel 2:12-14; Mic 7:18-20; Nah 1:2b, 3a; Mal 1:9a) and the sailors' inquiry about Jonah's origins and background (Jonah 1:8; Gen 24:23-24; 29:4; 42:7; Judg 19:17) offer good examples of traditional language used with variation throughout the Hebrew Bible. Similarly, Jonah's lament is composed in familiar imagery and formula patterns as befits traditional-style material, which any audience would recognize and to which composers have extemporaneous access.[24] These recurring words, turns of phrase, and formulas underscore critical emotions, plot actions, and themes in Jonah, linking this narrative to the wider tradition and culture.

---

21 For a brief discussion of style in Jonah (including the use of repetition and variation) as it relates to the work's simplicity in form and depth in meaning, see James E. Robson, "Undercurrents in Jonah," *TynBul* 64 (2013) 189-215. On the varieties of repetition in Jonah and the significance of repeated language for the creation of key themes, see Timothy L. Wilt, "Lexical Repetition in Jonah," *JOTT* 5 (1992) 252-64.

22 See the discussion of "evil" and other key terms in Fretheim, *Message of Jonah*, 40-50; and the excursus on רעע by Friedemann W. Golka, "Jonah," in George A. F. Knight and Friedemann W. Golka, eds., *Revelation of God: A Commentary on the Books of the Song of Songs and Jonah* (ITC; Grand Rapids: Eerdmans, 1988) 65-136, here 114-18. For the range of nuances conveyed by this term, see also James D. Nogalski, *The Book of the Twelve: Hosea–Jonah* (SHBC; Macon, GA: Smyth & Helwys, 2011) 442, 445. For a discussion of the root רעע with special reference to Jonah 4:1, see G. I. Davies, "The Uses of rʿʿ Qal and the Meaning of Jonah IV 1," *VT* 27 (1977) 105-11.

23 See Jonathan Magonet, *Form and Meaning: Studies in Literary Techniques in the Book of Jonah* (Bible and Literature 8; Sheffield: Almond, 1983) 14. See also Baruch Halpern and Richard Elliott Friedman, "Composition and Paronomasia in the Book of Jonah," *HAR* 4 (1980) 79-92; Christensen, "Jonah and the Sabbath Rest," 54-56; John F. Craghan, *Esther, Judith, Tobit, Jonah, Ruth* (OTM 16; Wilmington, DE: Glazier, 1982) 173-74; and Kenneth M. Craig, who emphasizes in particular the significance of recurring references to prayer and the vocabulary associated with it (*A Poetics of Jonah: Art in the Service of Ideology* [2nd ed.; Macon, GA: Mercer University Press, 1999] 106-10). In a study influenced by the techniques of Wolfgang Richter, Emmanuel Kojo Ennin Antwi also works closely with recurring language in Jonah (*The Book of Jonah in the Context of Post-Exilic Theology of Israel: An Exegetical Study* [ATSAT 95; St. Ottilien: Eos, 2013] 44-58).

24 On shared language variously explained, see Susan Niditch, *The Responsive Self: Personal Religion in Biblical Literature of the Neo-Babylonian and Persian Periods* (AYBRL; New Haven: Yale University Press, 2015) 57-63; Katharine J. Dell, "Reinventing the Wheel: The Shaping of the Book of Jonah," in John Barton and David J. Reimer, eds., *After the Exile: Essays in Honour of Rex Mason* (Macon, GA: Mercer University Press, 1996) 85-101; Sasson, *Jonah*, 160-80; Ehud Ben Zvi, *Signs of Jonah: Reading and Rereading in Ancient Yehud* (JSOTSup 367; London: Sheffield Academic Press, 2003) 47; Limburg, *Jonah*, 63-66.

The translation offered by the present volume seeks to capture the traditional nature of the language by employing whenever possible the same English words to convey recurring Hebrew vocabulary. The reader will also notice that the translation attempts to capture in English the syntax and cadences of the Hebrew. It is hoped that the resulting unexpected roughness in English alerts the reader to the word order that Israelites would have heard and spoken.[25]

It is also of note that much of Jonah, not only the lament in chap. 2, which is generally laid out in poetic lines, evidences what Albert Lord's teacher Milman Parry called an adding style, whereby the thought is complete at the end of the line even if the sentence continues.[26] There is a minimum of subordination, whereby imagery emerges in interlocking grammatical structures. To capture this quality of language I have generally laid out the text in lines, as do Everett Fox's translations of the Bible, and have occasionally employed indentation to mark subordination or another extender of the thought line. This interest in format as it conveys aesthetics and meaning is also related to Phyllis Trible's treatment of Jonah with its attention to the rhythms and repetitions of the narrative's rhetoric. This approach is found as well in Peter Weimar's German translation of Jonah, in which lines of text tend to be the same length and reflect what are perhaps natural pauses between, for example, a full clause that begins a sentence and a subordinate clause or lengthy prepositional phrase that continues the sentence.[27] Trible employs a complex system of indentation, grammatical markers such as semicolons and periods, dashes, underlining, and underlining with breaks to reveal the ways in which she perceives the author of Jonah to convey style, imagery, and meaning. She notes that her process is somewhat subjective,[28] and I will not attempt to imitate her style of mapping rhetoric. Nevertheless, Trible's interests—as well as those of Weimar—are shared and reflected in some of my formatting choices. The goal is to capture the rhythm of the narrative in its discrete pieces of content or imagery.

Questions of register reflected in form and format, the relation of "poetry" to "prose" and the meaning of these terms as they apply to ancient Israelite literature will arise, in particular, in the analysis of Jonah 2:3–10. As James Kugel has noted, categories of prose and poetry imposed on the biblical text by its interpreters and translators do not necessarily reflect or parallel ancient genres.[29] By ancient Near Eastern standards, the supposed "prose" portions of Jonah are characterized by a purposeful poesis in that self-contained brief lines often parallel the meaning of previous or subsequent lines. The language in chaps. 1, 3, and 4 is frequently rhythmic and

---

25 On the challenges in providing a literal translation of the Bible that takes seriously its oral qualities, see Everett Fox, *The Five Books of Moses: Genesis, Exodus, Leviticus, Numbers, Deuteronomy; A New Translation with Introductions, Commentary, and Notes* (Schocken Bible 1; New York: Schocken, 1995) ix–xxvi; and Robert Alter, *The Five Books of Moses: A Translation with Commentary* (New York: Norton, 2004) xxv–xxvii.

26 See Albert B. Lord, *The Singer of Tales* (HSCL 24; Cambridge, MA: Harvard University Press, 1960; repr., Cambridge, MA: Harvard University Press, 1988) 54. For a linguistic approach to register in Jonah that emphasizes the length of clauses and the completion of thought or action expressed by each clause, see Stanislav Segert, "Syntax and Style in the Book of Jonah: Six Simple Approaches to Their Analysis," in J. A. Emerton, ed., *Prophecy: Essays Presented to Georg Fohrer on His Sixty-Fifth Birthday, 6. September 1980* (BZAW 150; Berlin: de Gruyter, 1980) 121–30, here 124–26, 128. For a linguistic approach to possible sources in Jonah based on the statistical analysis of syllable frequencies and patterns, see Cornelius B. Houk, "Linguistic Patterns in Jonah," *JSOT* 77 (1998) 81–102.

27 Phyllis Trible, *Rhetorical Criticism: Context, Method, and the Book of Jonah* (Guides to Biblical Scholarship: Old Testament; Minneapolis: Fortress Press, 1994); Weimar, *Jona*, 44–51, 69, 109–10, 200–201, 279, 295–96, 391, 433. See also the transcription and translation by Antwi, *Book of Jonah*, 22–42. For a study of Jonah that explores the relationship between syntax, narrative function, meaning, and format, see Alviero Niccacci, "Syntactic Analysis of Jonah," *LASBF* 46 (1996) 9–32. See also the orientation in the commentary by Ursula Struppe, *Die Bücher Obadja, Jona* (NSKAT 24.1; Stuttgart: Katholisches Bibelwerk, 1996).

28 Trible, *Rhetorical Criticism*, 230–33.

29 James L. Kugel, *The Idea of Biblical Poetry: Parallelism and Its History* (New Haven: Yale University Press, 1981) 69–70.

parallelistic, for example, 1:8, 9, 14, 16; 3:6, 8; 4:3, 5. The language in Jonah 2 is more intense in this regard, but it is a matter of degree and register rather than a consistent and easily distinguishable difference in style that betokens poetry rather than prose.[30]

One other feature of Jonah's texture to which Jack Sasson has been especially sensitive, is its aural quality.[31] The author delights in the repetition of sounds and wordplay, an artistic and expressive feature.

Linguistic evidence is often cited in discussions of Jonah's date of composition. Arguments are frequently rooted in the presence of supposed Aramaisms and evidence of late biblical vocabulary and syntax. John Day, for example, points to "the sheer statistical fact that a number of forms are employed which are either only or predominantly attested in late works," for instance the word for "proclamation" (קריאה) in 3:2.[32] Day is convinced, moreover, of the presence of Aramaisms in Jonah and takes them as a sign of late linguistic influence.[33] Others, however, such as Karin Almbladh dispute the lateness of terms cited by Day, noting that some of these words are found in very ancient texts, perhaps reflecting northern Israelite forms.[34] She asks indeed whether in some cases an author is assuming a voice of more ancient Hebrew rather than reflecting a Persian-period vocabulary or syntax, suggesting, in addition, that certain linguistic features may indicate "stylistic" choices rather than date.[35] On the other hand, Almbladh does point to certain "expressions and constructions" as well as "idioms characteristic of post-exilic Hebrew," so that the "pastiche" that is the preserved Jonah does give hints of its date of composition or preservation.[36] Catherine L. Muldoon's thorough

---

30 Similar conclusions concerning the difficulty of distinguishing between prose and poetry and the importance of attention to relative degrees of heightened language in Jonah are drawn by Duane L. Christensen, "Narrative Poetics and the Interpretation of the Book of Jonah," in Elaine R. Follis, ed., *Directions in Biblical Hebrew Poetry* (JSOTSup 40; Sheffield: JSOT Press, 1987). Christensen explores "narrative poetics" in the book as a whole employing a particular variety of metrical analysis. He also offers a history of scholarship, citing previous efforts in this direction ("Narrative Poetics," 30 and nn. 4, 5, 6). Drawing comparisons with the book of Ruth, Raymond de Hoop describes Jonah 1 as "narrative poetry," emphasizing varieties of repetition and parallelism in the chapter ("The Book of Jonah as Poetry: An Analysis of Jonah 1:1-16," in Willem van der Meer and Joannes C. de Moor, eds., *The Structural Analysis of Biblical and Canaanite Poetry* [JSOTSup 74; Sheffield: JSOT Press, 1988] 156–71). In an earlier study, Rudolf Pesch points to repetition in language and content to produce a concentric structure in Jonah 1 with implications for meaning, message, and intertextual biblical connections ("Zur konzentrischen Struktur von Jona 1," *Bib* 47 [1966] 577–81).

31 See the several examples in Sasson, *Jonah*, 277, 291, 301, 304, 312.

32 John Day, "Problems in the Interpretation of the Book of Jonah," in A. S. van der Woude, ed., *In Quest of the Past: Studies on Israelite Religion, Literature and Prophetism; Papers Read at the Joint British-Dutch Old Testament Conference, Held at Elspeet, 1988* (OtSt 26; Leiden: Brill, 1990) 32–47, here 34; see also Alexander Rofé, *The Prophetical Stories: The Narratives about the Prophets in the Hebrew Bible, Their Literary Types and Their History* (Publications of the Perry Foundation for Biblical Research in the Hebrew University of Jerusalem; Jerusalem: Magnes Press, Hebrew University, 1988) 152–58.

33 See also Athalya Brenner, "Linguistic Criteria for Dating the Book of Jonah" [in Hebrew], *BetM* 79 (1979) 396–405; and for earlier scholarly examples, see Karl Marti, *Das Dodekapropheton* (KHC 13; Tübingen: Mohr Siebeck, 1904) 247; O. Procksch, *Die kleinen prophetischen Schriften nach dem Exil* (Stuttgart: Verlag der Vereinsbuchhandlung, 1916), who points to possible Aramaisms and to the emergence of forms of seafaring in the Persian period as hints of a fourth-century BCE date (90); and A. van Hoonacker, *Les douze Petits Prophètes* (EBib; Paris: Gabalda, 1908) 314. The use of -ש versus אשר to indicate subordination (e.g., Jonah 4:10) is one example of late usage cited (GKC §36), but Robert D. Holmstedt and Alexander T. Kirk argue that variation between the terms marks a meaningful form of code-switching ("Subversive Boundary Drawing in Jonah: The Variation of אשר and ש as Literary Code-Switching," *VT* 66 [2016] 542–55). See the relevant discussion in W. Dennis Tucker Jr., *Jonah: A Handbook on the Hebrew Text* (rev. and expanded ed.; Waco, TX: Baylor University Press, 2017) 11–14.

34 On this issue, see also Otto Loretz on Jonah's unusual vocabulary and Canaanite-Phoenician influence ("Herkunft und Sinn der Jona-Erzählung," *BZ* 5 [1961] 18–29).

35 Almbladh, *Studies in the Book of Jonah*, 44–45.

36 See the discussion by George M. Landes, "A Case

linguistic analysis of Jonah leads her tentatively to place Jonah in the early Persian period, that is, in the mid-sixth to early fifth centuries BCE.[37] Questions, however, about imitation of a classical Hebrew narrative style or origins in an early period remain unanswered or are perhaps unanswerable in any definitive way, as noted by Sasson.[38] Sasson carefully outlines the various examples adduced for late biblical style, and I will take account of the significance of these usages in vocabulary and syntax in notes on each passage. The prayer in chap. 2 raises questions about the nature of biblical poetry and parallelism and may hint at an aesthetic characteristic of works later than many classical works found in the Psalter and elsewhere in the Hebrew Bible. Nevertheless, we are wise to recall Sasson's reminder that the story of Jonah partakes in a lengthy and shared literary tradition. He concludes that "the process of assigning a date for Jonah may be a less useful enterprise" than is appreciation for the composed, inherited, "artfully narrated and sophisticated book."[39] Even so, it behooves us to try to appreciate the literary and sociohistorical settings, cultural concerns, theological orientation, and worldview not only of the author who crafted this particular story in this way but also those of his audience.

Jonah and the Twelve

What kind of prophet is Jonah? What does the depiction of Jonah as prophet reveal about the literary and religious sensibilities of the author of this tale, about that composer's assumptions concerning the role and demeanor of the prophets in ancient Israel? Those who collected the set of biblical writings in which Jonah is preserved evidently considered the book's hero to be a prophet and the narrative about him to be prophetic literature. These realizations lead to a discussion of Jonah as one work and one prophetic figure in the biblical corpus of the twelve "Minor Prophets."

In the 1990s and continuing into the twenty-first century, biblical scholars have immersed themselves in questions concerning the relationship between the writings of the so-called Minor Prophets, as currently situated in the Masoretic and Septuagintal versions of the canon. The case has been made that this collection of prophetic books is not a library or corpus but a whole, a distinct book in which the various parts relate to one another in a conscious authorial way. Influenced by canonical questions about "structure" and the final form of biblical works, scholars have suggested that the Twelve be treated "as a coherent collection every bit as deserving to be called a book as Isaiah, Jeremiah, or Ezekiel."[40] In the corpus of the Minor Prophets, they find a "theme, plot, and/or direction greater than the sum of its twelve parts."[41]

Various recurring interests emerge in this scholarly discussion of the Twelve's coherence and form. One concerns the historical, redactional, and literary implications of the differing order of prophetic books in each tradition. Jennifer Dines, for example, explores the means by which the various works have been combined.[42] Some have posited various stages and processes of development in the "Book of the Twelve," suggesting

---

for the Sixth-Century BCE Dating of the Book of Jonah," in Prescott H. Williams Jr. and Theodore Hiebert, eds., *Realia Dei: Essays in Archaeology and Biblical Interpretation in Honor of Edward F. Campbell, Jr. at His Retirement* (Scholars Press Homage Series 23; Atlanta: Scholars Press, 1999) 100–116, here 103–5; and George M. Landes "Linguistic Criteria and the Date of the Book of Jonah," *ErIsr* 16 (1982) 147–70, here 163.

37 Catherine L. Muldoon, *In Defense of Divine Justice: An Intertextual Approach to the Book of Jonah* (CBQMS 47; Washington, DC: Catholic Biblical Association of America, 2010) 49–63.

38 Sasson, *Jonah*, 22–23.

39 Ibid., 27–28. See also Phyllis Trible, "The Book of Jonah: Introduction, Commentary, and Reflections," *NIB* 7:463–529, here 466. For a fairly recent discussion of the possible date of Jonah that takes linguistic and other criteria into consideration and concludes that the Persian period is a reasonable *terminus a quo* for Jonah, see Martin Mulzer, "Die Datierung des Jonabuches: Eine Prüfung der Argumente," *BZ* 61 (2017) 230–48.

40 Paul A. Redditt, "The Formation of the Book of the Twelve: A Review of Research," in Paul L. Redditt and Aaron Schart, eds., *Thematic Threads in the Book of the Twelve* (BZAW 325; Berlin: de Gruyter, 2003) 1–26, here 3.

41 Ibid., 3.

42 Jennifer Dines, "Verbal and Thematic Links between the Books of the Twelve in Greek and Their Relevance to the Differing Manuscript Sequences," in Rainer Albertz, James D. Nogalski, and Jakob Wöhrle, eds., *Perspectives on the Formation of the Book of the Twelve: Methodological Foundations–Redactional*

that the LXX order (in which Jonah precedes Nahum) represents an original sequence dating to the early Persian period, whereas the MT ordering (in which Jonah precedes Micah) connotes concerns of the later Persian period of Ezra and Nehemiah with their emphasis on the restoration of Jerusalem.[43] Others posit a more complex set of stages from the late monarchic period through Hellenistic times.[44] As such discussions relate to Jonah, scholars seek to understand what sort of connections were made or imagined by those responsible for the MT order, Jonah followed by Micah, versus the order of LXX in which Jonah is followed by Nahum. They point as well to the Qumran manuscript 4QXII[a], in which Russell E. Fuller, the editor of the *editio princeps*, argued that Jonah is found at the very end of the collection of the Twelve, after Malachi, leading some to suggest that Jonah is a late addition to the corpus.[45]

Research on the Twelve has also intertwined with discussions of intertextuality, as variously defined.[46] Intertextuality is sometimes described as a matter of citation, quotation, or allusion so that one prophet alludes to another. Julia Kristeva's understanding of intertextuality, on the other hand, points more broadly and deeply to an awareness and presence of the wider tradition in every composition.[47] Her treatment of intertextuality relates well to folklorist John Foley's suggestions about immanent art whereby traditional-style literatures share language, imagery, and symbols, and each implicit cross-reference is a metonymic evocation of the larger tradition to which it belongs.[48] As related to Jonah, the intertextual orientation is reflected in the author's use of the so-called grace formula, versions of which are found in Exod 34:6; Joel 2:12–14; Mic 7:18–20; Nah 1:2b, 3a; and Mal 1:9a. Wöhrle suggests that a redactor reworked Jonah and inserted versions of the formula in four other books of the Twelve to provide a "theological superstructure" to the collection.[49] Aaron Schart suggests that the author of Jonah cites Joel in order to emphasize the theme of repentance.[50] "Jonah," he writes, "must be read with Joel in mind."[51]

A third important thread in scholarly discussions explores thematic links between the various pro-

---

43 See Marvin A. Sweeney, "Synchronic and Diachronic Concerns in Reading the Book of the Twelve Prophets," in Rainer Albertz, James D. Nogalski, and Jakob Wöhrle, eds., *Perspectives on the Formation of the Book of the Twelve: Methodological Foundations–Redactional Processes–Historical Insights* (BZAW 433; Berlin: de Gruyter, 2012) 21–34, here 25; see also, in the same volume, Walter Dietrich, "Three Minor Prophets and the Major Empires: Synchronic and Diachronic Perspectives on Nahum, Habakkuk, and Zephaniah," 147–56.

44 See Sweeney, "Synchronic and Diachronic," 21; Jakob Wöhrle, "So Many Cross-References! Methodological Reflections on the Problem of Intertextual Relationships and Their Significance for Redactional Analysis," in Albertz et al., *Formation of the Book of the Twelve*, 3–29.

45 See Aaron Schart, "The Jonah-Narrative within the Book of the Twelve," in Albertz et al., *Formation of the Book of the Twelve*, 109–28, here 115–16. For a discussion of ancient manuscript evidence and its implications for the redactional and compositional history of the Twelve as "a completed collection," see Russell Fuller, "The Form and Formation of the Book of the Twelve: The Evidence from the Judean Desert," in James W. Watts and Paul R. House, eds., *Forming Prophetic Literature: Essays on Isaiah and the Twelve in Honor of John D. W. Watts* (JSOTSup 235; Sheffield: Sheffield Academic Press, 1996) 86–101, here 86. For a challenge to the placement of Jonah at the end of 4QXII[a], see Philippe Guillaume, "The Unlikely Malachi-Jonah Sequence (4QXII[a])," *JHebS* 7 (2007) 2–10.

46 For an overview, see James D. Nogalski, "Intertextuality and the Twelve," in Watts and House, *Forming Prophetic Literature*, 102–24.

47 Julia Kristeva, *Desire in Language: A Semiotic Approach to Literature and Art* (ed. Leon S. Roudiez; trans. Thomas Gora et al.; European Perspectives; New York: Columbia University Press, 1980) 36–38, 66–69, 73.

48 John Miles Foley, *Immanent Art: From Structure to Meaning in Traditional Oral Epic* (Bloomington: Indiana University Press, 1991).

49 Wöhrle, "So Many Cross-References!," 13. See also Jakob Wöhrle, "A Prophetic Reflection on Divine Forgiveness: The Integration of the Book of Jonah into the Twelve," *JHebS* 9 (2009) 2–17.

50 Schart, "Jonah-Narrative," 109–28, esp. 121, 127.

51 Ibid., 112. See also Richard L. Schultz, "The Ties That Bind: Intertextuality, the Identification of Verbal Parallels, and Reading Strategies in the Book of the Twelve" in Redditt and Schart, *Thematic Threads*, 27–45, here 39; and, in the same volume,

phetic works, for example, the concern with theodicy (Crenshaw),[52] or attitudes toward the nations (Zapff),[53] or views of sin, repentance, and renewal (House).[54] Such studies make the case that the Twelve can be seen thematically as an integrated whole.

In contrast to those who suggest that the Twelve constitutes a work that is "not a mere collection of twelve individual books, but the product of a long-term redactional process,"[55] others such as David L. Petersen and Ehud Ben Zvi (1996) regard the collection as an "anthology."[56] I am sympathetic to conclusions reached by Petersen and Ben Zvi and share the reasoning behind them concerning the nature of the literature, its historical and social context, its authorship and intended audience. Differences in the ordering of biblical books are relevant to understanding the formation of LXX and MT traditions as a whole but are not necessarily indicators of a redactional process betokening the formation of a book of the Twelve. Shared language and imagery and patterns of content are indicators, moreover, of the traditional style of prophetic literature, of intertextuality in Kristeva's sense, rather than a key to ways in which final authors used cross-references and allusions to collate and combine disparate material to make a whole.

Jonah is such an unusual example of a prophetic book that, in fact, it figures less prominently in studies of the Twelve than some of the other works in the corpus. Nevertheless, the search for shared language and themes and the framing interest concerning what these books do or do not have in common are directly relevant to a study of Jonah. The discussion of what Jonah does or does not have in common with the Twelve leads to important larger questions about the very nature of the story of Jonah, about the sort of prophetic figure imagined, about the prophet's characterization, about the date of the little book, and about the meaning and message of Jonah in its literary and lived contexts. Therefore, reference to the work of those who have participated in debates about the Twelve will figure in the commentary even if the goal is not to search for the cohesion of the Twelve or the redactional place of Jonah in that process.

A thoughtful contribution that touches on such literary and contextual matters is that of Hyun Chul Paul Kim. He reviews many of the approaches mentioned above concerning redaction, placement of Jonah among the Twelve, and the various ways in which Jonah might be said to relate intertextually to other prophetic works of the Bible.[57] The links drawn by Kim between the tale of Noah preserved in Genesis and the story of Jonah will be discussed in some detail in relation to Jonah

---

52 Burkard M. Zapff, "The Perspective on the Nations in the Book of Micah as a 'Systematization' of the Nations' Role in Joel, Jonah and Nahum? Reflections on a Context-Oriented Exegesis in the Book of the Twelve," 292–312, here 311.

52 James L. Crenshaw, "Theodicy in the Book of the Twelve," in Redditt and Schart, *Thematic Threads*, 175–91.

53 Zapff, "Perspective on the Nations," 291–312; see also Gregory Goswell, "Jonah among the Twelve Prophets," *JBL* 135 (2016) 283–90.

54 Paul R. House, "Endings as New Beginnings: Returning to the Lord, the Day of the Lord, and Renewal in the Book of the Twelve," in Redditt and Schart, *Thematic Threads*, 313–38, here 328. Claude Lichtert suggests that Jonah functions within the Twelve to draw thematic, theological, and literary contrasts with the other prophetic works in the collection ("Entre rappels et reversements: Les particularités littéraires et théologiques du récit de Jonas," in Elena Di Pede and Donatella Scaiola, eds., *The Book of the Twelve–One Book or Many? Metz Conference Proceedings, 5–7 November 2015* [FAT 2/91; Tübingen: Mohr Siebeck, 2016] 134–44).

55 Wöhrle, "So Many Cross-References!," 3.

56 David L. Petersen, "A Book of the Twelve?," in James D. Nogalski and Marvin A. Sweeney, eds., *Reading and Hearing the Book of the Twelve* (SBLSymS 15; Atlanta: Society of Biblical Literature, 2000) 1–10; Ehud Ben Zvi, "Twelve Prophetic Books or 'The Twelve?': A Few Preliminary Considerations," in Watts and House, *Forming Prophetic Literature*, 125–56. See also Redditt, "Formation of the Book," 3–4; and Thomas Römer, "Introduction: The Book of the Twelve—Fact and Fiction?," in Ehud Ben Zvi and James D. Nogalski, eds., *Two Sides of a Coin: Juxtaposing Views on Interpreting the Book of the Twelve/ the Twelve Prophetic Books* (Analecta Gorgiana 201; Piscataway, NJ: Gorgias Press, 2009) 3–7.

57 Hyun Chul Paul Kim, "Jonah Read Intertextually," *VT* 126 (2007) 497–528. Another intertextual reading of Jonah by Yitzhak Berger understands the prophet as engaged in a search for Eden (*Jonah in the Shadows of Eden* [Indiana Studies in Biblical Litera-

3:5–10. Kim points to the dangerous waters in each account, to the attention paid to animals who will be saved or killed in a cataclysm, to the warning about the predicted destruction sent by the deity, and to shared vocabulary and imagery of "wind," "forty days," "dry ground," and "regretting/relenting." Kim, like others, points to Jonah's name and the *yônâ* or dove's role in the tale of Noah. Kim concludes that Jonah is an anti-Noah whose refusal to follow divine command contrasts with the obedience of the man who has found favor in God's eyes. Although many of these links in vocabulary and phrasing reflect shared traditional imagery and language rather than specific allusions, the story of Jonah may find specific resonances in the tale of Noah especially in relation to the human capacity for violence and the deity's range of emotional responses to the ways in which humans mistreat one another. The composers of these works offer quite different views of the divine response to the recurring problem of human corruption, framing their works with some similar language and motifs drawn from a lengthy literary and cultural tradition. As a receiver of the biblical tradition, the reader inevitably is drawn to each tale by the other.[58]

Jonah as Holy Man and Narrative Character

How is Jonah like other biblical prophets and leaders who have a special intimate connection to the deity, and how is he different from them? Does Jonah's characterization, in fact, point to important aspects of a particular author's attitudes to holy men, to views of the deity who interacts with holy people, and to the nature of divine revelation and messaging? And in what sort of literature is he presented?

As noted above, particular connections have been drawn between Jonah and other works because of their use of the so-called grace formula that invokes divine compassion (Nah 1:2b, 3a; Joel 2:12–14; Exod 34:6; also bits in Mic 7:18–20 and Mal 1:9a),[59] but what about matters of characterization and context? Comparisons have been drawn between the books of Jonah and Nahum because both works deal with the Assyrian enemy;[60]

---

ture; Bloomington: Indiana University Press, 2016]). Berger's creative approach explores language and imagery shared by Jonah, Ezekiel, Genesis, and other biblical works in a methodology evocative of traditional midrash. Focusing on the cosmogonic imagery of water described in recurring language, Alastair Hunter's intertextual study makes connections between Jonah 2 and the exodus theme employed in various biblical contexts ("Jonah from the Whale: Exodus Motifs in Jonah 2," in Johannes C. de Moor, ed., *The Elusive Prophet: The Prophet as Historical Person, Literary Character and Anonymous Artist* [OtSt 45; Leiden: Brill, 2001] 142–58). See also connections drawn by Joel Edmund Anderson between Jonah, Genesis 2–3, Genesis 6–9, and themes of new exodus, re-creation, and "cosmic temple" in a postexilic context ("Jonah's Peculiar Re-Creation," *BTB* 41 [2011] 179–88). On linguistic and thematic parallels between Jonah and the exodus account, see the sensitive study by Pnina Galpaz-Feller, *Jonah—A Journey to Freedom: A New Reading of the Book of Jonah* [in Hebrew] (Jerusalem: Carmel, 2009). For an analysis of language and imagery shared by Jonah and Esther with special attention to fasting and other images of self-abasement or mourning, see Ayelet Seidler, "'Fasting,' 'Sackcloth,' and 'Ashes': From Nineveh to Shushan," *VT* 69 (2019) 117–34. For a study that points to links between the Jonah narrative and Genesis 3–4, see Lena-Sofia Tiemeyer, "Jonah the Eternal Fugitive: Exploring the Intertextuality of Jonah's Flight in the Bible and Its Later Reception," in Jesper Høgenhaven, Frederik Poulsen, and Cian Power, eds., *Images of Exile in the Prophetic Literature: Copenhagen Conference Proceedings, 7–10 May 2017* (FAT 2/103; Tübingen: Mohr Siebeck, 2019) 255–68.

58   See also Noah Greenfield, "Jonah's Ark and Noah's Fish," *AJBI* 33 (2007) 37–72; and, building on the work of Hesse and Kikawada ("Jonah and Genesis 1–11," 3–19), Yael Shemesh, "'And Many Beasts' (Jonah 4:11): The Function and Status of Animals in the Book of Jonah," *JHebS* 10 (2010) 2–26.

59   See, e.g., Kim, "Jonah Read Intertextually," 508, 513. Mark E. Biddle compares and contrasts Micah, Joel, and Jonah regarding Yahweh's "patient mercy" ("Obadiah-Jonah-Micah in Canonical Context: The Nature of Prophetic Literature and Hermeneutics," *Int* 61 [2007] 154–66, here 158–61).

60   See R. B. Y. Scott, "The Sign of Jonah," *Int* 19 (1965) 16–25, here 19–20; Beate Ego, "The Repentance of Nineveh in the Story of Jonah and Nahum's Prophecy of the City's Destruction: A Coherent Reading of the Book of the Twelve as Reflected in the Aggada," in Redditt and Schart, *Thematic Threads*, 155–74. Ego also discusses the mention of Nahum in the longer Greek manuscript tradition of Tobit 14 and of Jonah

between the prophets Jonah and Elijah since both men despair and flee; between Jonah and Jeremiah,[61] because each complains to Yahweh about his mission and engages in lament; and between Jonah and Joel to contrast each work's attitudes to the nations that compete with or threaten Israel. One might add to the list of possibilities for comparison the biblical figures of Job, Moses, and Abraham.[62]

There are really two matters in play here. One deals with the perceived mission of the chosen human being whom the deity trusts with conveying his message, while the other has to do with the literary form of prophetic works and the typical plot elements and language, the content and structure, of such compositions. An overview of the book of Nahum that deals with the enemy Assyria and is often invoked in discussions of Jonah allows important contrasts to emerge concerning views of the prophetic role and the literature that shapes and presents such views.[63]

The introductory rubric of the work names the prophet, Nahum of Elkosh, and labels what follows "an oracle concerning Nineveh." We are thus informed of Nahum's origins in Elkosh, a presumed place whose location is unknown. Significantly, the corpus is called the book of the vision of Nahum of Elkosh, implying the existence of a document and his status as a visionary. The oracles that follow *are* the book.

These oracles dealing with the enemy Assyria condemn Nineveh, the capital, and declaim against this enemy with imagery of the divine warrior, whose power is typically manifested in the wind, the storm, and the waters (Nah 1:3). Traditional recurring biblical language is employed in parallel constructions (e.g., the Lord is slow to anger/will not free from guilt, the guilty [cf. Exod 34:6–7]). Mountains quake, hills melt (1:5). All of this power is directed against alien worshipers of multiple gods (1:14). Judah, the prophet's people, will be victorious with divine help. War imagery, including chariots, shields, and soldiers, characterizes the oracle of Nahum 2, betokening Nineveh's defeat, desolation, and status as plunder. Nahum 3 makes clear that Assyrians deserve this fate because of their utter depravity (3:4). The reader learns from these oracles that the prophet is skilled in the use of traditional and recurring media of expression, that his worldview is hotly anti-Assyrian and pro-Judean, and that he perceived the Assyrians as a consummate Other. We know nothing else about the prophet's identity, however constructed by an author; about his context; about

---

in the shorter version (156–58); see also Kim, "Jonah Read Intertextually," 508–12.

61 See, e.g., André LaCocque and Pierre-Emmanuel LaCocque, *Jonah: A Psycho-Religious Approach to the Prophet* (Studies on Personalities of the Old Testament; Columbia: University of South Carolina Press, 1990) 130–31, 151, 153. See also Bruce Vawter, *Job & Jonah: Questioning the Hidden God* (New York: Paulist Press, 1983) 113–14. Vawter suggests that Jonah 4:5-11 presents a "prophetic parody" of Elijah (1 Kgs 19:4–12). Emphasizing themes of despair and alienation from God, Walter Bührer draws comparisons with Jeremiah and Elijah, paying special attention to the terminology for the deity employed in Jonah ("Der Gott Jonas und der Gott des Himmels: Untersuchungen zur Theologie des Jonas-Buches," *BN* 167 [2015] 65–78). For another approach to the significance of key language shared by 1 Kings 19 and Jonah, see Gottfried Vanoni, "Elija, Jona und das Dodekapropheton: Grade der Intertextualität," in Erich Zenger, ed., *"Wort Jhwhs, das Geschah . . ." (Hos 1,1): Studien zum Zwölfprophetenbuch* (Herders biblische Studien 35; Freiburg: Herder, 2002) 113–21. For a comparative study of Jonah, Jeremiah, and Ezekiel, see Sheldon H. Blank, "The Prophet as Paradigm," in James L. Crenshaw and John T. Willis, eds., *Essays in Old Testament Ethics: J. Philip Hyatt, In Memoriam* (New York: Ktav, 1974) 111–30. A. A. Abela also draws thoughtful comparisons between Jeremiah and Jonah, prophets who feel beset by their commissions and their prophetic roles ("When the Agenda of an Artistic Composition Is Hidden: Jonah and Intertextual Dialogue with Isaiah 6, the 'Confessions of Jeremiah' and Other Texts," in de Moor, *Elusive Prophet*, 1–30, here 23).

62 Dell, "Reinventing the Wheel," 96–100. For a comparison with Job in particular, see Philip P. Jenson, "Interpreting Jonah's God: Canon and Criticism," in Robert P. Gordon, ed., *The God of Israel* (University of Cambridge Oriental Publications 64; Cambridge: Cambridge University Press, 2007) 229–45, here 232.

63 For a careful comparison of Nahum and Jonah in the context of a discussion of intertextuality and the role of these compositions in "The Twelve," see Charles Conroy, "Jonah and Nahum in the Book of the Twelve: Who Has the Last Word?," *PIBA* 32 (2009) 1–23, esp. 13–23; also Muldoon, *In Defense of Divine Justice*, 24–30.

his conversations with the deity apart from the reception of the oracles; or about the effect that his vision has on him. Allowing for significant differences in style, interest, and message, the essential form of Nahum—the identifying rubric followed by oracles—is typical of a number of the briefest prophetic works preserved in the Bible, Habakkuk, Zephaniah, Obadiah, and Joel.

The book of Jonah, however, stars the prophet, a much more fully inflected protagonist around whom a story is developed.[64] The divine word is directed to Nineveh, as in Nahum, but is alluded to only in a brief sentence in chap. 1, expressed explicitly in chap. 3. Heightened language rich in formulaic expression is found in chap. 2 but is framed within a plot—the prophet's lament as Jonah bemoans his imprisonment in the belly of the fish in a state that hovers between life and death. Despite the interest in Assyria, Jonah and Nahum are very different sorts of works, and, while Jonah is a lively character, Nahum is primarily identified as the messenger of particular oracles.[65]

Closer comparisons might be drawn between Jonah and Jeremiah, although there are clear differences. Jeremiah is described as having visionary experiences, conversations with the deity, and personal crises. His career, if one reads carefully, has a certain narrative arc punctuated by lengthy oracles, sign acts, symbolic visions, and other media not found in Jonah. As a reader of this lengthy work to which a series of composers have contributed, one has to work hard to follow the narrative. Not so with the tale of Jonah, where structure is easily outlined as noted above. Nevertheless, Jeremiah, like Jonah, is shown to interact with the deity in a personal and intimate way. As Robert R. Wilson observes, Jonah is about the relationship between the prophet and God.[66]

Like the leader Moses, the prophet Jeremiah hesitates to accept the divine charge to prophesy (1:6),[67] whereas Jonah downright refuses to act initially. Jeremiah articulates the way he feels when his message is rejected or mocked (15:15–18; 20:8–10); and, as with Moses, the deity urges him to accept his difficult charge (15:19). Jonah's negative response has a different cause than Jeremiah's. He seems to fear that his message will have an effect on the Assyrians and that his prediction of doom will be rendered false;[68] like Jeremiah, he expresses discontent about his calling, regarding it as a heavy burden. Jeremiah is portrayed as self-hating, wishing he had never been born (20:13–18), and Jonah asks to die. Jeremiah's confessions and complaints, like those of Jonah in chap. 2, share in formulaic language and content characteristic of the lament. In terms of characterization and the template of the unhappy prophet, therefore, Jonah shares much with Jeremiah. Jonah's story, however, is much more cohesive, a true narrative with beginning, middle, and end.[69]

---

64   See van Hoonacker, *Les douze Petits Prophètes*, 313; Gershom Scholem and Eric J. Schwab, "On Jonah and the Concept of Justice," *CritInq* 25 (1999) 353–61, here 356. On Jonah as narrative, see also Ben Zvi, *Signs of Jonah*, 83; Craghan, *Esther, Judith, Tobit, Jonah, Ruth*, 165. For a study that explores affinities between the content of Jonah and world folklore, biblical prophecy, and psalmic literature, see A. Feuillet, "Les sources du livre de Jonas," *RB* 54 (1947) 161–86; and for a discussion of Feuillet's conclusions, see Benoit Trépanier, "The Story of Jonas," *CBQ* 13 (1951) 8–16.

65   For contrasts between Nahum and Jonah, see Baruch A. Levine, "The Place of Jonah in the History of Biblical Ideas," in Stephen L. Cook and S. C. Winter, *On the Way to Nineveh: Studies in Honor of George M. Landes* (ASOR Books 4; Atlanta: Scholars Press, 1999) 201–17, here 208–9.

66   Robert R. Wilson, "Jonah in the Biblical Tradition," *Reflection* 76 (1978) 6–8, here 7.

67   On the motif of the "reluctant prophet," see Erica Brown, *Jonah: The Reluctant Prophet* (New Milford, CT: Maggid Books, 2017) 20–35.

68   Robert R. Wilson suggests that an important theme of Jonah has to do with accusations concerning false prophecy. Jonah's author shows that "God's prophets are not to be held responsible for the failure of the divine judgment to occur"—this in contrast to Deut 18:19–22 ("Jonah in the Biblical Tradition," 8). See also James L. Kugel, *How To Read the Bible: A Guide to Scripture, Then and Now* (New York: Free Press, 2007) 328; H. C. O. Lanchester, *Obadiah and Jonah* (CBSC; Cambridge: Cambridge University Press, 1918) 67.

69   On Jonah and Jeremiah as exemplars of the prophetic role, see Keller, "Jonas," 338. For an intertextual approach, see Gary Yates, "The 'Weeping Prophet' and 'Pouting Prophet' in Dialogue: Intertextual Connections between Jeremiah and Jonah," *JETS* 59 (2016) 223–39.

Tales of the Former Prophets, the most fully drawn of whom are Elijah and Elisha, read more assertively as episodic stories, although these tales are not set apart in a book devoted to the prophet. These narratives do provide additional comparative material for exploring where we might place Jonah in terms of the perceived function of the prophet and forms of prophetic literature. The Former Prophets are presented as miracle workers, critics of the establishment, pragmatic readers of political and historical situations, and conveyers of divine messages—the most important shared characteristic of all prophets. They deliver God's communications and indeed help to bring the messages about in verbal and nonverbal dramatic forms. Representations of Elisha and Elijah relate well to questions about Jonah; in each case details are provided about the personality and experiences of the prophet.

Elijah and Elisha are subject to angry outbursts and sullen behavior. The latter calls down a bear on children who mock his baldness (2 Kgs 2:23–25), while Elijah not only berates those he considers enemies of the Lord in typical prophetic fashion but also seems, like Jonah, to take issue with the deity himself. Fleeing from the queen Jezebel, who seeks his life, Elijah skulks off to the wilderness, sits down under a tree, and asks God to take his life, falling into a depressive sleep (1 Kgs 19:1–5). Indeed the similarities to Jonah's behavior make one wonder if Jonah is not modeled on the Elijah character, or perhaps certain holy men are expected to behave this way.[70]

The opening phrase of the book of Jonah ויהי דבר־יהוה אל יונה בן־אמתי לאמר, literally "and there was a word of Yahweh to Jonah son of Amittai, saying," identifies the work as prophetic, concerning a person chosen to deliver a divine message. This formulation is found frequently in stories of the Former Prophets, whose tales are collected in the Deuteronomistic History as well as in later biblical prophetic works such as Jeremiah (see the commentary on Jonah 1:1) and contrasts with the phrase דבר־יהוה אשר היה אל + [name of prophet], "the word of Yahweh that was to [name of prophet]," which functions as a heading for the oracles that follow, emphasizing "the message instead of informing us about the prophet who carries it."[71] The author of Jonah lets the reader know that a story is coming involving the message of God and his chosen messenger, who will turn out to be quite a protagonist and whose career offers interesting variations on the expected or conventional portrayal of the faithful prophet. A prophet named Jonah son of Amittai, in fact, appears in 2 Kgs 14:25, leading some scholars to suggest that the author of the book of Jonah alludes to the same servant of God or continues his story. The connection to 2 Kgs 14:25 is significant for understanding the genre of this work, its socioliterary context, and the implicit expectations of receivers of the tale of Jonah.

Matters of Context and Authorship

The Deuteronomistic History is punctuated by annalistic reports concerning the kings of Judah and Israel. 2 Kings 14:25 refers to a prophet, Jonah son of Amittai, who was from Gath-hepher, possibly to be identified with the location mentioned in Josh 19:10–13 in the tribe of Zebulun in the Galilee of Israel. This prophet is said to have predicted the restoration of Israel's border by Jeroboam, son of Joash, "from Lebo-hamath as far as the Sea of the Arabah," according to the word the prophet received from Yahweh, the God of Israel. The author of the book of Jonah seems to be identifying the prophet in his narrative with this figure, associated with Jeroboam II, the long-reigning and politically successful king of Israel (d. ca. 750 BCE) during a period just before Assyria's ascendancy and eventual conquest of the northern kingdom and subjugation of Judah in the late eighth century BCE. To be sure, the author's goal is probably not to create a historical novella that accurately reflects Assyria's position in the ancient world of the mid-eighth century. For the second-century BCE author of Judith, who mistakenly associates Nebuchadnezzar with Assyria, Assyria is an iconic symbol of a mighty enemy and its capital

---

70 In an overview of Yehezkel Kaufmann's approach to Jonah that focuses, in particular, upon reasons for his preexilic dating of the work, Haim Gevaryahu notes that Kaufmann draws comparisons between biblical portrayals of the Former Prophets and the story of Jonah ("The Universality of the Book of Jonah," *DD* 10 [1981] 20–27, here 25).

71 Sasson, *Jonah*, 67. See also Clifford John Collins, "From Literary Analysis to Theological Exposition: The Book of Jonah," *JOTT* 7 (1995) 28–44, here 31.

Nineveh an iconic great city, suggesting major historical events and responses to them. Assyria and Nineveh represent and evoke notions of greatness, cruelty, power, and otherness even centuries after any actual events that helped to shape and reinforce such meanings (see further the commentary on 1:2).

The adoption of the identity and name of a briefly mentioned prophet associated with an eighth-century BCE monarch, and the prophet's development as a character, betokens a kind of inner-biblical pseudepigraphy.[72] In an analogous way, the sixth-century BCE Isaiah 40–55 is folded into the corpus of the eighth-century BCE prophet Isaiah. The development of traditions about Jonah might be compared even more closely to postbiblical pseudepigraphic compositions in which a character from the Hebrew Bible is developed and recreated in works that have their own agendas and interests. Some of these compositions adopt the name and develop the persona of a major biblical character such as Moses or Ezra. Other works, however, develop minor characters like Jonah, who receive only brief mention in the Hebrew Bible. One thinks of Jeremiah's scribe Baruch or Enoch of the primeval genealogy in Genesis 5. What do the reuse and recontextualization of more obscure figures suggest?

We might conclude that the author is aware of a received piece of tradition, oral and/or written, about a prophet named Jonah son of Amittai, but that this tradition is open-ended and can be creatively developed.[73] As Yehoshua Gitay observes, the prophet in 2 Kings 14 is pictured as delivering a benevolent message to a king condemned by the larger Deuteronomistic tradition and other prophets (see Amos 7:10–17). Gitay suggests that, in choosing to identify his protagonist with the Jonah of 2 Kings, the author of Jonah displays particular interest in the themes of benevolence and forgiveness.[74] As noted by John Day, this is not to designate such reuse of biblical tradition as midrashic.[75] Midrash is a specific exegetical genre involving certain techniques and presuppositions not in evidence here, but it is important to emphasize the mentality of playful openness that informs both midrash and works such as the Genesis Apocryphon and the so-called additions to Daniel, and Jonah.[76] Jonah's exquisite sensitivity in verbal choices and scene creation, its orderly elegance of presentation, and its thematic cohesiveness suggest an author steeped in the tradition but free to innovate. This author expresses tolerance for foreigners, allowance for divine patience, and appreciation for mocking the demeanor of the condemnatory prophets that is often presented in the Hebrew Bible. At the same time, despite its often humorous tone, the work deeply comments on the big questions that define religious identity itself, questions concerning the relationship of mere mortals to a powerful deity,[77] about the nature of ethical behavior and interpersonal relationships, about

---

72   Philip Peter Jenson suggests that the author chooses "a relatively obscure pre-exilic prophet as the vehicle for a story with purposes other than the historiographic" (*Obadiah, Jonah, Micah: A Theological Commentary* [LHBOTS 496; London: T&T Clark, 2008] 30).

73   See the discussion by Sasson, *Jonah*, 86–87.

74   Yehoshua Gitay, "Jonah: The Prophecy of Antirhetoric," in Astrid B. Beck et al., eds., *Fortunate the Eyes That See: Essays in Honor of David Noel Freedman in Celebration of his Seventieth Birthday* (Grand Rapids: Eerdmans, 1995) 197–206, here 199. See also Julius A. Bewer, "Jonah," in Hinckley G. T. Mitchell, John Merlin Powis Smith, and Julius A. Bewer, *A Critical and Exegetical Commentary on Haggai, Zechariah, Malachi and Jonah* (ICC; New York: Scribner, 1912) 29.

75   Day, "Interpretation of the Book of Jonah," 38; George A. F. Knight does see midrash as a relevant designation (*Ruth and Jonah: Introduction and Commentary* [Torch Bible Commentaries; London: SCM Press, 1950] 51). Phyllis Trible also considers midrash to be "an appropriate Gattung for Jonah," a commentary on the common biblical credo, a version of which is found in Jonah 4:2 ("Studies in the Book of Jonah," 168). See also Julius Wellhausen, *Die Kleinen Propheten übersetzt, mit Noten* (SV 5; Berlin: Reimer, 1892) 211; and the suggestions of Karl Budde linking the tale of Jonah to the Midrash on Kings mentioned in 2 Chr 33:18 ("Vermutungen zum 'Midrasch' des Buches der Könige," *ZAW* 12 [1892] 37–51), an idea explored further by George Adam Smith, "Jonah," in *The Book of the Twelve Prophets Commonly Called the Minor* (2 vols.; EB; New York: Armstrong & Son, 1898) 2:491–541, here 505–6.

76   For a discussion of Jonah as midrash, see E. Nielsen, "Le message primitif du livre de Jonas," *RHPR* 59 (1979) 499–507, here 507.

77   On the role and varieties of prayers in Jonah as they relate to human beings' relationships with the deity

us versus them, about the consequences of evildoing, and about the capacity for forgiveness.[78] The author, moreover, is concerned with God's creation broadly defined and explores his and our obligations not only to humans of different varieties but also to animal and plant life.[79] The tale ends with concern for the life of the plant that the deity has mysteriously grown and causes to die and for the innocent animals that will die, should the deity be forced to punish Nineveh and its people.

In searching for context and authorship, a number of scholars have suggested that Deuteronomistic writers employ this tale to challenge the point of view represented in Amos, namely, that Israel is doomed because of the people's sinfulness. Despite certain verbal links between Amos and Jonah attributable to a shared tradition and linguistic palette, this theory concerning an anti-Amos polemic seems a bit far-fetched.[80] To be sure, these two works evince differences in worldview and reflect theological tensions in a larger history of thought in Judaism.

Lowell K. Handy argues that the context of Jonah's author is the "social world of scribal elites" in the Persian period,[81] for whom the temple in Jerusalem is perceived to be "the religious center of the world" and whose "norms, political and ethical, . . . are posited to be those of (his) ethnic and social circle."[82] For Handy, the story of Jonah is "told for the bureaucrats in a male-dominated hierarchical empire, in which authority is to be obeyed."[83] Handy sees references in Jonah 2:5 and 2:8 as important markers of this temple-centric orientation and the temple in Jerusalem as critical to the author's environment and that of his group. Although one wonders if such formulaic references to the divine abode (which I understand as the deity's court or palace, and not necessarily references to the temple in Jerusalem) are as significant as Handy asserts, the notion of a literary elite in the Persian period is pertinent.

In addressing matters of form and setting, the early work of Morton Smith is relevant.[84] Although one might take issue with the map of parties and politics that Smith finds reflected in the compositions of the Hebrew Bible, his reference to late biblical literati of a so-called "syncretistic" group seems pertinent here. Smith is one of the few scholars who sought to identify the worldview and context of those who composed or preserved some of the outlier, unusual books of the Hebrew Bible. Who might

---

and critical themes in the work, see Karin Schöpflin, "Notschrei, Dank und Disput: Beten im Jonasbuch," *Bib* 78 (1997) 389–404.

78 R. E. Clements views the possibility for forgiveness and repentance as the unifying theme of the work ("The Purpose of the Book of Jonah," in J. A. Emerton, ed., *Congress Volume: Edinburgh 1974* [VTSup 28; Leiden: Brill,1975] 16–28, here 21, 26, 28); see also Fretheim, *Message of Jonah*, 28. Suggesting that the postexilic audience of Jonah would be sympathetic to its hero, Serge Frolov views Jonah's central theme to be the tension between forgiveness of evildoers and support for the deservedly righteous ("Returning the Ticket: God and His Prophet in the Book of Jonah," *JSOT* 86 [1999] 85–105). Relating Jonah to current discussions of "reform" and deterrence," Étan Levine views the author as grappling with "the very nature of justice and the justification of punishment" (*Heaven and Earth, Law and Love: Studies in Biblical Thought* [BZAW 303; Berlin: de Gruyter, 2000] 78, 93). Influenced by trauma studies, L. Juliana M. Claassens finds a tragic dimension in the humor of Jonah ("Rethinking Humour in the Book of Jonah: Tragic Laughter as Resistance in the Context of Trauma," *OTE* 28 [2015] 655–73).

79 On the theme of God as creator, see also Elizabeth Achtemeier, *Minor Prophets 1* (NIBC; Peabody, MA: Hendrickson, 1996) 256, 277; Dreier, "JHWHs Grenzenlose Liebe," 235–55.

80 Annette Schellenberg, "An Anti-Prophet among the Prophets? On the Relationship of Jonah to Prophecy," *JSOT* 39 (2015) 353–71, here 361.

81 Handy, *Jonah's World*, 22.

82 Ibid., 123.

83 Ibid., 106–9.

84 Morton Smith, *Palestinian Parties and Politics That Shaped the Old Testament* (Lectures on the History of Religions n.s. 9; New York: Columbia University Press, 1971). On a postmonarchic setting and the role of literati, see also Ben Zvi, *Signs of Jonah*, 7–8, 116; Emil G. Kraeling, "The Evolution of the Story of Jonah," in *Hommages à André Dupont-Sommer* (Paris: Adrien-Maisonneuve, 1971) 305–18, here 306–7. For a discussion of a late-biblical narrative genre in 2 Kings and Jeremiah, "the historical short story," which is also exemplified by Jonah and Ruth, see Norbert Lohfink, "Die Gattung der 'Historischen Kurzgeschichte' in den letzten Jahren von Juda und in der Zeit des Babylonischen Exils," *ZAW* 90 (1978) 319–47.

have had interest in Song of Songs or Jonah? I think Smith's suggestion is apt and allows that such intellectuals would have been familiar as well with the works of Persian and Hellenistic writers. The composer of Jonah loves story, is skilled and deliberate in word choice, appreciates the narrative power of simplicity, and is sympathetic to the possibility that foreigners share his ethical, Yahwistically rooted humanistic concerns. Using deft short strokes, he is adept at the construction and development of characters, a narrative feature that is more typical of datably late biblical writers.

Smith's reference to a "syncretistic" party carries with it a certain amount of baggage in terms of defining the political and sociological setting of the postmonarchic period. Preferable in relation to the works composed and preserved by the literati that he mentions might be the designation "cosmopolitan realists." Gitay suggests that the point of view in Jonah suggests an attitude of "normalization" found in various forms, for example, in Jeremiah's "claim for coexistence in exile."[85] One might also make reference to the more inclusive aspects of oracles in late Isaianic material (e.g., Isa 56:6–7), Deutero-Isaiah's enthusiastic acceptance of Persian rulership, and passages that suggest a variety of religious universalism in which Yahweh is recognized as everyone's deity (Zech 8:20–23).[86] With attention to the colonialist setting of

---

[85] Gitay, "Jonah: The Prophecy of Antirhetoric," 206.

[86] A significant but dated characterization of worldview in Jonah that treats the work as a polemic against Ezra and Nehemiah, "a reaction against the intellectual provincialism and the religious fanaticism of some in Judah" in the postexilic period, is that of LaCocque and LaCocque, *Jonah*, 44. In this vein, Theodore H. Robinson draws a contrast between worldview in Ezra and Nehemiah and that in Jonah and Ruth (*Die zwölf kleinen Propheten: Hosea bis Micha* [HAT 1/14; Tübingen: Mohr Siebeck, 1954] 119). Some early- and mid-twentieth century works seem to veer toward a normatively informed, somewhat anti-Judaist description of this worldview, for example, Watts's description of "narrowly nationalistic attitudes to foreigners" (*Books*, 74). Jacob M. Myers writes of "a rebuke to their exclusiveness and to ours" (*The Book of Hosea, the Book of Joel, the Book of Amos, the Book of Jonah* [LBC 14; Richmond, VA: John Knox, 1959] 173). J. T. Erich Renner describes Jonah as a prophet who "cannot come to grips with the grace of God for others" (*In Times of Crisis: Commentaries on Joel, Jonah, and Habakkuk* [CRC; Adelaide: Openbook, 1995] 96); see also T. H. Hennessy, *Joel, Obadiah, Jonah and Malachi* (Cambridge: Cambridge University Press, 1919) 68. In a commentary that explores Jonah with a particular invitation to Christian readers, James Bruckner offers a critique of such explanations and takes issue with "anti-Semitic explanations" of the meaning of Jonah (*Jonah, Nahum, Habakkuk, Zephaniah* [NIVAC 13; Grand Rapids: Zondervan, 2004] 61). On such matters of worldview, see also James D. Smart, "The Book of Jonah," *IB* 6:875–94, here 872–73; and discussions by Rofé, *Prophetical Stories*, 160–61 and n. 63; Johan Ferreira, "A Note on Jonah 2:8: Idolatry and Inhumanity in Israel," *BT* 63 (2012) 28–38, here 34; and A. Feuillet, who views the context of Jonah as a fifth-century BCE ideological debate about universalism versus particularism ("Le sens du livre de Jonas," *RB* 54 [1947] 340–61, here 346, 350, 356). See also Friedrich Nötscher, *Zwölfprophetenbuch, oder Kleine Propheten* (Würzburg: Echter-Verlag, 1948) 82. Contrast A. S. van der Woude, "Nachholende Erzählung im Buch Jona," in Alexander Rofé and Yair Zakovitch, eds., *Isac Leo Seeligmann Volume: Essays on the Bible and the Ancient World* (3 vols.; Jerusalem: Rubenstein's Publishing House, 1983) 3:263–72; and the nuanced discussion by Wilhelm Rudolph, who takes note of suggestions that the work may be in debate with attitudes found in Ezra-Nehemiah and points to the author's concern with Israel's own sin as it relates to exile and to humanistic universalism in the work ("Jona," in Arnulf Kuschke and Ernst Kutsch, eds., *Archäologie und Altes Testament: Festschrift für Kurt Galling zum 8. Jan. 1970* [Tübingen: Mohr Siebeck, 1970] 235–37). Making a somewhat idiosyncratic argument that the work is meant to convince Jewish hellenizers to support the Seleucids, Jacques Vermeylen places Jonah in the Hellenistic period between the fourth and second centuries BCE ("Le livre de Jonas: Un écrit politico-religieux?," *ScEs* 54 [2002] 287–97). See also Weimar, who sees the author's context as third–century BCE Jerusalem (*Jona*, 65–66). Suggesting a quite late date for Jonah (about 250 BCE), Frank Zimmermann sees the work as "a plea for a rapprochement to proselytes" ("Problems and Solutions in the Book of Jonah," *Judaism* 40 [1991] 580–89, here 588–89). Rejecting notions about universalism in the sense of an outreach to non-Yahwists, Joel Rosenberg suggests that Jonah deals in complex ways with the tension between "a private, contemplative . . . absolutist . . . religiosity" and "a

Jonah, Gitay suggests that the work models "how to relate to the hated enemy."[87]

The author of Jonah shows interest as well in personal religion, that is, in the worldview of individuals whose religious sensibilities do not require institutional settings. Such people seem to make sense of their world and find their place in it in expressive ways that are rooted in family and culture without the explicit sanction of religious leaders. Jonah displays an exquisite ability to convey the sort of "lived religion" that emerges in relationships, and in verbal and nonverbal interactions. These qualities of sensitive characterization, of personal and lived experience, will emerge in commentary throughout the volume, but one brief analysis helps to set the scene.

Religion as Lived and Personal

Jonah 1:4–16 (see above under #2, "Group Punishment and Mollification") describes the events that take place once the fleeing Jonah is on the ship headed to Tarshish. The responses of the sailors to the storm sent by Yahweh, the interaction between them and Jonah, the characters' attitudes to deities, and their ritual actions are all revealing of worldview.[88] First, in their fear, the sailors cry out to their gods. The author sketches emotions and makes us feel the sense of panic onboard the vessel. They are "frightened," "cry out," and "hurl the cargo" (1:5). Jonah acknowledges the various religious cultures to which members of the crew belong and that it is natural for them, as for a Hebrew, to ask for help from the deity in times of crisis.[89] Religious action takes place on site, in the moment, extemporaneously. Jonah is missing from the action, and when the captain seeks him out, he finds Jonah in a deep sleep oblivious to the disaster around him. This scene is humorous; the captain yells at him and asks what's up with him, calling him a sluggard. Given that the captain asks Jonah to pray to his god as they have addressed theirs, the interaction suggests a kind of multi-culturalism; Jonah's deity may be able to master the sea. Religion is situated in interactions between people. They cast lots, a nice example of popular religion or religion as lived, a ritual action framed by the crisis of the moment and involving material means. The lot falls upon Jonah, indicating that he is the cause of the evil that has befallen them—all on the vessel would agree that there always is a cause, a fault, a reason. Then follow a formulaic interaction between strangers and a revelation of how Jonah has angered his deity. He asks to be thrown overboard so that he can save them, but they, decent human beings trying to do the right thing in a time of crisis, resist. They row harder, throwing objects overboard to lighten the ship's load, all to no avail. The author's language beautifully captures their frenetic activity, the feeling of panic, their physical exertion. They row, trying to reach dry

---

public, activist . . . pragmatic, tolerant . . . religiosity" ("Jonah and the Prophetic Vocation," *Response* 22 [1974] 23–26, here 25).

87   Gitay, "Jonah: The Prophecy of Antirhetoric," 206. With attention to the work's intended audience, David F. Payne suggests that the author is aware of but perhaps skeptical of an apocalyptic worldview appropriate to late biblical material ("Jonah from the Perspective of Its Audience," *JSOT* 13 [1979] 3–12, here 12). Although he does not take a stand on the date of the work, David Noel Freedman suggests that the concept of "reciprocal repentance" whereby the repentance of humans leads to "corresponding divine repentance" is not found in pre-eighth-century BCE biblical literature and that the Jonah narrative makes a case for this "new view," even while emphasizing divine compassion and independence in decisions concerning forgiveness and punishment ("Did God Play a Dirty Trick on Jonah at the End?," *BRev* 6 [1990] 26–31, here 29–31). On the efficacy of repentance as "a revolutionary concept," see also Jeffrey H. Tigay, "The Book of Jonah and Days of Awe," *CJ* 38 (1985–86) 67–76, here 74. On a transition in the nature of prophecy as it relates to repentance, see also Zalman Shazar, "Jonah: Transition from Seer to Prophet," *DD* 7 (1978) 1–8.

88   Lena-Sofia Tiemeyer discusses the significance of various forms of ritual action in Jonah performed by the sailors, Jonah, and the Ninevites ("Attitudes to the Cult in Jonah: In the Book of Jonah, the Book of the Twelve, and Beyond," in Lena-Sofia Tiemeyer, ed., *Priests and Cults in the Book of the Twelve* [ANEM 14; Atlanta: SBL Press, 2016] 115–29). See also Schöpflin, "Notschrei, Dank und Disput," 389–404.

89   Aaron Jed Brody, *"Each Man Cried Out to His God": The Specialized Religion of Canaanite and Phoenician Seafarers* (HSM 58; Atlanta: Scholars Press, 1998).

ground, but cannot, as the sea grows "more and more tempestuous" (1:13). These non-Yahwists care about the life of a stranger. Finally, they hurl him into the sea as he requests, but their action is punctuated by a feeling of guilt and a request to Yahweh to forgive them and not hold them responsible for innocent blood. Afterward, they sacrifice to Yahweh and vow vows (e.g., if you save us, we will do such and such), engaging again in lived religion in the context of crisis that arises in their work situation. In this way, as presented by this scene, religion involves individual prayer, the making of vows, the use of material divinatory means as a guide to action, the acknowledgment of divine powers, and the concern for every human life, even that of a foreigner. Religious actions and responses emerge in relationships, in everyday life. They are set in the workplace, miles from land or buildings or altars; yet there is a shared framework among all the men on the ship, including Jonah, for finding out truth, assessing blame, and addressing a crisis. The book of Jonah reflects an author's view of everyday religion, an interest in character development, and an emphasis on personal religion experienced by individuals[90]—qualities, I would argue, that are more typical of Ruth and Tobit than of many, or probably most, biblical narratives. I will make the case that these traits, together with linguistic considerations, implicit pseudepigraphy, and features of worldview, suggest that Jonah is a late biblical composition that points to directions in early Jewish literature.[91]

Worldview and Genre

Returning to questions concerning representations of the role of the prophet, the qualities of the piece of literature that is Jonah, and the orientation to life that informs both the work and the representation of its protagonist, we are able to offer certain preliminary observations regarding the work's genre and worldview. Jonah, like other biblical prophets and certain leaders, mediates between the deity and human beings. He receives and conveys messages about the future and the state of things in the present, offering reasons for what might happen. He is eccentric, an intimate of the deity—and yet he is self-doubting. Journey is part of his life, and the end of his life journey is left ambiguous and uncertain. In contrast to much prophetic literature, Jonah is a tightly constructed narrative with a clear structure. The lament in chap. 2 is a traditional Israelite literary form that fits the context beautifully. Jonah literally imagines himself drowning, as the author draws upon a favorite metaphor of the psalmists. Annette Schellenberg points to the author's use of "fairy-tale motifs,"[92] a matter to be addressed throughout the present volume, and considers him to be one of the "literary prophets."[93] Schellenberg suggests further that the genre in which this literary prophet works might be called "didactive narrative."[94] Many scholars similarly seek the

---

90 Johan H. Coetzee points to another important feature of personal religion in Jonah, namely, its emphasis on the body with images of his bound and contained body ("Jonah from the Perspective of Jonah: Embodied Theology Illustrated," *Scrip* 90 [2005] 850-58); and Coetzee, "And Jonah Swam and Swam and Swam: Jonah's Body in Deep Waters," *OTE* 17 (2004) 521-30. See also Philip J. Nel, "The Symbolism and Function of Epic Space in Jonah," *JNSL* 25 (1999) 215-24.

91 Codex Vaticanus (B) of Tob 14:3-4 alludes to Jonah's prediction of the destruction of Nineveh. Tobit warns his sons that war and destruction are coming so that they best flee Assyria and Babylonia. Codex Sinaiticus (א) has the prediction attributed to Nahum. Emil Kraeling suggests that the author of Tobit was aware of some "older version of Jonah" in which presumably the prediction of Jonah is not superseded by God's change of mind or in which the threat remains, awaiting fulfillment ("Evolution of the Story of Jonah," 318). While the use of this material to support a theory about the evolution of Jonah is questionable, the allusion to Jonah's oracle in a postbiblical work such as Tobit testifies to the vibrancy of the Jonah tradition and the way in which pieces of the Jonah tale were reapplied. For another discussion of possible reasons for the reference to Jonah in Vaticanus (B), see Mark Bredin, "The Significance of Jonah in Vaticanus (B) Tobit 14:4 and 8," in Mark Bredin, ed., *Studies in the Book of Tobit: A Multidisciplinary Approach* (LSTS 55; London: T&T Clark, 2006) 43-58.

92 Schellenberg, "Anti-Prophet among the Prophets?," 366.

93 Ibid., 371.

94 Ibid., 366; Golka, "Jonah," 73; see also R. B. Salters, *Jonah and Lamentations* (OTG 29; Sheffield: JSOT Press, 1994) 48.

right terminology to describe the work's genre.⁹⁵ Gitay's phrase is "prosaic narrative";⁹⁶ Uriel Simon's, "theological prophetic story."⁹⁷ Alexander Rofé offers "imaginary parable";⁹⁸ George M. Landes, "*mašal* in the form of an example story."⁹⁹ Handy employs "biblical short story" and, with comparisons to wisdom literature of the late biblical period such as Judith, Tobit, Esther, and Daniel 1–6, writes of Jonah as "entertainment with a purpose."¹⁰⁰ Jacob M. Myers describes Jonah as "a parable or perhaps a sermon,"¹⁰¹ while James Limburg in the same vein suggests that both the psalm and the larger narrative that employs it reflect "the presence of a listening congregation," its setting in the context of a "gathered community."¹⁰² Glenda Abramson explores the qualities of Jonah as a "dramatic work," with emphasis on "conflict, characterization, and action."¹⁰³ Douglas Stuart settles on "sensational didactic historical narrative."¹⁰⁴ Roger Syrén views Jonah as "a reversed Diasporanovella."¹⁰⁵

Jonah is a narrative about a prophet, deeply informed by traditional motifs and patterns, but one that individuates the protagonist and reveals the humanistic worldview of its author in startlingly modern ways.¹⁰⁶ Trible suggests that Jonah moves among genres.¹⁰⁷ Frequently found efforts to identify Jonah as allegory, parody, or satire¹⁰⁸ make the mistake of ignoring what folklorist Dan

---

95 For an overview of scholarly efforts to define the genre of Jonah, see T. Desmond Alexander, "Jonah and Genre," *TynBul* 36 (1983) 35–59; Mona West, "Irony in the Book of Jonah: Audience Identification with the Hero," *PRSt* 11 (1984) 233–42, here 235.

96 Gitay, "Jonah: The Prophecy of Antirhetoric," 206.

97 Simon, *Jonah*, xx.

98 Rofé, *Prophetical Stories*, 159–60. On Jonah's function as a kind of parable, see also Barbara Green, "Beyond Messages: How Meaning Emerges from Our Reading of Jonah," *WW* 27 (2007) 149–56.

99 Landes, "Case for the Sixth-Century," 148.

100 Handy, *Jonah's World*, 119–22; Craghan, *Esther, Judith, Tobit, Jonah, Ruth*, 167.

101 Myers, *Book of Jonah*, 162. See also Leslie C. Allen, who describes Jonah as a parable whose tone is satire or parody (*The Books of Joel, Obadiah, Jonah, and Micah* (NICOT; Grand Rapids: Eerdmans, 1976) 177–78). See also Bewer, "Jonah," 24. Brevard Childs suggests that the work functions as a parable in its canonical context ("The Canonical Shape of the Book of Jonah," in Gary A. Tuttle, ed., *Biblical and Near Eastern Studies: Essays in Honor of William Sanford LaSor* [Grand Rapids: Eerdmans, 1970] 122–28, here 127). M. E. Andrew provides an overview of studies of Jonah's *Gattung* and concludes that the work is a *Novelle* that becomes a sermon on divine mercy ("*Gattung* and Intention in the Book of Jonah," *Orita* 1 [1967] 13–18, 78–85).

102 Limburg, *Jonah*, 66. Robert J. Ratner suggests that the primary target audience of Jonah consisted of prophets concerned about their role and vocation in a time of national stress ("Jonah: Toward the Re-education of the Prophets," *DD* 17 [1988–1989] 10–18).

103 Glenda Abramson, "The Book of Jonah as a Literary and Dramatic Work," *Semitics* 5 (1977) 36–47, here 44.

104 Douglas Stuart, *Hosea–Jonah* (WBC 31; Waco, TX: Word Books, 1987) 438; Scholem and Schwab, "On Jonah," 354. See also Gerhard von Rad, *God at Work in Israel* (trans. John H. Marks; Nashville: Abingdon, 1980) 58–70; Alexander, "Jonah and Genre," 59; Alexander, "Jonah: An Introduction," 84; Trépanier, "Story of Jonas," 15; G. W. Wade, *The Books of the Prophets Micah, Obadiah, Joel and Jonah* (Westminster Commentaries; London: Methuen, 1925) lxxviii.

105 Roger Syrén, "The Book of Jonah: A Reversed Diasporanovella?" *SEÅ* 58 (1993) 7–14.

106 See James S. Ackerman's description, "short story," ("Jonah," in Robert Alter and Frank Kermode, eds., *The Literary Guide to the Bible* [Cambridge, MA: Belknap Press of Harvard University Press, 1987] 234). Jonathan Kaplan explores Jonah from the perspective of moral agency, inviting readers "to wrestle with how to balance the executive self in relationship to both self-control and external authorship" ("Jonah and Moral Agency," *JSOT* 43 [2019] 146–62, here 161).

107 Trible, "Book of Jonah," 474.

108 See Hans Walter Wolff, *Obadiah and Jonah: A Commentary* (trans. Margaret Kohl; Minneapolis: Augsburg, 1986) 84–85; see also Edwin M. Good, *Irony in the Old Testament* (Bible and Literature 3; Sheffield: Almond, 1981) 41, 51, 54; Johanna W. H. Van Wijk-Bos, *Ruth, Esther, Jonah* (Knox Preaching Guides; Atlanta: John Knox, 1986) 74–75; Michael Orth, "Genre in Jonah: The Effects of Parody in the Book of Jonah," in William W. Hallo, Bruce William Jones, and Gerald L. Mattingly, eds., *The Bible in the Light of Cuneiform Literature* (Scripture in Context 3; ANETS 8; Lewiston, NY: Mellen, 1990) 257–81. Drawing comparisons with "literary strategies" employed in scribal schools of late Bronze Age Syria, William W. Hallo views Jonah as a "parody of literary prophecy in general, and of Nahum in particular" ("Jonah and

Ben-Amos has called "ethnic genres"[109] and superimposing upon this work the genre designations that belong to other cultural and literary contexts.[110] Similar efforts have been made to impose terms such as "saga" on tales of Genesis. Such designations rooted in other cultures and time frames never quite fit.[111] On the other hand, Jonah as narrative has always appealed to receivers of the tradition, long after its inclusion in the biblical anthology and well beyond the audience for which its author wrote. Ultimately readers can identify with this man, because we all suffer anger and depression, feel like fools, or are betrayed at various points in our lives. The reception of Jonah is another thread in the treatments that follow.

Each section of analysis will conclude with one or more examples of the ways in which postbiblical Jews and non-Jews have understood and portrayed Jonah and his

---

the Uses of Parody," in John J. Ahn and Stephen L. Cook, eds., *Thus Says the Lord: Essays on the Former and Latter Prophets in Honor of Robert R. Wilson* [LHBOTS 502; London: T&T Clark, 2009] 285–91, here 290). On qualities of the humorous, incongruous, and ironic, see Willie van Heerden, "Humour and the Interpretation of the Book of Jonah," *OTE* 5 (1992) 375–88; and Bernhard Duhm, *The Twelve Prophets: A Version in the Various Poetical Measures of the Original Writings* (trans. Archibald Duff; London: Adam & Charles Black, 1912) 50–51, 263.

See also Abraham Z. Ephros, "The Book of Jonah as Allegory," *JBQ* 27 (1999) 141–54. Virginia Ingram points to inconsistencies in Jonah as exemplifying satire and a related "psychological condition of cognitive dissonance" ("Satire and Cognitive Dissonance in the Book of Jonah, in the Light of Ellens' Laws of Psychological Hermeneutics," in J. Harold Ellens, ed., *Psychological Hermeneutics for Biblical Themes and Texts: A Festschrift for Wayne G. Rollins* [London: T&T Clark, 2012] 140–55, esp.140).

109 Dan Ben-Amos, "Analytical Categories and Ethnic Genres," in Dan Ben-Amos, ed., *Folklore Genres* (PAFSBSS 26; Austin: University of Texas Press, 1976) 215–42. See also Thomas M. Bolin, *Freedom beyond Forgiveness: The Book of Jonah Re-Examined* (JSOTSup 236; Sheffield: Sheffield Academic Press, 1997) 51–52. For a critique of satirical readings of Jonah, see Yvonne Sherwood, "Cross-Currents in the Book of Jonah: Some Jewish and Cultural Midrashim on a Traditional text," *BibInt* 6 (1998) 49–79, here 60–61; and Jenson, *Obadiah, Jonah, and Micah*, 34. On the subjectivity and culturally contoured responses to what might be satirical or ironic, see also Jenson, "Interpreting Jonah's God" 232.

110 Influenced by the work Mikhail Bakhtin, André and Pierre-Emmanuel LaCocque (*Jonah*, 39–44) find parallels between Jonah and Menippean satire, pointing to literary and philosophical influences in the Hellenistic Mediterranean world. While such cross-cultural genre designations may be suspect, the comparative work itself does lead to sensitive observations about the literary qualities, character portrayals, and messages of the book. Judson Mather describes Jonah as "parodic and farcical" comedy, characterized by qualities of the burlesque ("The Comic Art of the Book of Jonah," *Soundings* 65 [1982] 280–91, here 290). See also John R. Miles Jr., "Laughing at the Bible: Jonah as Parody," *JQR* 65 (1975) 168–81; Arnold J. Band, "Swallowing Jonah: The Eclipse of Parody," *Prooftexts* 10 (1990) 177–95; Millar Burrows, "The Literary Category of the Book of Jonah," in Harry Thomas Frank and William L. Reed, eds., *Translating and Understanding the Old Testament: Essays in Honor of Herbert Gordon May* (Nashville: Abingdon, 1970) 80–107; John C. Hulbert, "The Deliverance Belongs to Yahweh! Satire in the Book of Jonah," *JSOT* 21 (1981) 59–81; James S. Ackerman, "Satire and Symbolism in the Song of Jonah," in Baruch Halpern and Jon D. Levenson, eds., *Traditions in Transformation: Turning Points in Biblical Faith; A Festschrift Honoring Frank Moore Cross* (Winona Lake, IN: Eisenbrauns, 1982) 213–46; Zev Garber and Bruce Zuckerman, "The Odd Prophet Out and In," in Frederick E. Greenspahn and Gary A. Rendsburg, eds., *Le-ma'an Ziony: Essays in Honor of Ziony Zevit* (Eugene, OR: Cascade, 2017) 175–202. For a nuanced critique of characterizations of Jonah as parody or satire, see Ben Zvi, *Signs of Jonah*, 26–28; David Marcus, *From Balaam to Jonah: Anti-prophetic Satire in the Hebrew Bible* (BJS 301; Atlanta: Scholars Press, 1995) 93–159. Barbara Bakke Kaiser provides an insightful comparison of major directions in Jonah scholarship in a delightful parody of a scholarly session held in the belly of the fish. Trible, A. LaCocque, P. LaCocque, Sasson, and Sherwood are pictured in debate about the form and meaning of Jonah ("Five Scholars in the Underbelly of the *Dag Gadol*: An Aqua-Fantasy," *WW* 27 [2007] 135–48).

111 For a problematic treatment in somewhat the same vein, see the effort to link the biblical Jonah to the legend of Semiramis in Eckhart Frahm, "Of Doves, Fish, and Goddesses: Reflections on the Literary, Religious, and Historical Background of the Book of Jonah," in Joel Baden, Hindy Najman, and Eibert Tigchelaar, eds., *Sibyls, Scriptures, and Scrolls: John Collins at Seventy* (2 vols.; JSJSup 175.1-2; Leiden: Brill, 2016) 1:432–50.

story. Our sources will be verbal and nonverbal, drawn from the rabbinic exegetical tradition and Jewish and Christian artistic representations of scenes from the narrative.[112]

---

[112] A number of valuable studies have been devoted to the study of the reception history of Jonah. Yves-Marie Duval explores treatments of Jonah in early Greek and Latin Christian literature (*Le livre de Jonas dans la littérature chrétienne grecque et latine: Sources et influence du commentaire sur Jonas de saint Jérôme* [2 vols.; Paris: Études Augustiniennes, 1973]). In a wide-ranging and erudite discussion, Elias J. Bickerman draws comparisons between aspects of Jonah and features of ancient Near Eastern and classical Greek and Latin works and explores interpretations found in subsequent Jewish and Christian sources ("Les deux erreurs du prophète Jonas," *RHPR* 45 [1965] 232–64). R. H. Bowers's brief but substantial book explores Jewish and Christian interpretations of Jonah, paying special attention to British writers' appropriations in the Tudor and Elizabethan periods, including a mention of the appearance of Jonah in examples of popular culture such as puppet plays on the streets of London in the sixteenth century (*The Legend of Jonah* [The Hague: Martinus Nijhoff, 1971]); for a brief overview of the interpretation of Jonah in premodern and Jewish sources, see Bolin, *Freedom beyond Forgiveness*, 13–33. Yvonne Sherwood explores appropriations of Jonah in art and literature employing a methodology grounded in comparative cultural studies. She seeks to understand the social and historical contexts in which certain portrayals and adaptations of Jonah were meaningful (*A Biblical Text and Its Afterlives: The Survival of Jonah in Western Culture* [Cambridge: Cambridge University Press, 2000]); see also the series of essays in Johann Anselm Steiger and Wilhelm Kühlmann, eds., *Der problematische Prophet: Die biblische Jona-Figur in Exegese, Theologie, Literatur und bildender Kunst* (Arbeiten zur Kirchengeschichte 118; Berlin: de Gruyter, 2011); and the brief overview by scholar of comparative literature Sol Liptzin, "The Literary Impact of Jonah," *DD* 7 (1978) 9–20. Robert C. Gregg compares Jewish, Christian, and Muslim appropriations of Jonah, one case study in an excellent work on the ways in which biblical tales are reshaped within these related religious traditions (*Shared Stories, Rival Tellings: Early Encounters of Jews, Christians, and Muslims* [Oxford: Oxford University Press, 2015] 329–454). For an earlier study of Jonah in these three traditions, see Uwe Steffen, *Die Jona-Geschichte: Ihre Auslegung und Darstellung im Judentum, Christentum und Islam* (Neukirchen-Vlyun: Neukirchener Verlag, 1994). See also the work of O. Komlós, who sets Jonah in the context of folk literature and then explores rabbinic and Islamic receptions ("Jonah Legends," in O. Komlós, ed., *Etudes orientales à la mémoire de Paul Hirschler* [Budapest: Allamosittt, 1950] 41–61). An article by Tamar Kadari focuses on the reception of key scenes in Jonah: "Aggadic Motifs in the Story of Jonah: A Study of Interaction between Religions," in Alberdina Houtman et al., eds., *Religious Stories in Transformation: Conflict, Revision and Reception* (Jewish and Christian Perspectives 31; Leiden: Brill, 2016) 107–25. Leonard S. Kravitz and Kerry M. Olitzky provide a commentary informed by the Targum and by scholars of the classical tradition, including Rabbi Solomon ben Isaac (Rashi), Abraham ibn Ezra, and Rabbi David Kimchi (Redak) (*Jonah: A Modern Commentary* [New York: URJ Press, 2006]). See also Israel Drazin, *Unusual Bible Interpretations: Jonah and Amos* (Jerusalem: Gefen, 2016). For two works that trace the treatment of Jonah in classical Jewish commentaries, see Meir Zlotowitz and Nosson Scherman, *Sefer Yonah/Jonah: A New Translation with a Commentary Anthologized from Talmudic, Midrashic and Rabbinic Sources* (Brooklyn, NY: Mesorah, 1978); and Steven M. Bob, *Go to Nineveh: Medieval Jewish Commentaries on the Book of Jonah Translated and Explained* (Eugene, OR: Pickwick, 2013); in this vein, see also S. Goldman, "Jonah," in A. Cohen, ed., *The Twelve Prophets* (London: Soncino Press, 1948) 136–50. For a popular retelling of Jonah from the perspective of talmudic and midrashic sources, see Yosef Deutsch, *Let My Nation Be Warned: The Story of Yonah, a Reluctant Prophet on a Mission of Repentance* (Nanuet, NY: Feldheim, 2014). In a similar vein, see the comments by Raphael Shuchat, "Jonah the Rebellious Prophet: A Look at the Man behind the Prophecy Based on Biblical and Rabbinic Sources," *JBQ* 37 (2009) 45–52. For an introduction to the portrayal of Jonah in Western art, see James Limburg, "Jonah and the Whale through the Eyes of Artists," *BRev* 6 (1990) 18–25. For an overview of representations of Jonah by twentieth-century book illustrators, see Mordechai Beck, "Dreaming of Jonah/Living in Tarshish: Two Images of Jonah," *Tikkun* 10 (1995) 73–74. Rosemary A. Nixon provides a popular work that presents Jonah to modern readers and points to its reception and interpretation in Judaism, Christianity, and Islam (*The Message of Jonah: Presence in the Storm* [Bible Speaks Today; Downers Grove, IL: InterVarsity Press, 2003]). For a nicely homiletic treatment of Jonah that draws upon Jewish interpretative tradition, see Brown, *Jonah: The Reluctant Prophet*. Louis H. Feldman's study of Josephus's reception of Jonah underscores the latter's attention

to the historical genre as he understood it; Feldman emphasizes ways in which the Jewish historian's version of the prophet's tale sought to please and not offend his Roman hosts and how it might have appealed to a Greek audience ("Josephus' Interpretation of Jonah," *AJSR* 17 [1992] 1–29). Pointing to the interests of Roman and Jewish readers, C. T. Begg closely explores the ways in which Josephus's rewriting of the story somewhat rehabilitates the prophet, as the ancient historian retells the prophet's story in reference to the career of Jeroboam II ("Jeroboam II and Jonah" *BETL* 145 [2000] 251–72). For an excellent brief recent commentary enriched by sidebars that point to the reception of Jonah, special attention to Christian appropriations, and visual examples, see Nogalski, *Book of the Twelve*. Beat Weber's study includes a nice overview of the reception of Jonah in literature and art from ancient times to recent decades (*Jona*, 125–84).

Commentary

1

Charge and Avoidance　　　　　　　　　　　　　　　*1:1–3*

Translation

1/ And the word of Yahweh came to Jonah, son of Amittai, saying,
2/ "Rise up, go to Nineveh, the great city,
　　and proclaim against it,ᵃ
　　for arisen has their evil before me."ᵇ
3/ But Jonah rose up to flee to Tarshish
　　from before Yahweh
　　and he went down to Joppa
　　and he found a ship bound forᶜ Tarshish.ᵈ
　And he paid its fare,
　　and he went down into it to go with them to Tarshish
　　from before Yahweh.ᵉ

Textual Notes

a 4QXIIᵍ (partially reconstructed), Mur, MT read וקרא עליה, "and proclaim against it," but G reads καὶ κήρυξον ἐν αὐτῇ, "and proclaim/preach in it." For an extensive exegetical discussion of the possible nuances that might be conveyed by these choices of preposition, see Sasson, *Jonah*, 72–75. Tg. renders the "call" verb as ואתנבי עלה, "and prophesy against it."

b 4QXIIᵃ 4QXIIᵍ MT Mur read כי עלתה רעתם לפני, "because arisen has their evil before me." Still, G has the more expansive subject ἡ κραυγὴ τῆς κακίας αὐτῆς, "the cry of her evil," evoking the sort of imagery found in the tale of Cain and Abel (Gen 4:9), "the voice of the blood of your brother cries to me from the earth," heightening the moral nuance. See below on the translation of the recurring root רעע connoting a bad action, situation, or experience in Jonah.

c 1:3 MT reads לבוא/באה rooted in "to go," but G varies the language of travel with two verbs, βαδίζον, "went," and πλεῦσαι, "to sail."

d Tg. interprets Tarshish, an unknown location, to be "the sea," ימא, both here and in numerous other prophetic texts that mention Tarshish (Isa 2:16; 23:1, 14; 60:9; 66:19; Ezek 27:12, 25; 38:13; Jon 4:2).

e Tg. interprets "away from Yahweh" to read "before he would prophesy in the name of the Lord," מן קדם דיתנבי בשמא דיוי, emphasizing Jonah's desire to avoid his mission.

Commentary

A typical commission by the deity of a prophet begins the Jonah narrative, but this charge does not lead to the prophet's fulfillment of his command. Instead, for unexplained reasons, he tries to flee and ends up at sea. In this way, at its very opening, the narrative underscores tensions and ambiguities that characterize the work as a whole.

■ 1 The opening rubric of the book, ויהי דבר־יהוה אל יונה בן־אמתי לאמור, literally, "and there was a word of Yahweh to Jonah, son of Amittai, saying," leads to consideration of date, genre, and goals. The rubric is employed to introduce an eighth-century BCE message to the prophet Isaiah (Isa 38:4), in which God responds to the prayer of King Hezekiah in his illness. In this scene, God agrees to extend the ill king's life for fifteen years, overturning a previous prophecy, because the prophet had petitioned the deity with reminders of his servant's faithfulness. More often, however, the rubric introduces stories of the Former Prophets, whose exploits are narrated in the Deuteronomistic History, and the rubric is also found in material that self-presents, for the most part, as late biblical in date in contexts framed by the Babylonian invasions and Persian-period return. The introductory framing language in Jonah 1:1 is thus found in 1 Sam 4:1 and 15:10 regarding communication received by the prophet Samuel; in 2 Sam 7:4 regarding a divine message to Nathan; in 1 Kgs 6:11 about God's communication to King Solomon; in 1 Kgs 12:22 concerning communication to "Shemiah, a man of God"; in 1 Kgs 13:20 concerning a message to an unnamed man of God; in

1 Kgs 16:1 concerning the prophet Jehu, son of Hanani (cf. 2 Chr 19:2-3, 7-10); and in 1 Kgs 17:2, 8; 21:17, 28 concerning Elijah. Other uses of this rubric formula are found in Jer 1:4, 11, 13; 2:1; 13:3, 8; 16:1; 18:5; 24:4; 28:12, frequently in chap. 29 and elsewhere in the Jeremiah corpus (33:1, 19; 34:12; 36:27; 37:6; 42:7; 43:8). Additional examples are found in Ezekiel (3:16; 6:1; 7:1; 12:8; 24:1), in Haggai (1:3; 2:20), and in the book of the prophet Zechariah (4:8; 6:9; 7:4, 8; 8:1).[1]

Much has been written concerning biblical narratives beginning with the phrase ויהי, literally, "and there was,"[2] including suggestions about the phrase's connections to founding tales of heroes and the epic genre. Douglas Stuart suggests that the sentence be regarded as comparable to "once upon a time."[3] Jack Sasson points out that the longer phrase in Jonah beginning with ויהי, examples of which are listed above, is "found only when contexts and circumstances regarding the prophet and his mission are already established in previous statements."[4] Thus, Wilhelm Rudolph concludes that the rubric links Jonah to the prophet of the same name mentioned in 2 Kgs 14:25.[5] This matter of allusion to previous circumstances does not seem to be in play in many of the references above. Still, it is part of and frequently the beginning of an account in which an oracle or oracles will figure and usually identifies the receiver of God's word as a prophet.

By contrast, Hosea, Joel, Amos, Obadiah, Micah, Nahum, Habakkuk, and Zephaniah all begin with variations on the formula דבר־יהוה אשר היה אל, followed by the name of the prophet, "the word of Yahweh was to [the named prophet]." Jonah's opening phrase functions, as Sasson notes, as a superscript to an oracle or oracles, emphasizing "the message instead of informing us about the prophet who carries it,"[6] the protagonist of the tale to follow. The textual tradition offers variant spellings of the prophet's name.[7]

As noted in the introduction, the name יונה בן־אמתי is attributed to a prophet in 2 Kings 14, said to serve the eighth-century BCE king Jeroboam II of the northern kingdom of Israel. Scholars generally agree that the author of Jonah perceives some sort of purposeful link between the two, but it is uncertain, however, how much the author intended receivers of the story to draw in terms of explicit historical connections. Does he situate the tale of Jonah in relation to the status of Assyria, with an eye to that kingdom's future ascendency and fall? Does the author of Jonah suggest, for example, that Assyrians repent only to do more evil and eventually be punished?[8] The possibility of such an orientation leads to further suggestions about the work's relation to other prophetic compositions among the Twelve and its placement in the LXX before Nahum, who unequivocally condemns Assyria. The view of this compiler would be that the Assyrians are temporarily spared (in Jonah) only to be brought down later, after their harsh treatment of

---

1   See also Hag 1:1 and Zech 1:1, in which the verb "to be" is used in the perfect: "[on such and such a date] the word of Yahweh was in the hand of Haggai the prophet/to Zechariah." For a discussion of the function of ויהי in prophetic literature and "the Twelve," see Diana V. Edelman: "Jonah among the Twelve in the MT: The Triumph of Torah over Prophecy," in Diana V. Edelman and Ehud Ben Zvi, eds., *The Production of Prophecy: Constructing Prophecy and Prophets in Yehud* (BibleWorld; London: Equinox, 2009) 150-67, here 151-52.

2   Susan Niditch, "The Challenge of Israelite Epic," in John Miles Foley, ed., *A Companion to Ancient Epic* (Blackwell Companions to the Ancient World: Literature and Culture; Oxford: Blackwell, 2005) 277-87, here 280-82; Niditch, *Judges: A Commentary* (OTL; Louisville: Westminster John Knox, 2008) 14-15; Yaira Amit, "There was a man . . . and his name was . . .": Editorial Variations and Their Tendenz" [in Hebrew], BetM 30 (1984-1985) 388-99; Sasson, *Jonah*, 66-68; Limburg, *Jonah*, 23, 37-38.

3   Stuart, *Hosea-Jonah*, 445.

4   Sasson, *Jonah*, 67.

5   Wilhelm Rudolph, *Joel, Amos, Obadja, Jona: Mit einer Zeittafel von Alfred Jepsen* (KAT 13.2; Gütersloh: Mohn, 1971) 335-36.

6   Sasson, *Jonah*, 67. See also McKenzie, "Genre of Jonah," 160.

7   See Sasson, *Jonah*, 68-69; and Trible, "Studies in the Book of Jonah," 10-11.

8   For a discussion of ways in which the eighth-century BCE prophet might have figured in the imagination of the writer and the receivers of his story, see Ben Zvi, *Signs of Jonah*, 48, 53-54.

Israel and Judah. While such connections are possible, it seems more likely that an author employs a figure from tradition, known by name and mentioned briefly in the Deuteronomistic corpus, to provide some verisimilitude to the character, a prophet of old situated in the north before the exile. Specifics about the Jonah of 2 Kings—that he was a central prophet during the reign of Jeroboam II and that, as a prophet to the crown, he predicted correctly that Jeroboam would restore the border of Israel (2 Kgs 14:25)—seem less relevant. Leslie Allen suggests, however, that because the Jonah of 2 Kings 14 is a nationalist, he offers a good model for the man who does not want to preach to Assyrians.[9] To be sure, the brief passage in 2 Kings 14 mentions Israel's distress and the divine promise to save Israel from utter destruction (2 Kgs 14:26–27), themes that might be expected to lurk in the mind of the recalcitrant hero of Jonah. Still, the book of Jonah does not need to be understood so closely in relation to 2 Kings 14 and moves in other creative directions.

Questions are also raised about the etymology of the name יונה בן־אמתי and its possible symbolic resonances. As Sasson notes, scholars have derived possible connotations from the root ינה, "to oppress" or "to suppress," from יון, "Greece," and other unlikely candidates.[10] The יונה is a dove, the lovely bird, comparable to terms for other creatures from the natural kingdom employed by parents for the names of children. The word אמתי, vocalized somewhat differently in the versions,"[11] is derived from the root אמן, "to confirm," and evokes the related term אמת, "truth." The *yod* (י) at the end functions perhaps as a hypocoristicon so that the name means "firm/true is Ya(hweh)."

While some scholars, for example, Alan J. Hauser and George A. F. Knight, view the dove name of the hero as essential to messages of the book, others such as Stuart do not see the the term "dove" as heavily symbolic.[12] The dove is a symbol of endearment in Song of Songs that references the beautiful eyes of the beloved or her person (1:15; 2:14; 4:1; 5:2; 6:9). One could also imagine such a name for a dear child, male or female. The dove is frequently a sacrificial animal in Priestly texts (Lev 12:6, 8; 15:14, 29; Num 6:10) and is used metaphorically to describe flightness, simple-mindedness (Hos 7:11), or the capacity to fly (Ps 55:7; Isa 60:8; Hos 7:11). Other biblical references refer to the moaning sound made by doves (Isa 38:14; 59:11; Ezek 7:16). Robert Alter suggests that perhaps the name in this prophetic work alludes to the story of Noah, where a dove is associated with the end of a "punitive cataclysm."[13] In Jonah, the disaster is avoided. The Eurasian rock dove has homing capacities, and so may be an appropriate image both for the tale of Noah and for the name of a prophet who serves as an intermediary and conveyer of messages.

■ **2** As noted by Sasson and W. Dennis Tucker, the opening two verbs of 1:2, imperatives in form, create a phrase in which the first verb, קום, literally, "rise up," functions as an auxiliary to the command, "go" (לך).[14] The term "rise" lends the command urgency, insistence, or immediacy.[15] In addition to Jonah 1:2, the command (קום +) is used in such a phrase in Jonah 1:6 and 3:2, and with לך, "go," in 3:2 to indicate a commission to the prophet. Similar commission language is addressed by the deity or his messenger to Elijah (1 Kgs 17:9; 21:18; 2 Kgs 1:3), to Jeremiah (Jer 13:4, 6), and to Ezekiel (Ezek 3:22). The language evoking a formulaic call to the prophet

---

9 Allen, *Joel, Obadiah, Jonah, and Micah*, 179.
10 Sasson, *Jonah*, 69.
11 See Sasson, *Jonah*, 69; Trible, "Studies in the Book of Jonah," 11.
12 Knight, *Ruth and Jonah*, 56–57; Alan Jon Hauser relates the dove to themes of flight and passivity ("Jonah: In Pursuit of the Dove," *JBL* 104 [1985] 21–37, esp. 22–23); Stuart, *Hosea–Jonah*, 447. See also Robert Alter, who weighs these possibilities (*Strong as Death Is Love: The Song of Songs, Ruth, Esther, Jonah, and Daniel; A Translation with Commentary* [New York: Norton, 2015] 135–36).
13 Alter, *Strong as Death*, 135. On the implications of Jonah's name, see also the discussion by Ben Zvi, *Signs of Jonah*, 41–43.
14 Sasson, *Jonah*, 69–70; Tucker, *Jonah*, 13.
15 See also Trible, "Studies in the Book of Jonah," 204–6; Trible, *Rhetorical Criticism*, 125; GKC §120g. Moshe Pelli discusses the use of קום in Jonah in the context of the work's emphasis on movement and entrapment ("The Literary Art of Jonah," *HS* 20/21 [1979–1980] 18–28, esp. 19–20).

in Jonah suggests a traditional biblical pattern, and often after the deity commissions his servant, the latter attempts to refuse—so Moses and Jeremiah—and yet here the refusal involves the prophet's flight (see overview below).[16]

Nineveh, one of the most important cities and the eventual capital of the Assyrian empire, is located on the east bank of the Tigris River, within the suburban outskirts of the Iraqi city of Mosul, which figured so prominently in the twenty-first-century battles for the control of Iraq. The history of the city reaches back to the seventh millennium BCE, but its reputation as an imposing, beautiful city is associated with Sennacherib (705–681 BCE), the invader of Judah, who chose the site as his capital. Sennacherib expanded Nineveh with a variety of magnificent improvements in infrastructure, including walls, gates, gardens, canals, aqueducts, and buildings, the most famous project being his own "Palace without Rival." This palace was decorated with more than two thousand artistically innovative reliefs that allowed for "perspective and narrative exploration."[17] The scenes depicted on the reliefs are exquisite tools of propaganda emphasizing the power and inevitability of Assyrian ascendancy. Historian of Assyrian art John M. Russell describes the audience of these reliefs portraying Assyrian victory and control: gods, captive workers, foreign visitors such as diplomats, interpreters, bearers of tribute, the king himself, senior officials, royal attendants, scribes, household staff, diviners, and singers.[18] Similarly, art historian Irene Winter notes that "right from the beginning there was a heterogeneous, ethnic and cultural audience for the palace reliefs" and that the diverse audience grew as the empire expanded.[19]

Sennacherib's son Esarhaddon and his grandson Ashurbanipal would rule after him and would add to the city's splendor, the latter famous for his vast library. But political turmoil and decline followed Ashurbanipal's death in the late seventh century BCE, and in 612 BCE Nineveh fell to allied forces of the Babylonians, the Persians, and the Medes.[20]

The phrase "Nineveh, the great city" in Jonah 1:2 raises questions about the author's historical and ideological orientation, as does the possible identification of Jonah with the eighth-century BCE prophet mentioned in 2 Kings. A common thread in Jonah studies is to assume a synecdochic identification between Nineveh and Assyria; this leads to questions about God's care for Nineveh and the prophet's effort to resist a mission to the inhabitants of this Assyrian city that might result in their being spared divine wrath. The second line of thought in scholarship questions whether Nineveh is a cipher or symbol for a particularly vicious enemy, one whose tactics are extremely aggressive. Assyria's totalistic prosecution of war is portrayed in ancient Near Eastern literature, including the Hebrew Bible, and in artistic visual representations of the behavior of Assyrian conquerors.[21] Indeed André LaCoque and Pierre-Emmanuel LaCoque describe a mission to Nineveh as a virtual descent into hell and regard the resonances of "Nineveh" for ancient Israelites as comparable in negative connotations to the mention of Auschwitz for contemporary Jews.[22] Alternatively, is Nineveh to be

---

[16] On the call narrative, see N. Habel, "The Form and Significance of the Call Narrative," *ZAW* 77 (1965) 297–323; Martin J. Buss, "An Anthropological Perspective on Prophetic Call Narratives," *Semeia* 21 (1981) 9–30.

[17] Russell, "Sennacherib's Lachish Narratives," 60.

[18] John M. Russell, *Sennacherib's Palace without Rival at Nineveh* (Chicago: University of Chicago Press, 1991) 238–40.

[19] Irene Winter, "Royal Rhetoric and the Development of Historical Narratives in Neo-Assyrian Reliefs," *SVC* 7.2 (1981) 2–38, esp. 30.

[20] For a recent political overview of the Assyrian empire, see Mario Liverani, *Assyria: The Imperial Mission* (trans. Andrea Trameri and Jonathan Valk; Mesopotamian Civilizations 20; Winona Lake, IN: Eisenbrauns, 2017).

[21] See Michael G. Hasel, "Assyrian Military Practices and Deuteronomy's Laws of Warfare," in Brad E. Kelle and Frank Ritchel Ames, eds., *Writing and Reading War: Rhetoric, Gender, and Ethics in Biblical and Modern Contexts* (SBLSymS 42; Atlanta: Society of Biblical Literature, 2008) 67–81.

[22] LaCoque and LaCoque, *Jonah*, 37, 73–74. See also Limburg, who views the meaning of Nineveh in Jonah in reference to condemnations by the prophets Zephaniah and Nahum (*Jonah*, 41–42); and Gitay, "Jonah: The Prophecy of Antirhetoric," 200.

identified by audiences with some faraway metropolis of the past, opulent, powerful, and now defunct? The emphasis on Nineveh's size, greatness, and significance is conveyed by the language of bigness, העיר הגדולה, here in 1:2 and also in 3:2–3 and 4:11. Thomas Bolin equates the view of Nineveh in Jonah with Hellenistic representations of "the idyllic great city of long ago, full of gross excess and exotic opulence"; he rejects the notion that receivers of the story would have considered the reference as representing "the cruel Assyrian empire, Israel's bitterest enemy."[23] Both nuances may be in play.[24] "Nineveh" may stand for "Assyria," as references to Washington, DC, often synecdochically connote the United States.

Nineveh is identified as Sennacherib's royal residence in 2 Kgs 19:36 and its parallel text in Isa 37:37, the place of his assassination according to this biblical tradition.[25] Genesis includes a mythological tradition that Nineveh was built in Assyria by the hero Nimrud (10:11). Finally, oracles are directed against Nineveh by the prophets Zephaniah (2:13) and Nahum (1:1; 2:8). Nahum 2:9 refers to this Assyrian capital as wealthy but doomed (cf. Nah 3:7). Describing the end of Assyria's power, Zeph 2:13 also juxtaposes Nineveh with Assyria in poetic parallelism and describes the righteous glee of those who witness its fall (Zeph 2:15). The suggestion that Nineveh can stand for the larger Assyrian polity does seem justified, and the range of biblical references seems to point both to the rise and deserved fall of a savage enemy from an Israelite perspective, and to the city's international and even timeless status as iconically grand. So Babylon, so Rome.[26] (See further the overview and comments on chap. 3).

The verb "to call" (קרא) here translated as "proclaim," is frequently employed by the author of Jonah in reference to prayers (1:6; 2:3; 3:8). The phrase "proclaim," literally, "'call' against her," continues the prophet's commissioning. "To call" is found with a divine command to action or initiation in Zech 7:7, 13, directed to prophets in Isa 49:1 (cf. Isa 42:6), to a new ruler in Isa 22:20, and to Cyrus in Isa 41:9. The use of the preposition על lends the verb an antagonistic nuance.[27] In Deut 15:9, a neighbor cries (קרא) to the Lord against (על) oppressors; in 1 Kgs 13:2 a man of God proclaims (קרא) against (על) Jeroboam's altar by the word of God; in Ezek 38:21, God calls forth (קרא) a sword against (על) Gog. Similarly, Jer 49:29 proclaims (קרא) against (על) Kedar "terror all around," and in Jer 25:29, God summons (קרא) a sword against (על) all inhabitants of the land. In Jonah, the prophet is commissioned to proclaim against Nineveh.

The phrase כי עלתה רעתם לפני, "for arisen has their evil before me," has several interesting implications for the worldview of the author and the theme of the book. The term "evil" (רעע) is used seven times throughout the narrative, and it is frequently translated into English with varying vocabulary to capture the nuance of wrongdoing: "wickedness" (NRSV 1:2), "calamity" (NRSV 1:7, 8; 3:10), "evil" (NRSV 3:8, 10), being "displeasing" (NRSV 4:1), sending calamity (NRSV "punishing," 4:1),

---

23 Thomas M. Bolin, "'Should I Not Also Pity Nineveh?' Divine Freedom in the Book of Jonah," *JSOT* 67 (1995) 109–20. Bolin in fact dates Jonah to the Hellenistic period in part based on this view of Nineveh in Hellenistic literature. Carey Walsh comments that Jonah, like the Persian-period work Esther, "takes place in strange lands" ("Between Text and Sermon: Jonah 3," *Int* 69 [2015] 338–40, esp. 338).

24 Wolff, *Obadiah and Jonah*, 99, 147; Allen, *Joel, Obadiah, Jonah, and Micah*, 203.

25 See Simo Parpola, "The Murder of Sennacherib," in Bendt Alster, ed., *Death in Mesopotamia: Papers Read at the XXVIe Rencontre Assyriologique Internationale* (Mesopotamia 8; Copenhagen: Akedemisk, 1980) 171–82. See also Andrew Knapp, "The Murder of Sennacherib, Yet Again," *JAOS* 140 (2020) 165–81.

26 See Allen, *Joel, Obadiah, Jonah, and Micah*, 203.

27 See Sasson, *Jonah*, 74–75; and compare Jonah 3:2, which employs the preposition אל rather than על. Douglas K. Stuart offers an alternate translation of Jonah 1:2 that nuances the understanding of God's purpose and suggests a more sympathetic portrayal of the Ninevites than suggested by many scholars: "Go to the important city, Nineveh, and speak to it, for their trouble concerns me" ("'The Great City of Nineveh' [Jon. 1:2]," *BibSac* 171 [2014] 387–400).

or "discomfort" (NRSV 4:6). The ancient translators, too, made an effort to capture differences in nuance and meaning through various vocabulary choices for the root רעע.

I have translated this root throughout as "evil" and think it necessary to note that calamity or wrongdoing or suffering discomfort are all forms of evil, whether deserved or underserved, a way of acting or an experience. All these notions are perceived as somehow connected to divine expectations for proper behavior, which are sometimes ambiguous, or a sentence imposed by the deity, fair or not, including flood, storm, illness, and death.[28] As Alan Cooper and Thomas M. Bolin have noted, the Jonah tale suggests that the treatment of human beings, to forgive or not, to punish or not, may be a matter of "divine caprice."[29] As the sailors say to Yahweh in their prayer, "that which you desire, you do" (1:14).[30] Bolin points out that, in this respect, the worldview of Jonah shares much with ideas expressed in late biblical works such as Ecclesiastes and Job.[31] A consistent translation of terms derived from רעע as "evil" thus not only seeks to capture the purposefully delimited traditional-style use of vocabulary in Jonah but also important qualities of its message and meaning.

The nature of the "evil" to which Yahweh refers in 1:2 seems to be akin to the "violence" (חמס) referenced in 3:8, where the king of Nineveh, through his proclamation, acknowledges the violence or ethical shortcomings in the ways in which people treat one another in Nineveh.[32] The image of this evil rising up to God has important implications and leads to a number of inner-biblical comparisons.

Most important, it is assumed and emphasized that the deity observes, hears, and will address evil promulgated by individuals and groups. God hears the cries of the oppressed (Exod 22:22); the blood of a murdered brother cries out to God from the ground (Gen 4:10); God sees that great is the evil of humanity (Gen 6:4); and the cries of violence in Sodom come to the deity (Gen 18:21). The person beset by enemies asks in his lament that the evil they do to him "come before you [God]" (cf. Pss 88:3; 102:3). The cry of the city Ashdod rises toward heaven, for the people suffer from tumors after the arrival of the captured ark (1 Sam 5:12). The deity is always within reach and watches over individuals, cities, and social groups, and their complaints and suffering come to him, as does knowledge of actions that cause the suffering of others. Such information about the disposition of individuals or groups is sometimes said to rise as in Jonah 1:2, suggesting that God is above, in the world visited by various prophets such as Isaiah and Micaiah, the place from which and to which the angels seen by Jacob in his dream vision descend and ascend (Gen 28:2). So too, the Israelites' archetypal cry for help

---

28 For a discussion of modes of being described as evil in prophetic literature, see Handy, *Jonah's World*, 76–77. On ways in which this root contributes to purposeful lexical enigma in Jonah, see Ernst Wendland, "Recursion and Variation in the 'Prophecy' of Jonah: On the Rhetorical Impact of Stylistic Technique in Hebrew Narrative Discourse with Special Reference to Irony and Enigma (Part Three)," *AUSS* 36 (1998) 81–110, esp. 103–4.

29 Alan Cooper, "In Praise of Divine Caprice: The Significance of the Book of Jonah," in Philip R. Davies and David J. A. Clines, eds., *Among the Prophets: Language, Image and Structure in the Prophetic Writings* (JSOTSup 144; Sheffield: JSOT Press, 1993) 144–63, here 150. Bolin, "'Should I Not Also Pity Nineveh?,'" 110. See also Elias Bickerman, *Four Strange Books of the Bible: Jonah, Daniel, Koheleth, Esther* (New York: Schocken, 1967), 47.

30 On the verb's morphology, see textual note s on 1:14.

31 Bolin, "'Should I Not Also Pity Nineveh?,'" 120.

32 Harry Orlinsky draws a distinction between lawlessness and political oppression perpetrated by Assyria against Israel and other conquered peoples ("Nationalism, Universalism and Internationalism in Ancient Israel," in Harry Thomas Frank and William L. Reed, eds., *Translating and Understanding the Old Testament: Essays in Honor of Herbert Gordon May* [Nashville: Abingdon, 1970] 206–37, here 231). See also Tigay, "Days of Awe," 70. See also Simon, who draws a distinction between the way citizens treat one another and Assyrian imperialism, the former being the emphasis here in his view (*Jonah*, 5); in a similar vein, see H. L. Ginsberg, *The Five Megilloth and Jonah: A New Translation* (Philadelphia: Jewish Publication Society, 1969) 115–16.

rises up to God as they groan under Pharaoh's slavery (Exod 2:23). The small phrase in Jonah 1:2 concerning evil rising up before the deity thus suggests much about worldview and ethos; the implicit message about divine attention helps to make sense of the world, providing hope for the oppressed and a warning to oppressors.[33]

■ **3** Jonah 1:3 reprises the language of קום, "to rise up." Jonah, however, rises up and runs away rather than following divine directions of the commission language in 1:2. His goal is to flee to Tarshish. The term תרשיש is found numerous times in the Hebrew Bible, and these usages provide an instructive range of meanings that may inform Jonah 1:3. One set of texts treats תרשיש as a mineral or a golden-colored gem. It is the stone located in the four rows of precious stones on the priestly breastplate (Exod 28:20; 39:13). It is the material that characterizes the wheels of the divine throne observed by the prophet Ezekiel in his mystical initiation vision כעין תרשיש, the gleaming or sparkling of beryl or jasper (Ezek 1:16; cf.10:9). This mineral is also listed among the gems in the bejeweled paradise lost by the king of Tyre in Ezekiel's alternate and urbane vision of the Garden of Eden and the fall (Ezek 28:13). The body of the man clothed in linen in the vision of Dan 10:6 is also *taršîš*-like, as are the arms of the male lover in Song of Songs 5:14.

The second set of texts treats Tarshish as a coastal location, or, as BDB suggests, "a distant port, site not certainly known" (Isa 23:6).[34] Some have suggested that Tarshish is to be equated with an actual port in the Western Mediterranean, perhaps its sound-alike Tartessus in southern Spain.[35] Sasson offers a review of etymological options for the meaning of the name. He lists the various actual place identifications suggested by scholars, concluding that Tarshish must have been an actual place at some period, "the geographical and directional opposite of Nineveh," a location in the far west.[36]

In the Hebrew Bible, Tarshish is presented as a place that produces merchants (Ezek 27:12; 38:13) and trades in precious commodities such as silver (Jer 10:9; cf. Ezek 27:25). It is a city-state, one of the distant nations in Isa 66:19, who have not heard God's name or seen God's glory. In Ps 72:10, Tarshish is imagined to have kings, a somewhat mythical place like Sheba, with which it is listed. The phrase "ships of Tarshish" (Isa 2:16; 23:1, 14; 60:9; Ezek 27:25; 1 Kgs 10:22, 23; 22:49; Ps 48:8 [7][37]) refers to a type of seafaring vessel or to vessels from this port. According to the Targum, Jonah's journey is not "to Tarshish" but "to the sea" (see textual note d on 1:3). How do these various references illuminate the imagining of the author of Jonah?

Tarshish seems to suggest an actual port that might welcome and send off ships that go to and fro, transporting wares in the ancient Mediterranean world. Like other places worldwide, however, the name also connotes mystery, a faraway place that few of one's neighbors have visited, a source of luxury items, where no one worships Yahweh—at least not yet.

The phrase translated as "from before Yahweh," is understood by John Walton to indicate a departure from an official audience with the deity, initiated in 1:1 by the divine voice. Walton draws comparisons with scenes in Gen 41:46 and 2 Kgs 5:27 in which a character of lesser status leaves the presence of a superior.[38] Most commentators, however, emphasize instead the intent and direc-

---

33 The quasi-legal framework for God's making sense of the world has been recognized by Patrick D. Miller (*They Cried to the Lord: The Form and Theology of Biblical Prayer* [Minneapolis: Fortress Press, 1994]) and Shalom Holtz (*Praying Legally* [BJS 364; Providence, RI: Brown Judaic Studies, 2019]).

34 BDB, s.v. "תַּרְשִׁישׁ II."

35 See Hardy, *Jonah's World*, 27–31.

36 Sasson, *Jonah*, 79; also 82–83, 92. See also Wolff, *Obadiah and Jonah*, 100–101; Ackerman, "Jonah," 235; Allen, *Joel, Obadiah, Jonah, and Micah*, 204 n. 10. Ackerman suggests that Tarshish and Nineveh are "geographic antipoles," both in location and in connotation ("Jonah," 235). See also LaCoque and LaCoque, *Jonah*, 75; Limburg, *Jonah*, 43; Simon, *Jonah*, 5. Arcadio del Castillo suggests that Tarshish is to be identified with an area close to the Red Sea and points to the Nile canal opened by Darius I, which he believes was in use in the time of Jonah's author ("Tarshish in the Book of Jonah," *RB* 114 [2007] 481–98).

37 References to Psalms are to the MT chapter and verse; numbers in square brackets indicate the English versification when it differs from the MT.

38 John H. Walton, "Jonah" in Bryan Beyer and John H. Walton, *Obadiah, Jonah* (BSC; Grand Rapids: Zondervan, 1982), 14.

tion of hasty escape suggested by the phrase here and in 1:10, where it is repeated. Furthermore, Trible points to repeated words and phrases in 1:3, such as Tarshish, "from before the presence of Yahweh," and "went down," and finds a purposely chiastic arrangement for this verse.[39]

The deity from whom Jonah flees is called Yahweh (YHWH), but the Israelite God is called Elohim in many other places in Jonah. Much has been written concerning this variation. Elizabeth Goldstein suggests that Yahweh is employed here, as in 1:4, when the deity engages with an Israelite but that Elohim is found to describe relationships or interactions between the deity and non-Israelites.[40]

The verb ירד, "to go down," is another of the frequently employed words in Jonah's purposeful economy of language (1:3, 5; 2:7). Jonathan Magonet suggests that this verb, as employed in Jonah, has both physical and spiritual dimensions.[41] Alter points out that the direction of Jonah, the character, is to move farther and farther downward.[42] To build on his suggestion, Jonah first heads down to the coast (1:3), then into the ship (1:3), then farther into the recesses of the ship when the storm grows wild (1:5), then into the sea, then into the fish (where the verb ירד itself is not employed although the downward motion continues), then metaphorically into the bowels of the earth itself, a descent into Sheol, in the lament of chap. 2 (see 2:6).

Joppa, northwest of Jerusalem (modern Jaffa; Tel Aviv-Yafo), is the local port where Jonah hopes to connect with a vessel headed to Tarshish. An ancient site with evidence of human habitation and culture going back to the Neolithic period, the coastal port of Joppa is mentioned in Ezra 3:7; 2 Chr 2:15; 1 Macc 10:76 and is associated with sea stories in ancient Mediterranean lore, including those featuring monsters (see the overview below on folk motifs).[43] Jacob Kaplan notes that archaeological evidence of Persian-period Joppa indicates "economic prosperity and expansion" in the latter part of the fifth century BCE by which time the port is a Phoenician city.[44]

My translation treats באה, "going," as a feminine singular active participial form, an attributive participle modifying "ship," with the nuance of being about to do something.[45] The existence of merchant ships plying the Mediterranean in the first millennium BCE is well attested in archaeological and representational evidence for the material culture of seafaring.[46] Merchant ships "tended to be broad and heavy," "roomy enough to take passengers as well as profitable cargo," and they relied

---

39 Trible, *Rhetorical Criticism*, 129.
40 Elizabeth Goldstein, "On the Use of the Name of God in the Book of Jonah," in Sarah Malena and David Miano, eds., *Milk and Honey: Essays on Ancient Israel and the Bible in Appreciation of the Judaic Studies Program at the University of California, San Diego* (Winona Lake, IN: Eisenbrauns, 2007), 77–83.
41 Magonet, *Form and Meaning*, 17; see also Peter C. Craigie, *Twelve Prophets*, vol. 1: *Hosea, Joel, Amos, Obadiah and Jonah* (DSB; Louisville: Westminster John Knox, 1984) 219.
42 Alter, *Strong as Death*, 140.
43 See Wolff, *Studien zum Jonabuch*, 26; M. Avi, "Jonah, Perseus and Andromeda at Joppa" [in Hebrew], *Yediot* 31 (1967) 203–10; J. Kaplan, "The Archaeology and History of Tel Aviv-Jaffa," *BA* 35 (1972) 66–95, esp. 87.
44 Kaplan, "Archaeology and History," 87. For further discussion, see Handy, *Jonah's World*, 25–26. See also Martin Peilstöker and Aaron A. Burke, eds., *The History and Archaeology of Jaffa, 1* (Monumenta Archaeologica 25; Los Angeles: Cotsen Institute of Archaeology Press, University of California Los Angeles, 2011); Aaron A. Burke, Katherine Strange Burke, and Martin Peilstöker, eds., *The History and Archaeology of Jaffa, 2* (Monumenta Archaeologica 41; Los Angeles: Cotsen Institute of Archaeology Press, 2017).
45 See Norman H. Snaith, *Notes on the Hebrew Text of Jonah* (London: Epworth Press, 1945) 10. For an alternate possibility that emphasizes the verb's typical meaning of coming toward rather than away from, see Sasson, *Jonah*, 82; also Tucker, *Jonah*, 16.
46 For an illuminating discussion of ancient seafaring based on underwater archaeological evidence, see Robert Ballard, Lawrence Stager, et al., "Iron Age Shipwrecks in Deep Water off Ashkelon, Israel," *AJA* 106 (2002) 151–68. The authors shed light on the varieties of cargo carried, the structure of vessels, and the sort of routes chosen by ancient mariners and link their findings to biblical allusions.

on sails and wind for locomotion. Due to their bulk, they "were rowed, ineffectively, only when absolutely necessary."[47] James Limburg draws comparisons with the image of a Tyrian vessel in the oracle against Tyre in Ezek 27:5-7; the text describes the sort of wood used to construct the ship's planks, mast, oars, and deck, and the linen of which its sail is made.[48]

Some modern scholarly literature and traditional Jewish commentaries that deal with Jonah's hiring a vessel or paying for his fare discuss the cost of such a journey in ancient times, whether Jonah is to be imagined a wealthy man, and whether he hired the whole ship or just purchased passage for one. Sasson suggests that the phrasing translated here as "to go with them" suggests that Jonah joined the crew, hoping to hide among them.[49] Allen offers that, since Israelites were generally "landsmen," going to sea must have been a desperate move on Jonah's part.[50] All of these concerns perhaps fail to appreciate the traditional narrative qualities of the description. Are such questions relevant to the hiring of guides in other traditional-style narratives, for example, by Tobias in the Book of Tobit and Telemachus in the *Odyssey*, whose guides are actually disguised divine beings? Alexis, "the man of God," a fifth-century CE Syrian saint, avoids marriage by running to the port, finding a ship, getting on board, and sailing to Seleucia in Syria.[51] Scholars of early Christianity do not generally ask how Alexis paid for passage or how much it cost. The important point in all these narratives is that the hero is about to undertake a journey. More specifically, in the Jonah narrative, a prophet, called to action by God, tries to run away, becoming an example of the folk motif of the the runaway servant. This motif intertwines with the theme of "death takes a holiday." These internationally recognized pieces of traditional narrative content are important to an overview of this first scene in Jonah.

Overview of Jonah 1:1-3, Comparative Folklore, and Reception

The opening scene of Jonah begins with a call to the prophet, as do many biblical narratives about divinely sent emissaries charged with delivering God's message or undertaking other tasks. This call to action by the deity can be met with differing reactions by the summoned servant—obedient undertaking of what is asked, or the attempt to avoid the charge, often for reasons of self-doubt as in the cases of Moses and Jeremiah. Jonah's reaction is to run away and refuse his charge without explanation.[52] When the prophet Elijah flees to the mountain, it is to escape Jezebel, who seeks his life; but the reader has no idea why Jonah seeks to escape his charge. In this way, the opening verses set up a major problematic of the book and encourage the reader to learn more about this odd protagonist and his motivations.[53]

Jonah, a servant of the deity, assumes the character motif of the runaway servant, a protagonist of various

---

47 See George F. Bass, *A History of Seafaring Based on Underwater Archaeology* (London: Thames & Hudson, 1972) 41. See also the erudite discussion by Sasson, *Jonah*, 80-81; and also Lionel Casson, *Ships and Seamanship in the Ancient World* (Princeton, NJ: Princeton University Press, 1971) 157-218.

48 Limburg, *Jonah*, 49.

49 Sasson, *Jonah*, 83-84.

50 Allen, *Joel, Obadiah, Jonah, and Micah*, 205.

51 Robert Doran, *Stewards of the Poor: The Man of God, Rabbula, and Hiba in the Fifth-Century Edessa* (Cistercian Studies 208; Kalamazoo, MI: Cistercian Publications, 2006) 19-20.

52 Timothy L. Wilt attempts to relate Jonah's flight and other narrative motifs in chap. 1 to patterns of content found in ancient Near Eastern battle accounts ("Jonah: A Battle of Shifting Alliances," in Davies and Clines, *Among the Prophets*, 164-82). On the motif of the prophet's refusal of his mission and the cascade of responses and events related to this act of disobedience, see John Kurichianil, "Jonah, A Disobedient Prophet," *ITS* 52 (2015) 163-76.

53 Robin Payne describes Jonah as "a type of anti-prophet" ("The Prophet Jonah: Reluctant Messenger and Intercessor," *ExpTim* 100 [1989] 131-34, esp. 132). Meir Sternberg treats Jonah's unexplained reaction to the divine command as exemplifying a "surprise gap" that "controls the reader's progress over a whole book" (*The Poetics of Biblical Narrative: Ideological Literature and the Drama of Reading* [Indiana Literary Biblical Series; Bloomington: Indiana University Press, 1985] 318).

folktales, one extremely popular in African American folklore in which the slave has obvious reasons to escape his servitude.[54] Similarly, folktales such as Snow White include the flight of the young girl threatened by her powerful and murderous stepmother. We might also include the figure of Ahiqar, forced to flee from his ruler when false rumors of treachery are spread about him by his evil nephew.[55] The relative status of the one who runs and the person from whom they are running is common and applies, to be sure, to a prophet who flees his god. The motif is also found in other contexts, for example, the Thompson Motif K 1951.2, the "runaway cavalry hero."[56] Integrated into a narrative pattern, this runaway soldier is comically portrayed as "a sham hero" who becomes a real hero through a series of events that begins when his unruly horse takes off with him. Jonah partakes of some of these nuances of an anti-hero. At the same time, the image of running off, regardless of whether it is an action under the protagonist's own control, initiates a wide range of traditional narrative patterns.

The runaway servant motif in Jonah also includes the nuance of "death takes a holiday," perhaps best known from British author W. Somerset Maugham's 1933 retelling of "The Appointment in Samarra." Escape is not possible, and, ironically, by running away the one who flees becomes trapped, unable to escape his fate. It is important to emphasize that, at this point in the narrative, the audience or reader does not know the reason for Jonah's assuming the role of the runaway servant whose fate is inescapable no matter how much the prophet seeks to avoid it. The narrative defies expectations for the behavior of God's servant, producing tension and anticipation in the receiver of the story. The first case of action and reaction in the story immediately raises issues pertaining to human disobedience in the face of divine power, creates a setting involving the sea, and emphasizes the journey, physical and metaphysical, that its protagonist will experience.

Rabbinic commentaries grapple in creative ways with these challenges in message and meaning and the significance of setting, offering case studies in the reception of Jonah.[57] Mekilta de-Rabbi Ishmael, the Tannaitic midrash on portions of Exodus 12–35, commences exegesis at Exod 12:1, a rubric concerning the location of divine revelation and its receivers, "And the Lord spoke to Moses and Aaron in the land of Egypt, saying. . . ." The midrash that follows underscores that, whereas the holy land has a special status as a locus of divine communication, divine revelation cannot be contained by geographic boundaries. God is everywhere and can reach all locations, all interlocutors, a critical message in postmonarchic times when many Jews live outside the homeland.

Jonah enters the discussion because "Jonah arose to flee to Tarshish from before Yahweh" (Jonah 1:3). The

---

54 Ben Zvi also takes note of the author's use of the motif of the runaway servant or slave but delves into the possible sociohistorical environment in which such a protagonist might have had relevance and meaning for a Persian-period author and audience (*Signs of Jonah*, 65–79). Robert J. Ratner explores the runaway servant in the context of ancient Near Eastern legal texts and relates these materials to the message of Jonah ("Jonah, the Runaway Servant," *Maarav* 5–6 [1990] 281–305).

55 J. M. Lindenberger, "Ahiqar: A New Translation and Introduction," in James H. Charlesworth, ed., *The Old Testament Pseudepigrapha* (2 vols.; Garden City, NY: Doubleday, 1983–1985) 2:479–507. For recent relevant discussions, see Seth A. Bledsoe, "Ahiqar and Other Legendary Sages," in Samuel L. Adams and Matthew Goff, eds., *Wiley Blackwell Companion to Wisdom Literature* (Wiley-Blackwell Companions to Religion; Hoboken, NJ: John Wiley & Sons, 2020) 287–309; Saul Olyan, "The Literary Dynamic of Loyalty and Betrayal in the Aramaic Ahiqar Narrative," *JNES* 79 (2020) 261–69.

56 See Stith Thompson, *The Motif-Index of Folk Literature* (6 vols.; Bloomington, IN: Indiana University Press, 1955–1958).

57 For a thoughtful theological and literary study of rabbinic treatments of Jonah, see Gerda Elata-Alster and Rachel Salmon, "The Deconstruction of Genre in the Book of Jonah: Towards a Theological Discourse," *LitTheo* 3 (1989) 40–60. See also Gregg, *Shared Stories*, 335–61, and for Gregg's treatment of Mekilta Pisha 1:84–87, see 336–37. On the treatment of Jonah in Mekilta, see Sherwood, "Cross-Currents," 66–67; and Sherwood, *A Biblical Text and Its Afterlives*, 120–23.

rabbis present various proof-texts to point to the infinite reach of God, but they comment that Jonah said, "I will take myself outside the land, a place where the divine presence is not revealed."[58] In the view of the midrash, Jonah attempts to avoid divine reach for Israel's sake, reasoning that, if foreigners are inclined to repent, Israel will appear even more guilty of sin and unrepentant by comparison. The Mekilta suggests that Jonah mistakenly believes that there are places where God cannot go. They comment that no one can hide from God, and, in any event, God has agents who can track people down to do his bidding. In Jonah, the agent is the sea (1:4).

The midrash goes on to describe three varieties of prophet, those who respect the father (God) and the son (Israel) equally, those who respect the father more than the son, and those who respect the son more than the father. For them, Jonah exemplifies the third category. The rabbis emphasize that Jonah tries to avoid making trouble for Israel, lest the Israelites seem morally inferior to the Ninevites. As a result, they conclude, he receives fewer divine communications than Jeremiah, who respects father and son, for God spoke with Jonah a second time (Jonah 3:1), but not a third time! Rabbi Nathan is cited to conclude this section with a critical transition in the midrash. Jonah's asking the sailors to hurl him into the sea is interpreted as reflecting his desire or willingness to become a martyr for the sake of his people. The rabbis go on to place him in the company of other biblical characters such as Moses and David who were willing to sacrifice themselves for Israel's sake (Exod 32:32; Num 11:15; 2 Sam 24:17). "Everywhere you find that the ancestors and the prophets offer their lives for the sake of Israel."[59]

How has Jonah been reshaped, reframed, and understood in this Tannaitic composition? He is not a petulant anti-hero but a champion and protector of his people who does not want them to be morally outdone by foreigners, disreputable Assyrians at that! Jonah is willing to die rather than let the people be seen in a bad light. He is, in short, normalized and rehabilitated.

The rabbis affirm the ubiquity of divine reach. Thus, despite what they interpret as Jonah's good intentions, there is no hiding from God, surely a normative theological theme and one important to people under colonialist rule, many or (increasingly) most of whom live outside the land of Israel. The rabbis affirm the importance of respecting God and Israel, but are sympathetic to what they portray as Jonah's good intentions. In contrast to the views of the author of Jonah, for the rabbis, foreigners—non-Yahwists—really are the "Other." The implication is that if such people can repent, it puts enormous pressure on Israel.

Similarly, implicit in the rabbis' interpretation may be an unwritten but shadowy suggestion that perhaps the deity is not fully upholding his end of the eternal promise to Israel. Yahweh takes care to warn and rehabilitate Ninevites, but what about the salvation of his people now living under Rome or Persia, members of a diaspora even within their own land, as pointed out by Fergus Millar.[60] Finally, Jonah is placed in the postbiblically popular category of a martyr. As Henry Fischel has noted, in the rabbinic tradition all the great leaders—prophets, kings, and patriarchs—come to be regarded as martyrs. They are all presented in midrash as willing to sacrifice themselves for the sake of Israel.[61] The overriding theme of Mekilta Pisha 1 is that martyrdom itself has become a valued form of religious expression and identity, a sign of merit, a means of atonement, and a way to attract divine sympathy and forgiveness for God's people. Jonah is thus reinterpreted and recontextualized to provide a message about salvation in which the role of the prophet is not merely to serve as an intermediary between God and humans or as a critic of the people's sin, but rather as a martyr willing to offer up his own person for their sake. Jonah's fleeing, his near-drowning, and his willingness to die are all seen in this context, and he is thereby transformed from anti-hero into a sympathetic role model.

---

58 Jacob Z. Lauterbach, *Mekilta de-Rabbi Ishmael* (3 vols.; 1933–1935; repr., Philadelphia: Jewish Publication Society of America, 1976) 1:84–87.
59 Lauterbach, *Mekilta de-Rabbi Ishmael*, 1:105–13.
60 Fergus Millar, "Transformations of Judaism under Greco-Roman Rule: Responses to Seth Schwartz's 'Imperialism and Jewish Society,'" *JJS* 57 (2006) 139–58.
61 Henry Fischel, "Martyr and Prophet," *JQR* 37 (1947) 265–80, 363–86.

1

Group Punishment and Mollification   *1:4–16*

Translation

4/ But Yahweh hurled[a] a great wind at the sea,
and there was a great[b] tempest in the sea,
and the ship threatened[c] to break.
5/ And frightened were the sailors,
and cry out did each man to his god,[d]
and they hurled the cargo that was in the ship into the sea
  to lighten their load,
but Jonah went down into the recesses of the vessel,
and he lay down and fell into a deep sleep.[e]
6/ And approach[f] him did the captain[g]
and he said to him,
"What's with you, deep sleeper?[h]
Rise up, call to your god.
Maybe the god will give a thought[i] to us
and we will not perish."
7/ And say did they, each man to his mate,
"Let's go and cast lots,
so that we may know
  on whose account has this evil happened to us."[j]
And they cast lots,
and fall did the lot upon Jonah.
8/ And they said to him,
"Tell us, please,
  on whose account has this evil happened to us?[k]
What is your occupation, and from where do you come,
what is your country, and from what people are you?"
9/ And he said to them.
"A Hebrew am I,[l]
and Yahweh, God of the heavens,[m] I fear,
  the one who made the sea and the dry ground."
10/ And the men feared a great fear,
and they said to him,
"What is this you have done?"
For know did the men that from Yahweh he was fleeing,[n]
for he had told them.
11/ And they said to him,
"What can we do about you
so the sea quiets from upon us,
for the sea is growing more and more tempestuous."
12/ And he[o] said to them,
"Lift me and hurl me into the sea,
so the sea will quiet from upon you,
for I know
  that it is on my account this great tempest is upon you."
13/ And row[p] frantically did the men
  to return to the dry ground,[q]
but they could not,
for the sea was growing more and more tempestuous upon them.
14/ And they called to Yahweh
and they said,
"We beseech you, Yahweh,
please let us not perish for the life of this man,
and do not set against us innocent blood.[r]
For you are Yahweh,
that which you desire, you do."[s]
15/ And they lifted Jonah
and they hurled him into the sea
and the sea stood down from its fury.[t]

16/ And the men feared a great fear toward Yahweh,
and they sacrificed a sacrifice to Yahweh,
and they vowed vows.ᵘ

Textual Notes

a   Mur MT הטיל from טול, "to hurl," is poetically rendered in G ἐξήγειρε, as in "arouse," "wake up," in relation to the great wind. Translations of the verb in S and Tg. suggest upward motion: Tg. reads ארים. S reads ʾrmy. For suggestions concerning the Aramaic traditions' possible reading of the verb nṭl, see Almbladh, *Studies in the Book of Jonah*, 18.

b   Some Greek manuscripts do not include the modifier "great."

c   *IBHS* renders as a middle, "the ship threatened to break" (§a1.2.32). Mur and MT read חשבה a term rooted in thought. G reads ἐκινδύνευε, "was in danger" or "ran the risk."

d   Tg. omits "to his god" reading ובעו גבר מן דחלתיה, "each man prayed out of his fear," making explicit the cause of their prayer but leaving the object of their prayer unstated. Tg. adds וחזו ארי לית בהון צריך, "but they saw there was no profit in them." Kevin Cathcart and Robert P. Gordon posit that the pronoun "them" implicitly refers to "idols" kept on ships to whom prayers are addressed in this crisis (*The Targum of the Minor Prophets: Translated with a Critical Introduction, Apparatus, and Notes* [ArBib 14; Wilmington, DE: Glazier, 1989] 105 n. 9; see also É. Levine, *Aramaic Version of Jonah*, 60 nn. 4, 5).

e   Mur MT read וירדם from the root "to sleep." G reads rather more comically ἔρρεγχε, "and he snored."

f   4QXIIᶠ Mur MT G read ויקרב, "he approached" or "came near." Th. reads κατέβη, "he went down from."

g   4QXIIᵍ Mur (partially reconstructed) MT read רב החבל, literally "the chief of the rope," implying a leadership role in the crew, translated here as "captain." G reads ὁ πρωρεύς, which LS translates as "the officer in command at the bow" (s.v. "πρῷρα") and Casson describes as the "first mate" (*Ships and Seamanship*, 318–19). Some Greek manuscript traditions read κυβερνήτης, which LS translates as "the officer in command at the stern" (s.v. "κυβερνήτης"). Casson translates as "executive officer," literally, the "one who steers" or navigating officer (*Ships and Seamanship*, 310). Vg. reads *gubernator*, "helmsman" or "pilot." Tg. reads רב ספניא, "the captain of the ship," and S *rb mlḥʾ*, the chief of the sailors, i.e., the captain.

h   Mur MT read "What's with you, deep sleeper"—נרדם with implications of a sluggard or lazybones. As in 1:5, G refers to snoring: ῥέγχεις "Why are you snoring?"

i   Mur MT יתעשת, usually taken to mean "give a thought," in G is translated as διασώσῃ, "save." The conditional "perhaps" is also not employed in G. Rather, Jonah should pray "so that the god might deliver us," suggesting more confidence that God hears the prayers of those who call upon him (see Daniela Scialabba, "The LXX Translation of Jonah 1:6: Text-Critical and Exegetical Considerations," in Siegfried Kreuzer, Martin Meiser, and Marcus Sigismund, eds., *Die Septuaginta–Orte und Intentionen, 5: Internationale Fachtagung veranstaltet von Septuaginta Deutsch, Wuppertal 24.–27. Juli 2014*, [WUNT 361; Tübingen: Mohr Siebeck, 645 [2016-54]). Tg. interprets מא אם יתרחם מן קדם יוי עלנא, "perhaps there will be mercy from the Lord upon us," avoiding the impression that "God might change his mind" (Cathcart and Gordon, *Targum of the Minor Prophets*, 106 n. 17; see also É. Levine, *Aramaic Version of Jonah*, 16).

j   MT reads הרעה הזאת לנו literally "this evil ours" or "to us." G reads ἐν ἡμῖν, "in us," "in our midst." Other Greek manuscripts read "upon us" ἐφ' ἡμῖν / ἡμᾶς.

k   Some Greek manuscripts omit באשר למי הרעה הזאת לנו, "on whose account has this evil happened to us?" (see Trible, "Studies in the Book of Jonah," 22; the discussion by Almbladh, *Studies in the Book of Jonah*, 21; the note by Paul Joüon ["Notes philologiques sur le texte hébreu de Osée 2, 7, 11; Joël 1, 7, 15 (= 1S. 13, 6); Jonas 1, 8; Habacuc 2, 2; Aggée 2, 11-14; Zacharie 1, 5; 3, 9; Malachie 1, 14," *Bib* 10 [1929] 417–20, esp. 418], and text-critical choices offered by Wolff, *Obadiah and Jonah*, 107). 4QXIIᵃ reads בשלמי, not באשר למי, probably through assimilation with v. 7 (thus BHQ).

l   G omits עברי אנכי, "a Hebrew I am." In G, Jonah describes himself as Δοῦλος κυρίου, "a servant of the Lord." Wolff suggests scribal variation due to the similarity of the Hebrew letters *dalet* and *resh* (*Obadiah and Jonah*, 107). Tg. reads יהודאה אנא, "a Jew I am," indicating that, for the targumist, Hebrew identity is synonymous with Jewish identity. See also Almbladh (*Studies in the Book of Jonah*, 21) for wider links with the rabbinic tradition; also É. Levine, *Aramaic Version of the Bible*, 189.

m   Mur MT and G describe the deity יי אלהי השמים, κύριον θεὸν τοῦ οὐρανοῦ, "Yahweh God of the heavens (or sky)." 4QXIIᵃ (as reconstructed) and a few Greek manuscripts describe the deity as יי אלהי השמים והארץ / κύριον θεὸν τοῦ οὐρανοῦ καὶ τῆς γῆς, "Lord God of the sky and the earth." The traditions thus evidence traditional style variation in epithets for the deity. See Sasson, *Jonah*, 116, 119; Trible, "Studies in the Book of Jonah," 24.

n   As in 1:3, Tg. reads מן קדם דיתנבי בשמא דיוי, "before he would prophesy in the name of the Lord," emphasizing Jonah's reason for his flight from God.

o   Mur MT employ the verb without a subject, "he said," ויאמר. G mentions the prophet by name καὶ εἶπεν Ιωνας, "and said Jonah."

p   Mur MT ויחתרו, "and row," with nuances of digging or boring in this case through water is rendered in G as καὶ παρεβιάζοντο, a term that has the nuance of force or violence, "struggling to do a thing against nature" (LS, s.v. "παραβιάζομαι")—in this case beating back the sea.

q   Mur MT יבשה, "the dry land," is rendered by G as τὴν γῆν, "the earth," which diverges from its translation of the same Hebrew at the end of v. 9.

r   MT Mur read דם נקיא, "innocent blood," and Tg. expands to "the guilt of innocent blood" חובת דם זכי. On implicit links to biblical texts pertaining to bloodguilt, see Almbladh, *Studies in the Book of Jonah*, 23.

s   G translates the last phrase of the verse concerning the deity's actions in the perfect tense, following the perfective verbs, ὃν τρόπον ἐβούλου πεποίηκας, "you did whatever you wish," but in the Hebrew, the verb can have the nuance of continuing to do what is habitual, that is "you do in the manner that you wish" (see Sasson, *Jonah*, 135; Trible, "Studies in the Book of Jonah," 29–30; *IBHS*, §30.4.b). Tg. reads "as it is pleasing before you," כמא דרעוא קדמך, somewhat softening the view of the deity's decision-making. In a similar vein, see É. Levine, *Aramaic Version of Jonah*, 69.

t   Mur MT זעפו, "his raging" or "fury," is rendered by G as σάλου, "tossing."

u   Mur MT וידרו נדרים, "and they vowed vows," is rendered by G as καὶ εὔξαντο εὐχάς, "and they prayed prayers." Tg. expands to "they promised to offer a sacrifice," ואמרו לדבחא דיבח, rather than "offered," perhaps suggesting that the proper locus of mediation is not outside the chosen place in Jerusalem (so Cathcart and Gordon, *Targum of the Minor Prophets*, 106 n. 29) or that the targumists considered a sacrificial fire on board ship to be logistically problematic (so Trible, "Studies in the Book of Jonah," 31). On midrashic implications of this expansion, see Almbladh, *Studies in the Book of Jonah*, 24.

Commentary

Jonah 1:4–16 focuses on the interactions between Jonah and the crew members before and in the midst of a life-threatening storm sent by God. The captain rouses Jonah from an escapist slumber in the hold, and the sailors try to save the vessel, finally agreeing to throw Jonah overboard in an effort to appease the deity, master of all nature, who has churned up the sea in his displeasure. References to prayer, vows, sacrifices, and divinatory technique enrich the scene with qualities of lived religion. A favorite subject of postbiblical visual media, the events at sea raise critical questions about the relationship between Yahweh and non-Yahwists, between Hebrews and non-Hebrews, and between Jonah and his deity.

■ **4** Jonah 1:4 is characterized by three parallel lines that describe the terrifying tempest stirred up by Yahweh: his hurling of wind, the violent storm at sea, and the danger that the ship would break up. The verb "hurl" (טול), though not frequent in the Hebrew Bible, is employed four times in this chapter (vv. 4, 5 12, and 15). It creates in each instance an image of great intensity and emotion. Deities exhibit their power in nature in the Levantine and Mediterranean worlds; they manifest their authority and express their displeasure with tempests and wild seas (cf. Jer 23:19, 20).[1] One thinks of Poseidon sending Odysseus off course with great blasts of wind (*Odyssey* 5.291-296; see also Vergil, *Aeneid* 1.81-91).

The root connected with storm or tempest (סער) is employed both as a verb (1:11, 13) and as a noun (1:4, 12) in the chapter. Sasson suggests that the verbal use reflects the sailor's perspective and the noun, that of the narrator and Jonah.[2]

The term here translated as "was about to" (the *piel* form of חשב) literally means "thought to" or "considered." When the subject of this verb is a person, which it almost always is in the Hebrew Bible, the nuance is one of intent, as in Gen 50:20 (Joseph's words to his brothers about their intending to do him harm) and 1 Sam 18:25

---

1   On connections between imagery in Jonah 1 and the mythic complex describing the battle with the sea, see Kurtis Peters, "Jonah 1 and the Battle with the Sea: Myth and Irony," *SJOT* 32 (2018) 157-65.

2   Sasson, *Jonah*, 95. For a discussion of narrative perspective in Jonah within the theoretical framework of focalization studies, see Benjamin Lyle Berger, "Picturing the Prophet: Focalization in the Book of Jonah," *SR* 29 (2000) 58-68.

(Saul's intent to do away with his rival David). In Jonah, the verb has the effect of personifying the ship, as is common in portrayals of seafaring vessels.[3]

■ **5** This verse employs some of the frequently used terminology in Jonah: the root ירא, "to fear," occurs also in 1:10 and 1:16, emphasizing the emotion that punctuates this scene. Imagery of an enemy's fear and trembling is captured by a metaphor that describes reactions to the east wind's breaking up ships of Tarshish in Ps 48:8 [7]. The terms for "breaking up" and "ship" (Jonah 1:4) and the mention of the maritime site Tarshish (1:3) point to the traditional fund of imagery from which the author of Jonah draws.

The term "hurl" found in 1:4 appears again in 1:5, as the men desperately try to lighten the ship's load to ease their journey in the storm, and in 1:15, when the sailors finally hurl the miscreant Jonah into the sea, at his own insistence, in hopes of mollifying the angry god (see below). Jonah has descended into the recesses of the ship, tracing the downward journey mentioned above (see commentary on 1:3). The scene thus comes alive by means of emotional and kinetic dimensions conveyed by recurring language.

That each sailor calls out to his god for help in this life-threatening crisis and that this entreaty is presented in a nonjudgmental way suggest an interesting cosmopolitanism and empathy on the part of the narrator and a deep understanding of personal religion.[4] The sailors experience fear and call out to their gods for help.

The term for the sailors, מלחים, found also in Ezek 27:9, 27, 29, probably derives from a Sumerian loanword in Akkadian that relates to a "sailor" or "boatman," rather than from the sound-alike Hebrew term for salt (מלח), as some have suggested.[5] As noted by Karin Almbladh, this term for sailor is attested in Phoenician sources and is associated with Phoenicians in Ezekiel 27, which explains its entry into a Hebrew author's vocabulary.[6]

The verb for "hurl" reprises terminology of 1:4, evidencing the economy of language that characterizes the book. The term translated as "cargo items" (כלים) can also mean instruments, in this case nautical equipment, or containers.[7] The latter nuance seems the more likely one. The sailors' efforts to jettison their cargo has been treated as a kind of sacrificial offering by a number of scholars.[8] Sasson views the narrator's use of the preposition אל rather than על as telling, an effort "to appease the sea with offerings," and he draws parallels with 1:12, 15, involving the throwing over of Jonah himself.[9] On the other hand, the reference to "lightening" might suggest a more literal meaning, the effort to save themselves and the ship by lightening their load. Ironically, while disaster threatens and the sailors respond with frenetic activity, Jonah sleeps.

The translation of the clause conveying Jonah's going down into the hold is a matter of debate. Grammarians note that the placement of the subject, Jonah, at the beginning of the clause may indicate anterior activity, "a break in sequencing," one signaled by the disjunctive *waw*, so that many translate "had gone down."[10] W. Dennis Tucker suggests, "in the meantime, Jonah had gone down," whereas Snaith proposes, as in the present

---

3   See Sasson, *Jonah*, 96–97; Simon, *Jonah*, 8; Limburg, *Jonah*, 48; David Noel Freedman, "Jonah 1:4b," *JBL* 77 (1958) 161–62.

4   See Brody, "Each Man Cried Out to His God," 9–85.

5   See Eva Strömberg Krantz, *Des Schiffes Weg Mitten im Meer: Beiträge zur Erforschung der nautischen Terminologie des Alten Testaments* (ConBOT 19; Lund: Gleerup, 1984) 182–84; Sasson, *Jonah*, 97. On terminology for various roles and statuses of members of the crew, see Wolff, *Obadiah and Jonah*, 111.

6   The term may be a loan from Akkadian; see *CAD* M1, s.v. malāḫu A; Paul V. Mankowski, *Akkadian Loanwords in Biblical Hebrew* (HSS 47; Winona Lake, IN: Eisenbrauns, 2000), 149, 156; on the Phoenician connection, Almbladh, *Studies in the Book of Jonah*, 19. For an interesting discussion of ancient "merchant marines," see Handy, *Jonah's World*, 67–74. On seafaring in rabbinic sources as relevant to scenes in Jonah, see Raphael Patai, "Jewish Seafaring in Ancient Times," *JQR* 32 (1941) 1–26, esp. 12.

7   See Ballard, Stager, et al., "Iron Age Shipwrecks."

8   Robert P. Carroll explores other possible ritual actions in Jonah, emphasizing 1:16, 2:9, and 3:6–8 ("Jonah as a Book of Ritual Responses," in Klaus-Dietrich Schunck and Matthias Augustin, eds., "'Lasset uns Brücken bauen . . .': Collected Communications to the XVth Congress of the International Organization for the Study of the Old Testament, Cambridge 1995* [BEATAJ 42; Frankfurt am Main: Peter Lang, 1995] 261–68).

9   Sasson, *Jonah*, 94.

10 Tucker, *Jonah* (2006), 22.

translation, "but Jonah went down" to convey the idea that the break in sequence indicates that he acts "differently from all the rest."[11] This understanding of the chain of events is important in the creation of Jonah's characterization as an anti-hero with a particular emotional makeup and worldview, to be discussed more fully in the overview below.

A reconstruction of the precise layout of ancient ships is a challenging enterprise, as Sasson notes, so that we cannot be sure what it meant physically to descend into its recesses.[12] Like Douglas Stuart, he points to psychological as well as physical dimensions of Jonah's descent.[13] The phrase ירכתי הספינה evokes two biblical images, the descent into the pit or Sheol (ירכתי בור), a reference to death or being hauled down into the underworld (Isa 14:15; Ezek 32:23), and to ירכתי צפון, the far reaches of the north where the gods are imagined to dwell (Ps 48:3; Isa 14:13; Ezek 38:6).[14] Some have suggested wordplay between the unusual term for ship sĕpînâ (ספינה) and the word for north ṣāpôn (צפון).[15] The link to the underworld seems more likely in play here than the link to the divine realm, but the terminology and the descent suggest passage to a nether realm and a transformation to follow.

The unusual word for ship (ספינה), in contrast to אניה (Jonah 1:3), is used only here in the Hebrew Bible. It is one of the terms that scholars have attributed to Late Biblical Hebrew and the influence of Aramaic,[16] but Sasson notes that this term is attested in various Semitic languages and is found in a seventh-century BCE Assyrian text. One need not, therefore, necessarily conclude that it provides evidence of Late Biblical Hebrew or an "Aramaism," which is often used to suggest lateness.[17] Uriel Simon suggests links to the root spn, meaning "to cover" or "to panel" (1 Kgs 7:3, 7) and hypothesizes that the vessel "had a full deck and covered hold."[18]

The term for sleep is רדם, rather than the more usual biblical term ישן. Here רדם is coupled with the verb שכב, "to sleep," "to lie down." It is this sort of deep sleep (תרדמה) that God causes to fall upon the first man when God takes the man's rib to form the woman (Gen 2:21). It is the state in which Abram has a vision of God in the covenant-making scene of Gen 15:12, a sleep associated with terror and great darkness. It is the state of deep sleep, "a deep sleep of Yahweh," placed upon Saul and his men that allows David, God's new favorite, to steal the king's spear and water jar in a manifestation and assertion of his divinely ordained power over the supporters of Saul and the king himself (1 Sam 26:12). This is no mere sleep, but a kind of stupor state. Similarly, the Canaanite general Sisera sleeps in a state of utter exhaustion (Judg 4:21), enabling Jael to creep up on him and kill him.

Sleep, of course, can be a form of escapism, a sign of psychological depression, an inability or lack of desire to cope, as Stuart points out.[19] The verb רדם is also found in Proverbs (19:15, 10:5), where it seems to point to what Sasson dubs "the sleep of the irresponsible," a sleep associated with laziness and idleness.[20] Perhaps capturing this nuance, G translates "snore," creating a rather antiheroic portrait. This same nuance seems to attach to the captain's description of Jonah in 1:6. The image of a deeply sleeping prophet avoiding the crisis thus bears multiple connotations, including descent and rite of passage, psychological state of mind, and avoidance of duty.

■ **6** The phrase translated here as "captain" literally means "chief of the rope," probably the person in charge

---

11 Ibid., 18; Snaith, *Notes on the Hebrew Text of Jonah*, 13. See also Sasson, *Jonah*, 99.
12 Sasson, *Jonah*, 100.
13 Sasson, *Jonah*, 100; Stuart, *Hosea-Jonah*, 458. For a thoughtful critical review of psychoanalytical approaches to Jonah, see Stuart Lasine, "Jonah's Complexes and Our Own: Psychology and the Interpretation of Jonah," *JSOT* 41 (2017) 237–60.
14 See Alter, *Strong as Death*, 140; Ackerman, "Jonah," 235–36.
15 See Ackerman, "Jonah," 229–30.
16 See Wolff, *Obadiah and Jonah*, 110.
17 Sasson, *Jonah*, 101.
18 Simon, *Jonah*, 9. For a similar suggestion, see the brief but meaty discussion by Martin Mulzer concerning the structure and type of the vessel, the term's possible etymology in Hebrew, and the location of Jonah as he sleeps (הספינה [Jon 1, 5] [gedeckter] Laderaum," *BN* 104 [2000] 83–94).
19 Stuart, *Hosea-Jonah*, 458. On Jonah's frame of mind, see also more broadly Ackerman, "Jonah," 236; LaCocque and LaCocque, *Jonah*, 88; Abraham D. Cohen emphasizes the link between anger and depression in the story of Jonah ("The Tragedy of Jonah," *Judaism* 21 [1972] 164–75, esp. 171).
20 Sasson, *Jonah*, 102.

of the crew. John Walton suggests "first mate" or "chief petty officer."[21] The manuscript traditions offer various understandings of the terminology, describing the role of this sailor with differing degrees of specificity and significance attached to the nautical use of ropes.[22] Ezekiel 27:8, 28 refer to "your rope handlers" or "your rowers" in a seafaring context. The oars perhaps function by means of ropes, a material critical on any vessel for various functions. Ezekiel 27:29 juxtaposes the term for "rope" referring to a sailor or type of sailor with מלחים (see 1:5 above). At the very least, the use of this term—like the vocabulary for ships, mention of an inner part of the ship where passengers might sleep, and terminology for crew members and reference to their activities—suggests use of appropriate local color in narrating a sea story (see overview below).

The question begins with the formulaic idiom מה־לך, literally, "what's with you," that always precedes a tense situation, for example, an accusation of wrongdoing or an expression of frustration or concern with the person addressed, an indication that something is awry or out of place. This language introduces God's interaction with Hagar when she and Ishmael have been cast out (Gen 21:17). So Caleb addresses his daughter Achsah after she bounds down from her donkey, perturbed about water rights to land (Josh 15:18; Judg 1:18), and so David addresses Bathsheba when she comes to complain about the succession (1 Kgs 1:16). See also 2 Sam 14:5; 2 Kgs 6:16; Ezek 18:2; Judg 18:23.

Most translate נרדם, a participial form, as "an accusative of state," as in Sasson's suggestion "what's with you being in a trance."[23] I am treating the participle as a vocative. Finding Jonah incongruously asleep in the watery crisis at sea, the captain essentially says, "What is with you sluggard?" or perhaps "lazy-bones?" For nuances of the verb רדם, see v. 5 above.

Notice that the captain's urging of Jonah to act, "rise up, call to your god," reprises the verbs of command used by Yahweh at the opening of the book (v. 2) and emphasizes the contrast between Jonah's supine state and the command of the captain.[24]

Various options present themselves for the translation here rendered "your god" and "the god." The verb of this clause is in the singular so that the writer intends readers to see the "calling out" as an appeal to a god, but is it Yahweh/God or some other deity, "the god?" It is difficult to ascertain whether the biblical writer is governed by his own worldview, in which האלהים, "the god," means God Yahweh, or whether he is assuming the identity of the foreign sailor for whom the deity is unknown or generic. It is also difficult to know how various audiences might have understood the term. Sasson suggests that the definite article may be taken as a "mild demonstrative," implying "that god of yours."[25]

The verb translated "give a thought" (יתעשת) is unusual, found only here in the *hithpael* form of the verb. The root עשת occurs in the Aramaic portion of Daniel as a passive participle (Dan 6:4), meaning "inclined to . . .," and for this reason some consider the terminology an Aramaism and therefore further proof for the late date of Jonah.[26] H. L. Ginsberg suggests the verb means "to take favorable thought," with the nuance of being positively disposed toward a particular action, also basing his understanding on Aramaic examples.[27] He translates the occurrence in Jonah 1:6 as "will be gracious." David Clines points to biblical passages in the *qal* with the nuance of devising or planning in the context of wicked deeds (Isa 32:6 [if לעשת is emended to לעשת]; Jer 5:28) and to the noun עשתון in Ps 146:4 and Sir 3:24 meaning "thoughts." He translates the verb עשת in Jonah as "bear in mind."[28]

---

21 Walton, "Jonah," 15, 18.
22 See textual note g on 1:6; Wolff, *Obadiah and Jonah*, 111; Sasson, *Jonah*, 102–03.
23 Sasson, *Jonah*, 103.
24 See Tucker, *Jonah*, 24; Wolff, *Obadiah and Jonah*, 113; Sasson, *Jonah*, 103. Elizabeth Achtemeier finds irony in the parallel between the captain's command and that of the deity in Jonah 1:2 (*Minor Prophets 1*, 263).
25 Sasson, *Jonah*, 104; see also 93. On the invocation of deities by sailors at sea in the Levantine world, see Brody, "*Each Man Cried Out to His God*," 82.
26 See Bewer, "Jonah," 34.
27 H. L. Ginsberg, "Lexicographical Note," in Benedikt Hartmann et al., eds., *Hebräische Wortforschung: Festschrift zum 80. Geburtstag von Walter Baumgartner* (VTSup 16; Leiden: Brill, 1967) 81–82.
28 *DCH* 6, s.v. "עשת II."

■ **7** The interaction between the crew members is an important indicator of worldview. As noted in the discussion of the translation "evil," for the words related to the basic root meaning "bad" (רעע), Jonah's characters are portrayed as sharing with members of many traditional cultures the belief that misfortune is not just bad luck or happenstance, being in the wrong place at the wrong time. Rather, whether fairly or unfairly, some higher power is against you or someone has cursed you—and curses, like blessings, have power. There is a cause, and the affected person may be directly or indirectly responsible for what has happened. Once he has discovered the source the problem, he may be able to address this cause and improve the situation. We thus find the sailors on the overlapping borders of what the great anthropologist Bronislaw Malinowski tried to delineate as "magic, science, and religion."[29] Numerous traditional means can be employed to ascertain which deity has been offended, who is one's enemy, or which individual's actions have brought down wrath upon the group—the case here.

Divinatory activities and media are traditional aspects of lived culture in the ancient Levant. Their purpose is to seek out underlying reasons for some occurrence or to predict future events in the hopes of protecting an individual and allowing him or her to prepare for what lies ahead. In contrast to the thread of the Jonah narrative that might be interpreted to view the decisions of Yahweh as somewhat inscrutable (e.g., the turning of predicted wrath away from repentant Ninevites even while Jonah's oracle of destruction was divinely sent and seemingly certain), the thread involving the casting of lots is less ambiguously understood as allowing human beings to adjust their situation and avoid disaster.

Divinatory know-how can be quite sophisticated, involving the study of omens such as bird signs or mantic knowledge about the meaning of dream symbols or the shape of an animal's entrails. Only the well-trained person can exercise this variety of divination, and it often involves the participation of a skilled professional.[30] Other forms of divination seem to have been more accessible to all members of a community, for example, the use of lots employed to provide a yes-or-no answer to a specific question or to serve as a binary sort of selection device. It is not known what material lots would have been made of or what sort of markings would have distinguished them, how they would have been cast or drawn, and so on; nor is it entirely clear what their relationship was to the frequently mentioned Urim and Tummim associated with divinatory procedures (e.g., 1 Sam 14:42–43).[31] Limburg suggests that the lots may be stones, and he relates the term גורל to the Arabic in which *jarila* is "to be stoney"; *jarwal* is a "small stone, pebble."[32]

---

29 See Bronislaw Malinowski, *Magic, Science, and Religion and Other Essays* (Garden City, NY: Doubleday, 1954).

30 On divinatory methods, see Jeannette C. Fincke, "Divination im Alten Orient: Ein Überblick," in Jeannette C. Fincke, ed., *Divination in the Ancient Near East: A Workshop on Divination Conducted during the 54th Rencontre Assyriologique Internationale at Würzburg, 20–25 July 2008* (Winona Lake, IN: Eisenbrauns, 2014) 1–20; Frederick H. Cryer, *Divination in Ancient Israel and Its Near Eastern Environment: A Socio-Historical Investigation* (JSOTSup 142; Sheffield: JSOT Press, 1994) 141–295; Susan Niditch, *The Symbolic Vision in Biblical Tradition* (HSM 30; Chico, CA: Scholars Press, 1980), 15–17; Burke O. Long, "The Effect of Divination upon Israelite Literature," *JBL* 92 (1973) 489–97; A. Leo Oppenheim, "Perspectives on Mesopotamian Divination," in *La divination en Mésopotamie ancienne et dans les régions voisines: 14e Rencontre assyriologiques internationale (Strasbourg, 2-6 juillet 1965)* (Paris: Presses universitaires de France, 1966) 35–43, esp. 37; Strawn, "Jonah's Sailors," 68–71 and nn. 5–11.

31 See Cryer, *Divination*, 273–77; for suggestions concerning divinatory procedures, see Johannes Lindblom, "Lot-Casting in the Old Testament," *VT* 12 (1962) 164–78, esp. 168, 170 for suggestions concerning markings on the lots.

32 Limburg, *Jonah*, 51; *HALOT*, s.v. "גורל." On linguistic and anthropological dimensions of the lot-throwing scene as described in Jonah, see Sasson, *Jonah*, 108–9. Strawn suggests that the terminology for the casting of lots employs specifically Israelite language, evoking a popular Israelite practice meant to clothe the sailors "in Israelite garb" ("Jonah's Sailors," 71–72). Here, as in the repentance of the Ninevites in chap. 3, "foreigners are portrayed in particularly pious ways" (ibid., 76). On the casting of lots by seafarers at sea, see Brody, *"Each Man Cried Out to His God,"* 84.

Verbs used with the word for lot (גורל) tend to suggest a throwing or tossing motion, for example, ירה, "to throw" or "to shoot" (Josh 18:6) as with an arrow, or שׁלח, "to send," in the *hiphil* with the sense of "send out" or "throw" (Josh 18:8). In Jonah 1:7 the verb root is נפל, "to fall," employed in the *hiphil* to mean "let fall" or "drop." The same verb (נפל) is employed to describe what is done with lots in several other passages (cf. 1 Chr 24:31; 25:8; 26:13; Neh 11:1; Isa 34:17). The phrase "to let drop lots" here translated as "cast lots" (also Esth 3:7; 9:24) suggests throwing of dice-type objects.

The drawing or casting of "lots" (גורלות) is pictured in the Hebrew Bible as a means of apportioning land (Josh 18:6) or boundaries (Josh 15:1), as well as of assigning responsibilities (1 Chr 24:5). It also functions as a means of selecting a person from a group, whether for possible benefit or for punishment, as portrayed in the case of Saul's elevation as king (1 Sam 10:20–21). Also relevant is the case of Jonathan, where the process appears to involve divinatory instruments that are said to be cast or made to drop but the actual term for lot is not employed (1 Sam 14:41–42). In the book of Esther, Haman infamously casts lots to select the day for the Jews' destruction (9:24). In all cases, the lot is believed to reflect divine will (not Yahweh's will in the case of Haman, to be sure), providing information of what is the proper course, the desired result—desired, that is, by "extra-human sources."[33] This means of calling upon a sign concerning divine decision-making or cosmic will avoids human conflict over ownership or responsibility and resolves issues that could be destructive of the group. In the case of the planned destruction of the Jews in Esther, the practice perhaps allows Haman and the powers that back him to distance themselves somewhat from their actions. The address to "fate" underscores the eventual reversal and setting matters aright, as Haman is ultimately destroyed and the Jews saved.[34]

A process of elimination involving lots is assumed to be the means of identifying the member of the community who has caused the Israelite defeat in the battle for Ai, although as in the story of Jonathan the term "lot" is not employed. Rather the people are told to "come near" (Josh 7:14), but the tale nicely exemplifies the situation calling for such an intervention (cf. 1 Sam 14:41–42). In a direct word oracle, God tells Joshua that someone has taken war spoil forbidden to individuals under the ban in the battle of Jericho (Joshua 6–7). Reference is made to ascertaining guilt, between tribe and tribe, then clan and clan, and then household and household, finally between person and person. These groupings are to "come near" and then finally the one is "taken" (7:14-17). Achan confirms what he has done in stealing God's war prizes. He is then eliminated with his household, and equanimity is restored, with Israelite victories to follow. It is interesting that the deity is not pictured as identifying the miscreant, although the deity is said to identify the reason for defeat. The ritual process of divination is somehow imagined as being necessary to restore the community and make things right. Moreover, defeat is attributed not to the ineptitude of the enemies or their superior force but to the commission of an offense. Military defeat causes recriminations and self-doubt and threatens the cohesion of the group. A cause, a scapegoat, must be identified, and divination is the means. Achan is identified, group confidence is restored, and victory is made possible.

The situation on the ship for the casting of lots touches on several of the issues described above. A wild storm threatens to destroy the crew and the ship, and the sailors suspect that something is awry between one of the human beings on the ship and the cosmic powers who control wind and water. Some force must be annoyed. They cast lots to see if they can learn who is to blame, and the lot falls upon or picks out Jonah. The author then turns the sailors' and readers' attention to the protagonist. Who is this man and how does he self-identify?

■ **8** The language of the sailors has the quality of entreaty and politeness, as the introductory verb, "tell us," is employed with the particle נא, here translated as "please." Many scholars suggest that the phrase באשר למי־הרעה הזאת לנו, which might be literally translated as "because of whom is this evil ours,"[35] is an interpolation, since it seems to be a close variant of a similar phrase

---

33 Cryer, *Divination*, 213.
34 See Sasson, *Jonah*, 109.
35 See Sasson, *Jonah*, 113.

in v. 7 and is omitted in some Old Greek manuscript traditions.[36] The suggestion is frequently made that the lot has already selected Jonah as the cause of the deadly storm, so there is no need for the question to be asked again. The sailors, however, may be pictured as asking a different question, namely, "Who has a grudge against you that has the power to create such havoc?" Or, to put it colloquially "Who has it in for you?" As noted above, there are causes for misfortune—or we, as human beings, like to think that there are. The subsequent questions of the sailors to Jonah about his origins and identity seek to discern who this magnet for trouble is. Their questions and Jonah's response that he is a follower of Yahweh are not, as Wolff suggests, a strange pause for a "biographical sketch" in the midst of a life-threatening crisis.[37] Rather, the questioning ascertains and explains the ultimate cause of the crisis so that it can be properly addressed. And once the sailors hear who is behind the tumult, their fear and apprehension only grow.

The questions about occupation, place of origin, and ethnicity partake of formulaic language seen in the encounters between Abraham's servant and Rebekah at the well (Gen 24:23–24); between Jacob and the shepherds (Gen 29:4); between Joseph and his brothers, a scene in which the brother sold into slavery feigns not knowing the men's identity (Gen 42:7); and between the host and the traveling Levite (Judg 19:17). The term used for occupation (מלאכה) might be translated as "trade," "mission," or "business." Parallels are found in Prov 18:9 referring to slackness in work habits, in Prov 22:29 in terms of skill in one's job, and in Ps 107:23 in reference to those engaged in the shipping business.

The requests for information about a person in the scenes from Genesis and Judges involve people who turn out to be related by kinship or ethnicity. In Jonah 1, the encounter is between those whose relationship is forged in the shared danger of the experience, in the immediacy of the moment, and in the confined setting of the ship at risk.[38] The scene is riveting for this reason, and the relationship all the more surprising, for these men are strangers.

■ **9** The author further builds the scene with Jonah's self-revelation. Jonah declares himself to be "a Hebrew," one who literally "fears" or reverences Yahweh, God of the heavens, the creator God who, significantly, has created the dry ground and the sea, a reference to the purview of Yahweh's power as relevant to their present situation (cf. Ps 89:9; Nah 1:4; Hab 3:8; Hag 2:6). The vocabulary evokes the creation myth of Genesis and the people-creation of Exodus (Gen 1:9; Exod 14:16, 22). As Trible observes, Jonah answers the last question about his people first.[39] This rhetorical technique highlights the issue of peoplehood and personal identity.[40]

The epithet "God of heaven/the heavens" is a Northwest Semitic designation for the deity that is attached not only to Yahweh but also to Baal, a deity of the Canaanite/Phoenician pantheon. Baal's identity intertwines with that of Yahweh in the Israelite tradition even as he figures as a false or powerless rival god condemned by the prophets and the dominant biblical tradition (e.g., Hosea 2). This ancient epithet found in Gen 24:3, 7 becomes particularly popular as a designation for Yahweh in the Persian period in passages such as 2 Chr 36:23; Ezra 1:2; and Ps 136:26. Wolff notes that nineteen of these designations are found in Ezra, Nehemiah, and Daniel and that twelve are in Aramaic. The phrase is

---

36 See, e.g., Bewer, "Jonah," 37. For a review of possible treatments of the phrase, see Allen, *Joel, Obadiah, Jonah, and Micah*, 209, n. 31. Trible views the repetition as linking "incidents as they move the plot" (*Rhetorical Criticism*, 139). Takamitsu Muraoka points to different forms of the compound particles employed in 1:7, 12 and in 1:8, the former examples being in "a lower register," an example of vernacular Hebrew, whereas v. 8 employs standard classical Hebrew ("A Case of Diglossia in the Book of Jonah," *VT* 62 [2012] 129–31).

37 Wolff, *Obadiah and Jonah*, 114.

38 Israel Drazin nicely points to the "fearful emotion" reflected in this "staccato series" of questions (*Unusual Bible Interpretations*, 14).

39 Trible, *Rhetorical Criticism*, 140.

40 For a discussion of the role of this verse in the hypothesized chiastic or concentric structure of Jonah 1:4–16, see the discussion and review of scholarship offered by Carl J. Bosma, "Jonah 1:9: An Example of Elenctic Testimony," *CTJ* 48 (2013) 65–90, here 69–72. Bosma himself treats Jonah 1:9 as "elenctic testimony" and a key turning point in the narrative (ibid., 65–90).

also found nine times in the Aramaic Elephantine correspondence.⁴¹

Jonah's describing himself as a "Hebrew" is significant. The term, or its origins, has been associated with the Akkadian *hapiru/apiru*, meaning those who are landless or who have a stateless status, but there is much debate among Semitists about the accuracy of this equation.⁴² As Marvin Sweeney points out, the designation "Hebrew" appears to be used when the biblical characters' status is not yet clearly associated with the land of Israel and a national identity (Gen 14:13 concerning Abram), or when they are strangers in a strange land (Joseph and his brothers in Egypt, Gen 39:14; 43:32) and the slaves in Egypt (e.g., Exod 1:16, 19; 3:18), or when they are under another group's control (e.g., that of the Philistines in 1 Sam 4:6, 9; 13:19; 14:21).⁴³ It has also been suggested that the designation "Hebrew" is often placed in the mouths of non-Israelites rather than functioning as an Israelite self-description.

Jonah's declaration that he is a "Hebrew" is directly followed by his self-description as a fearer of Yahweh. Are the two identities meant to be synonymous? That is, Jonah is a member of the עם, the "people," the Hebrews, and therefore is defined in part by the worship of Yahweh. If so, the term in Jonah now has implications for religious and ethnic identity, much as being Jewish eventually comes to be disassociated from one's ancestors' origins in Judea.⁴⁴ In 2 Macc 7:31, the soon-to-be-martyred mother thus refers to her people as "Hebrews" (cf. 11:13; 15:37). As Paula Fredriksen has written in relation to identity in late antiquity, "'religion' ran in the blood."⁴⁵ Jonah's declarations that he is a Hebrew and that he worships Yahweh are interrelated and integral to the question "from what people are you?"

■ **10** Tucker notes that henceforward the sailors are called simply "men," perhaps heightening the sense of shared humanity on the ship.⁴⁶

Language of fear and bigness again points to the author's purposefully delimited vocabulary.

The men's question מה זאת עשית ("What is this you have done?") is idiomatic language used to accuse one of wrongdoing or to indicate disapproval of one's behavior. The foreign ruler who has been led to believe that the patriarch's wife is his sister in the tales of Gen 12:10–20; 20:1–18; and 26:1–16, thus addresses the husband who has deceived him. This language is used formulaically at the same point in each variant of the tale after the revelation concerning the true relationship between Abraham or Isaac and his wife. It is also used by the fleeing Israelites to question Moses's leadership in Exod 14:11, as the powerful Egyptians pursue them. This question is also addressed by Balak to Balaam when the latter, paid to curse the Israelites, blesses them instead (Num 23:11). By means of this language, the Ephraimites accuse Gideon of denying them an opportunity to join in battle (Judg 8:1), and the men of Judah accuse Samson of angering the Philistines, so that this enemy, more powerful than they, threatens them (Judg 15:11).

In Jonah, we learn that the sailors now know that Jonah has angered this powerful deity bringing down his wrath upon them all, "for he had told them."⁴⁷ This phrase in the *qal* perfect is usually treated as a past

---

41 Wolff, *Obadiah and Jonah*, 115. For a discussion of this epithet as its use relates to a dating of Jonah and its theme, see Bezazel Porten, "Baalshamen and the Date of the Book of Jonah," in Maurice Carrez, Joseph Doré, and Pierre Grelot, eds., *De la Tôrah au Messie: Études d'exégèse et d'herméneutique bibliques offertes à Henri Cazelles pour ses 25 années d'enseignement à l'Institut Catholique de Paris (Octobre 1979)* (Paris: Desclée, 1981) 237–44.

42 See Marvin A. Sweeney, *The Twelve Prophets* (2 vols.; Berit Olam; Collegeville, MN: Liturgical Press, 2000) 1:314; see Deut 15:12; Jer 34:9, where the social and economic status of the "Hebrew" is an issue.

43 Ibid., 1:313–14.

44 See Robert Doran, *2 Maccabees: A Critical Commentary* (Hermeneia; Minneapolis: Fortress Press, 2012) 300; and for an overview, see Graham Harvey, *The True Israel: Uses of the Names Jew, Hebrew, and Israel in Ancient Jewish and Early Christian Literature* (AGAJU 35; Leiden: Brill, 2001) 104–10.

45 Paula Fredriksen, "Christians in the Roman Empire," in David S. Potter, ed., *A Companion to the Roman Empire* (Blackwell Companions to the Ancient World: Ancient History; Chichester: Wiley Blackwell, 2010), 590.

46 Tucker, *Jonah*, 33.

47 Bolin and others emphasize the ways in which the recurring conjunction כי, "for/because," links 1:10–14 (*Freedom beyond Forgiveness*, 85). Some have regarded the phrase as an explicating gloss (see BHS), but there is no manuscript evidence for its deletion (see BHQ).

perfect because it is employed in a causal clause, and the verb in the main clause has to do with a previous situation or event. A translation in the simple past tense perhaps emphasizes better the immediacy of the situation: because he told them.

From a storytelling perspective, the omission of the important detail about Jonah's fleeing from God in the prophet's own speech in v. 9 and its mention in v. 10 suggests a few interesting possibilities. One is the option of "Homer's nodding"; that is, the storyteller omits an important detail which is then filled in by him or a later contributor to the narrative tradition. Alternatively, one can imagine that listeners or readers, knowing from the opening of the tale that Jonah has fled, are not expected to be uncomfortable with this seeming lacuna, and some versions of the narrative might simply have omitted it. The manuscript traditions, however, do all reflect the reference to this backstory in 1:10. Simon treats the reference to Jonah's flight as a flashback in a chiastic structure.[48]

■ **11–12** The sailors address Jonah, asking, "What's to be done about you?" so that the sea would quiet down. The verb שתק, "to quiet," is used in Ps 107:30 in reference to the calming of raging seas in a storm.[49] The repetition about the sea's raging uses the root סער, "to grow stormy," which occurs in a noun form in 1:4, heightening one's capacity to identify with the panic of the crew, caught in this violent tempest. Noting that the idiomatic phrase literally states that "the sea was walking and storming," James Nogalski points to the author's lending the storm "an almost personified quality."[50]

Do the sailors ask for Jonah's advice because they now know he is the cause of their problem? Do they respect his status as a messenger of the God of heaven who might know what to do, or are they seeking permission to eliminate him? Jonah's own advice requests the third option, and his language evokes previous verses. He asks that they "lift" and "hurl" him into "the sea" so that it "quiets." God hurled the great wind at the sea (1:4), and the sailors earlier attempted to hurl cargo into the sea to lighten their load (1:5) and perhaps allow the ship to stay afloat. Jonah suggests this action will "quiet" the seas as they had hoped, using similar language (1:11). And again, the tempest is expressed by the noun form of the root סער employed in vv. 4, 11.

Uriel Simon suggests that Jonah is requesting "passive suicide," and he draws comparisons with other biblical heroes' requests or readiness to die, for example, Abimelech in Judg 9:54, Samson in Judg 16:30, and Saul in 1 Sam 31:4.[51] These cases are not necessarily comparable in motivation to one another or to the case of Jonah. Abimelech and Samson seek to avoid an ignoble death, Samson seeks vengeance against his enemies and to die in a noble way that causes them to die with him. Some scholars suggest that Jonah is not sacrificing himself at all, but, quite to the contrary, that he seeks to avoid God's charge in an emphatic way. Others see Jonah as taking responsibility for the sailors' troubles.[52] It is also suggested that Jonah expresses a death wish (cf. 4:3, 8),[53] evoking Elijah (see Introduction). LaCoque and LaCoque explore the psychoanalytical dimensions of Jonah's behavior as rooted in a kind of depression.[54] Ultimately the narrator may intend to have readers perceive Jonah's advice as suggesting a way to mollify or pacify the angry deity. Alter points to the theme of sacrifice, a means of appeasing the deity.[55] It is significant that Jonah does not simply jump overboard, committing himself to death (see the rabbinic interpretation of his flight in the commentary on 1:1–3 above) but rather tells the sailors to rid themselves of him. From the actions that follow, the impression is that the sailors themselves need to undertake action to save themselves, and the jettisoning of the one who angered the deity is their last guilty choice, perhaps perceived by them as a necessary act of human sacrifice.

---

48 Simon, *Jonah*, 13.
49 See the discussion by Sasson, *Jonah*, 122.
50 Nogalski, *Book of the Twelve*, 420.
51 Simon, *Jonah*, 13.
52 See Wolff, *Obadiah and Jonah*, 118; and compare with Stuart, *Hosea–Jonah*, 462; and Allen, *Joel, Obadiah, Jonah, and Micah*, 211. Reading אניה, "ship," instead of אני, "I," William J. Horwitz suggests that the "ship," perhaps the crew, knows him to be guilty. Thus, in Horwitz's unusual reading, Jonah is, in fact, not taking responsibility ("Another Interpretation of Jonah 1 12," *VT* 23 [1973] 370–72).
53 Limburg, *Jonah*, 55.
54 LaCocque and LaCocque, *Jonah*, 88.
55 Alter, *Strong as Death*, 142. See also Bewer ("Jonah," 39), who calls attention to a folk theme involving sailors' pacification of the angry sea.

■ **13–16** The final four verses of chap. 1 are dedicated to the men's reaction to Jonah's words and reveal important aspects of religious ethics and humanistic responsibility. They also draw upon folk motifs to be discussed below and motivate rabbinic speculation about Jonah's entry into the sea.

Instead of immediately heeding Jonah's request to throw him overboard, the crew members work even harder to row to shore. The verb חתר literally means to "dig" or "bore." Frantic effort is conveyed as the men dig or bore into the sea—hence the translation "row frantically." Tucker notes that the verb is used in Amos 9:2 to suggest a "futile" action and in Job 24:16 to connote "illicit entry"; Tucker translates the verb in Jonah 1:13 as "rowed desperately."[56] The verbal form for "tempest" is again employed (1:4, 11, 12, 13) with the nuance of escalation, "growing more and more" (as in v. 11) to impress upon the reader the desperation of the situation.

In 1:14, the phrase ויקראו אל, "And they called to . . . ," reprises language that refers to calling upon God's help in v. 6 (see also "proclaim" in v. 2). The prayerful calling here commences a set of motifs evoking the biblical lament, a literary form found in full blossom in chap. 2. The opening language אנה יהוה, employs a particle of entreaty, literally "ah, now Yahweh," here translated figuratively as "we beseech you, Yahweh," which expresses the desperate anxiety that lies behind the appeal.[57] Thus Joseph's brothers begin their address to their powerful brother in Egypt (Gen 50:17; see also the pleas of King Hezekiah facing death from his illness in 2 Kgs 20:3; Isa 38:3). The petition to the deity employing אנה יהוה is somewhat common in the Hebrew Bible (Exod 32:31; Neh 1:5, 1; Pss 116:4, 16; 118:25; Dan 9:4). This particle is an appropriate opening of the lament, and, in Jonah 1:14, the sentiment is reinforced by the additional particle of entreaty that precedes the request, אל־נא, "please do not. . . ."

The lament is a prayer to the deity that presumes or describes a dire situation experienced by the petitioner, sometimes including an insistence that the petitioner does not deserve this fate; or it may be the opposite, a confession of guilt, followed by a hope for vindication and a promise or vow to repay the deity with praises or sacrifices.[58] The essential form can be expanded or abbreviated, but in Jonah 1 nuances of lament beautifully capture the situation faced by the sailors and anticipate Jonah's own crisis and response in chap. 2.

The sailors face death at sea, to be sure, but it is noteworthy that their description of their situation emphasizes not fear of perishing from the sea but rather fear that their killing the traveler to save themselves will also result in divine wrath and their deaths. The term translated "living being," נפש, sometimes rendered as "soul," connotes the life force, the very living essence of a person (see commentary on 2:6, 8 below). The language of "innocent blood" is found in Deut 19:10, 13; 21:8; 27:25; Jer 26:15, and elsewhere in the Hebrew Bible. Scholars frequently find the sailors' plea ironic or satirical, as Jonah has confessed that he is responsible for the dire situation that they face.[59] The author recognizes, however, that it is not an easy matter to place oneself in the role of God's avenger or executioner. As human beings, they resist being the immediate cause of this man's death. The sailors' prayer points to motifs of the lament both in the request for relief and in their readiness to take blame for wrongdoing.

Their final words in v. 14, "that which you desire, you do" (כאשר חפצת עשית), make sense in this context as an acknowledgment of divine power and ultimate responsibility. Avi Hurvitz relates this phrase to an Aramaic legal formula "authorizing the relevant person 'to do whatever he pleases.'"[60] Some suggest that the sailors' comment on God's doing as he desires refers not to God's power in general but specifically to this scene in which they are

---

56 Tucker, *Jonah*, 40; see also Sasson, *Jonah*, 130. For alternate suggestions concerning the difficult root חתר, see Christopher Meredith, "The Conundrum of *ḥtr* in Jonah 1:13," *VT* 64 (2014) 147–52.

57 See also *IBHS*, §40.2.5.c: "it is used before imperatives and in similar contexts" (and indeed here before a cohortative). On the interjection, see also BDB, s.v. "אנה."

58 See Niditch, *Responsive Self*, 55–63.

59 See, e.g., Wolff, *Obadiah and Jonah*, 120.

60 Avi Hurvitz, "The History of a Legal Formula: *kōl ʾašer-ḥāpēṣ ʿāśāh* (Psalms CXV 3, CXXXV 6)," *VT* 32 (1982) 257–67, esp. 261.

fulfilling God's will.[61] More likely is Sasson's interpretation that the phrase refers to "God's limitless freedom."[62] This formula concerning divine power is found also in Pss 115:3 and 135:6, where God's power over nature is specifically emphasized, in particular, the sea and the deep, translated as "primeval ocean" in Jonah 2:6. That this formula is a confession of faith indicating conversion on the part of the foreign sailors cannot be proved. Their declaration does evoke a common biblical motif of the foreigner who appreciates God's power (e.g., Jael [Judg 4:17], Naaman [2 Kings 5], the Gibeonites [Joshua 9], and Rahab [Joshua 2]), whereby the biblical writers declare the rightness of their own belief and the power of their deity, for even strangers acknowledge him.

The men lift Jonah and hurl him into the sea. As noted, "hurl" is another of the frequently found words in Jonah, employed in 1:4 in reference to God's hurling the wind, and in 1:5 in reference to the sailors' efforts to get rid of their cargo. The sea calms down, literally, "stands (down)" (עמד), and its fury abates. The men are said to fear or respect God greatly, offering sacrifices and vowing vows. The sacrifice and the vow, implicitly promising further acts of dedication to the deity, conclude the pattern of the lament as in Ps 54:8 [6]. The scholarship reflects a peculiar debate about logistics, namely, whether sacrifice could be offered onboard the ship, and if so what might have been sacrificed? Had they not thrown all cargo overboard? Do they offer sacrifices onboard and promise future offerings in accordance with their vow?[63] It seems much more likely that the parallel phrases, "and they sacrificed sacrifices to Yahweh // and they vowed vows" invoke the poetry of the lament as well as an expected message concerning God's saving acts and human beings' obligation to give reverential thanks.

Overview of Jonah 1:4–16, Comparative Folklore, and Reception

This section of Jonah describes the tempest sent by Yahweh and the series of responses by those onboard the ship. Delimited vocabulary of evil, hurling, fright, tempest, and calling to the deity captures the heightening anxiety and panic. The sea forms the constant backdrop of this portion of the narrative, with references to the wild water itself, the ship, and the roles of the seafaring crew. The contrast between these non-Israelite crewmen and Jonah is trenchant. They call to their gods; Jonah is silent. They attempt to save the ship, but Jonah sleeps in a trance. They are clearly non-Yahwists; Jonah is a Hebrew who fears the great creator God who made sea and land. He runs from his responsibility, hides asleep in the hold, and finally asks to be sent to his almost certain death. In contrast, the crew members desperately try to save the ship, themselves, and their passenger, even once they realize that he is the cause of their woes. Winding throughout the passage are threads in personal religion: the address to one's god to save one's life; the belief that troubles may be the result of some god's wrath or some curse and removal of the offense may lead to removal of one's problems; the use of divinatory techniques to reveal the underlying cause; and emphasis on a relationship with deities confirmed by personal sacrifices and vows. Yahweh is presented as the all-powerful creator of the cosmos who controls the entire natural world and hurls a storm at the sea to do his bidding, and yet this deity has special relationships with individuals, sometimes fraught relationships, as in the case of his messenger Jonah. Sacrifice is a recurring theme: the sacrifice of Jonah to save the crew and the crew's sacrifices to Yahweh; and vows implying future ritual action. The view of the sailors is humanistic throughout; they seek to do the best they can in a difficult situation, conscious that they must not offend further the powerful deity who has sent the storm but reluctant to take it upon themselves to kill a man.

By the end of Jonah 1 readers know why there is a storm and who is responsible for angering the god who controls the sea and dry ground, but not why the prophet fled. This piece of content, critical to the plot and to the message of the narrative, is the nagging problem of the book. Why does Jonah attempt to flee? For the answer to this question we must read on.

---

61 E.g., Stuart, *Hosea–Jonah*, 464.
62 Sasson, *Jonah*, 150.
63 See, e.g., Stuart, *Hosea–Jonah*, 464–65; Limburg, *Jonah*, 57–58, Sasson, *Jonah*, 139–40; Simon, *Jonah*, 15. On nautical votives, see Brody, "Each Man Cried Out to His God," 41.

At the center of this portion of Jonah are motifs found in an international fund of folklore: a storm at sea caused by the actions of an individual on the ship who has committed some offense and is being punished by divine powers, and the related motif that describes throwing the offending person overboard thereby quieting the sea.

The Thompson Motif and Type Indices offer a fund of parallels to the stuff of folk narrative, catalogued by content. When one searches under "Storm" one finds a host of examples of "storms caused by the breaking of a tabu" (C984; C984.2; C984.3). For Thompson, "breaking a tabu" includes a wide range of actions that transgress implicit or explicit boundaries, rules, or orders believed to be set by some supernatural being. Taboo breaking may also be seen less theologically as the defiance of a culturally shared, implicit set of customs for right and wrong behavior. In Jonah, of course, the prophet defies God's orders to go to Nineveh by boarding a ship bound for Tarshish, and the storm takes place at sea. Another motif or motif cluster involves the effort to calm the storm and quiet the sea, whatever its cause. Sometimes the sea is stilled by prayer to a superhuman being, a saint for example (V254.2). Many tales, however, depict acts of sacrifice that quiet the storm, and the sacrifice can be throwing a person overboard, as in Jonah. The person who is sacrificed is not always the cause of the disaster. For example, Motif S264.1.2 is a Japanese tale in which "a woman drowns herself as a sacrifice to the water gods to save her husband's boat from capsizing." The closest parallel to the Jonah tale is Motif S264.1/Type 973 "Man thrown overboard to placate the storm." Under Type 973, Thompson lists an Icelandic example, a Pali version, a Korean narrative, a Scottish ballad, among other sources. The ballad, "Brown Robyn's Confession" (Child 57), is especially interesting for purposes of comparison because its pattern of content is quite similar to that of Jonah. Editor's notes to the classic nineteenth-century collection by Francis James Child of English and Scottish ballads, in fact, ponder whether the ballad is based on the biblical book, but he decides not, for the plot is so common in his view.[64] This ballad, found also in several Scandinavian versions, tells of a prediction of the hero's death at sea, but he, not fearing the danger, pays no heed and sets out on a lengthy voyage in a splendid ship. A year or two into the journey, a disaster strikes, often in the form of a storm. The crewmen assume someone's sin is to blame and cast lots. The lot falls on Brown Robyn, who asks that they throw him overboard in order that they and the ship may be released from the danger. They do, and, as he tries to stay afloat in the ocean, he is met by "Our Blessed Lady," to whom he confesses his sin. He is absolved, and she offers him a choice of whether to return to the ship or to ascend to heaven; he chooses the latter.

The international presence of these motifs points to a shared respect for the power of the sea and its danger and again to the human tendency to ascribe reasons for disaster apart from weather, currents, or chance. Implicit are strong desires to find an explanation for misfortune and an often-related belief in the deservedness of punishment. Lying beneath this aspect of worldview is also speculation about the efficacy of human sacrifice. Each account, of course, is culturally and artistically specified. For the writer of Jonah, the stock folk pattern allows for an examination of human relationships forged among strangers in times of crisis, the emphasis on Yahweh as absolute lord of the sea and earth, a contemplation on events that follow when one's own sense of proper behavior or preferred action is at odds with the expectations of this powerful God, and an exemplar concerning the personal and complicated relationship between God and his designated representative, the prophet.

Pirqe de-Rabbi Eliezer is a pseudepigraphic work attributed to Rabbi Eliezer, described in Tannaitic literature as a student of Rabbi Johanan ben Zakkai, an influential rabbi of the first century CE. The date of this compilation of midrashim is probably as late as the eighth or ninth century. Its tenth chapter deals with Jonah.[65] A

---

64 Francis James Child, *The English and Scottish Popular Ballads in Five Volumes* (Boston: Houghton, Mifflin, 1885), 2:14.

65 For a fuller discussion of this work and its attribution to R. Eliezer, see the discussion of its treatment of Jonah's encounter with the fish in the commentary below on Jonah 2.

midrashic passage that allows for further exploration of ways in which the later tradition receives and revises the biblical text was probably motivated by the two verbs in 1:15 translated as "lift and hurl" (see also 1:12). The authors of the midrash do not allow for mere idiom, and the use of two verbs in the text must mean something of import. It is, as James Kugel suggests in discussing the motivations of rabbinic exegesis, a rough edge, an intriguing opening, that the rabbis address in meaningful and creative ways revealing some of their vital concerns and the challenges to their worldview posed by the biblical tale of Jonah.[66]

The midrash describes the sailors' throwing Jonah into the sea as a matter of stages of immersion—hence perhaps implicitly the two verbs. First, they cast Jonah into the sea up to his knees and the sea-storm abates. Then they bring him back onboard and the sea again becomes agitated. They cast him in again up to his neck, and again the sea abates. Again they bring him back on the ship and "the sea was again agitated against them, until they cast him in entirely and forthwith the sea-storm abated, as it is said, 'So they *took up* Jonah, and *cast him forth* into the sea: and the sea ceased from her raging.'"[67] The verbs italicized above suggest to the midrashists that the sailors are truly torn about sacrificing their passenger, moving forward with hesitation, taking back their action and seeing if a temporary dousing will be adequate to still the storm, but to no avail. The rabbinic interpretation reinforces the impression conveyed by Jonah 1:13, in which the men are described as trying at all costs to avoid being the cause of Jonah's death, and 1:14, in which they essentially beg God to forgive them for taking innocent blood. The rabbis thus express empathy concerning the dire situation in which the crewmen find themselves and appreciate their desperation in taking steps short of causing Jonah's death. The midrash in Pirqe de-Rabbi Eliezer captures the humanistic moral dimensions of the scene.[68] The deity, of course, is not through with Jonah, who will be saved by other means.

---

66 James L. Kugel, "Two Introductions to Midrash," *Prooftexts* 3 (1983) 131–55, esp. 144–45.

67 Gerald Friedlander, *Pirke de Rabbi Eliezer (The Chapters of Rabbi Eliezer the Great) according to the Text of the Manuscript Belonging to Abraham Epstein of Vienna: Translated and Annotated with Introduction and Indices* (New York: Benjamin Blom, 1971) 69.

68 A similar point is made by Gregg, *Shared Stories*, 342.

2

Individual Punishment, Petition, and Forgiveness

2:1–11

Translation

1a/ And assign[b] did Yahweh a great fish[c] to swallow Jonah,
and Jonah was in the innards of the fish three days[d] and three nights.
2/ And Jonah prayed to Yahweh his god from the innards of the fish
3/ and he said,
"I call out from my distress to Yahweh,[e]
and he answers me.[f]
From the belly of Sheol[g] I cry out for help,
and you hear my voice.[h]
4/ And toss me does the Deep in the heart of the seas,[i]
River[j] surrounds me,
all your breakers and billows above me pass.
5/ And I, I say, 'I am driven out from your sight.[k]
Even so, might I yet[l] look to your holy temple?'
6/ Encompass me do the waters to the extent of my very being,
the Primeval Ocean surrounds me,
the End[m] is twisted around my head.
7/ At the foundations of the mountains I descend into the earth,[n]
its bars around me for eternity,[o]
but my life you bring up from the pit,[p]
Yahweh my god.
8/ As my living being grows faint for me,
Yahweh I remember,
and go[q] to you does my prayer,
to your holy temple.
9/ Those who devote themselves to false vapors,[r]
forsake their access to loving-kindness.[s]
10/ But I in a voice of thanksgiving[t] shall sacrifice to you,
that which I vowed I shall fulfill,[u]
salvation is Yahweh's.[v]
11/ And Yahweh spoke[w] to the fish,
and he vomited[x] Jonah up onto the dry ground.

Textual Notes

a Note that G S and Vg. number 2:1 as 1:17.
b G renders the Hebrew term found in Mur MT וימן, "appointed, assigned," as προσέταξε, which has more the nuance of "command." So OL *praecepit*; Vg. *preparavit* suggests "prepared," a nuance reflected also in Tg. וזמין and S *wtyb*.
c G employs the term κῆτος for the sea creature, which often refers to a seal, monster, or serpent.
d OL omits "three days."
e G OL Tg. expand "Yahweh my God," as in 2:2.
f Tg. reflects "he answers/answered me" with וקביל צלותי, "he received my prayer."
g Whereas the Hebrew and Greek traditions refer to Sheol or Hades, Tg. naturalizes the watery setting as "the deep" (תהומא), perhaps because the term has such resonances elsewhere (e.g., Gen 1:2).
h MT Mur (reconstructed) read שועתי שמעת קולי as "I cry out for help. You hear my voice." G OL read κραυγῆς μου ἤκουσας φωνῆς μου / *clamoris mei exaudisti vocem meam*, literally, "you heard my cry of my voice," emphasizing Jonah's personhood. See comments by Martin Mulzer, "Satzgrenzen im Jonabuch im Vergleich von hebräischer und griechischer Texttradition," *BN* 113 (2002) 68–16, esp. 62.

i MT Mur can be translated to personify the Deep and read ותשליכני מצולה בלבב ימים as "and toss me does the Deep in the heart of the seas." G OL read the verb "toss" or "throw" in the second person and add the preposition "in.": G ἀπέρριψάς με εἰς βάθη καρδίας θαλάσσης / OL *proiecisti me in altitudinem cordis maris*, "You threw me into the depths of the heart of the sea."
j 4QXII[g] Mur MT נהר, "river," is plural in G καὶ ποταμοί. The phrase "your breakers" in Mur MT משבריך is rendered with a term that contains nuances of "upheaval" οἱ μετεωρισμοί, "upwellings," or the like.
k Mur MT G מנגד עיניך, "from your sight," in Tg. is rendered מן קדם מימרך, "from your Memra," to avoid anthropomorphizing the deity. See Almbladh, *Studies*

l   Mur MT G "surely" or contrastively "yet" (אך) in θ´ is πῶς, "how."

m   Mur MT סוף is taken by G as an adjective ἄβυσσος . . . ἐσχάτη, "deepest abyss." Tg. reads דסוף ימא, "the Red Sea," alluding to the exodus. S reads "in the bottom of the sea was bound my head" bʾšth dymʾ ʾtḥbš ryšy. For the translation "End," see the commentary.

n   G has the beginning of v. 7 as preserved in Mur MT apply to the final colon of v. 6 with "head" as subject: ἔδυ ἡ κεφαλή μου εἰς σχισμὰς ὀρέων. "My head sank into the crevices of the mountains." (See comments by Mulzer, "Satzgrenzen im Jonabuch," 66–67). This image is reminiscent of a rabbinic description of the defeat of Og of Bashan (b. Ber. 54b). OL reads similarly *postremo demersit caput meum in fissuras motium*, "Afterwards my head sank into the fissures of the mountain," taking סוף as an adverb, "afterwards."

o   Mur (reconstructed) "her bars around me for eternity" (בריחה בעדי לעלם) in G is rendered as ἧς οἱ μοχλοὶ αὐτῆς κάτοχοι αἰώνιοι, "whose bars are eternal bonds." Vg. adds a verb *terrae vectes concluserunt me in aeternum*, nicely translated by Sasson as "the bolts of the earth have locked me in forever" (*Jonah*, 188).

p   Mur (reconstructed) MT reads ותעל חיי משחת, "but my life you bring up from the pit." G reads καὶ ἀναβήτω φθορὰ ζωῆς μου, "Let the destruction of my soul be taken away." OL reads *et ascendat corruptio vitae meae ad te*, "Let the corruption of my life rise toward you." See Sasson, *Jonah*, 191. BHQ assesses the readings of G and OL as lexical errors.

q   G reads ἔλθοι, the optative: "may my prayer come to you." See discussion by Bolin, *Freedom beyond Forgiveness*, 109.

r   Tg. expands the seeming reference to unbelievers with לא כעממיא פלחי טעותא דמאתר דמטוב להון לית אנון ידעין, "I am not like the nations . . . who do not know the source of their welfare" (so Cathcart and Gordon, *Targum of the Minor Prophets*, 107).

s   S reads "your mercy forsake," mrḥmnwtk šbqyn.

t   MT reads אני בקל תודה, "I with a voice of thanks," but G reads more expansively "I with a voice of praise and confession," ἐγὼ δὲ μετὰ φωνῆς αἰνέσεως καὶ ἐξομολογήσεως.

u   MT ליי / ישועתה אשר נדרתי אשלמה, "that which I vowed I will fulfill / salvation is Yahweh's," in G is ὅσα ηὐξάμην, ἀποδώσω εἰς σωτηρίαν μου τῷ κυρίῳ, "What I have vowed I will repay for my salvation to the Lord." OL reads "to my savior, the Lord: *salvatori meo*.

v   Tg. reads פורקן נפשי בצלו קדם יוי, "the deliverance of my life is through prayer before the Lord."

w   G omits "and Yahweh said" (ויאמר יי) (a phrase that seems to be missing an object as in the story of Cain and Abel, MT Gen 4:8) and has προσετάγη, "it was commanded," in the passive. The verb "command" in G is the same one that is employed in 2:1. S reads wpqd mryʾ, "and the Lord commanded."

x   MT Mur read ויקא, "he vomited." G reads καὶ ἐξέβαλε, "and he threw." The same verb is used in G 1:15.

Commentary

Jonah 2 contains the best-known portion of the narrative, beginning with Jonah's being swallowed by a big fish and concluding with the fish's spewing forth the recalcitrant prophet. In between is a traditional-style lament in a poetic register, partaking of formulaic language and imagery that beautifully express Jonah's description of his trials and his prayerful request for release.

■ **1** The verb מנה in the *piel* form translated here as "assign" is rooted in counting or apportionment. The verb in Dan 1:5, 10, 11 also conveys the meaning of "appointing" or "assigning." Here, as in Jonah 4:6, 7, 8, it conveys a message about God's total control of the cosmos, in which all animate and inanimate creations are subject to his orders.[1] The use of a swallowing sea creature as the means of containing and maintaining Jonah, who continues to live within the fish for three days, is an Israelite example of a motif found in an international fund of folklore to be explored in detail below. This motif is a favorite in pictorial representations of Jonah and has captured the imagination of countless artists, ancient and modern. Examples of this rich reception history are presented in the final section on this chapter.

Sasson provides an overview of animals who appear in the Hebrew Bible and discusses their roles as God's servants.[2] The most important threads emphasized by

---

1   See Limburg, *Jonah*, 60; Sweeney, *Twelve Prophets*, 1:316.

2   Sasson, *Jonah*, 144–46; on natural phenomena as characters in Jonah, see Person, *In Conversation with Jonah*, 58–59.

this verse and its imagery seem to be the continued interest in the sea that dominates a good portion of the book; the role of its larger-than-life legendary creatures; the act of swallowing, which is associated with death in ancient Near Eastern mythology; and the liminal condition of being swallowed and yet not digested, dissolved, and killed so that the hero emerges whole and live three days later.

The sea provides the author with a symbol of creation and chaos, death and rebirth that will be beautifully developed in the lament to follow in this chapter.[3] Enriching this imagery of the waters is the big fish, the adjective echoing its numerous uses in chap. 1. Scholars have worried about the identity of the fanciful big "fish," variously rendered in artistic representations as a whale or a shark or a sea dragon.[4] The author leaves room for the imagination, and his use of a general term need not be attributed to his lack of precise or taxonomic knowledge concerning sea life. Such openness to the reader or listener and implicit invitation to co-create the narrative are typical of oral traditional literature.

The specific image of swallowing in the Levantine tradition is suggestive of death. So Mot, Death, swallows up the god Baal in the Canaanite epic. So Yahweh is imagined to swallow up Death in the apocalyptic imagery of Isa 25:6–8. So the underworld Sheol swallows people alive (Prov 1:12). So the earth swallows up Dathan and Abiram, those who would challenge God's favorites, Moses and Aaron, for leadership (Num 16:30–34; Deut 11:6; Ps 106:17). So enemies threaten to swallow the people (Ps 124:3).

The fish itself has been compared to a variety of biblical sea monsters that inhabit ancient Israelite myth such as Leviathan. The term for fish is masculine in 2:1 but feminine in 2:2, leading some scholars to suggest nuances of the womb or images of pregnancy or to emphasize themes of rebirth.[5] Lena-Sofia Tiemeyer suggests, however, that Jonah 2:2 preserves a rare lengthened nominal form attested also in Job 34:13; 37:12; and Ezek 8:2 and that the masoretes did not recognize this archaic form of the noun, rendering it instead as a feminine singular.[6] We will have more to say about the fish motif in the comparative study that follows close work with the verses of chap. 2. In fact, the fish, which has the potential to devour the man, is also pictured as sustaining him. A folklorist might point to the way in which the antagonist of the narrative, in fact, becomes a helper.[7] The inward parts of the fish (מעי הדג) might be translated as "womb" (Gen 25:23) or "entrails" (2 Sam 20:10), "belly," or "innards." They initially appear to be a burial place for Jonah but turn out to be a temporary holding cell that in fact spares him from the ravages of sea. It is a marginal place for a marginal man, at odds with his God, uncertain of his future, uncomfortable with his role, and ready to die.

The three days and three nights may simply be a stock reference to a duration of time as in the periods of fasting in 1 Sam 30:12 and Esth 4:16[8] (cf. "forty days

---

3   On the fish, sea monsters, creation, and chaos as they relate to matters of political conquest and the deity's capacity for transformation, see Jan-Dirk Döhling, "Jona und des Meeres Wellen: Zum problemgeschichtlichen Horizont und zum traditionsgeschichtlichen Hintergrund der Schöpfungsdynamik in Jona 1 und 2," *BN* 158 (2013) 17–37.

4   On the influence of the Greek translation (see textual note c above) on later Christian receptions of the scene, see Wilson, "Jonah in the Biblical Tradition," 8. For a discussion of fish and sea creatures with which the author of Jonah might have been familiar and their typologically monstrous associations, see Handy, *Jonah's World*, 83–88. For a treatment of Mediterranean Sea life and traditional associations made between the big fish and whales, see Paul Haupt, "Jonah's Whale," *PAPHS* 46 (1907) 151–64.

5   See Simon, *Jonah*, 19; Sasson's overview, *Jonah*, 155–56; Sweeney, *Twelve Prophets*, 1:317; and the nice summary by Tucker, *Jonah*, 49; on the fish as "a womb fantasy," see Zimmermann, "Problems and Solutions in the Book of Jonah," 582. On rabbinic midrashim that address the issue of the fish's gender, see É. Levine, *Aramaic Version of Jonah*, 71–72 n. 5.

6   Lena-Sofia Tiemeyer, "A New Look at the Biological Sex/Grammatical Gender of Jonah's Fish," *VT* 67 (2017) 317–23.

7   See Bickerman, *Four Strange Books*, 11–12; also David Gunn and Danna Nolan Fewell, *Narrative in the Hebrew Bible* (Oxford: Oxford University Press, 1993), 134.

8   See Johannes B. Bauer, "Drei Tage," *Bib* 39 (1958) 354–58.

and forty nights," Exod 24:18; 1 Kgs 19:8). Three-day journeys are referenced frequently in the exodus tradition, as it will be also later in Jonah (Exod 3:18; 5:3; 15:22). Some scholars have suggested that the three days and three nights might relate to various Mediterranean stories of antiquity involving descents to the underworld, whether referring to the length of time until the hero's release or to the length of time it takes to reach the other world. Comparisons have been drawn, for example, with tales of Heracles and Inanna.[9]

■ **2** In Jonah 2:2 comes a reversal, an expressed desire by Jonah to emerge from the divinely mandated liminal state. Jonah's prayer from inside the fish is a lament, a literary form in which the following motifs are common: an indication of need or request, often with anticipatory hope of fulfillment (2:3), followed by the speaker or singer's description of the dire straits in which he finds himself (2:4-8); a declaration of faith in the power of the one true God, evocative of the wisdom tradition (2:9); and, finally, a reference to gifts that the speaker promises to the rescuing deity—sacrifice, vows of sacrifice, or other gifts such as praise (2:10).[10] Scholars have found a chiastic structure in the prayer, and there is no doubt that recurring language and content serve to frame the piece and underscore its messages.[11] Several key points and questions surround this prayer by Jonah and will be addressed in notes that follow. First, this piece is deeply mythological, describing chaos in watery terms appropriate to the larger narrative context. Just as the turbulent sea is the backdrop to the opening shipboard events, so the sea—as "the Deep," breakers and billows, the heart of the sea, and the Primeval Ocean—confront the hero in chap. 2. References to Sheol, the End, the inner earth, the foundations of the mountains, and the pit also capture the poetic imagination, underscoring the challenge to Jonah's very life presented as a cosmogonic confrontation, a conflict between creation and chaos.

A second important issue involves style or texture and register. As scholars note, Jonah 2 shares language with many biblical psalms.[12] While some see the song as a pastiche, less than "original,"[13] the important point rather is that there are no absolute "originals" in this sort of rhythmic prayer. Content as expressed reflects variations on the way such things are said and imagined in a culturally situated ethnic genre, an immersion in a tradition in which certain ideas are articulated in certain ways.[14] The traditional nature of this lament, thus, is characterized not only by the expected pattern of content described above but also by the language in which the motifs are expressed.

In addition to formulaic patterns in content and language, Jonah 2 evidences the impressionistic parallelism typical of poetry in the ancient Levant, so that the meaning, imagery, and syntax of one line are repeated

---

9   See Wolff, *Obadiah and Jonah*, 132-33; George M. Landes, "The Kerygma of the Book of Jonah: The Contextual Interpretation of the Jonah Psalm," *Int* 12 (1967) 3-31, esp. 10-13; Landes, "The 'Three Days and Three Nights' Motif in Jonah 2:1," *JBL* 86 (1967) 446-50. For a brief but thoughtful study of the significance of formulaic durations of time in Jonah, see Erik Eynikel, "One Day, Three Days, and Forty Days in the Book of Jonah," in Patrick Chatelion Counet and Ulrich Berges, eds., *One Text, A Thousand Methods: Studies in Memory of Sjef van Tilborg* (BibInt 71; Leiden: Brill, 2005) 65-76. Eynikel suggests that "three days" sometimes suggests the limits of human endurance (68-71).

10 On the lament in Jonah 2, see William P. Brown, *Obadiah through Malachi* (WeBC; Louisville: Westminster John Knox, 1996) 23.

11 See Trible, *Rhetorical Criticism*, 163-73; Sasson, *Jonah*, 167; Steven T. Mann, "Performance Prayers of a Prophet: Investigating the Prayers of Jonah as Speech Acts," *CBQ* 79 (2017) 20-40; Van Wijk-Bos, *Ruth, Esther, Jonah*, 86-88.

12 See Robinson, *Die zwölf kleinen Propheten*, 123; Sasson, *Jonah*, 171-74, 192; Patrick D. Miller, "Trouble and Woe: Interpreting Biblical Laments," *Int* 37 (1983) 32-45, esp. 34.

13 Citing parallels in Psalms, R. B. Salters suggests that the work could have been composed by "borrowing phrases" (*Jonah and Lamentations*, 31). This suggestion fails to take account of the traditional-style register of the work (see the Introduction above). Robert D. Wilson seeks to make a case for the preexilic dating of Jonah through an examination of its texture and content. In the process he provides a detailed analysis of formulaic language shared by Jonah 2 and other biblical material ("The Authenticity of Jonah," *PTR* 16 [1918] 433-43).

14 In a similar vein, see Bolin, *Freedom beyond Forgiveness*, 118-19; Moshe Greenberg, *Biblical Prose Prayer: As a Window to the Popular Religion of Ancient Israel* (TLJS 6; Berkeley: University of California Press, 1983) 7, 37; and R. E. Clements, *The Prayers of the Bible* (London: SCM Press, 1986) 122.

with variation and nuance in the next to create a richer and deeper image. The lines are also characterized by an "adding style,"[15] so that the thought is often complete at the end of the line, even if the sentence continues. These three criteria, attention to formulaic language, to parallelism, and to adding style, have influenced the formatting of chap. 2 in the present volume, the location of line breaks, for example, and other choices made to underscore the traditional nature of the lament. Also important is Frank Moore Cross's observation that the work reflects a limping or *qînâ* meter so that one line of each set (usually a bicolon) is generally longer than the other.[16] The limping meter is typical of mourning songs and reflects the emotional state of the speaker, who intones a dirge to mark the death of a loved one or who experiences another difficult situation, expressed in the more wide-ranging lament. The prayer's heightened stylistic qualities also distinguish it from the surrounding narrative, and this difference in register has implications for questions about context and about the relationship of the prayer to Jonah as a whole.

The switch in register has a dramatic effect at this moment in the book.[17] Because the language of the lament is such a culturally shared medium, perhaps one that was employed in liturgical settings, the reader or listener is fully able to identify with the sufferer, with Jonah, odd, even disagreeable person though he seems to be. As Esther Menn has written about laments, "The suggestive vagueness of this stereotypical imagery appears to be a deliberate strategy that allows people facing any number of horrors to adapt the psalm for ritual use."[18] Receivers of Jonah's lament need to pause at the shift in register to look at him in a different light, perhaps to empathize with him, to appreciate the complexity and ambivalence of his character. This change in register creates heightened drama.[19] Will Jonah, praying to God and asking to be spared, live or die, and do we care more about him as we listen to his song? The role of v. 9, the critique of idolaters, again a stock motif common in the lament, plays a particularly interesting role in forcing the reader to rethink Jonah, a matter to be discussed below. The lament thus plays an important role in the narrative as it now stands.

An unanswerable question is whether Jonah 2 was created by the author of the book, a person immersed in the lament tradition, or was a self-standing composition that was added at an appropriate location to the larger work concerning the fleeing prophet.[20] Hugh S. Pyper explores the notion that the psalm may have been "the generative source for the narrative."[21] Others, such as

---

15 Lord, *Singer of Tales*, 54.
16 Frank Moore Cross, "Studies in the Structure of Hebrew Verse: The Prosody of the Psalm of Jonah," in H. B. Huffmon, F. A. Spina, and A. R. W. Green, eds., *The Quest for the Kingdom of God: Studies in Honor of George E. Mendenhall* (Winona Lake, IN: Eisenbrauns, 1983) 159–67. Additional close studies of the prosody of Jonah 2 and its significance for the messages, meanings, and poetic structure of the song in the context of the Jonah narrative are Duane L. Christiansen, "The Song of Jonah: A Metrical Analysis," *JBL* 104 (1985) 217–31; and J. T. Walsh, "Jonah 2, 3–10: A Rhetorical Critical Study," *Bib* 63 (1982) 219–29. See also Ackerman, "Satire and Symbolism," 221. For an interesting attempt to have the English translation reflect the posited rhythm of the Hebrew, see Wade, *Books of the Prophets*, 143.
17 For a reflection on possible reasons for this switch, see K. A. D. Smelik, "The Literary Function of Poetical Passages in Biblical Narrative: The Case of Jonah 2:3–10," in Janet Dyk, ed., *Give Ear to My Words: Psalms and Other Poetry in and around the Hebrew Bible; Essays in Honor of Professor N. A. van Uchelen* (Amsterdam: Societas Hebraica Amstelodamensis, 1996) 147–59.
18 Esther Menn, "No Ordinary Lament: Relecture and the Identity of the Distressed in Psalm 22," *HTR* 93 (2000) 301–41, here 308.
19 See also Athalya Brenner, "Jonah's Poem out and within Its Context," in Davies and Clines, *Among the Prophets*, 183–92, esp. 190.
20 Walter Bührer discusses Jonah 2 as part of a larger study of the narrative, seeking to establish whether various threads in the work point to a redaction history and various contributors. He concludes that the work, including Jonah 2, is a unified literary whole ("Untersuchungen zur literarischen Gestaltung des Jona-Buches," *BN* 166 [2015] 29–50).
21 See Hugh S. Pyper, "Swallowed by a Song: Jonah and the Jonah-Psalm through the Looking-Glass," in Robert Rezetko, Timothy H. Lim, and W. Brian Aucker, eds., *Reflection and Refraction: Studies in Biblical Historiography in Honour of A. Graeme Auld* (VTSup 113; Leiden: Brill, 2007) 337–58, here 342; also Kugel, *How to Read the Bible*, 631.

R. B. Salters, do not consider the psalm original to the book.[22] As noted by Douglas Stuart, the inclusion of a poem within a prose narrative is a common device in the Israelite literary tradition, a classic comparable case being the song of Hannah in 1 Samuel 2.[23] The "hook" for the latter is 1 Sam 2:5, the reference to the barren woman who gives birth. The links in Jonah 2 include the supplicant's physical situation in the sea; a metaphor of near-death employed in many laments that is portrayed in actual physical terms in the book; Jonah's desire or willingness to die and the prayer's overt references to Sheol, life, and death; and the reference to the belly/womb (בטן) of Sheol (2:3), evocative of the innards of the fish (2:1, 2), although different vocabulary is employed. George Landes makes the case that the poetic prayer or song of lament was composed by a different artist than the author of the story that surrounds it but that it is integral to the message and meaning of the book.[24] What does this song contribute to the book of Jonah?

The song reemphasizes that Jonah is under the sea. The metaphor of drowning with references to the Deep, breakers, the waters, and the Primeval Ocean is common in the language of laments (Pss 42:8 [7], תהום; 69:2–3 [1–2], מים/מצולה; 88:7–8, 18 [6–7, 17], משבריך/מצלות).[25] However, given that the surrounding story literally sets Jonah inside a fish under the sea,[26] the imagery of Jonah 2 allows for added realism and depth, albeit within the fantasmic imaginary of the narrative. The lament's theme of descent into the sea and resurgence onto dry land also enriches the peaks and valleys in this tale in which a man who expects to die is brought back to the living and a condemned city is spared.[27] The lament placed in the hero's mouth, moreover, enhances qualities of personal religion in the tale and, by doing so, our capacity to identify with him.[28] Like other laments, the song is set in the first person, so that however formulaic its content and words, the reader or listener hears the speaker talking about himself or herself. A further contributor to the speaker's projection of a self is embodied references, also the stock-in-trade of the lament. He is tossed around by the Deep, he feels the breakers and billows over him, the End is twisted around the speaker's head, he descends. The term נפש, translated "being" at 2:6, 8, and "life" at 1:14, could also be translated "up to my neck" in 2:6 or as "soul," "self," "life," "life-force" in either verse, and is also a frequent term in the laments.[29] The language thus emphasizes the person or self.

■ 3 The texture of Jonah 2:3 anticipates and exemplifies the textural qualities of the lament in 2:3–10 as a whole. The present tense is used in translating the verbs, in agreement with Sasson's astute observations concerning the grammatical acceptability and elegance of such a choice and the presence in chap. 2 of "a remarkable smor-

---

22 Salters, *Jonah and Lamentations*, 28; Nogalski, *Book of the Twelve*, 427.
23 Stuart, *Hosea–Jonah*, 470; Hartmut Gese, *Alttestamentliche Studien* (Tübingen: Mohr Siebeck, 1991) 138. See also Bickerman, who suggests that the prayer predates the current form of the book but that it had already been attributed to or associated with Jonah (*Four Strange Books*, 12–13). For thoughtful reflections on the relationship between Jonah 2 and the larger work, see Steven Weitzman, *Song and Story in Biblical Narrative: The History of a Literary Convention in Ancient Israel* (Indiana Studies in Biblical Literature; Bloomington: Indiana University Press, 1997) 57–58, 60, 109, 111, 113.
24 Landes, "Kerygma," 30–31. See also Von Rad, "The Prophet Jonah," in *God at Work in Israel* (trans. John H. Marks; Nashville: Abingdon Press, 1980 [essay originally published in 1950]) 58–70, here 68. Brenner views the lament as a parody that contributes to satirical dimensions of the book ("Jonah's Poem," 189); see also Ackerman, "Satire and Symbolism," 216–17; Good, *Irony in the Old Testament*, 54. Kenneth M. Craig Jr. makes a case for the role of the prayer in the structure of the Jonah narrative ("Jonah and the Reading Process," *JSOT* 47 [1990] 103–14).
25 Drawing connections between language and imagery shared by Jonah 2 and a number of psalms, P. Kyle McCarter points to the relevance of "the river ordeal" in Israelite and other ancient Near Eastern literatures ("The River Ordeal in Israelite Literature," *HTR* 66 [1973] 403–12, esp. 403–6).
26 On "literalization" in Jonah 2:1–2, see Muldoon, *In Defense of Divine Justice*, 123–24.
27 On the "topography" of the psalm that contrasts death and life, calamity and salvation, see Beat Weber, *Jona*, 80.
28 See comments by R. E. Clements, *The Prayers of the Bible* (London: SCM Press, 1986) 117.
29 See Niditch, *The Responsive Self*, 58; and Pss 17:9; 31:10 [9]; 70:3 [2], for some examples.

gasbord of verbal sequences."³⁰ Present tense allows the prayer a quality of immediacy, but the shifts from perfect to converted imperfect (with *waw*-conversive) in 2:3, 4, 7, 8, although translated in the present, do signal "crucial junctures."³¹ The shift from perfect in the verb "call" to *waw*-conversive with the imperfect in the verb "answer" is a frequently found juxtaposition of tenses in prayers expressing an appeal and a divine response (e.g., Ps 30:3 [2]). The switch may have the nuance of "but," that is, "I am in trouble *but* my God is trusted to come to my aid."

The way in which the text of v. 3 is formatted in the present English translation (laid out in five lines) produces a very long first line and a second line half as long, with ten and four syllables each. Most scholars, for example, Frank Moore Cross, break the line after "distress,"³² but I have chosen to let the adding style dominate, with the thought complete at the end of the line rather than having the prepositional phrase, "to Yahweh," begin a second line. In this first verse of the prayer and subsequently, adherence to the adding style and the interests of parallelism lead to some very uneven lines, and the present verse is a case in point.

In this respect, the format suggested in the translation differs from that of Cross's influential study of Jonah 2, which analyzes this prayer as an example of biblical poetry characterized by a limping meter. Like many commentators, Cross suggests that one line of each set is generally a syllable or two longer than its partner, as is typical in classical Israelite laments. The process of laying out the text involves certain decisions about line pairs and, in one case in v. 4, a reading based on variants in the textual tradition.³³ It is possible, however, that the juxtaposition of quite long lines with significantly shorter lines, suggested for Jonah 2 in the present volume, reflects the uneven register of a late biblical aesthetic found, for example, in Isa 1:21-31 and Isa 63:7–64:11.³⁴

Language of "calling out" reprises the captain's plea to Jonah to try to contact his deity for help (1:6) and the introduction to the prayer of the sailors for forgiveness (1:14). Appeals to Yahweh are frequently framed with language of calling out, as in Ps 18:7 [6] (cf. 2 Sam 22:7); 120:1; 130:1-2; Lam 3:55-56, passages that also include additional formulaic language of the lament found in Jonah 2, for example, words from the root for distress (צרר, "to bind, tie, be restricted") which occurs also in Jonah 2:3; Pss 18:7 (6); 120:1.

The lines in Ps 18:6-7 (5-6) characterized by parallelism share key images and vocabulary with Jonah 2:3, offering a useful comparison that underscores the traditional-style texture of the prayer. In addition to the root צרר, "to bind, tie, be restricted," and the reference to being trapped by Sheol, the Israelite version of Hades (see more below), the use of the *piel* of שׁוע, "cry out for help," a term frequently employed for appeals to the deity (see also Pss 5:3 [2]; 18:7-8, 42 [6-7, 41]; 30:3 [2]; 31:23 [22]; 119:147), the verb for "call," (קרא) and the phrase "hear my voice" are the stock from which the lament is drawn (see also Ps 120:1; Hab 1:2-4). A formula pattern is shared by the opening words of Ps 18:7 [6] and Jonah 2:3, which combines "distress" (root צרר) with "calling" (root קרא + the naming of the deity to whom the address is made, יהוה). Similarly, ויענני, "and he answers me," שמעת קולי, "you hear my voice" (Jonah 2:3), and Ps 18:7, ישמע מהיכלו קולי, "from his temple he heard my voice," are variants of a formula that indicates divine response.

Like the Greek Hades, Sheol is both a personified being and a place, the realm of the dead and in some sense Death itself. Thus, Isa 14:15 equates Sheol with the "Pit" (בור), the underworld, as in the parallelism of Ps 88:4-5 (3-4). Sheol also "rumbles toward" the deceased person to "greet" his coming and rouses his fellow dead, "the shades," to greet him (Isa 14:9). Although full-blown

---

30 Sasson, *Jonah*, 163, 170. See also Joüon §118.
31 Sasson, *Jonah*, 170.
32 Landes, "Kerygma," 9; Cross, "Studies in the Structure," 161; Michael Barré, "Jonah 2, 9 and the Structure of Jonah's Prayer," *Bib* 72 (1991) 237-48, here 242.
33 Cross, "Studies in the Structure," 162.
34 On a postexilic date for Isa 1:21-31, see Susan Niditch, "The Composition of Isaiah 1," *Bib* 61 (1980) 509-29, here 526-27. Niditch points to the contrast in content, vocabulary, and texture between the dirge in the eighth-century B.C.E. Isa 1:10-15 and material in Isa 1:21-31. Similarly, concerning the content and meter of the lament in Isa 63:7–64:11, see Paul D. Hanson, *The Dawn of Apocalyptic* (Philadelphia: Fortress Press, 1975) 79-92, esp. 87.

concepts of resurrection appear only later in the biblical corpus (e.g., Dan 12:2), death leads to some sort of shade-like existence in an underworld, usually portrayed as a gloomy, dark place experienced in an unenviable state (Job 10:22, 26).[35] Thus, Samuel, after his death, can appear to the ghost-whisperer or spirit medium of 1 Samuel 28 when she invokes the now dead prophet for Saul. The location of the realm of the dead is generally described as subterranean, under the earth (Num 16:30; Jonah 2:7) or beneath the primeval oceans (Job 26:6). The brush with Sheol, sometimes poetically paired with "Death" (Ps 18:6 [5]) or "the Pit" (Pss 30:4 [3]; 88:4–5 [3–4]) beautifully describes the experience of the lamenter, who presents himself as trapped, drowning, near death due to his current life challenges. In contrast to the collection of prayers in the Psalms, which can be uttered in any life-threatening or diminishing situation, the metaphoric language of the lament in Jonah 2 literally fits the narrative content. Jonah is a man thrown overboard, swallowed by a fish, in danger of drowning, dying.

The parallelistic and formulaic style continues with a pairing of "call out" with "cry out," and "answers me" with "hear my voice," as discussed above.

■ **4** The subject in the present translation is the Deep, מצולה, a personified force and feminine noun as in Pss 68:23 [22]; 69:3, 16 [2, 15]; 88:7 [6]; 107:24, the cosmic waters, although the ancient versions and most interpreters translate the verb שׁלך in the second person, as part of Jonah's address to the deity.[36] Some commentators eliminate or abbreviate the phrase "in the heart of the seas" due to metric considerations and place the preposition before "Deep" (e.g., Cross: "You cast me into the depth of the Sea").[37] The leggy line is as noted above perhaps a mark of late biblical compositions in the *qînâ* register.

The "Deep" is paired with נהר, "River," another personified watery force, a synonym for ים, "Sea," in Canaanite mythology.

The third colon in 2:4, parallel in meaning to the first two in the present formatting, is again a very long line. A formula is repeated with a traditional term for powerful waters, "Deep," or "River," or "breakers and waves" and a verb and object that indicate the lamenter or object's almost drowning, being thrown into the seas, surrounded, experiencing the waves passing over him. Language of breakers and/or waves is employed under similar thematic circumstances in Ps 42:8 [7]; 88:8 [7]. Again, such a recurrence of language is not a matter of quotation or anthologizing but an indication of an author's immersion in a culturally shared corpus of traditional means of expressing particular moods, emotions, settings, or other content.

■ **5** The phrase ואני אמרתי, "and I say," further enriches the sense of selfhood in play in the lament. As Sasson notes, the language suggests, "I say to myself" or "I ponder," enhancing nuances of self-reflection.[38] In Jonah, the lament form contributes to a quality of personal religion as a man, speaking in the first person in language and forms however conventionalized, expresses the way he feels, what he whispers to himself in a time of extreme alienation and impending doom.[39] This attention to the interiority of the protagonist runs throughout the book and is a marker of biblical narrative literature in the Persian period (see discussion in the overview below).

Comparisons can be drawn with lament language in Ps 31:23 [22] and Lam 3:54. Ps 31:23 [22] and Jonah 2:5 share a formula pattern: "I say" + term of distancing from the deity, "driven out" in Jonah and "cut off" in the psalm + "from your sight." The formulaic quality of the composition continues.

---

35   See Christopher B. Hays, *Death in the Iron Age II and in First Isaiah* (FAT 79; Tübingen: Mohr Siebeck, 2011); Matthew Suriano, *A History of Death in the Hebrew Bible* (New York: Oxford University Press, 2018).

36   For a discussion of links between the underworld, death, and images of water in biblical and ancient Near Eastern contexts, see A. R. Johnson, "Jonah II. 3–10: A Study in Cultic Phantasy," in H. H. Rowley, ed., *Studies in Old Testament Prophecy: Presented to Theodore H. Robinson by the Society for Old Testament Study on His Sixty-Fifth Birthday, August 9th, 1946* (Edinburgh: T&T Clark, 1957) 82–102.

37   Cross, "Studies in the Structure," 161.

38   Sasson, *Jonah*, 178.

39   On the emotional dimension of this phrase, see also Limburg, *Jonah*, 67.

The demonstrative adverb אך, which sometimes operates temporally ("just as"), and at other times as an emphatic ("surely"), here functions in a third way as a "restrictive."[40] Thus, Sasson suggests "nevertheless," "for all that."[41] The idiom employing a *hiphil* imperfect form of יסף, "to add," + an infinitive conveys repetition of an act, "to continue" to do something or do it/experience it "again." Some scholars who read the imperfect as implying a future event translate assertively, for example, Landes's "Nevertheless, I shall gaze upon. . . ."[42] The case is made that Jonah's veering back and forth between desolation and hope is part of the structure of the lament. From a narrative perspective, given the imagery that follows in 2:6–8, it seems likely that the prophet, talking to himself, is portrayed as continuing to express self-doubt and alienation, although the very asking about the possibility of continued contact with his deity anticipates reversal of his situation. The present translation attempts to convey both doubt and a ray of hope, employing "yet" to suggest both the notion of "continuing" and future orientation.

The hope that Jonah will again look upon "your holy temple/court/palace" (היכל) is usually understood as a reference to the Jerusalem temple, the place where God's holy presence dwells, the locus of mediation between people and deity via ritual activity. It is not necessary to overliteralize or historicize this reference, asking whether the temple still existed at the time of the composition of the prayer or the story to which it now belongs. Nor is it helpful to point out that the northern prophet of 2 Kings, the possible pseudepigraphic persona of the protagonist, might not have been concerned about the Jerusalem temple.

Wolff, like most scholars, does consider the reference to היכל קדשך as meant to evoke "the sanctuary at Jerusalem."[43] Scholars point to the use of this phrase in psalms describing the physical place, as in Ps 79:1, where it refers to the defiled temple, and Pss 5:8 [7] and 138:2, where the composer describes his worship. Yet the reference to the divine temple or palace in Ps 18:7 [6] is more equivocal. In Ps 18:7, as in Jonah 2:5, the composer describes his distress and calling to God, his crying out, in formulaic language shared with Jonah 2:3 (see above). He asserts (Ps 18:7) that God hears his voice from his היכל. Has the author of the psalm made petition at the temple Jerusalem? Is he pictured as praying "toward it" as in 1 Kgs 8:29, 42? Is reference to the temple in this psalm and in Jonah 2, however, meant to evoke a literal building? Isaiah's initiation vision takes place in the heavenly palace or היכל, the divine realm, which is echoed or paralleled in the manmade building in Jerusalem (Isa 6:1). As Ps 11:4 notes, Yahweh is in his holy temple/palace/court, literally "in the temple of his holiness," בהיכל קדשו. The bicolon in Ps 11:4 continues and specifies the location of this temple or palace: "Yahweh, in heaven is his throne," יהוה בשמים כסאו. It is possible that the composer of Jonah 2 entertains the possibility that the prophet imagines communion with God on high as a part of his prophetic role and status.[44] A comparison might be drawn with Ps 34:5–6 [4–5], in which the speaker in the first person describes his seeking God and the deity's answering him, and recommends to others, "Look to him, and shine."

■ 6 The prayer continues imagery of watery chaos found in v. 4, a use of traditional, mythological, and conventionalized speech and scenery often found in laments that capture the "literal" essence of Jonah's situation. The water that threatens "his very life," encompassing him עד־נפש (sometimes translated as "up to my neck"[45] or "throat,"[46]), is paired with the primeval waters or abyss תהום, here translated as "Primeval Ocean," that surrounds him. It is the תהום and primeval waters that

---

40 For demonstrative אך, see *IBHS* §17.2.b; for the restrictive use of the adverb, see §39.3.5.c.

41 Sasson, *Jonah*, 179–80. Similarly Tucker, *Jonah*, 54; Snaith, *Hebrew Text of Jonah*, 26.

42 Landes, "Kerygma," 21; see also Allen, *Joel–Micah*, 115.

43 Wolff, *Obadiah and Jonah*, 135. See also Sasson, *Jonah*, 179–80. So too Nogalski, *Book of the Twelve*, 430, who views the reference as possible evidence of a southern composer for the lament.

44 For questions concerning the identity and location of this sacred space, see the discussion by Lasine, "Jonah's Complexes," 243. See also J. Anderson for suggestions concerning a "cosmic temple" ("Jonah's Peculiar Re-Creation," 183).

45 E.g., Sasson, *Jonah*, 160.

46 Wolff, *Obadiah and Jonah*, 126. For a nice treatment of embodied emotions in Jonah 2, see Johnson, "Jonah II. 3–10," 85.

open the scene of cosmic creation in Genesis 1. This term, related to Tiamat, the female manifestation of procreative chaos in the Mesopotamian creation myth, Enuma Elish, is also employed in the lament in Ps 42:8 [7], paired with the "breakers and billows" seen also in Jonah 2:4. The composer thus has available a rich fund of traditional language from which to draw in creating his own composition, a set of material with which his audience is completely familiar as they identify with Jonah. They, like him, are caught up in a mythic complex that evokes intense anxiety and portrays the confrontation with death itself.

The common translations of סוּף in the third colon of 2:6 as "reeds" or "seaweed"[47] or "kelp"[48] are inadequate and fail to capture the typological and insistent scenery of chaos. Building on the work of Norman Snaith and others, Bernard Batto makes the case that the translation of יָם סוּף as "Sea of Reeds" is completely misguided and often rooted in a desire to link the archetypal scene of crossing in the exodus tradition with a particular ecological, topographical location.[49] He derives the meaning of the term from the basic root סוּף, "to come to an end," "to cease to exist,"[50] and points to the parallelism in Jonah 2:6 between the images of watery chaos, the Abyss, and סוּף. He notes further the parallels between the use of verbs אפף, "to surround" or "to encompass," and סבב, "to surround," in Jonah 2:6, 4 and Ps 18:5–6 [4–5] (cf. 2 Sam 22:5; Ps 116:3). In each case, this language expresses the situation of the lamenter. The passive participle of the verb חבש, here translated as "is twisted around," is also employed in Job 40:13 in relation to being bound "in the hidden place (i.e. the underworld)."[51]

■ **7** This verse is the turning point of the lament, for descent into the realm of chaos and death (note again the use of the root ירד, as found in Jonah 1:3, 5) is followed by ascent and release. Following imagery of chaos as a watery environment, being dragged under the sea or overwhelmed by primeval waters, v. 7 describes an under-the-earth netherland also associated with death and chaos, an alternate cosmological dimension. In this way, Jonah 2 partakes in a mythic geography, a worldview revealing culturally shared imagery concerning the structure and features of the cosmos as well as its mythological ecosystem.

The descent into the earthen underworld begins at לקצבי הרים, here translated as "At the foundations of the mountains." The term קצב is related to a verb that signifies to "shear off" or "cut"—hence BDB's suggestion for קצבי, "extremities,"[52] and the ancient translator's suggestions, "crevices" (G), "fissures" (OL). In 1 Kgs 6:25 and 7:37, the noun refers to a shape or form or "cut" of decorative features in the temple, namely, cherubim and stands. With good attention to the ancient cosmology implicit in this imagery, Wolff suggests that the term refers to "'the anchorages' of the mountains which let them stand firm above the primeval waters (cf. Ps 24:2)."[53] Parallels might be drawn with the "foundations of the mountains" in Deut 32:22 and the "roots" of the mountains in Job 28:9 (cf. Sir 16:19).

The inner earth is paralleled in v. 7 by שחת, "the pit" or "grave," a term that can be understood as the individual's grave or as the underworld where the shades dwell (Isa 38:17; Pss 30:10 [9]; 49:10 [9]; 103:4). In a philological tour de force, Marvin Pope draws upon a range of comparative material from the ancient Near East to examine the possible connotations and origins of שחת, with special reference to Job 9:29–31. His attention to nuances of "putrescence" in play in the word's use in various

---

47 Allen, *Joel-Micah*, 214.
48 Sasson, *Jonah*, 182.
49 Bernard Batto, "The Reed Sea: Requiescat in Pace," *JBL* 102 (1983): 27–35; Norman H. Snaith, "The Sea of Reeds: The Red Sea," *VT* 15 (1965): 395–98.
50 BDB, s.v. "סוּף." See David J. A. Clines (*DCH* 6:133–34), who offers examples from Qohelet, Sirach, and Qumran texts of the association between this term and death itself. This connotation works well in the context of the lament in which the chords of death frequently surround the lamenter.
51 Batto, "The Reed Sea," 34.
52 BDB, s.v. "קָצֵב."
53 Wolff, *Obadiah and Jonah*, 136; on the "geography of the underworld," see also Ackerman, "Satire and Symbolism," 233–34. For an erudite and close analysis of terminology and imagery shared by Jonah 2:7 and Mesopotamian mythology, see Shalom M. Paul, "Jonah 2:7: The Descent to the Netherworld and Its Mesopotamian Congeners," in Marilyn J. Lundbert, Steven Fine, and Wayne T. Pitard, eds., *Puzzling Out the Past: Studies in Northwest Semitic Languages and Literatures in Honor of Bruce Zuckerman* (CHANE 55; Leiden: Brill, 2012) 131–34.

sources helps one to imagine the gloom of decomposition in the underworld portrayed by the ancient composers.[54] This term, used in synonymous parallelism with Sheol in Ps 16:10, also implies the realm of the dead in Jonah 2:7. In death one descends into the dust (Ps 22:30 [29]), the pit (בור, Ps 28:1; 30:4), the underworld Sheol (Ps 55:16 [15]), the utter silence of death (דומה, Ps 115:17), or, as here, into the earth. Wolff points out that Akkadian *erṣetu* refers to the underworld,[55] as implicit in the apocalyptic imagery of Isa 26:19, where the earth is said to cast forth or to give birth to (literally, "let drop") the shades. The innermost part of the earth can also be presented as a place of creation, as in Ps 139:15.

The phrase that further describes the lamenter's condition in the underworld, translated as "its bars around me for eternity," suggests an eternal prison-like fortress from which there is no escape. The word for "bar," בריח, found in phrases such as "bars of iron" (Isa 45:2; cf. Ps 107:10), suggests strength, as one might expect. The "bars of your gates" in Ps 147:13 images protection and the capacity to keep unwanted visitors out, whereas in Jonah 2 the bars that surround the lamenter imply permanent captivity reminiscent of the "gates of Sheol" (Isa 38:10) or the "gates of death" (Pss 9:14 [13]; 107:18; Job 38:17). The postbiblical composer of Qumran Hymn 9 reveals familiarity with and continued use of the traditional cache of ancient Israelite parallel and formulaic phrases, for example, "the doors of שחת" and "the eternal bars" (1QH^a XI, 18). In Jonah 2:7, bars are also said to be eternal, forever (לעולם), but in the next colon comes the reversal.

As the descent into a netherworld is associated with death, so ascent is associated with renewal. Salvation is to rise or be redeemed from שחת or the gates of death or Sheol (cf. Pss 9:14 [13]; 30:4 [3]; 71:20; 103:4; 71:20). After this turning point in the lament, the speaker alludes to his successful petition to the saving God (2:8), implicitly distinguishes himself from those who do not worship the one God (2:9), and finally makes a vow to thank the deity for his act of kindness toward himself as sufferer, a typical conclusion to the traditional lament (2:10).

■ **8** The root עטף in the *hithpael* generally is understood to mean "faint" as in an infant's faintness due to hunger (Lam 2:19; also 2:12), and Tucker, translating "ebbing away," notes that the term "often signals the onset of death (Lam 2:12) or serves as a precursor to death (Ps 143:3–4, 7)."[56] Elsewhere the root connotes "to physically wrap" or "cover oneself" (Ps 65:14 [13]). The root in Jonah 2:8 thus may function in a multivocalic way to create a visceral image of life ebbing away as the person's נפש, the life force or soul, wraps itself around him in a kind of suffocation. The language is formulaic, as noted by Sasson. This verb is linked with "a word for the human vital force," either נפש or רוח, "spirit," as in the laments in Pss 104:4; 142:4 [3]; 143:4–5; 77:4 [3].[57] In fact, the Hebrew manuscript traditions of Jonah evidence the two variants.[58] As in Pss 77:4 [3] and 143:4–5, the lamenter's desperate situation relates to a kind of remembering, remembering God or days past, and in this self-reflective frame of mind his prayer goes to God, to God's holy temple. The language that expresses the prayer going to or reaching God is a common formula in the psalms, communion with a sympathetic deity being the quintessential goal of prayer (cf. Pss 18:7 [cf. 2 Sam 22:7]; 88:3 [2]; see also 2 Chr 30:27).

As in the case of 2:5, most scholars interpret the reference to the temple as connoting the Jerusalem temple, the locus on earth of God's holy presence, the place to which people, Israelites and foreigners, are to direct their prayers and confessions of sin (1 Kgs 8:35, 38, 46–51). In 1 Kings 8 the prayers toward the temple intertwine with the deity's hearing them in his heavenly dwelling (1 Kgs 8:30, 36, 39, 45, 49). It seems entirely possible that the reference need not be to a physical building on earth but to God's divine dwelling, or that the two, so connected in ancient Israelite cosmology, are evoked by the phrase היכל קדשך, "your holy temple/palace" (or literally, "temple of your holiness"). See on 2:5 above.

■ **9** This verse declares that people who devote themselves to mere illusion and not to the true God lose out

---

54 Marvin H. Pope, "The Word שחת in Job 9:31," *JBL* 83 (1964) 269–78.
55 Wolff, *Obadiah and Jonah*, 136.
56 Tucker, *Jonah* (2017), 59.
57 Sasson, *Jonah*, 193.
58 See Trible, "Studies in the Book of Jonah," 38.

on חסד, a term that encapsulates the concept of divine favor.⁵⁹ Translated as "loyalty," "faithfulness," "kindness," "love," or "mercy,"⁶⁰ the term is deeply associated with positive relationships or bonds whereby a person or deity offers kindness, often selflessly, for the sake of others. Quintessential biblical examples of divine חסד include the formation of the unconditional covenant with Abraham in Genesis 15 and God's rescue of Israel from Egyptian bondage (Exod 15:13).⁶¹

The verbal roots שמר, "to keep" or "preserve," and עזב, "to leave" or "forsake," are paired in biblical poetry (cf. Pss 89:31–32 [30–31]; 119:87–88) to contrast adherence to God's commandments and disregard of them.⁶²

The phrase הבלי שוא literally means "vapors of emptiness or nothingness." The former word is used in Qohelet (1:2) and is frequently translated as "vanity" or "absurdity," and the latter term is often employed in reference to empty speech or falsehood (cf. Pss 12:3 [2]; 41:7 [6]; Prov 30:8).⁶³ The term הבל is traditionally paired with a reference to hewn images, icons, or "idols," in the aniconic thread of Israelite tradition, foreign objects of devotion, or "no-gods" in the view of the Israelite author (cf. Deut 32:21; Jer 8:19). The contrast between the speaker of a lament and the ill-willed enemies who surround him is an essential component of the genre (Pss 38:20 [19]; 41:6 [7]; 42:10–11 [9–10]). More broadly, biblical prayers in the collection of Psalms frequently emphasize contrasts between the holy and the unholy, the faithful and the sinner, Yahweh loyalists and the devotees of other gods (Pss 38:20 [19]; 41:5–6 [4–5]; 42:9–10 [8–9]; 73:27). Psalm 31:7 employs the same epithet for God's enemies as that found in Jonah 2:9; they are השמרים הבלי־שוא, and the psalmist contrasts these devotees of empty vapors with himself, one who trusts in Yahweh.

As noted throughout close work with Jonah 2, the author thus draws upon the typological language and imagery of the lament.⁶⁴ This verse, however, is especially relevant to questions about the relationship between the prayer and the larger book. Just as imagery of watery chaos is a formulaic feature of the lament that has special relevance for the plot of Jonah, the contrast drawn between those who have faith in Yahweh and access to his favor versus the devotees of vapors who cannot expect Yahweh's support, while formulaic and conventionalized in message and meaning, has special relevance to this tale about foreigners who also need and can apparently receive divine help. Are readers to think about the non-Israelite sailors in Jonah 1, who are ethically self-aware and at pains not to sacrifice Jonah to save themselves, as the devotees of vapors? Does their respect for Jonah's deity, the one God, and their sacrifices and vows to Yahweh identify them as those who have or seek access to חסד even though they are not Israelites? Are they to be compared with the foreigners mentioned in 1 Kgs 8:41–43 who seek out God? While neither 1 Kings 8 nor Jonah 1 is to be interpreted as a pro-conversion piece, each of these late biblical compositions, like some other Israelite works such as the book of Ruth written after the Babylonian conquests, does breathe a certain openness. The stock material in Jonah 2:9 thus has particular pertinence to themes with which the larger work grapples. The presentation of and attitudes to the supposed "Other" both in looking back to chap. 1 and ahead to the actions of the Ninevites in chap. 3, God's

---

59   Katharine Doob Sakenfeld suggests that the term refers most often to specific acts rather than to generic divine favor (*The Meaning of Hesed in the Hebrew Bible: A New Inquiry* (HSM 17; Missoula, MT: Scholars Press, 1978) 230–31, 234–39.

60   *DCH* 3, s.v. "חֶסֶד."

61   For a history of scholarship on חסד and a study rooted in lexical field studies, see Gordon R. Clark, *The Word Hesed in the Hebrew Bible* (JSOTSup 157; Sheffield: JSOT Press, 1993). Noting that חסד can refer to human kindness and compassion, Johan Ferreira suggests that 2:9 be read to declare that "by following idols the people of Israel are abandoning basic humanity and kindness" ("Note on Jonah 2:8," 36).

62   Pointing to the absence in the biblical corpus of other examples of שמר in the *piel* form, Michael Barré suggests reading the preposition מן, "from," and a *qal* participle, translating "From (among) those who hold to faithless practices//who abandon/disregard their covenant fidelity" ("Jonah 2:9," 237–48). This reading in turn requires a particular view of the lament's poetic structure.

63   For a discussion of the meaning of הבלי־שוא in the context of the verse, the lament, and the larger narrative, see Nathan Patrick Love, "Translating Jonah 2:9: Looking for a Breath of Fresh Air," *BT* 64 (2013) 266–83.

64   See also Craigie, *Twelve Prophets*, 225–26.

response, and in turn Jonah's response to the deity's saving actions in chap. 4, all relate to the questions about us versus them, "real" versus false religion, true divinity, and who has access to this God. These are central concerns in the work as a whole.

■ **10** The final verse of Jonah's prayer concludes with the sufferer/petitioner's vow to make an offering in thanks to Yahweh, a typical feature of the lament (Pss 54:8 [6]; 66:13-14; 116:17-18). Alter notes that the meaning of the tense in v. 10 is to be understood in the "optative mode." The speaker "wishes" to offer sacrifice.[65] The promise to offer to God underscores the hopeful element of the lament, which is ultimately a prayer emotionally informed not only by despair but also by nuances of wish-fulfillment. As Tony Cartledge has emphasized, moreover, implicit in the vow is a concept of reciprocity. The speaker promises to sing to Yahweh (Ps 13:6 [5]) or to bless him in public assemblies (Ps 26:12) or to offer sacrifice (Ps 54:8 [6]; 66:13-14; 116:17-18) in response to or expectation of the deity's act of kindness toward him.[66] And perhaps psychologically the declaration that the vow will be fulfilled by him is a way to assure himself that he will be rescued and all will be well. Indeed, in Jonah 2:11, the big fish expels Jonah at God's word so that he finds himself safe on dry ground.

The final phrase of the verse, "salvation is Yahweh's," is a formulaic refrain, confirming the message of the foregoing events, found also in Ps 3:9 [8].

■ **11** An actual quotation that would typically follow the introductory phrase ויאמר יהוה לדג, "and Yahweh said to the fish," is missing. Tucker, agreeing with Cynthia Miller, suggests that the "content and purpose of the speech event may be inferred from the subsequent events" and that this formulation is a means of narrative condensation.[67]

The verbal root קיא meaning "vomit" or "disgorge" often employed metaphorically in Hebrew Bible, for example, in Lev 18:28 and 20:22 concerning the land's vomiting out its inhabitants, here appears to be quite literal.[68]

Overview of Jonah 2:1-11, Comparative Folklore, and Reception

This section of Jonah begins with the prophet's being swallowed by the fish, his descent and punishment, and concludes with his emergence live from the fish and surrounding waters as he is saved by order of God. The section is dominated by the lament in 2:3-10, marked by formulaic language, parallelism, and the long-short meter typical of biblical laments. Throughout, the choice of language and language patterns partake in a traditional fund shared with other biblical compositions to describe essential content, for example, the underworld and facing death, the address to God for relief, and the salvific divine response. This traditional language provides a means and a style of composition and reflects key cultural ideas and imagery.[69] The verse-by-verse analysis above draws comparatively upon the psalms of lament, for Jonah 2:3-10 is a typical biblical lament built from motifs including the description of the speaker's dire situation, often with imagery of drowning, the request to Yahweh for salvation, the release or hoped-for release, and the vow to offer thanks for the speaker's vindication.

The switch to the more formalized register in 2:3-10 serves to emphasize the prophet's own journey and the

---

65 Alter translates "let me sacrifice . . . let me pay" (*Strong as Death*, 147).
66 Tony W. Cartledge, *Vows in the Hebrew Bible and the Ancient Near East* (JSOTSup 147; Sheffield: JSOT Press, 1992) 23. For the link between music, voice, and thanksgiving in such formulaic promises, see Nissim Amzallag, "Praise or Antiphonal Singing? The Meaning of להודות Revisited," *HS* 56 (2015) 115-28.
67 Tucker, *Jonah* (2006), 62.
68 With reference to Gerhard Sauter's ("Jonah 2: A Prayer out of the Deep," in Brent A. Strawn and Nancy R. Bowers, eds., *A God So Near: Essays on Old Testament Theology in Honor of Patrick D. Miller* [Winona Lake, IN: Eisenbrauns, 2003] 145-52, here 146-47) insistence on the work's irony, Brent Strawn considers that the vomiting fish "is sick of/on *Jonah's false piety*, his misplaced psalm of thanksgiving" ("On Vomiting: Leviticus, Jonah, Ea(a)rth," *CBQ* 74 [2012] 445-64, esp. 453).
69 Ben Zvi suggests somewhat woodenly that the author creates "a pastiche of different verses" from "existing Psalms," quoting and combining to create a new composition (*Signs of Jonah*, 107 n. 27).

capacity of all human beings for transformation and renewal. The piece enhances qualities of personal religion characteristic of Jonah with its emphases on outer, embodied physicality and inner psychological turmoil.

More specifically, metaphorical imagery of the waters typical of laments is relevant to the literal content of the work in which a man is sent overboard into the sea. The contrast drawn between the Yahweh-faithful and the "Other" in v. 9, again a typical feature in the psalms, also has special relevance for this work, for the distrust and differences between ethnic groups and the shared humanity of all people are thematic counterpoints.

Comparative Folklore

Among the folk motifs of Jonah, the fish swallowing a man has the largest number of international parallels and holds the greatest fascination for appropriators of the tale.[70] The fish swallowing Jonah figures in a wide array of artistic renderings in various media and periods and is a source of lively literary and theological elaboration. Fanciful stories about sea worlds and their inhabitants have always been sources of human speculation, whether the focus is the environment with its underwater castles, its lost kingdoms such as Atlantis or its inhabitants including mermaids, mermen, monstrous dragons, and other sea creatures. Tales about such worlds and beings no doubt reflect both an innate attraction to the life-teeming water and a fear of its enormous capacity to overpower even the sturdiest of ships and cleverest of captains. In its own way, like the storm-tossed scene of chap. 1, Jonah 2 shares in some of these very human responses to the sea and its inhabitants. To shine an instructive comparativist light specifically on Jonah's use of the motif of the fish that swallows a man, good places to begin are Stith Thompson's catalogue of folktale patterns and its expanded three-volume edition by Hans-Jörg Uther (the types) and Thompson's multivolume catalogue of individual pieces of content (the motifs);[71] Theodor Gaster's collection of parallels to biblical tales, based on James George Frazer's earlier work;[72] and the material collected by Hans Schmidt.[73]

Hans Schmidt's work reflects an early 20th century effort to place Jonah in the context of an international fund of folklore. He pays special attention to classical sources and offers a host of visual representations from the Western tradition. Astutely, Schmidt suggests that the fishes in various Jonah-like tales be examined as enemies, rescuers, and as embodying a kind of underworld.[74] Among the dangerous sea creatures and personifications of the sea itself are an array of biblical characters such as Rahab and Leviathan, the Canaanite "Prince River," and the Mesopotamian Tiamat. In folktales collected by Thompson and his students, fish themselves, in fact, are usually treated as benevolent helpers, frequently playing a role in tales of rescue, granting the hero a wish (B375.1.1), rescuing a ship (B541.5), recovering a lost object from the sea (B548.2.5), pricking and defeating a monster (L315.8), and swallowing a man to rescue him (B541.1.1). Examples in the B540's are all variants on "animal rescuers." A set of tales is also listed under B470, "Helpful Fish," and finds its place among tales of other helpful animals in B400–B499. In these various tales, humans explore the relationship between human and other life forms on earth. As Gaster

---

70 An earlier and briefer presentation of some of the comparative material that follows appears in Susan Niditch, "Fish Swallows Man: The Tale of Jonah and Its Reception History in Folkloristic Perspective," in Peter Machinist et al., eds., *Ve'Ed Ya'leh (Gen 2:6): Essays in Biblical and Ancient Near Eastern Studies Presented to Edward L. Greenstein* (2 vols.; WAWSup 5–6; Atlanta, GA: SBL Press, 2021) 2:1079–95.

71 Stith Thompson, *The Types of the Folktale: A Classification and Bibliography* (FFC 184; Helsinki: Suomalainen Tiedeakatemia, 1973); Hans-Jörg Uther, *The Types of International Folktales: A Classification and Bibliography, Based on the System of Antti Aarne and Stith Thompson* (3 vols.; FFC 284–286; Helsinki: Suomalainen Tiedeakatemia, 2004); Thompson, *Motif-Index*.

72 Theodor H. Gaster, *Myth, Legend, and Custom in the Old Testament: A Comparative Study with Chapters from Sir James G. Frazer's Folklore in the Old Testament* (1969; repr., 2 vols.; Gloucester, MA: Peter Smith, 1981).

73 Hans Schmidt, *Jona: Eine Untersuchung zur vergleichenden Religionsgeschichte* (FRLANT 9; Göttingen: Vandenhoeck & Ruprecht, 1907). See also Komlós, "Jonah Legends," 43–47; and Ernst Sellin, who is sensitive to the folkloric qualities of the narrative (*Das Zwölfprophetenbuch: Übersetzt und erklärt* [2 vols.; Kommentar zum Alten Testament 12; Leipzig: Deichert, 1922] 1:238–39).

74 Schmidt, *Jona*.

explains, scholars frequently compare the experience of Jonah to that of several classical heroes including Phalanthus, the hero of Brundisium and Tarentum, rescued by a dolphin, Eikadios, Korianos, and Arion.[75] More malevolent images are provided by the representation of Jason on an Etruscan mirror, depicting the hero, sword drawn, battling a huge snake that seeks to swallow him, and an Attic vase that depicts the hero emerging from the enormous gullet of a sea monster.[76] The fish in Jonah is not described as particularly benevolent or malevolent, an important ambiguity to keep in mind.

The action features of the motif, swallowing and disgorging, lead to an additional set of comparative material in the Indices. Motif F910 includes a long list of "extraordinary swallowings," for example, F911 "person (animal) swallowed without killing." Examples of the story pattern involving the extraordinary swallowing are found under the type classifications Aarne-Thompson-Uther (ATU) 123, 333, 700. The stories to which one is led describe an animal swallowing a man, but "not fatally." ATU 1889G specifically points to a type of story "fish swallows man" and to related motifs such as F911.6 ("all-swallowing monster"), F913 ("victims rescued from swallower's belly"), F914 ("person swallowed and disgorged"), and X1723.1 ("swallowed person discovered in animal's body still alive"). Type 1889G significantly is catalogued in the Type Index under "tales about lying," and the related motif X1723.1 is considered a building block of a kind of humorous tale.

Folklorist I. A. Ben-Josef describes some of the specific tales to which the Indices lead, implicitly pointing to the overlaps and classificatory subjectivities that underlie this useful but sometimes frustrating scholarly resource.[77] Parallels in pieces of content and plot as seen in the above overview are often not perfect, but such variation and improvisation are at the heart of traditional works. The Historic Geographic School to which Thompson was such an important contributor sought to use the compilations of motifs and types to trace the geographic and historical origins and development of traditional narratives. Many folklorists and biblicists do not share this particular goal, suggesting that there are no "original versions," an orientation reflected in my commentary on Jonah. Nevertheless, the comparative work enabled by the Indices is useful as we think about message and meaning in Jonah, about the book's tone and effect on audiences, and about the ways in which it is like other versions of stories about men swallowed by creatures of the sea, and ways in which it is unique.

A few of the Jonah-like stories to which the Thompson Indices point are instructive as well as entertaining, leading to questions about the relationship between content, context, and theme. Each of these tales includes a sea creature, the act of swallowing a human or humans, and their emergence from the belly of the creature unharmed. The release may be by disgorging, by the machinations of the human protagonist(s) from inside the creature, or by the intervention of others, who often carve the prisoner(s) out of the creature's belly or who find him/them there unexpectedly when cutting up the sea animal on dry ground. Two Canadian tales are especially apt.

In one tale reported by E. W. Baughman, a huge fish follows a ship in the midst of a storm. The crew associates the fish with their dire situation and seeks to appease him, first by throwing over crates of oranges, then by throwing in three sailors in an apparent act of sacrifice to the beast, and finally by tossing overboard an old woman strapped to a rocking chair! The fish eventually washes ashore and within it they find the lady "sitting rocking selling oranges to the sailors for five cents apiece!"[78] A French-Canadian tale that shares the

---

75 Gaster, *Myth, Legend, and Custom*, 654 nn. 22–25; see also Uwe Steffen, *Das Mysterium von Tod und Auferstehung: Formen und Wandlungen des Jona-Motivs* (Göttingen: Vandenhoeck & Ruprecht, 1963). On Arion, see also Watts, *Books*, 83.

76 Schmidt, *Jona*, 24, illustrations 4 and 5. See also Hamel, "Taking the Argo," 351.

77 I. A. Ben-Josef, "Jonah and the Fish as Folk Motif," *Semitics* 7 (1980) 102–17. On folkloric patterns in the Jonah narrative, see also the observations of Wilhelm Nowack, *Die kleinen Propheten* (GHAT; Göttingen: Vandenhoeck & Ruprecht, 1922) 185.

78 Ernest W. Baughman, *Type and Motif-Index of the Folktales of England and North America* (IUFS 20; Bloomington: Indiana University Press, 1966) 579. See a summary of this tale (X1723.1.2b) and variants in Ernest W. Baughman, "A Comparative Study of the Folktales of England and North America" (2 vols.; PhD diss., Indiana University, 1953) 2:1071–73. A briefer variant that originates from

essential morphology with variations in specific content motifs is provided by folklorist C. Marius Barbeau. This account features Petit-Jean, a favorite hero of traditional lore who is both resourceful and often too daring for his own good, although he always manages to survive, like his British counterpart Jack the Giant Slayer. Known also as Ti-Jean, he slays giants and undertakes various bold adventures, a successful underdog with whom audiences can identify. In the Jonah-like tale he is given a sleep potion at sea by sailors who throw him overboard whereupon he awakens in the belly of a whale. He manages to lead the whale to beach itself on the shore, whereby he regains his freedom.[79]

A third relevant tale presented by folklorist Martha Beckwith features the boy hero Punia, another resilient underdog who combats and outwits the king of the sharks, who is incensed because the boy stole all the good lobsters for his mother and his village. He tricks the shark into swallowing him whole and lives in its belly for ten days making himself fully at home, cooking provisions he has brought on a fire, and carving out the shark itself from within. Understandably, the shark weakens, heads for shore, and, once he is beached, the villagers come and dig the boy out.[80]

Such tales share with Jonah the following pattern: danger at sea; the throwing of the human or humans overboard; the presence of the sea creature; survival of the human(s) within the creature; and eventual emergence. In this rich trove of folklore, the reason for the threat at sea may differ or be unstated; the nuance of appeasement of the creature may or may not be found; the activities of the human in the creature are various, as are the ways the person escapes; but the swallowing, survival, and emergence are always found. Indeed, in a variant of the first example above, a deceased person actually comes back to life.[81]

This comparative material, located by means of the cataloging work of Thompson, his students, and subsequent folklorists, underscores humanistic universals and culturally, author-specific interests in the book of Jonah, shared meanings and messages, and those especially important in a particular biblical and ancient Jewish context. First, contemplation of the mysterious and not fully understood creatures of the sea, like the depths of the ocean itself, expresses human fear and awe of an unfathomable and vast universe. The numerous variants of tales about the sea creature that swallows a man also may serve as a kind of whistling in the dark. The majority of these tales are not terrifying but comic, filled with grannies who sell fruit in the confines of the fish, or men who light a fire with the animal's tallow, or workmen who continue to ply their trade. The ordinary world, in other words, continues in the confines of this peculiar and potentially frightening place, inside the fish or shark

---

a Welch informant by way of a Canadian collector is found in Herbert Halpert, "Three Tales from Gwent," *JAF* 58 (1945) 51–52, esp. 52. A lengthy and amusing variant preserved to capture the accent and dialect of the Caribbean informant is found in Elsie Clews Parsons, "Spirituals and Other Folklore from the Bahamas," *JAF* 41 (1928) 453–524, esp. 519. In this account, the woman and others simply fall overboard and are retrieved by chance when a shark caught by the sailors is being prepared for dinner. The sacrifice nuance is particularly strong, however, in a West Virginian version reported by a traveling salesman in Ohio. The old woman in the rocking chair is described as a "noble soul," and she begs the sailors to throw her overboard to appease a monster fish. This version and others are found in Lowell Thomas, *Tall Stories: The Rise and Triumph of the Great American Whopper* (New York: Funk & Wagnalls, 1931) 71–76. See also Richard Dorson, "Yorker Yarns of Yore," *NYFQ* 3 (1947) 5–27, esp. 20. In this account, a dead sailor weighed down with a grindstone and a carpenter's axe has been buried at sea whereupon his son jumps in after him. Both seem to be lost. The sailor is revived in the sea creature that swallows them, in this case a shark, and sets at sharpening the axe on the grindstone turned by the boy, as they work to cut themselves out.

79 C. Marius Barbeau, "Contes Populaires Canadiens," *JAF* 29 (1916) 1–136, here 11. An American tale about a folk hero named Tom Stasil also involves being swallowed by a whale and turning the huge creature into a kind of vessel; this version has the hero think of Jonah in the midst of his predicament! (B. A. Botkin, ed., *A Treasury of American Folklore* [New York: Crown, 1944] 637).

80 Martha Beckwith, *Hawaiian Mythology* (New Haven: Yale University Press, 1940) 443.

81 See n. 78 above.

or whale. Life goes on. In fact, in one version listed above, a dead person comes back to life in this marginal, liminal, and potentially revivifying place.[82] The tales also emphasize the theme that human beings do have some control, ways in which they can act to save themselves in the face of danger. The person is often thrown overboard to save other people, the sacrifice being regarded as a means of appeasing the source of the threat. Many of the swallowed heroes also work within the creature to survive and free themselves. An optimism and faith in human invention informs these tales, for the end is never really the end. Qualities of surprise, chance, and humor infuse the tales. What does Jonah's version of this internationally evidenced story reveal about the Jonah author's orientation and message?

As elsewhere in Scripture, the sea creature is a powerful and antagonistic force of nature, but the big fish in Jonah 2 has been appointed by God; it is a tool of the divinity, who also controls the end of Jonah's ordeal, speaking to the fish so that the fish vomits out the prophet. Jonah's activity inside the fish is also revealing. He engages in prayer, addressing the master of the fish, acknowledging the deity's power, and petitioning for rescue in the typological form and language of the lament. He is not pictured as plying a trade, like some of the other swallowed people in comparable tales. Yet his very prayer, ending formulaically in the mention of promises or vows, suggests hope for release and some of the same optimism that is evident in more typical tales. For the prophet, his trade is communication with God and mediation between God and humans, a mission he will resume once he is released. People have hopes of rescue and often take actions that might lead to that outcome. In this case, the action is sincere prayer. The consummate control of the deity and the belief in the efficacy of prayer come of course as no surprise in biblical literature about a prophet. Yet the Jonah tale, so evocative of a range of international tales that do not feature principal roles for a deity, also shares some of the qualities of comedy and serendipity in these other tales. Scenes relating to the fish swallowing a man help to build the portrait of a thoroughly quirky biblical character, in part because of other tales like it. The appeal, charm, and narrative attractiveness of Jonah is reinforced by the odd situation in which the prophet finds himself. Scenes involving Jonah and the fish are further developed by postbiblical contributors to the tradition, and this theme is perhaps the most popular and popularized aspect of the book.

Appropriations

A Jewish Hellenistic work written in Greek and probably dated to the late first century BCE or first century CE of the Roman era, 3 Maccabees has nothing to do with the Maccabees or the Maccabean revolt. Like the tales of Daniel 1–6 and the book of Esther, 3 Maccabees is concerned with forms of resistance and the maintenance of cultural and religious identity in dealing with the situation faced by Jews in exile.[83] There may also be a link to the tales in 2 Maccabees of martyrs who resist their foreign oppressors.

Set in Ptolemaic Egypt, the work includes a prayer by an elderly and venerable Jewish priest named Eleazar, who petitions God to spare the Jews from the persecutions of Ptolemy.[84] The speech includes reference to various nodal points in the biblical tradition when God has intervened to save his people, for example, in the case of Sennacherib's invasions (3 Macc 6:5) or to rescue his prophets, Daniel (6:7) and Jonah (6:8). Jonah is described as rescued or restored after his suffering in the belly of "a huge fish living in the deep." The Greek term for the fish is the same as that found in the Septuagint of Jonah 2:1 meaning, "sea monster, huge fish, seal, or serpent" (see textual note c on 2:1). Eleazar addresses God's treatment of Jonah in his prayer saying, "You have shown him forth unharmed to all his household"

---

82 See n. 72 above.

83 For a discussion of 3 Maccabees in its sociohistorical context with special attention to the work's connections to the book of Esther, see Noah Hacham, "3 Maccabees and Esther: Parallels, Intertextuality, and Diaspora Identity," *JBL* 126 (2007) 765–85. Hacham mentions the reference to Jonah in 3 Maccabees 6 as he explores the way in which its author alludes to and reappropriates the tradition (771).

84 On the prayer of Eleazar and the role of the reference to Jonah, see N. Clayton Croy, *3 Maccabees* (SCS; Leiden: Brill, 2006) 97–102.

(6:9). The Hellenistic writer thus imagines the prophet to have a household or family to which to return, and pictures him implicitly as a worthy recipient of divine mercy, released from undeserved suffering. This thread in the exegetical tradition in a sense contributes to the rehabilitation of Jonah, a thematic direction also found in rabbinic sources. The emphasis on rising from the deep, a saved man, is also of particular interest in early Christianity.

Jonah's interaction with the fish as developed in the rabbinic work Pirke de-Rabbi Eliezer (Pirqe R. El.), discussed earlier in relation to the sailors' hesitant jettisoning of Jonah, evokes some of the folktale themes explored above. Pirqe R. El. adds a cosmogonic thread that reshapes the biblical account in richly mystical directions and further reveals the midrashist's own understanding of the biblical tale, the problems it presents, and the vital concerns that are suggested by its content. More needs to be said about Pirqe R. El. as it relates to this portion of reception history.

Pirqe de-Rabbi Eliezer is an expansive work pseudepigraphically attributed to Rabbi Eliezer (ben Hyrcanos), one of the older group of rabbis of the second generation of early rabbis, the Tannaim, whose leadership and scholarly roles flourished in Judaism from 90 to 130 CE in the period following the destruction of the Second Temple by the Romans in 70 CE. Eliezer is said to have lived in Lydda, a town northwest of Jerusalem about eleven miles southeast of Joppa; he is frequently described in the rabbinic corpus debating with his contemporaries Rabbis Yehoshua ben Hananyah and Aqiba. Eliezer is featured as a controversial figure in the well-known debate among the rabbis concerning the purity of the oven of Akhnai, a matter that ends with Rabbi Eliezer's excommunication. In this halakic debate, the winning side defends the view that the ruling is with the majority of rabbis, rational human beings here on earth, whereas Eliezer appears to endorse a more mystical notion of direct divine revelation. He is, in fact, associated with wider cosmological interests concerning the makeup of the cosmos and its creation, a salient theme in Pirqe R. El. and its commentary on Jonah and the fish.[85] In b. B. Bat. 74b Eliezer and Joshua are on a ship, and Eliezer identifies a light seen by Joshua as the eye of Leviathan! This interest in the great sea monster associated with creation and the end-time figures prominently in the section of Pirqe R. El. involving Jonah and the fish.

Eliezer is an exemplar of rabbinic piety manifested in love for Torah, as discussed by Jacob Neusner in his study of the ways in which Eliezer is presented in the tradition.[86] It has been suggested that the attribution of Pirqe R. El. to R. Eliezer is merely due to the work's opening biographic tales about the young Eliezer's burning desire to study Torah, and yet that opening framework (Pirqe R. El. 1), like Eliezer's association with cosmological speculation, does influence the way in which the reader approaches the larger work. Eliezer's passion for Torah might suggest that he is driven to uncover its deepest messages and meanings, and this passion appropriately frames the work's reflections on the cosmological implications of Jonah's interaction with the fish, who is linked to the very creation of the cosmos.

Like many holy men and women from various cultural traditions, including the Buddha, Simeon Stylites, and the Aggadic representation of Abraham, the tales of the hero's youth include a kind of conversion account in which the protagonist seeks to break with convention and the way of his fathers or family to pursue a special calling. In this case, Rabbi Eliezer's father finds his son shedding tears while at work with the plough, because of his passion to leave agricultural pursuits to study Torah. He tells his father that he does not want to till the land, and he rejects his father's advice to marry and lead a more conventional life. Eliezer then fasts for two weeks, whereupon the prophet Elijah appears to him and urges him to go Jerusalem to study with Rabbi Johanan ben Zakkai. Eliezer's pious fasting and family tensions continue until, ultimately, he receives his father's understanding and his blessing to lead a scholarly rabbinic life. This opening biographic account is followed by a series of expositions on the biblical creation, of which chap. 10, an excursus on Jonah, is a part.

---

85 See Jacob Neusner, *Eliezer ben Hyrcanus: The Tradition and the Man* (2 vols.; SJLA 3–4; Leiden: Brill, 1973) 2:403, 406, 409.

86 Neusner, *Eliezer ben Hyrcanus*, 285, 302.

In terms of genre, Pirqe R. El. is a narrative midrash that retells and enriches portions of biblical myth, including not only the creation but also the experiences of the patriarchs and matriarchs, and the exodus. It draws upon various midrashic traditions and, in Hermann Strack's view, reflects the narrative creativity of a particular author whose core work has been further expanded by various additions.[87] As noted above, Pirqe R. El. probably dates to the eighth or ninth century, for it makes reference to Arab rule and alludes to Islamic foundation narratives, and to Islam's heroes and heroines, and holy sites.

The section concerning Jonah in Pirqe R. El. 10 and the fish begins by quoting Jonah 2:1 in the typical style of exegetical midrash, whereby a verse of Scripture is quoted and then explained and expanded by rabbinic techniques, bringing to bear other relevant biblical verses: "And assign did Yahweh a great fish to swallow Jonah." R. Tarphon links this verse with the creation of Genesis 1, an account rich in allusions to the sea and to divine commands concerning the cosmogonic process. Tarphon declares that the fish was prepared for Jonah from the time of the six days of creation, emphasizing not only the way in which God plans ahead, but also the links between Jonah's experience and the mythological traditions of world creation reflected in the Hebrew Bible and developed in rabbinic and Jewish mystical traditions. A reflection of this link between Jonah's being swallowed by the fish and the creation of the world by means of divine commands is also emphasized in Gen. Rab. 5:5. God's separating the waters from the dry land in Gen 1:9 is explored with biblical texts understood as assignments by God to aspects or creatures of the natural world. Thus, the ravens are commanded to feed Elijah, the fire not to harm Hananiah, Mishael, and Azariah, the lions not to harm Daniel, the heavens to open before Ezekiel, and the fish to vomit out Jonah. The midrash in Pirqe R. El. on Jonah 2:1 is followed by reflections on the physical environment in which Jonah finds himself in the fish. The rabbis ask implicitly, as do several of the traditional storytellers mentioned above, what does it look like inside the sea creature? What does the hero experience?

Entering the mouth of the fish is compared to entering the great synagogue, possibly, in Gerald Friedlander's view, a reference to the Great Synagogue in Alexandria.[88] Jonah stands within the apparently ample space in this architectonic comparison. The eyes of the fish are compared to "windows of glass giving light to Jonah."[89] Thus the space is not a dark hole or a womb-like enclosure but a well-lit building of sorts. Light imagery is further developed in an interpretation attributed to R. Meir, who states that "one pearl was suspended inside the belly of the fish and it gave illumination to Jonah, like the sun which shines with its might at noon." In this way, the Jonah of Pirqe R. El. shares with the swallowed heroes in the international range of folklore discussed above an unexpected continuation of recognizable reality in the fish, if existing inside a sea creature can ever be considered to be realistic. Jonah's experience moves even further beyond the mundane, for the pearl is described as a kind of crystal ball that reveals cosmological truths: "It showed to Jonah all that was in the sea and in the depths as it is said, 'Light is sown for the righteous' (Ps 97:11)." As Adam in the midrashic tradition is shown all future generations (Gen. Rab. 24:2) and the mantic seers of classical Judaism participate in tours of the hidden cosmos,[90] Jonah is given a tour of the watery

---

87 H. L. Strack and Günter Stemberger, *Introduction to the Talmud and Midrash* (trans. and ed. Markus Bockmuehl; Minneapolis: Fortress Press, 1992) 329. For an excellent discussion of the section of Pirqe R. El. that pertains to Jonah, see Rachel Adelman, "Through the Looking Glass: Pirqe de-Rabbi Eliezer's portrait of an Apocalyptic Prophet," *Journal of the Faculty of Religious Studies, McGill University* 39 (2011) 79–92. For further detail concerning the manuscript tradition, see Rachel Adelman, *The Return of the Repressed: Pirqe de-Rabbi Eliezer and the Pseudepigrapha* (JSJSup 140; Leiden: Brill, 2009) 193–239, and for a critical Hebrew edition, see Appendix I, 299–302.

88 Friedlander, *Pirke de Rabbi Eliezer*, 69 n.8

89 Jastrow, s.v. "אמפוביות, אמפומיות."

90 See Martha Himmelfarb, *Tours of Hell: An Apocalyptic Form in Jewish and Christian Literature* (Philadelphia: University of Pennsylvania Press, 1983); Himmelfarb, *Ascent to Heaven in Jewish and Christian Apocalypses* (New York: Oxford University Press, 1993).

underworld. One thinks here of the fascination with water worlds in Western classics such as *Twenty Thousand Leagues under the Sea*, the various folk traditions about mermaids and their dwellings, and the tradition of the lost kingdom of Atlantis. The proof-text from Psalm 97 that points to Jonah's illuminating experience asserts that Jonah is deserving of this tour because he is among the righteous. The composer of the midrash thus puts a positive spin on the hero's characterization, significantly altering the biblical tale and implying that the rabbis may have been concerned that a man such as the biblical Jonah was considered to be a prophet of the Lord whose story is preserved among the minor prophets.

The opening architectonic and cosmological content of this midrashic excursus on Jonah 2:1 is followed in Pirqe R. El. by a conversation between Jonah and the fish, initiated by his captor. The fish, who of course talks, says to Jonah, "Do you not know that my day is coming to be eaten in the mouth of Leviathan?" Thus, the creature who swallowed Jonah is imagined to reveal to the prophet that he himself is about to be devoured, and this information continues the revelatory aspect of the midrash. The fish knows what is coming and reveals to Jonah that the fish himself and the still-living man within the fish will soon be consumed by a gigantic sea monster associated in the biblical and postbiblical mythological tradition pertaining to world creation and the end of time. In the narrative of the midrash, Jonah offers to intercede to save the fish and himself, saying "lead me next to it." In addressing Leviathan, Jonah self-identifies with the one who will put a rope in Leviathan's tongue, a mythic motif found in Job 40:25 [41:1], and as one who will prepare Leviathan as food for the messianic banquet. It is, he tells the beast, for the very purpose of interacting with Leviathan that he had descended into the sea. The midrash thus truly transforms biblical Jonah's character from an atypical and unwilling messenger of God into a willing participant in divine machinations as they relate to cosmic events. In Job, Yahweh himself is the one who can ensnare Leviathan; it is only Yahweh who can accomplish such a feat,

further proof of divine power. It is no small matter that the human prophet is associated with this accomplishment, a player in the myth whose biblical protagonist is the deity himself.[91] Jonah shows Leviathan the seal of Abraham, commanding the sea monster to look at the "covenant"; and, like a protective icon, the seal seems to repel the monster, for "Leviathan flees away from Jonah," covering some distance, "a walking journey of two days."

The final section of the narrative midrash is framed as a tour of the watery underworld led by the fish, a theme that reprises the more abbreviated revelations to Jonah by the light-bearing pearl suspended in the fish. Jonah requests this tour as compensation for having rescued the fish from Leviathan: "Behold, I have saved you from the mouth of Leviathan. Show me all that is in the sea and the depths." The Jonah of Pirqe R. El. thus has an interest in mantic wisdom, in knowledge of the unknown. The midrashist creates this tour of the unknown realms by means of interpretations of details in the prayer of Jonah 2. The great rivers of the ocean connect to Jonah 2:6, the paths of the Reed Sea to 2:6, the place from which flow forth the sea's breakers and billows to 2:4, the pillars of the earth to 2:7, the lowest Sheol to 2:2, Gehinnom to 2:7, and that which lies beneath the temple of God to 2:7. The temple locus is part of the essential cosmos, integral to an eternal creation.

In the final section of the tour, knowledge is imparted concerning Jerusalem's resting on seven hills, its foundation of stone rooted in the depths. And here, in this sacred, thoroughly mythologized locus, Jonah sees the hereditary priests, the sons of Korah "standing and praying over it [i.e., foundation of stone]." They transcend mere history and place, fixtures of the holy place. The fish tells Jonah that he is standing beneath the temple of God: "Pray and you will be answered." Jonah asks the fish to stay where he is because he wishes to pray. Does the fish provide a witness? Does the presence of this mythological creature assure that the vision experienced will not evaporate? His unmoving presence is somehow

---

91 On the transformation of the character of Jonah into a heroic rather than an antiheroic figure, see Gregg, *Shared Stories*, 344. Gregg sets this transformation in the context of an "apocalyptic urgency" that he sees at work in an eighth-century setting. See also Adelman, "Through the Looking Glass," 90, 91.

necessary for the success of Jonah's petition. The fish remains stationary and Jonah prays that the deity who kills and makes alive might bring him back from death. His prayer is not answered, according to Pirqe R. El., until he reiterates his vow to offer up Leviathan before God on the day of Israel's salvation. This promissory vow is linked to Jonah 2:10. At this point God "offers a hint" to the fish and the fish vomits up Jonah onto dry land as the midrashist returns to the biblical text (Jonah 2:11).

In a narrative midrash influenced by cosmogonic and mystical interests, Pirqe R. El. thus transforms the story of "fish swallows man" found in the biblical tale of Jonah, providing a creative variant within the contours of Jewish tradition. The basic outline of the story remains the same: a fish swallows the man, who is not digested or killed in its belly, and then the man is vomited out. The tale in Pirqe R. El. shares with an array of international versions of this vignette the architectonic interest in the environment inside fish, the nature of the lighting, the presence of windows. As in many of these tales, life goes on within, but the experience of Jonah is that of a visionary. The framing of the version in Pirqe R. El. is exegetical, tying the tale to the text of Jonah with special interests in chap. 2. Pirqe R. El. transforms Jonah into a rescuer, a righteous person worthy of seeing divine light and of participation in the end-time events involving Leviathan that inaugurate the messianic era. Jonah, moreover, takes the role of a seer who is led on a tour of the cosmos by the fish whose rescuer he has become due to the prophet's power over the monster Leviathan. The tour concludes with a stop at the foundations of the holy temple, a sacred place that is rooted in the structure of the earth and the very creation itself. There Jonah's prayer ascends and he is released from the fish. The medieval midrashist thus seems to rehabilitate the biblical Jonah, placing him among the visionary prophets, a holy person whose own rise from a watery underworld anticipates the end-time and the resurrection itself.[92] Early Christians had made this significant transition in interpreting the characterization and story of Jonah already in New Testament times, explaining the popularity of visual images of Jonah among Christians of late antiquity, who linked Jonah's experience to that of Jesus.

The key text is Matt 12:38–42, especially v. 40, a verse that explicitly equates Jonah and his story with the sacred narrative about Jesus's death and resurrection.[93] The larger context of Matthew 12 points to a debate between the Jewish establishment, represented by the Pharisees, and Jesus concerning Jesus's position on the law and other matters as they relate to his role as miracle worker or holy man and expectations for the end of time. In a frequently employed framework in Matthew that contrasts the scribes and Pharisees with Jesus, the former groups ask Jesus for a sign, presumably a sign about the final judgment alluded to in 12:36–37, or a sign confirming Jesus's status as a true prophet (cf. Deut 18:15–22). Jesus responds that there will be no sign except the sign of the prophet Jonah.

Just as Jonah was three days and three nights in the belly of the sea monster,[94] so for three nights the son of man will be in the heart of the earth (Matt 12:40). Matthew 12:41 offers further application of the Jonah story to the issue of repentance, but it is v. 40 that provides an interpretation of the motif of the fish that swallows a man. The message of v. 40 draws upon the foundational credo found in 1 Cor 15:4 that Jesus rose on the third day in accordance with the Scriptures. The Scriptural foundation for 1 Cor 15:4 is generally taken to be either Jonah 2:1 (G 1:17) or Hos 6:2, a verse that makes reference to reviving in two days and raising up in three. For the author of Matthew, Jesus's resurrection after three days foreshadows and confirms that the end-time is at

---

92 On the recasting of Jonah in a more positive light in rabbinic appropriations, see also Bezalel Narkiss, "The Sign of Jonah," *Gesta* 18 (1979) 63–76, esp. 63.

93 Cf. Matt 16:4; Luke 11:29. For a discussion of these various uses of the Jonah tale and the motif of the sign of Jonah by early Christian writers and their significance for variations in worldview, see Gregg, *Shared Stories*, 371–72; Golka, "Jonah," 129–31; Scott, "Sign of Jonah," 17–18; James Swetnam, "No Sign of Jonah," *Bib* 66 (1985) 126–30.

94 See the textual note d on Jonah 2:1. The New Testament employs the same term for the sea creature κῆτος (MT דג, "fish") that is employed in G.

hand with its promise of raising the dead, and this sign is anticipated by the experience of Jonah.⁹⁵ What does the New Testament author's treatment and application of the scene concerning the sea creature and Jonah indicate about his understanding and interpretation of the story of the Hebrew prophet?

Jonah is implicitly presented as a fairly typical biblical prophet associated with themes of repentance and salvation. In contrast to some early Jewish exegesis preserved, for example, in the Tannaitic Mekilta de-Rabbi Ishmael, the Matthean author does not seem concerned with or seek to explain Jonah's efforts to avoid his call. The emphasis on periods of three days is shared in Jewish tradition and is related to freedom, covenant, and God's saving acts: Exod. Rab. 23:6 points to Exod 19:16, the scene at Sinai, the receiving of Torah, "And it happened on the third day . . ."; Gen. Rab. 91:7 offers a midrash on Gen 42:18, concerning the imprisonment and freeing of Joseph's brothers in Egypt: "And said to them did Joseph on the third day . . . ." Genesis Rabbah 56:1 presents a commentary on Gen 22:4, the introduction to the binding of Isaac tale: "On the third day Abraham raised his eyes . . . ." Genesis Rabbah, which probably dates to the first half of the fifth century C.E.,⁹⁶ preserves in midrashic scholastic style a catalog of biblical references to significant events in the tradition linked to a third day or to the passing of three days (Gen. Rab. 56:1). This passage includes Gen 42:18 and Exod 19:16, mentioned above, and explicitly relates these passages and others, including Hos 6:2 and Jonah 2:1, to themes of salvation, the merit of the ancestors, and resurrection—all associated with the binding of Isaac in a lengthy rabbinic tradition.⁹⁷ In this Jewish matrix, preserved in a text no later than the fifth century C.E., we thus see the constellation of associations that animate the author of Matthew 12.

Artistic Representations

The artistic cultures of late antiquity and the work of thirteenth- to fifteenth-century European illustrators of sacred books offer two excellent touchpoints for exploring the portrayal in visual media of Jonah's experience with the fish. Jewish and Christian artists of these creative periods produced objects and settings for the communities well versed in the biblical tale of Jonah and receptive to its illustration and visual retelling. In particular, early Christian artists embraced images of Jonah, whose experience with the fish and under the shade of the planting are among the most common representations in early Christian art.⁹⁸

Evidence for visual imaginings of Jonah and the fish in late antiquity can be found in various media including mosaics, painted scenes on plaster or frescoes, and carved work. Mosaics featuring Jonah are of special interest in the present study, and appreciation for the medium and the orientation of the artists requires some introduction. Mosaics are constructed from chips of stone or terra-cotta in various natural or glazed colors that are set in a surface layer of mortar resting on base layers of coarse mortar.⁹⁹ As noted by art historian Roger Ling, the principal function of mosaic pavements was aesthetic, "to enhance the spaces that contained them."¹⁰⁰ He writes, "Tiny pieces of different coloured materials, when viewed from a distance, would merge to

---

95 Caroline Walker Bynum traces the way in which early Christian writers from the second through the fifth centuries treated Jonah's emergence from the fish unscathed as an exemplar concerning the material incorruptibility of that hero's body and future resurrected bodies (*The Resurrection of the Body in Western Christianity, 200–1336* [American Lectures on the History of Religions; New York: Columbia University Press,1995] 29, 36, 75).

96 See the discussion in Strack and Stemberger, *Introduction to the Talmud and Midrash*, 279.

97 See Shalom Spiegel, *The Last Trial: On the Legends and Lore of the Command to Abraham to Offer Isaac as a Sacrifice; The Akedah* (New York: Schocken, 1969).

98 See Robin Margaret Jensen, *Understanding Early Christian Art* (London: Routledge, 2000) 172. See also Jeffrey Spier, ed., *Picturing the Bible: The Earliest Christian Art* (Fort Worth, TX: Kimbell Art Museum, 2007) 7, 102, 120, 173–74, 186–87, 207. See also examples explored by Gregg, *Shared Stories*, 361–67, 395–407.

99 See the description and diagrams in Roger Ling, *Ancient Mosaics* (Princeton, NJ: Princeton University Press, 1998) 11.

100 Ibid., 10.

create gradations and modulations of tone that mimicked the mixing of pigments on a traditional painter's panel."[101]

As to content, Rachel Hachlili points to the theme of salvation implicit in Jewish portrayals of Aaron, Abraham, Daniel, and other biblical heroes and sees such scenes as "symbolizing traditional historical events, divine intervention, the covenant between God and his chosen people, and his protection of some and his punishment of others."[102] Roger Ling and Hachlili both describe the traditional, formulaic or conventionalized nature of the portrayals and suggest that artisans had at their disposal pattern books.[103] Ling mentions a third-century B.C.E. Egyptian papyrus that refers to a pattern sent to a mosaicist at Philadelphia in the Fayum as a "guide" for his project.[104] For all traditional artists working in verbal and nonverbal media, such patterns eventually become "inscribed on the heart" while being open to individual creative adaptations influenced by personal and local tastes.[105] Mosaics could be applied to walls and vaults as well as to pavements, although the latter are far more common due to the cost of applications on high-up surfaces and the dangers involved in this sort of work. In such difficult-to-reach places, paintings or stucco reliefs would be more practical media,[106] although one example of a Christian Jonah mosaic does decorate, along with other representations, a fourth-century vault in the mausoleum at Centcelles near Tarragona in Spain.[107] The mosaics, Jewish or Christian, are placed in "buildings of high prestige."[108]

Differences in Jewish and Christian orientations may inform, to a degree, the use made of Jonah in late antique settings, in mosaics as well as in other media. Hachlili notes, for example, that Jews employed various biblical scenes in floor mosaics, allowing portrayals of the biblical tradition, its events and heroes, to be integral features of synagogues' decorative art and the buildings' substance, places where worshipers walked. Christians generally did not place such scenes on floors but employed them as part of sacred paraphernalia such as sarcophagi or as wall paintings in catacombs. An imperial decree of 427 explicitly banned "signs of Christ" on floors, and Roger Ling suggests that, from the fifth century on, a taboo may have arisen against walking on biblical scenes.[109] Exceptions include two mosaics involving Jonah, the mosaic pavement of a Byzantine church at Beit Guvrin (fifth–sixth century) and a mosaic at the Cathedral of Bishop Theodore in Aquileia dated 313–319 C.E., the latter discussed below.[110]

In addition to differences in placement, Hachlili suggests that the art functioned differently in each tradition, reflecting differences in worldview. For Jews, she suggests, portrayals of scenes and heroes from the Hebrew Bible were "reminders of the tradition of biblical stories," whereas for Christians the scenes of the Hebrew Bible are employed as prefigurations of individual salvation, thus, for example, illustrations of Moses, Daniel, and Jonah.[111] She writes that "Jews distinguish their places of worship from those of Christians" by means of artistic choices.[112] The case could be made, for example, that the very popularity of the motif of Jonah's being swallowed and then released as a model or adumbration of Jesus, specifically mentioned in the New Testament itself, may have made the same depiction less popular among Jews. On the other hand, it is difficult to argue from limited evidence. As noted above, for example, Christians, like Jews, have placed some mosaics of biblical heroes on floors of sacred spaces. At

---

101 Ibid.
102 Rachel Hachlili, *Ancient Mosaic Pavements: Themes, Issues, and Trends; Selected Studies* (Leiden: Brill, 2009) 96.
103 Ling, *Ancient Mosaics*, 13; Hachlili, *Ancient Mosaic Pavements*, 92, 94.
104 Ling, *Ancient Mosaics*, 13.
105 Robin Jensen points to the similarities between North African maritime mosaics and the scenes depicted in the floor mosaic of the Christian basilica at Aquileia, discussed below (*Understanding Early Christian Art*, 48).
106 Ling, *Ancient Mosaics*, 8.
107 Ibid., 107.
108 Ibid., 8.
109 Ibid., 98.
110 Hachlili, *Ancient Mosaic Pavements*, 91, 92, 227. See André Grabar, *The Beginnings of Christian Art, 200–395* (trans. Stuart Gilbert and James Emmons; Arts of Mankind 9; London: Thames & Hudson, 1967) 22, fig. 19.
111 Hachlili, *Ancient Mosaic Pavements*, 228.
112 Ibid., 284.

least in one case Jews did include a mosaic of Jonah in an early synagogue at Huqoq, in Israel's eastern Lower Galilee,[113] and so things are often more complex than they seem.[114] Scenes depicting the theme of "fish swallows/disgorges man" associated with Jonah may have not have been completely ceded to Christians; and, while each tradition treats the subject of salvation in its own way, it is entirely possible that Jews of late antiquity did associate the tale of Jonah with end-time matters, as do the midrashists of Genesis Rabbah and the later compilers of Pirqe de-Rabbi Eliezer. To be sure, for Matthew the three days of Jonah's stay in the fish relate to the specific Jesus narrative, for the tradition holds that Jesus rises from the dead after three days. An important characteristic of the Matthean tradition is the search for confirmation in Hebrew Bible of the truth of the Jesus story shared by Christians, and the Jonah tale contributes to this interpretative thread. Nevertheless, it is entirely probable that Jonah's experience with the fish was a manifestation to Jews in late antiquity of God's capacity to forgive and save, a confirmation of God's ability to raise the dead, even if Jesus was not, to Jews, the "firstfruit" in this process. A close look at Jewish and Christian representations of Jonah and the fish in mosaics and other media provides an excellent case study in reception history.

Jewish Mosaics of Late Antiquity and Jonah

The excavation of Huqoq in Israel's eastern Lower Galilee has yielded a magnificent find relevant to the study of Jonah, a synagogue dated by its excavators to the early fifth century decorated with a variety of colorful mosaic pavements. Of special interest for the present study are panels at the northern end of the building's nave depicting biblical scenes: Noah and his animal passengers; the encounter with Pharaoh's soldiers at the Red Sea; Jonah being swallowed by the fish (fig. 1, p. 82); and the building of the tower of Babel. The Red Sea scene, like the Jonah scene, portrays sea creatures, the sea, and men, and partakes in a formulaic cache of maritime motifs found in mosaics of Roman late antiquity.[115] Relevant to our study of Jonah, one of the soldiers in the Red Sea scene at Huqoq, spear still in hand, is being consumed feet first by a huge fish whose gaping maw has already swallowed the man's body up to the chest. Only one arm, neck, head in helmet, and half of the upper chest remain free. Horses are overthrown, bodies lie in various contortions, as the mosaic evokes vibrant images of Exodus 15.

The Jonah mosaic also includes the fish-swallowing-man motif evoking a central motif of the narrative. In this case, Jonah has entered the fish head first. His legs and feet trail beyond the fish, and another fish appears to nip at his toe. Significantly, Jonah is being swallowed by a huge fish who is being swallowed by another bigger fish who is being swallowed by a still larger fish! Karen Britt and Ra'anan Boustan count "almost a dozen species of fish, including perhaps red snapper, sea bass, bream, and mullet," as well an octopus and dolphin.[116] Noting that several of the images depict everyday maritime scenes and activities, such as an eel winding itself around a long thin fish, other fish of many species swimming along, a bare-chested fisherman casting a net from a boat, and another who appears to be wringing out a

---

113 See Jodi Magness et al., "The Huqoq Excavation Project: 2014–2017 Interim Report," *BASOR* 380 (2018) 61–131.

114 See also Gregg's discussion of challenges faced in identifying iconography that includes images of Jonah as explicitly Christian rather than Jewish. He points to the possibility of shared conventions employed by artists in late antiquity and ponders why none of the works extant in 2015 (when he writes) are identified as possible reflections of Jewish interpretation (*Shared Stories*, 361–67); see especially his comments on two artifacts, figs. 10.2 and 10.3. The new find from Huqoq confirms his suspicion that works featuring Jonah could be created explicitly for Jews (Magness et al., "Huqoq Excavation," 114).

115 See Karen Britt and Ra'anan Boustan in Magness et al., "Huqoq Excavations," 105, for comparisons to other Jewish and Christian art of late antiquity and a discussion of "the artistic repertoire drawn upon by Jewish and Christian communities far beyond Galilee" (p. 114) and "macro-regional trends" (p. 115). In particular, Britt and Boustan point to parallels to decorative art employed in the building at Mopsuestra, in the church at Beit Guvrin, and in the basilica at Aquileia (p. 114). Relevant for the maritime scenes at Huqoq and Aquileia are the mosaics of Lod (p. 111 n. 74).

116 Britt and Boustan in Magness et al., "Huqoq Excavations," 111.

fishing net, the authors describe in detail the immediate scene involving Jonah.

Prominently represented in the center of the scene is a large sailing ship manned by five sailors, two of whom are climbing the mast.[117] A bearded, partially balding, gray-haired man in the center of the ship—perhaps the captain—is lowering into the water a rope with a loop at the end. Immediately below the rope, Jonah's legs and feet can be seen dangling from the mouth of a large fish, which is being swallowed by two successively larger fish.

The presence of a looped rope, which presumably was used to lower Jonah into the sea, is evocative of a midrash preserved in Pirqe de-Rabbi Eliezer. According to the homilist, the sailors are so loath to sacrifice Jonah in order to save themselves and the ship that they try at first to lower him only partially into the water (presumably via some means of retrieving him such as the looped rope pictured in the mosaic). First they cast him into the sea as far as his knee (earlier manuscripts read "up to his navel"), and sure enough the sea calms down, but as soon as they pull him out, the tempest resumes. Then they lower him up to his neck, the sea calms, they raise him, and again the seas grow wild. So finally with regret they let him go, "and the sea ceased from her raging."[118] It could well be that the visual midrash of the mosaic is picturing this means by which Jonah is repeatedly lowered and raised and finally the loop on the tether is empty, for Jonah has been let go.

Another midrashic nuance may also be implicit in the motif of the multiple fish. Always alert to rough edges in the biblical text, whether a potential contradiction or repetition in content or a grammatical incongruity,[119] the rabbis, like modern commentators, point to the masculine form of the word fish in Jonah 2:1, 11 and the feminine form in 2:2. Various midrashic traditions grapple with these masculine and feminine forms, lighting upon the notion of Jonah's being swallowed by more than one fish. Tractate Nedarim in the Babylonian Talmud suggests that Jonah was vomited forth by a large male fish and then swallowed by a smaller female one. Some midrashim suggest that Jonah prays only when he finds himself in the small fish because he is uncomfortable in the confined space.[120] Given that the word for belly and womb are the same, Midrash Jonah suggests that the innards of the female fish make the situation in the fish's "belly" dire indeed; Jonah feels extreme discomfort due to the "defilement" and "filth" or "decay" in the environment.[121] Finally, as noted by Britt and Boustan, Midrash Jonah also seems to allude to a tradition of a large male fish appointed by God to swallow Jonah and a female fish, perhaps implying a succession of swallowings.[122] Indeed the image of fish swallowing

---

117 For a comparative discussion of representations of sailing vessels, see Magness et al., "Huqoq Excavations," 111 n. 75.

118 For the full text in translation, see Friedlander, *Pirqe de Rabbi Eliezer*, 69.

119 James L. Kugel, *The Bible as It Was* (Cambridge, MA: Belknap Press of Harvard University Press, 1997) 3–5.

120 See Zlotowitz and Scherman, *Sefer Yonah/Jonah*, 108. A midrashic tradition rediscovered by Tamar Kadari, the Midrash of the Repentance of Jonah the Prophet, which Kadari suggests circulated during the eleventh century in northern France, pictures the female fish as pregnant with myriad little fish, making the environment even more unbearable ("Aggadic Motifs," 111). Shemaryahu Talmon links midrashic traditions concerning the female fish to a fanciful depiction of a mermaid in a thirteenth-century Jewish manuscript illustration of Jonah ("A Unique Depiction of a Scene from the Book of Jonah in a 13th Century Illuminated Hebrew Manuscript," in Jan Heller, Shemaryahu Talmon, and Hana Hlavackova, eds., *The Old Testament as Inspiration in Culture: International Academic Symposium, Prague, September 1995* [Trebenice: Mlýn, 2001] 72–95).

121 See Adolf Jellinek, ed., *Bet ha-Midrasch: Sammlung kleiner Midraschim und vermischter Abhandlungen aus der ältern jüdischen Literatur* (6 vols.; Leipzig, 1853–1877; repr., Jerusalem: Bamberger & Wahrmann, 1938) 98:1. The androcentric rabbinic tradition is replete with such negative associations between uncleanness and the womb (e.g., b. Šabb. 152a), a priestly orientation found already in the biblical imagery of Ezekiel's boiling pot (Ezek 24:6–13). Midrash of the Repentance of Jonah the Prophet also describes the belly of the fish as a kind of hell in which burning heat destroys the prophet's hair and clothes (Kadari, "Aggadic Motifs," 117–19). See also Narkiss, "Sign of Jonah," 65.

122 See Magness et al., "Huqoq Expedition," 99. The Midrash of the Repentance of Jonah also includes a succession of three fish, one for each reference in Jonah 2 (Kadari, "Aggadic Motifs," 111).

fish is a favorite in an international fund of folk art and popular culture. That the first fish has swallowed a man is a twist on the pattern.

Art historian Robin M. Jensen has taken stock of the popularity of representations of Jonah among early Christians. "In the pre-Constantinian era Jonah occurs more than seventy times of which at least thirty are series of three or four episodes."[123] These works offer a window into the reception of Jonah's experience with the sea and the fish and into the interpreted significance of the scene from Jonah 4 picturing the prophet under the shade of the planting miraculously created by God. An example in the mosaic medium points to major issues in aesthetics and worldview.

The well-preserved mosaic of the Cathedral of Bishop Theodore (fourth century) in Aquileia (fig. 3, p. 83), an ancient Roman city located at the northern end of the Adriatic Sea, provides a variation on the conventional scene preserved also at Beit Guvrin, in which a person is thrown from a boat to be swallowed by a sea creature.[124] As at Huqoq, the scenes at Aquileia are part of a larger mosaic collage featuring maritime elements: boats, various sailors, lines evoking waves of water, an array of fishes and other sea creatures including octopuses and anemones. The fishes, in particular, although formalized and similar in design, actually have differing expressions depending on the placement and shape of the mouth or the placement of the eye. The mosaic, however formulaic, thus reveals the fanciful artistic sensibilities of the mosaicist. The number of fins and the tail end of the fishes also suggest different species, as appears to be the case at Huqoq.[125] Some of the sailors manning these open, skiff-like vessels seem to have wings like angels or cherubs. In the scene of interest for the study of Jonah motifs, three men (without wings) stand in the boat, an open vessel that itself looks like a sea creature, perhaps a bird, with a beak at the bow and a tail at the stern. Decorative tiles mark the rim on the side. A sailor or passenger stands on one side in orans pose, his arms raised. He is dressed in a robe-like tunic with long sleeves, decorative markings at the wrist, neck, and chest. He looks toward the other two on the vessel. One man, naked, at the opposite side employs a pole or oar, while the central figure, also naked, seems to feed a human to a large sea creature at the side of the boat, head-first. The sea creature is a dragon, different from the fish and other smaller creatures in this fanciful ocean. It has a curling tail, claw feet, scaled back, and open maw. Tones of blue, tan, and brown dominate, with darker tiles for outlines that set creatures, humans, and vessels apart from the sea. Figures face front and exhibit "isocephaly," that is, the heads of the figures are lined up on the same level. As noted by Ling, "what matters" in this period and genre "is not the truth to visual appearances but the clear presentation of a message."[126] The message of this scene, as is true of the folk motif of fish-swallows-man, suggests vulnerability to the great unknown forces that inhabit the vast oceans and the complicit role that humans play in "feeding the beast." The larger mosaic, however, also includes the scene of the same dragon vomiting up the man, who emerges as if shot from a cannon, face forward, arms stretched out like those of a diver, feet still in the dragon's mouth. As in the folktales explored above, a stay in the belly of the sea creatures does not necessarily imply certain death—quite the contrary. Given the Christian context and the association of the Jonah version of "fish-swallows/disgorges-man" with the Jesus story, the message of these scenes reinforces hopes for resurrection and belief in the central Christian credo that Jesus rose on the third day.

That the mosaicist has Jonah in mind seems to be confirmed by another section of the larger mosaic. Next

---

123 Jensen, *Understanding Early Christian Art*, 172.
124 The mosaic situated in a round medallion in the south isle of the church at Mahat el-Urdi at Beit Guvrin (fifth–sixth century) is one of two maritime scenes that may represent portions of the tale of Jonah. The Greek inscription in an additional medallion actually identifies a figure reclining under the planting as Jonah. The round maritime medallion in the south isle is damaged but seems to depict two figures in a boat that are pushing out another figure toward a sea creature next to the vessel (see Hachlili, *Ancient Mosaic Pavements*, 91, fig. IV-24b).
125 Noted by Britt and Boustan in Magness et al., "Huqoq Excavations," 111.
126 Ling, *Ancient Mosaics*, 98.

to the image of the disgorged man is the scene of a nude figure, stretched out, arm raised, hand touching his head, under a gourd trellis (discussed in more detail in the commentary on 4:6–11). A figure in the same pose is carved on the third-century sarcophagus in Santa Maria Antiqua, an ancient Roman church. The pose and model are those of the Greek hero Endymion, but on the sarcophagus, as in the "fish swallows/disgorges" mosaics of Aquileia, the figure represents Jonah, who here, as in the mosaics, is pictured with a sea monster—in this case a particularly curvaceous and animated one (fig. 2, p. 82).[127] Jensen suggests that images of water and nudity link such interpretations of Jonah to baptism. Two sailors are in the boat above Jonah and the creature, and the boat bears carved markings suggesting waves of water.[128] The boughs of a tree hang over the reclining figure, combining motifs of garden and sea and make clear the link to episodes in the Jonah tale. This fanciful but purposeful combining of motifs is evident also in the Aquileia mosaic, where the scene of Jonah under the planting is surrounded by maritime imagery—fishes, for example. The scene of Jonah under the planting in various late antique imaginings will be discussed in greater detail in the commentary on Jonah 4:6–11, but we note here that the Aquileia mosaic with its three scenes concerning Jonah is an impressionistic and eclectic seascape richly imbued with Christian resonances.[129] Is it possible that the "sailors" with wings are "fishers of men?" The fish itself is a symbol of Christ, for the letters of the Greek word for "fish" form an acrostic for "Jesus Christ Son of God, Savior."[130] This mosaic offers particularly rich examples of early Christian visual appropriation of the book of Jonah's version of "fish swallows man."[131]

---

127 Gregg emphasizes that Christian viewers of the figure were thinking of Jonah and not Endymion (*Shared Stories*, 398).

128 See Jensen, *Understanding Early Christian Art*, 49, fig. 13a; and, for comments on the symbolism of water and nudity, 177.

129 Jensen also comments that "often the presence of water seems to unify the artistic motifs" and suggests that "fish and fishing images also might have functioned as broader symbols of the sacrament of baptism" (*Understanding Early Christian Art*, 48).

130 See ibid., 51, 57, and above for connections between the fish of Jonah, the end-time banquet, and Leviathan in Pirqe de-Rabbi Eliezer

131 For a selection and discussion of other representations of Jonah in Christian art of late antiquity, see Ling, *Ancient Mosaics*, 106–7; Bickermann, *Four Strange Books*, 5; Spier, *Picturing the Bible*, 71, 173, 186–87; Jensen, *Understanding Early Christian Art*, 172; Gregg, *Shared Stories*, 395–407. The following are excellent examples: a fourth-century vault mosaic from a circular mausoleum at Centcelles near Tarragona in Spain, in which one of the biblical scenes includes Jonah in three episodes (Ling, *Ancient Mosaics*, 107); a scene of Jonah and whale along with other biblical scenes on "upper parts of walls," in the late third-century Mausoleum of the Julii (Tomb M) in the necropolis under the Basilica of St. Peter in Rome (Ling, *Ancient Mosaics*, 105–6); Jonah in mouth of sea monster, a painted fresco, from the Catacomb of Priscilla, Rome, fourth century (Spier, *Picturing the Bible*, 71, fig. 52); a fresco in the Catacomb of Callixtus, Rome, dated ca. third century, depicting a big fish as "hippocampus" (Bickermann, *Four Strange Books*, 5; Spier, *Picturing the Bible*, 173–74, figs. 3A and 3B); a late third-century sarcophagus in Santa Maria Antiqua, Rome, depicting Jonah thrown into the sea "and reclining" (Jensen, *Understanding Early Christian Art*, 48–49 and figs. 13a–c); the Jonah sarcophagus, now in Vatican Museo Pio Cristiano, from the late third century picturing "Jonah being tossed overboard" (Jensen, *Understanding Early Christian Art*, 172, fig. 63); a statuette of Jonah thrown from the ship, dated to the fourth century, in marble, depicting both swallowing and vomiting him out (Spier, *Picturing the Bible*, 187, fig. 15); a gold glass medallion with Jonah from the second half of fourth century, a beautiful dragon-like figure with massive tail (glass also has images of Jonah vomited forth and reclining under gourds before city of Nineveh), in the Louvre (Spier, *Picturing the Bible*, 186, fig. 14). For an overview of many of the representations of Jonah in Jewish and Christian art, see Narkiss, "Sign of Jonah," 63–76. For a discussion of representations of scenes of Jonah in Roman Balkan art, in particular a mid- to late-fourth-century sarcophagus excavated in Belgrade, see Sanja Pilpović and Ljubomir Milanović, "The Jonah Sarcophagus from *Singidunum*: A Contribution to the Study of Early Christian Art in the Balkans," *Classica et Christiana* 11 (2016) 219–45.

European Jewish medieval manuscript illustrations offer a second site for a brief examination of visual reception of the fish and Jonah. One beautiful illustration is found at the opening of the book of Jonah in the Cervera Bible (in Hebrew), an "important example of early Castilian Bibles," dating to the late thirteenth century and held by the National Library of Portugal.[132] In a final colophon, the artist declares "I, Joseph ha-Zerefati ('the Frenchman') illustrated this book and completed it" (fol. 449). As in the imagery of many of the mosaics of late antiquity, a ship carries three sailors, and Jonah has been thrown overboard into the sea, right into the gaping maw of a huge fish (fol. 304). As Narkiss notes, the artists used certain formulaic designs and no doubt had access to sketch books.[133] As in the case of the verbal examples of the motif and Roman-period mosaics, these portrayals are part of a traditional repertoire. While the existence of sketch books or previous versions of "fish swallows man" can be assumed, one need not imagine the storyteller's need to use such models in a rote form of copying. Rather, much as in John Foley's concept of immanent art in the production of epic texts, with their formulaic imagery and expression, ancient and medieval artists, verbal and nonverbal, shared a medium, a formulaic and expressive library rooted in a lengthy cultural tradition.[134]

In the example from the Cervera Bible, the deep-bellied ship has a sail and a vertical architectural structure on one side reminiscent of medieval castle defenses, a little tower with small window openings and two additional turrets at its roof. The sea is a pile of rolling shaded waves in which a smaller fish swims. The sailors' expressions, though conventionalized, perhaps suggests a range of anxiety or concern, while the bearded Jonah himself looks determined rather than fearful as he enters the large fish, whose own demeanor and expression are neutral. This charming depiction draws upon medieval imagery and alerts readers that they are about to enter the narrative world of Jonah. Nevertheless, as with the mosaics discussed above, the attitude of the artist to the sailors, Jonah, and the fish is somewhat masked due to the typological nature of the maritime portrayal.

Another beautiful manuscript illumination of Jonah and the fish, influenced by the style of Joseph ha-Zerefati, was produced in 1476 in Corunna, where the Cervera Bible originated. Folio 305 of the Kennicott Bible (also in Hebrew), now housed in the Bodleian Library, contains a bold and ornate rendering of the ship, the sailors, and the sea (see fig. 4, p. 84). The fully unfurled sails are striped, and the ship itself and its rigging bear a brick pattern. The upper bodies of the two sailors in the ship are visible in profile—they appear to be sitting down, one arm folded at the elbow is visible and each is beautifully clothed in renaissance-style garments. The sailors are smooth-shaven and long-haired, wearing dapper hats, and give the impression of courtiers. One opens his mouth as if to speak, and the hand of the other makes some sort of gesture. The large open-mouthed fish has a round eye and a stripe down its side tracing its curved, sweeping contours. Jonah, dressed in a striped robe, enters the mouth head-first, as is typical in depictions of the scene, his mouth slightly open, but no panic or any emotion can be discerned in the expressions of the sailors or the victim or the predator. The sea is depicted by symmetrical rows of undulating lines, also not giving the impression of storm or torrent. The imagery is stylized, beautiful, and controlled. Rather than interpreting the scene or offering commentary, as the rabbinic texts do, these fanciful drawings enliven the biblical narration and allow the viewer to imagine how Jonah, the ship, and the sailors might be imagined in the visual patois of the times. The tone of each is fanciful and colorful, drawing in the reader to the story of this unusual prophet.

One final example of Jewish visual portrayals of Jonah worthy of note is offered by a thirteenth-century German Bible held in the British Library. This work, known as the Yonah Pentateuch, contains the Pentateuch, the Haftarot, the Five Scrolls, and Job, as well as Targum Onkelos and masorah magna and parva. The image of the fish disgorging Jonah is in the margin of a folio containing the biblical text of chap. 2 of Jonah (Add. MS 21160, fol. 292; see fig. 5, p. 85). This is a particularly popular work, as it is the haftorah for the after-

---

132 Bezalel Narkiss, *Hebrew Illuminated Manuscripts* (Jerusalem: Keter, 1969) 52.

133 Narkiss, *Hebrew Illuminated Manuscripts*, 16.
134 See Foley, *Immanent Art*.

noon service of Yom Kippur. The decoratively scaled fish lies on his back, his mouth open, and the emerging Jonah is visible from about the knee up. His face and body are in profile, his arms are raised in prayer, his eye is focused on a distant spot, and he wears a small goatee. The artist is emphasizing the prayer of Jonah here, heard by God, who then has released him. What most distinguishes this depiction and places it among comparable German illustrations is the use of micrography, minute script that often forms "geometrical or floral designs surrounding a page of conventional script or to form a whole carpet page," the decorative and often geometric opening page of a biblical book. Narkiss notes that this tiny writing is "not necessarily legible or comprehensible" but that it preserves the "masorah apparatus," that is, "the marginal lists of irregularities in writing or spelling, and reading the Bible" that reflect the Jewish transmission tradition.[135] Micrography marks the Jonah figure's hair, the outline of his shirt, and the folds of his robe. It outlines the great fish's mouth and decorates his tail. The Hebrew word "Jonah" floats above the figure's head. The text thus becomes a part of the visual representation which here emphasizes the important role of prayer in the process of salvation, as Jonah is depicted as a pious man whose petition to God allows him to escape certain death. So the worshiper stands on the Day of Atonement, hoping that his sincere prayer leads to forgiveness and a renewal of life.

---

135 Narkiss, *Hebrew Illuminated Manuscripts*, 16. See also Stanley Ferber, "Micrography: A Jewish Art Form," *JJA* 3–4 (1977) 12–24, esp. 18–19 concerning the illustration of Jonah.

Figure 1. Huqoq synagogue, Jonah mosaic panel.
Photo by Jim Haberman. Courtesy of Jodi Magness.

Figure 2. Sarcophagus of Santa Maria Antiqua: front frieze.
Courtesy Robin M. Jensen.

Figure 3. Detail of a mosaic floor depicting the stories of Jonah at the Cathedral of Bishop Theodore in Aquileia, by DEA / A DAGALI ORTI. Copyright Agephoto 2022, e Agostini Editore collection.

Figure 4. Folio 305r of the Kennicott Bible.
With permission of the Bodleian Library,
University of Oxford.

Figure 5. Image of Jonah, from a thirteenth-century Bible known as the Yonah Pentateuch.
Add. MS 21160, folio 292. British Library.

3

Charge and Fulfillment

3:1-4

Translation

1/ And the word of Yahweh came to Jonah a second time saying,
2/ "Rise up, go to Nineveh, the great city,
and proclaim to it
the proclamation that I speak to you."ᵃ
3/ And Jonah rose up and he went to Nineveh,
according to the word of Yahweh.ᵇ
Now Nineveh was a great city of God,ᶜ
a walking journey of three days.
4/ And he began to go into the city,
a walking journey of one day.
And he proclaimed and said,
"Another forty daysᵈ and Nineveh will be overturned."

Textual Notes

a   MT Mur read וקרא אליה את־הקריאה אשר אנכי דבר אליך, "and proclaim to it the proclamation that I speak to you." G reads the command to Jonah with slight variation: "and proclaim in it [ἐν αὐτῇ] according to the former proclamation [τὸ ἔμπροσθεν] which I spoke [ἐλάλησα]." 4QXIIᵃ reads הקרי[אה כזאת, "the proclamation as follows." See the discussion by Bolin, *Freedom beyond Forgiveness*, 122.

b   MT Mur read כדבר יי, "according to the word of Yahweh." G vocalizes καθὼς ἐλάλησε, "as spoke. . . ." See also BHQ, 99*, n. at 3:2.

c   MT Mur לאלהים could be read "of the gods" or "of/to God," but G reads the latter τῷ θεῷ. Tg. reads קדם יוי "before the Lord."

d   MT Mur read ארבעים יום "forty days" (so also Ḥev, Vg., Tg., S). G reads τρεῖς ἡμέραι, "three days" (so also OL). Both readings employ common numbers indicating a set time, and the differences are further evidence of traditional-style variation, which makes it difficult to discern the original.

Commentary

After surviving within the fish, Jonah is again ordered by Yahweh to go to Nineveh and proclaim God's message, and this time Jonah obeys. The message is that Nineveh will be overturned after forty days, but the verb employed suggests and anticipates some ambiguity about the events to follow.

■ 1–2 The language of 3:1–2, the charge to Jonah, reprises with some variation the charge of 1:1–2. In traditional style, the recurring formula signals both a new plot move and a resumption of the work's central thread involving the mission to Nineveh. See the commentary above for a discussion of this formulaic language of commission to the prophet in the context of the larger biblical tradition. The repetition of and variation on this language in Jonah underscore the stylistic and literary orientation of the author while raising questions about characterization and theme.

Jonah 3:1 abbreviates, leaving out Jonah's father's name in identifying the prophet and adds that God's word came שנית, "a second time." The command in 3:2, moreover, is to proclaim to it (אליה), that is, "to Nineveh," whereas 1:2 reads "against it" (עליה), which leads Alter to suggest that the message the prophet is to convey in chap. 3 "may not have an altogether hostile purpose."[1] The variation in the preposition may or may not be significant. Similarly, whereas 1:1 makes reference to the reason for the proclamation—namely, Nineveh's evil–3:2 reads more generally "the proclamation that I speak to

---

1   Alter, *Strong as Death*, 148. See Ben Zvi's discussion of the possible significance of the two prepositions (*Signs of Jonah*, 34–35, 38–39).

you."[2] It is uncertain whether this variation has implications for a possible softening of the message, the content of which was not yet specified in 1:1 and is likewise still pending in 3:1.

The important thematic point underscored by the repetition with variation is that Jonah is given a second chance to play the role expected of him, to serve as God's messenger,[3] conventionalized expectations that are thwarted in Jonah 1. The reader thus begins the third chapter of the book wondering if the story will proceed more typically this second time. The inclusion of the word שֵׁנִית, "a second time," while a common way to describe a second, related encounter or event (e.g., Gen 41:5; 1 Kgs 9:2, related to dream experiences; Lev 13:6–7, related to a skin examination; Josh 5:2, concerning circumcision; and Gen 22:15; Jer 1:13; 13:3; 33:1, on cases of divine communication), also points to a tension in characterization and builds drama. How will Jonah respond this time, and is the cause to which the deity refers the same one as that expressed in 1:2? With her deep interests in rhetorical criticism, Phyllis Trible sees the repetition as a marker of two major divisions in the narrative, while others suggest that the story appears to start over.[4] A number of scholars emphasize that Jonah now goes to Nineveh without question, but as Douglas Stuart and Uriel Simon note it is not clear that he is any more dedicated to the mission.[5] We must read on to hear Jonah's rendition of what he has been charged to say.

■ **3** This time, like a more typical prophet, Jonah rises up and goes to Nineveh in accordance with the divine command.

On Nineveh, the city, as a historical-geographic designation and as a symbol, see 1:1 above. The term rooted in גדל, "great" or "big," is one of the most frequently found adjectives in the book: big storm (1:4, 12); big fish (2:1 [1:17]); big wind (1:4); big fear (1:10, 16); big city (1:2; 3:2, 3; 4:11); big evil (4:1); big joy (4:6). On some level, the narrator describes things to be bigger than life, over the top, and the simple repeated adjective serves over and over to create this impression of hyperbole. The phrase in MT Mur עיר־גדולה לאלהים in reference to Nineveh might be translated as "and Nineveh was a great city of the gods" or "of God" or "to the gods" or "to God." The ancient Greek translation reads the latter, while the Targum translates "before the Lord." Jack Sasson explores the various options and their implications settling upon "Nineveh was a large city *for/to* God" seeing the phrase as a comment on ubiquitous divine control.[6] Others view the phrase as a superlative (e.g., Wolff, "a great city even for God"),[7] related to the three-day time they think it takes to walk across it. The translation in this volume allows for the purposeful ambiguity conveyed by the Hebrew. All belongs to Yahweh, and so it is a great city of God; the deity takes an interest in it and so it is great to him; it is an iconic place perceived to be of interest to the many gods of the Assyrian pantheon whose temples it houses; and it is physically large as well as great in the sense of prominent.

Most scholars treat the three-day journey as a measure of time with parallels to biblical passages such as Gen 30:36; Exod 3:18; and Num 10:33. Drawing on Hebrew and Akkadian parallels, David Marcus suggests

---

2   The term קריאה translated as "proclamation," rooted in a common verb קרא, "to call," is found only in Jonah in the Hebrew Bible, although it appears frequently in rabbinic literature (Sasson, *Jonah*, 226).

3   See also Limburg, *Jonah*, 75.

4   Trible, "Studies in the Book of Jonah," 185; Simon, *Jonah*, 25–26; Stuart, *Hosea–Jonah*, 482. Exploring further these two sections of Jonah, Trible points to conflicting portrayals of an unpredictable deity and tensions in the work that remain unresolved ("Divine Incongruities in the Book of Jonah," in Tod Linafelt and Timothy K. Beal, eds., *God in the Fray: A Tribute to Walter Brueggemann* [Minneapolis: Fortress Press, 1998] 202, 208). For an alternate approach to the significance of repetition and variation in the deity's two commissions, see James A. Loader, "Jonah's Commission," *OTE* 22 (2009) 589–604.

5   Wolff, *Obadiah and Jonah*, 140; Stuart, *Hosea–Jonah*, 482–83; Simon, *Jonah*, 26.

6   Sasson, *Jonah*, 229–30. Similarly, see Alter, *Strong As Death*, 149.

7   Wolff, *Obadiah and Jonah*, 148. To convey nuances of Assyria's "monstrous" capacity to crush its enemies, Johanna W. H. van Wijk-Bos translates "godawful big" ("No Small Thing: 'The Overturning' of Nineveh in the Third Chapter of Jonah," in Cook and Winter, *On the Way to Nineveh*, 218–38, here 225).

that the three-days' journey refers to "a journey involving a long time" versus a one day journey, which is an idiomatic reference to a short distance.[8] Marvin Sweeney suggests that the number three evokes the stay in the belly of the fish thereby linking the last two chapters of Jonah with the first two.[9] Influenced by D. J. Wiseman, Stuart translates the term מהלך rooted in הלך, most basically "to walk," not as "a linear measure" but as the length of time for a planned visit, as in Neh 2:6.[10]

■ **4** Jonah walks a day's worth into the city and issues the proclamation in a perfunctory, peremptory fashion. The reference to forty days is a formulaic measure of time in the Hebrew Bible (e.g., Gen 7:12, 17; Num 14:33; Deut 9:18, 25; Judg 3:11; 1 Kgs 19:8).[11] The term נהפכת here translated as "will be overturned" is, as noted by Sasson, "purposefully ambiguous."[12] The connotation of overturning in terms of the destruction of a city is found in the root's use in Gen 19:21, 25, 29 concerning Sodom and Gomorrah and elsewhere in the Hebrew Bible (cf. Deut 29:22; Jer 20:16; 49:18; Lam 4:6; Amos 4:11).[13] See also the dream of the round barley bread turning over and over in the enemy encampment, knocking down "the tent," a symbolic dream that is interpreted to mean that Gideon will vanquish or overturn his Midianite enemies (Judg 7:13–14). The root, however, can also mean "turn" in the sense of changing the mind (cf. Hos 11:8), also signaling the transformation in Saul's status and demeanor (1 Sam 10:6-10). Sasson suggests, in fact, that the biblical author seeks to remind the reader that what Jonah considers a promise of destruction may not be what God plans or what the Ninevites do in the hopes of altering their fate.[14] In fact, the style of Jonah's brusque, perfunctory prophecy suggests that he is still not happy with his role in God's plans and that he is meant to be

---

8 David Marcus, "Nineveh's 'Three Days' Walk' (Jonah 3:3): Another Interpretation," in Cook and Winter, *On the Way to Nineveh*, 42–53, here 45.

9 Sweeney, *Twelve Prophets*, 1:325.

10 D. J. Wiseman, "Jonah's Nineveh," *TynBul* 30 (1979) 29–51; Stuart, *Hosea–Jonah*, 487.

11 On the significance of MT "forty days" versus G "three days," see R. W. L. Moberly, "Preaching for a Response? Jonah's Message to the Ninevites Reconsidered," *VT* 53 (2003) 156–68. On the text-critical and thematic implications of this variation among manuscript traditions, see Kristin De Troyer, "The Freer Twelve Minor Prophets Codex—A Case Study: The Old Greek Text of Jonah, Its Revisions, and Its Corrections," in Larry W. Hurtado, ed., *The Freer Biblical Manuscripts: Fresh Studies of an American Treasure Trove* (SBLTCS 6; Atlanta: Society of Biblical Literature, 2006) 75–85, esp. 81–82.

12 Sasson, *Jonah*, 234–35; Alter, *Strong as Death*, 149; Stuart, *Hosea–Jonah*, 49; Ben Zvi, *Signs of Jonah*, 24, 112; Gitay, "Jonah: The Prophecy of Antirhetoric," 201–3; Christensen, "Jonah and the Sabbath Rest," 51. Halpern and Friedman suggest that Jonah himself "does not fathom the delphic nature of his oracle" ("Composition and Paronomasia," 87). On the double nuances of נהפכת, see Bolin, *Freedom beyond Forgiveness*," 124; and Brown, *Obadiah through Malachi*, 25. See also Yitzhak Peleg "'Yet Forty Days and Nineveh Shall Be Overthrown' (Jonah 3.4): Two Readings (Shtei Krie'ot) of the Book of Jonah," in J. Harold Ellens et al., eds., *God's Word for Our World*, vol. 1: *Biblical Studies in Honor of Simon John De Vries* (JSOTSup 388; London: T&T Clark, 2004) 262–74.

13 For thematic and linguistic comparisons with the tale of Sodom and Gomorrah, see T. A. Perry, "Changing God's Mind: Abraham versus Jonah," in Diana Lipton, ed., *Universalism and Particularism at Sodom and Gomorrah: Essays in Memory of Ron Pirson* (AIL 11; Atlanta: Society of Biblical Literature, 2012) 43–52.

14 Sasson, *Jonah*, 236–37. See also the discussion by Sherwood, *Biblical Text and Its Afterlives*, 117; Schellenberg, "Anti-Prophet among the Prophets?," 356; Eynikel, "One Day," 75–76. Employing an approach influenced by the work of Meir Sternberg, George M. Landes explores the many gaps, dissonances, ambiguities, and incongruities that challenge readers of Jonah and enrich the narrative ("Textual 'Information Gaps' and 'Dissonances' in the Interpretation of the Book of Jonah," in Robert Chazan, William W. Hallo, and Lawrence H. Schiffman, eds., *Ki Baruch Hu: Ancient Near Eastern, Biblical, and Judaic Studies in Honor of Baruch A. Levine* [Winona Lake, IN: Eisenbrauns, 1999] 273–93). Yair Zakovitch raises questions about the connection between Jonah's commission by God and what the prophet actually says. He takes note of the double meaning of הפך and suggests that God's message is "refracted through the prism of his [Jonah's] self." ("Did Jonah Proclaim What God Told Him?," in Yair Hoffman and Frank H. Polak, eds., *A Light for Jacob: Studies in the Bible and the Dead Sea Scrolls in Memory of Jacob Shalom Licht* [Jerusalem: Bialik Institute, 1997] 55–60, here 59–60).

portrayed as not all at sure about the worth of his prophecy or its claim to determine the city's future.

Jonah 3:1–4 and Comparative Folklore

This small section of Jonah includes versions of common international folk motifs that contribute to the tone of the work and its effect on readers. Attention to these motifs in the context of comparative folklore allows the reader to recognize dimensions of the story that hold universal appeal and the ways in which those shared narrative features are framed in culturally and individually specific ways, the more fully to appreciate Jonah's range of meanings and messages.

The prophetic and doom-saying aspects of Jonah's activity as the messenger of a higher power are not of course unique to ancient Judaism. The unfavorable prophecy (Motif M340) or the prophecy of great misfortune (M340.6) are the stock-in-trade of narrative folklore, whether the curse of the fairy who was not invited to the christening of "Sleeping Beauty" in the German version of the tale (Grimm 50) or the prediction in a traditional tale from Korea that a young man's wife will die.[15] A negative prediction that functions as a curse against a named city is also represented in folklore, as in the Irish tale of Colman Mac Lenini's dooming the walls of a city named Ressad.[16] Also common in an international fund of traditional narratives is the prediction that destruction will occur in a certain length of time (M341.1.6.3).

Perhaps the most interesting evocation in Jonah 3:1-4 of an international folk motif is the ambiguous or enigmatic nature of the prediction (M306.1). A talmudic reference to this motif in the tale of Jonah interprets astutely, "Nineveh will be overturned/turned over, they said, but he did not know whether for good or for bad" (b. Sanh. 89b).[17] Both Moses Gaster and Theodor H. Gaster collected a variety of tales that include the enigmatic prediction that can be misunderstood or variously interpreted. Theodor Gaster cites the Jewish tale of the man who was told that he would "end his days in Jerusalem," but he dies not in the holy city but in the Jerusalem Chamber, a room added to Westminster Abbey in the fourteenth century. He also includes the tale preserved by Apollodorus in which an oracle predicts an invasion by the Heraclids into the Peloponnesus "at the third sowing." The prediction is interpreted to mean the third year, and the defenders mistakenly launch an expedition. The prediction, however, had really meant "the third generation."[18] Moses Gaster provides a translation of a rabbinic vignette, found in a number of sources, in which the son of Simeon b. Yohai is sent by his father to the academy for the scholars to bless the lad.[19] The blessing, a series of sayings beginning with "What thou sow thou shalt not reap," can be interpreted as curses and are so understood by the concerned son. His father, however, interprets the rabbis' words with a positive spin. The very placement of a particular interpretation upon the words is the difference between a blessing and a curse, both of which have the power to bring about what they predict. As in the saying attributed to R. Hisda in the talmudic "dream-book" of b. Ber., dream symbols "follow the mouth." This fascinating collection of omens, dream interpretation techniques, and sayings reveals attitudes concerning the efficacy and real-life implications of dreams. The implication of R. Hisda's saying is that dreams follow the interpretation placed upon them (b. Ber. 55b–56a). Those interpretations have the power, according to some rabbis, to bring about what they are said to predict. So too in this talmudic passage and in Jonah, the enigmatic prediction can be understood in a positive way or in a negative way and can have implications for the future of the characters addressed.

---

15   Zong In-Sob, "The Young Man and the Priest," in *Folk Tales from Korea* (London: Routledge & Kegan Paul, 1952) 73–75.

16   Vernam Hull, "Conall Corc and the Corco Luigde," *PMLA* 62.4 (1947) 887–909, esp. 900. Note that the translator is not certain of the city's name.

17   B. Sanh. 89b: נינוה נהפכת אמרי ליה איהו לא ידע אי לטובה אי לרעה.

18   Theodor H. Gaster, *The Oldest Stories in the World* (Boston: Beacon, 1952) 205.

19   Moses Gaster, *The Exempla of the Rabbis: Being a Collection of Exempla, Apologues and Tales Culled from Hebrew Manuscripts and Rare Hebrew Books* (London: Asia Publishing, 1924; repr., New York: Ktav, 1968) 87 n. 144. See also a range of tales including enigmatic predictions in Haim Schwartzbaum, *Studies in Jewish and World Folklore* (Fabula Supplement B.3; Berlin: de Gruyter, 1968) 122.

The motifs of doom pronouncement over a city and the mention of the time frame in which that prophecy will be fulfilled build drama, as the audience of readers anticipates the possible cataclysm. In traditional works, the drama is rebuilt and reexperienced each time the work is performed. It does not matter that everyone knows how the story goes. The knowing allows for a kind of informed and wise participation in the pattern of events. When the prediction, however, is enigmatic, an additional thread is introduced into the drama. In a number of the tales employing the motif of enigmatic prediction, the characters of the tale and perhaps also the audience or reader does not know about the potential plot twist until the story's conclusion. This possibility of surprise animates the plot. That the prophecy has the potential to be ironic or the opposite of expectations gives one pause and adds a riddling nuance to the interaction. The ambiguous verb in Jonah's prophecy rooted in the word הפך, "to turn," leads the reader to ask who thinks what. How do the Ninevites understand the prediction? How does the deity mean it? How does Jonah interpret the proclamation he has been charged to deliver? Is it not merely pique but uncertainty concerning the apparent turn of events that leads Jonah in 4:5 to skulk off and still wait to see what will happen to Nineveh? The uncertainty lingers even though the deity is said to have changed his mind in 3:10, for God's actions can turn once again, and his message is tinged with uncertainty.

The enigmatic nature of the prophecy and the author's use of this traditional folk motif in Jonah serves to remind the reader that the tale is not merely about the compassion of God, who is much more forgiving than his human messenger. Nor is the tale merely about the power of repentance, a theme that surely contributes to Jonah's place as the *haftorah* reading for the Day of Atonement. Like Job, Ecclesiastes, and Ruth—all late biblical works—Jonah is about the inscrutability of the deity and about the challenges of a theology that promises blessings to the good and punishment for the evil. Job is without sin and yet loses his children, his health, and the respect of his community. Ecclesiastes emphasizes how unpredictable and unfair are the ways of the world. The book of Ruth, despite its happy ending, speaks to the pain of personal suffering and loss. Bad things happen to decent people for seemingly no reason that we as human beings can comprehend. And apparently good things can happen to those who commit evil. Jonah too attests to and explores divine unpredictability. The folk motif of the enigmatic prophecy speaks to a recognition by human beings that there is no clear road map; life contains ironies and surprises. By means of this motif, Jonah radically insists that the world created by Yahweh is characterized by irony and a lack of moral clarity. In this respect, the folkloristically influenced interpretation offered here takes issue with some who find the book's message to suggest that "God does not exercise his power arbitrarily and discriminatorily."[20]

---

20   Stuart, *Hosea–Jonah*, 496.

3

Repentance and Forgiveness

3:5–10

Translation

5/ And trust did the men of Nineveh God,ᵃ
and they called a fast
and they dressed in sackcloth,
   from their greatest to their smallest.
6/ And the word reached the king of Nineveh,
and he rose up from his throne,
and he took off his mantle,ᵇ
and he covered himself in sackcloth
and sat upon the dust.
7/ And he cried out and said in Nineveh,ᶜ
according to the resolution of the kingᵈ and his grandees
   saying,
"Humans and animals, the cattle and the sheep, shall not
   taste a thing,
they shall not feed,
and water they shall not drink.
8/ And they shall cover themselves in sackcloth, the human
   beings and the animals,
and they shall call out toᵉ God with force,ᶠ
and let everyone turn back from his evil wayᵍ
and from the violenceʰ that is in their hands.ⁱ
9/ Who knows, God may turn back and feel regret,
and turn backʲ from his burning anger,
and we will not perish?"
10/ And see did God their actions,ᵏ
that they turned back from their evil way,
and God was regretful about the evilˡ
   that he had declared to do to them,
and he did not do it.

Textual Notes

a   As in 3:3, MT Mur באלהים could be read to say "in God" or "in the gods," but G chooses the former: τῷ θεῷ. Tg. expands to במימרא דיוי, "in the Word of God." The term "Memra" is often used in the Targums as a respectful substitute for the divine name. See Tg.'s reading of 2:5.

b   Tg. expands to מכורסי מלכותיה, "from his royal throne," and לבושי יקריה, "precious robes." Instead of "robes" S reads "and he lifted off his tiara," wšql tgh mnh, a typical variation.

c   MT Mur read בנינוה ויאמר ויזעק, "And he cried out and said in Nineveh...," whereas G employs the passive "it was proclaimed and it was said," καὶ ἐκηρύχθη καὶ ἐρρέθη. OL reads "it was proclaimed in Nineveh from the king and the leaders of his city, saying," *et praedicatum est in nineve: a rege et a maioribus civitatis eius dicens.*

d   The somewhat unusual MT Mur מטעם, "according to the [lit.] taste [or will/authority] of the king" (see Sasson, *Jonah*, 240), is rendered in G by παρά and in OL by *a* "from." Vg. has *ex ore*, "from the mouth." Note that the root טעם is found in the verb for the command not to eat or to fast in MT Mur v. 7.

e   MT and G OL read אל, "to," whereas Mur varies the preposition with "upon" (על) and Tg. reads "before."

f   MT בחזקה, "with strength," "strongly," is rendered by G as ἐκτενῶς, "assiduously," "zealously," "eagerly." OL reads similarly *ad deum vehementer*. S reads *bḥngtʾ*, "with a groan," providing an alternate emotional nuance.

g   MT Mur read with reference to man and beast, "They shall be covered ... and call ... and return" (ויתכסו... ויקראו... וישבו); G reads, καὶ περιεβάλοντο ... καὶ ἀνεβόησαν ... καὶ ἀπέστρεψαν, "put on sackcloth and cried to the Lord, etc." OL reads "the men covered ..." *et cooperuerunt se cilicia homines*, omits "beasts," and continues "and the men and beasts cried out etc.," *et proclamaverunt homines et iumenta.*

h   MT Mur read חמס, "violence." G reads ἀδικίας, "injustice," and OL reads *iniusta*, "the unjust things."

i   G adds λέγοντες, "saying." OL reads *dixerunt*, "they said."

j   G omits ישוב. Tg. somewhat complicates the image of God's turning back and regretting as follows: מן ידע דאית ביריה חובין יתוב מנהון ויתרחם עלנא מן קדם יוי "Whoever knows that there are sins on his conscience let him repent of them and we will be pitied before the Lord." Cathcart and Gordon link this nuanced translation to an implicit midrash on this verse and Joel 2:14 that emphasizes "the efficacy of repentance" and "remove(s) from both verses the suggestion that God 'repents'" (*Targum of the Minor Prophets*, 108 n. 11). See also Almbladh, *Studies in the Book of Jonah*, 35. É. Levine views Tg. as emphasizing the liturgical function of Jonah, read on Yom Kippur (*Aramaic Version of Jonah*, 89).

k   Tg. reads וגלן קדם יוי עובדיהון, "And revealed before Yhwh were their deeds," perhaps to avoid anthropomorphizing the deity. See Cathcart and Gordon, *Targum of the Minor Prophets*, 108 n. 13 and Almbladh, *Studies in the Book of Jonah*, 35.

l   Note that G here translates the same MT word הרע appearing twice in this verse with two terms: τῶν πονηρῶν, "wicked ways," in reference to human actions דרכם הרעה, and τῇ κακίᾳ, "evil," with reference to the punitive harm that the deity decides not to carry out after all—the bad things God was about to do. The former term has a more explicit moral nuance.

Commentary

This passage describes embodied manifestations of repentance by the inhabitants of Nineveh, including the king and all his realm, old and young, aristocrats and commoners, animals and humans. The hope is that the deity, seeing these signs, will pull back from his planned destruction, and indeed he does.

■ **5** The Ninevites respond collectively with repentance, an action that is also a reaction, and the deity responds by relenting from the evil he had planned (3:5–10).

The motif of the foreigner's expression of belief in the might of the Israelite God Yahweh is a salient one in Hebrew Scriptures. The popularity of this motif perhaps speaks to Israelite insecurities in the face of formidable and aggressive neighbors and frequent political and military threats to their independence and well-being. The success of the nation is bound up with notions about the power and potency of its national deity, a matter of deep concern to biblical writers in the wake of Assyrian and Babylonian conquests. Whether it is the benign Pharaoh in the tales of Joseph (Gen 41:37) or the tyrant of the exodus and his entourage, who intermittently acknowledge Yahweh's dominance (e.g., Exod 10:7, 17–20), foreigners' admissions concerning the authority of Yahweh send an important self-assertive message. Admittedly, writers also acknowledge in the exodus account, for example, that such appreciation for God by the Other may be fleeting, as the tyrant returns to a state of "hardened heart" imposed by Yahweh himself. Nevertheless, Rahab in Joshua 2, the Gibeonites in Joshua 9, Naaman the leper in 2 Kings 5 are all foreigners who acknowledge the power of Yahweh and testify to the respect that he commands. In Jonah, the sailors of 1:14, 16 join the list of those who come to fear God, as do the Ninevites and their king in Jonah 3.

The verb used in Jonah 3:5 translated as "trust" is a *hiphil* form of the root אמן + the preposition ב, "in," meaning "to believe in," or "trust." This phrase is used in Exod 19:9, where Moses is told by God that the Israelites will believe in or trust Moses. In 1 Sam 27:12, Achish the Philistine is said to trust David. Most frequently, the phrase describes human beings' belief in Yahweh, the rescuer and patron of Israel. So Abraham trusts in the Lord (Gen 15:6), as do the people Israel after the exodus experience (Exod 14:31). So Jehoshaphat urges the people threatened by invaders to trust in God (2 Chr 20:20). In contrast, the rebellious people are said to be without trust or belief in Num 14:11; 20:12; Deut 1:32; and 2 Kgs 17:14. In Jonah, the point seems to be that the Ninevites trust or believe in God because of the word delivered by Jonah. They are fully convinced that Nineveh truly faces destruction, and they respond accordingly. To read the verb as an indication of mass religious conversion moves in the wrong direction, as seen by Stuart, Alter, John H. Walton and others.[1]

---

1   See Stuart, *Hosea–Jonah*, 483; Alter, *Strong as Death*," 150 n. 5; John H. Walton, "The Object Lesson of Jonah 4:5–7 and the Purpose of the Book of Jonah," *BBR* 2 (1992) 47–57, here 53–54; Christensen, "Narrative Poetics," 37. For a discussion of the verb אמן in the *hiphil* employed with the preposition ב before the object, see A. Jepsen, "אמן," *TDOT* 1:298–309; and Alter, *Strong as Death*, 150). The presence of the preposition that can be translated "in" does not require the translation "believed in,"

The people's declaring a fast and the wearing of sackcloth are material expressions of mourning and self-abasement, as in Gen 37:34; 1 Sam 7:6; 2 Sam 3:31; 1 Kgs 21:27; 2 Kgs 19:1–2; Ezra 8:21–23; Esth 4:1–3; Jer 36:9; and Joel 1:13, 14; 2:12. Conventionalized language describes dressing in sackcloth (Jonah 3:5; Esth 4:1) or covering/clothing in/putting on sackcloth (Gen 37:34; Jonah 3:6; 2 Kgs 19:1) and often includes ashes that are worn (Esth 4:1) or sat upon (Jonah 3:6).[2]

Sackcloth is a coarse uncomfortable material, unpleasant to wear. As Sasson notes, the term שׂק might be translated as "hair shirt," "rags," or "tatters."[3] The change in eating habits and clothing marks identity and aspiration, an expression of genuine repentance and hope for forgiveness. An impending or current disaster is understood to be punishment from God. Thus, the Israelites fast and confess sins at Mizpah when facing the approach of Philistine enemies (1 Sam 7:6; see also Jdt 4:9–15).[4] The pattern in the Hebrew Bible of threat, physical expression of penitence, forgiveness, and avoidance of disaster is, as Allen notes, recurring.[5] So Ahab is pictured in 1 Kgs 21:27–29 as repenting and being granted a reprieve from God. It is of note in Jonah 3 that the people themselves react with these signs of self-abasement, as if by sudden popular uprising or communal agreement, from "great" to "small," a reference to all members of society whatever their age or social status.[6] In 3:6, the king learns of Jonah's prophecy and further engages himself and his people in the effort to reverse God's decree, going beyond fasting. Given the mention of the people's acts of self-abasement in 3:5, some have suggested that the following verse is a "flashback,"[7] but Sasson's reading of a more simple sequence is preferable.[8]

■ **6** The term דבר here translated as "word," understood as a "matter," is rooted in terminology of "speech" and is used for divine commissions in this and other prophetic works (e.g., Jonah 1:1; 3:1, 2, 3, 10).

The phrase מלך נינוה is unusual, without any direct equivalence in the Assyrian royal titulary. The composer does not refer to the monarchic head of state as king of Assyria, a typical designation in the Hebrew Bible for the Assyrian ruler (cf. 2 Kgs 18:11, 19; Isa 7:17, 20; 8:7; 36:15, 16, 18; 37:8, 10; Nah 3:18). Perhaps the formulation "king of Nineveh" is generated by analogy with the very common designation מלך בבל, "king of Babylon," that is used so frequently in the Hebrew Bible.[9] Sasson provides an overview of possible reasons for this kingly epithet, rejecting various historical explanations that have been offered for the terminology and pointing out that, throughout the Hebrew Bible, "labels for rulers" reveal considerable variation and extemporization. He notes, for example, that the writer of Judith refers to the Babylonian Nebuchadnezzar as king of Assyria.[10] The goal of these writers is literary and thematic rather than historiographic. Assyria in the book of Judith functions as a symbol of the ancient Levant's most vicious enemy, and, in Jonah, Nineveh the magnificent city with an international reputation for grandeur and power (see discussion in chap. 1 above) serves as a metonym for Assyria and the Assyrians, the archetypal enemies of Israel and oppressive aliens par excellence. It is against "Nineveh" that Nahum is said to direct his anti-Assyrian oracle (Nah 1:1).[11]

---

in the sense of conversion. Jepsen suggests (305) "they took Jonah's message seriously as a message which actually came from God."

2   On the possible significance of linguistic and visual connections between similar scenes in Esther and Jonah, see Seidler, "'Fasting,' 'Sackcloth,' and 'Ashes,'" 117–34.

3   Sasson, *Jonah*, 245.

4   For examples of this ritual behavior and the worldview behind it in the wider Levant, see Sasson, *Jonah*, 245. The rabbinic tractates on fasts, m. Taʿan and b. Taʿan, exhibit a similar typology in belief.

5   Allen, *Joel, Obadiah, Jonah, and Micah*, 223; see also Sweeney, *Twelve Prophets*, 1:326.

6   See Sasson, *Jonah*, 246; Limburg, *Jonah*, 81.

7   See Wolff, *Obadiah and Jonah*, 145; Person, *In Conversation with Jonah*, 126.

8   See Sasson, *Jonah*, 247.

9   David S. Vanderhooft, "Biblical Perspectives on Nineveh and Babylon: Views from the Endangered Periphery," *JCSMS* 3 (2008) 83–92, esp. 86.

10 Sasson, *Jonah*, 247–50.

11 For more on the references to Nineveh in Nahum and other prophetic materials of the Hebrew Bible, see Peter Machinist, "Nahum as Prophet and as Prophetic Book: Some Reconsiderations," in Heinz-Josef Fabry, ed., *The Books of the Twelve Prophets: Minor Prophets, Major Theologies* (BETL 295; Leuven: Peeters, 2018) 103–29; Machinist, "The Fall of Assyria in Comparative Ancient Perspective," in

The phrase "king of named city" also, however, infuses the tale with the nuances of ancient archetypal and mythological historiographic accounts of the interactions of the ancestors with various enemy peoples and their leaders. In many instances the place named is a city-state, and so its ruler is king of that city and beyond, for the geographic designation often includes "its villages," as in Num 21:25, in reference to Heshbon, and Judg 11:26, in reference to Aroer. In the patriarchal narratives, Gen 14:8 refers to the king of Sodom, and to Abimelech as king of Gerar (Gen 20:2). In the conquest tales, there are references to the king of Jericho (Josh 2:3), to Adonizedek, king of Jerusalem (Josh 10:1, 3, 5), to the king of Lachish (Josh 10:23; 12:11) and the king of Gezer (Josh 12:12). Most relevant to the royal epithet in Jonah 3 is the reference to Sihon, king of Heshbon (Deut 2:26; see also Num 21:27). Sihon is the king of the Amorites, but more specifically king of Heshbon (Judg 11:19). In an archaizing way, the king of the Assyrians is similarly designated in Jonah as the king of its major city Nineveh. From a narrative, literary perspective the emphasis on the people and the king, who are identified with a specific city, also focuses the reader's attention on the scene within that geographic area and allows for Jonah to leave and perch himself in sight of a particular place to see what would happen (4:5).

As for his people, the king's change in clothing marks his immersion into a state of supplication and self-abasement. Here the transformation or ritual passage is even more pronounced, for the king rises from his throne (literally, his seat)[12] and sits instead upon ashes, על־האפר (ʿal hāʾēper), a substance that bears a resemblance to the term, עפר (ʿāpār, "dust"). He removes his kingly garb, a mantle or cloak, and dons sackcloth (see above). The phrase "his mantle," אדרתו (ʾaddartô), as Alter notes, may play on the root אדר (ʾdr) with its nuances of glory or magnificence.[13] The term for the item of clothing itself may be rooted in notions of ampleness and breadth.[14]

■ **7-8** The king "cried out," a verb (זעק), that lends the image of the king's speech extra intensity.

The sentence structure is ambiguous in v. 7. Does the king "cry out in Nineveh" or does he cry out, "In Nineveh . . ."? Sasson makes the case for the latter translation, emphasizing that orders or pronouncements generally follow directly after the verb אמר. Citing Cynthia Miller, however, Tucker notes that, where two verbs (in this case זעק and אמר) precede the לאמר ("saying") frame, then the quotation follows the frame word.[15]

The term טעם most basically means "taste" and plays on the king's declaration that neither man nor animal "taste anything" in a communal fast, but the term is also employed to suggest discernment or wisdom, sensibility with nuances of perception (e.g., 1 Sam 25:33; Ps 34:9 [8]; Prov 31:18) or feeling (Job 12:20; Ps 119:66). Acceptable translations might be "resolution" or "determination" in the sense of issuing a wise decision.[16]

The fast is to be undertaken by the community of humans and animals alike—hence the parallelism of verb טעם for humans, again "from great to small" as in 3:5, and רעה, literally "to graze," a term for food consumption generally applied to the animal kingdom (e.g., Isa 5:17; 61:5; Mic 7:14).[17] Similarly, the animals, like the human beings,

---

Simo Parpola and R. M. Whiting, eds., *Assyria 1995: Proceedings of the 10th Anniversary Symposium of the Neo-Assyrian Text Corpus Project, Helsinki, September 7-11, 1995* (Helsinki: Neo-Assyrian Text Corpus Project, 1997) 179-95.

12 Interestingly, 2 Kgs 19:36 insists that Sennacherib, "the king of Assyria," returned (*wayyāšob*) to Nineveh after his failed assault on Jerusalem; the king then "sat [enthroned] [*wayyēšeb*] in Nineveh." Does the Jonah reference to the king rising from his throne here allude to this passage?

13 Alter, *Strong as Death*, 150.

14 BDB, s.v. "אָדַר."

15 Sasson, *Jonah*, 235; Tucker, *Jonah* (2006), 75-76; and Cynthia Miller, ed. *The Verbless Clause in Biblical Hebrew* (Winona Lake, IN: Eisenbrauns, 1999) 196.]

16 Gesenius thinks it is probably a loanword from Akk. *ṭēmu*, "Befehl," that is, "order" or, with BDB, "decree" (s.v. טעם). The irony of using what may be a homophonous Akkadian loanword for "resolution" is interesting. Some have suggested that this is an Aramaism; see Sasson, *Jonah*, 253-54. Perhaps the writer is aware of the dual meaning.

17 On the possible wordplay or pun between the root *rʿh* (רעה) for "graze" or "pasture" and the recurring root *rʿʿ* (רעע), "to be evil," and its structural significance, see Duane L. Christensen, "Anticipatory Paronomasia in Jonah 3:7-8 and Genesis 37:2," *RB* 90 (1983) 261-63.

are to be covered in sackcloth. Scholars cite the parallel in Jdt 4:10–12 where the response to Holofernes's threatened invasion of Jerusalem involves all members of the community and their cattle, which are pictured, along with the people, as being wrapped in sackcloth. Wolff draws parallels with Herodotus *Hist.* 9.24, in which the Persians express mourning for a deceased leader by shaving their horses and draught animals.[18] Alter suggests that the image of animals in mourning in Jonah 3 is "bizarre" and "farcical," whereas Wolff describes it as satirical.[19] Limburg and others, however, emphasize the ways in which the connection between humans and animals as shared members of God's creation are drawn in the Hebrew Bible, for example, in the image of animals sighing or groaning, crying out to God, in times of drought (Joel 1:18, 20).[20] Jeremiah 12:4 expresses deep empathy for the animals and birds who are swept away because of the wickedness of human beings that brought divine wrath upon all nature (see also Hab 2:17). The image of mourning animals, moreover, anticipates the final phrase of the Jonah narrative, which suggests concern for the animal residents of Nineveh.[21]

All are to call out to God "with force" (בחזקה), terminology that suggests force, strength, and violence (e.g., Judg 4:3; 1 Sam 2:16). "Calling out" is what the prophet is commanded by God to do in 1:2 and 3:1 and describes the petitioning by the sailors on the churning sea in 1:14 (see also 1:6 and the discussion at 1:2 above). Each member of the community is to repent and reform. Terminology connoting turning back and badness conveys, in the purposely delimited vocabulary employed throughout Jonah, the hope for transformation. The root שוב, "to turn back," employed in 1:13 to express the sailors' desperate efforts to return to shore is used intensely in 3:8–10 to express the king's urging of Nineveh to repent and the hopes that the deity will turn from his anger and forgive and see Nineveh's change of path. The term translated "evil" in this volume, rooted in the basic meaning of bad (רעע), is found throughout Jonah with connotations ranging from misfortune to moral shortcoming (see the discussion on 1:2 above). Tucker notes that the image of "turning" plays on the doubly meant language of Jonah's pronouncement in 3:4 employing the root הפך (see the discussion above).[22]

The translation takes דרך ("way") as a feminine noun modified by הרעה, the term for "evil."[23] The phrase is used with the masculine form רע in Prov 2:12 (מדרך רע), where the author writes of saving from the bad path, and in Prov 21:16 with a modifier השכל, "being prudent," which connotes the good or wise way to act.

Jonah 3:8 reflects a formulaic pattern: verb שוב ("to turn back") + a person/a bad person + מדרכם/מדרכו (from his or their path) + adjective meaning evil or bad.[24] With variation, the pattern is found in Jer 18:11; 23:22; 25:5; 26:3; 35:15; 36:3, 7; Ezek 3:18, 19; 13:22. This language of turning back from the evil path expresses formulaically the quintessential desire of the moral leader for his people's repentance. Whether prophet or political leader, Yahwist or foreigner, the speaker realizes and accepts that the current misfortune of his people is rooted in their actions of wrongdoing. It is particularly arresting that the voice of moral awareness in Jonah 3 is that of an Assyrian and that the author implicitly attributes to him a covenantal theology of blessings and curses. The self-awareness of an imagined leader of Assyrians, famous for their martial cruelty and vicious treatment of enemies, a matter self-proclaimed in propaganda works such as the Lachish reliefs, is surely a critical theme in Jonah and one meant to shock, surprise, and make the listener think deeply about the human capacity for reason and repentance.

---

18 Wolff, *Obadiah and Jonah*, 153; see also Allen, *Joel, Obadiah, Jonah, and Micah*, 224 n. 23 on Plutarch, *Alex.* 72.

19 Alter, *Strong as Death*, 150–51; Wolff, *Obadiah and Jonah*, 152.

20 Limburg, *Jonah*, 83. See also Shemesh, "'And Many Beasts,'" 20–26.

21 See also Phyllis Trible, "A Tempest in a Text: Ecological Soundings in the Book of Jonah," in Cook and Winter, *On the Way to Nineveh*, 187–200, here 192; Ken Stone, *Reading the Hebrew Bible with Animal Studies* (Stanford, CA: Stanford University Press, 2018) 159–60; Carey Walsh, "Between Text and Sermon," 339.

22 Tucker, *Jonah*, 79.

23 See Robert J. Ratner, "*Derek*: Morpho-Syntactical Considerations," *JAOS* 107 (1987) 471–73, a frequently cited discussion of דרך as a masculine and feminine noun.

24 For a thoughtful discussion of "turning" as a key term and concept in Jonah and its reception history, see Gregg, *Shared Stories*, 355.

The phrase concerning turning away from the evil path is balanced by a parallel image, ומן־החמס אשר בכפיהם, "and from the violence that is in their hands." The term for violence (חמס) has nuances of ethical and physical abuse suffered by human beings at the hands of others. The term is used, for example, in relation to warring, often illicit, behavior (e.g., Gen 49:5; Judg 9:24). It evokes a kind of ruthlessness and viciousness. Thus the deity describes the way of human beings on earth in the biblical Noah narrative (Gen 6:11, 13). Biblical characters describe their feelings of having been mistreated with the language "my violence/abuse" (e.g., Sarah [Gen 16:5]; the inhabitants of Zion mistreated by Babylonia [Jer 51:35]). The possession or embodiment of the mal-treatment is visceral. The term translated "hand" (כף) is literally the hollow or flat of the hand, the palm, and so one has an image of violence having been scooped up and held. This image suggests beautifully human responsibility, for the violence is something one might control, one's fault, suggestive of Isaiah's imagery in the lawsuit of chap. 1, "your hands are full of blood" (Isa 1:15). The phrase "violence (חמס) + in/of their/my/your + hands/palms" is another formula pattern found in Job 16:17; Ps 58:3 [2]; and Isa 59:6. In 1 Chr 12:18 [17], the speaker, David, insists that there is no violence in his hands. The language suggests ownership of an ethical violation, rejection of behavior expected of decent human beings. Here the king asks his community to turn away from this sort of inhumanity, the cause of threatened divine retribution.

The two parallel phrases juxtapose the singular "his path" with the plural "their hands." Such variation may not be connotatively significant, although Trible suggests that the alternation allows the author to point to individual wrongdoing and to the behavior of the larger community.[25] Biblical passages dealing with blessings and punishment, actions and their consequences, often do alternate between descriptions of individual choices and consequences experienced by those individuals and matters concerning the tone and tenor of society at large, for example, Ezek 18:5-24 versus Ezek 18:25-32; and Deut 27:15-26 versus Deut 28:12, 20.[26]

■ 9 The phrase "who knows?" introduces a conventionalized pattern of speech that carries the hope that God will relent, forgive, or rescue. The phrase "who knows" or "perhaps" is followed by a verb that indicates a change in attitude or behavior by the deity and then by a description of the hoped-for outcome. In Jonah 3:9, "who knows" is followed by a form of שוב, "to turn back" (see above in 3:8 and 3:10) and the *niphal* of נחם, "to be sorry or console oneself," terminology betokening self-regret or change of mind (see 3:10; 4:2).[27] This image of forgiveness is extended by additional embodied idiomatic language betokening divine pulling back from anger (literally, "the burning anger of his nostrils"), and finally the goal, "we will not perish" or literally "be lost" (לא נאבד). A close parallel is found in Jonah 1:6, in which the sailors facing death at sea hope for rescue. In 1:6, אולי, "perhaps," functions in the same way as "who knows" followed by the unusual verb here translated as "give a thought" to us, and finally the goal, "we will not perish," as in 3:9. Variants on this formula pattern are found in 2 Sam 12:22, where David fasts and hopes that God will spare the child born to Bathsheba, and in Joel 2:14, as the prophet hopes that repentance will lead to relief from the invasion of locusts described so viscerally in Joel 1. Like Jonah 3:9, Joel 2:14 employs forms of שוב and נחם in the formula pattern that describes a hoped-for change of heart on the deity's part.[28]

The root נחם is especially evocative of divine emotion as well as action. Rooted in the feeling of being sorry and the effort to console oneself, the verb can also mean to repent or be aggrieved over one's actions. Limburg offers a careful taxonomy of the various meanings that seem to be attributed to the root in biblical literature,[29] but such connotations do not exhaust the meaning of the term. The reader is well served by awareness that the deity's "changing his mind" or "relenting" is informed

---

25   Trible, *Rhetorical Criticism*, 186.
26   See the discussion in Niditch, *Responsive Self*, 17–31.
27   For a theological approach to this verb that draws on metaphor studies, see Terence E. Fretheim, "The Repentance of God: A Key to Evaluating Old Testament God-Talk," *HBT* 10 (1988) 47–70.
28   See also Esth 4:14. For a discussion of the phrase "who knows" and its range of meanings and applications in the Hebrew Bible, see James L. Crenshaw, "The Expression *mî yôdēaʿ* in the Hebrew Bible," *VT* 36 (1986) 274–88.
29   Limburg, *Jonah*, 84–85.

by notions of sorrow or the need for comforting self-consolation. The author in this way offers a complex portrayal of the deity and his motivations, attributing to God the mixed emotions that often accompany human action and response. Perhaps the most evocative use of this verb in relation to divine decisions is found in the biblical tale of the flood in which God is described in the third person as sorry that he created humankind, who has turned out to be such a violent disappointment. The image of God's somehow consoling himself is juxtaposed with the image of his being pained to his heart in Gen 6:6 (ויתעצב אל־לבו). He is pictured saying in the first person (Gen 6:7), "I am sorry that I made them" (נחמתי כי עשיתם). The use of the term נחם together with the description of human beings' violence via the loaded term חמס employed to describe people's reprehensible behavior in Gen 6:11, 13 may have the effect of juxtaposing the tale about the destruction faced by the people of Nineveh with the foundational story of the flood when all on earth, animal and human, are destroyed, except for those on the ark. Significantly, in the tale of Noah no option exists for repentance, and the salvation of a cosmos filled with life-forms is apparently based on one man's previous good record. In Jonah, the message is different. God may listen if people repent, any people. In one of the conclusions of the tale of the flood in Gen 8:21, God declares that human beings by their very nature are so prone to evil, that if the deity wants a cosmos filled with humans and animals, he will need to take utter and complete destruction off the list. The possibility of repentance by particular groups and temporary divine relenting may fall somewhere between the options considered by God in the tale of Noah.

It is always difficult to establish the nature of the relationship between extant biblical versions of material, as the introductory discussion of Jonah among the Twelve indicates.[30] To be sure, the juxtaposition of these relatively uncommon terms for violence and regret, involving humans and God, is at the very least suggestive of ways of thinking about the relationship between the deity and his imperfect human creations and about modes of expressing these thoughts in a traditional medium. Awareness of the Israelite version of the flood narrative with its emphasis on human malfeasance and divine disappointment enriches the reader or listener's response to subsequent plot moves in the tale of Jonah.[31]

■ **10** This verse once again employs the root נחם, indicating that God does indeed relent or think better about the punishing destruction that he had commanded Jonah to declare against Nineveh. Here one can compare Exod 32:14, which shares with Jonah 3:10 formulaic language involving quite precise repetition of the same words; in the Exodus text, after hearing Moses's remonstrations, God relents from the punishment he had planned in response to the incident of the golden calf. The two examples evidence slight variations: in Exodus, the deity is called יהוה, the divine name, whereas in Jonah the deity is אלהים, God. In addition, Jonah 3:10 lengthens the relenting act with the phrase ולא עשה, "and he did not do it." In Exodus, the change of heart is a response to Moses's intervention, his reminder that God has a reputation to uphold among the Egyptians and a promise to keep to Israel. Another example of the same conventionalized language describing divine relenting in regard to punishment is found in Jer 18:8 (to be contrasted with the variant in Jer 18:10 declaring that the deity may change his mind in regard to positive or salutary plans).

God leads the prophet Jeremiah to a potter whose clay pots are shown to be malleable; the spoiled pot can be reshaped and made good. In the same way, human nations can be transformed, can indeed transform themselves, allowing the deity to relent. In Jer 18:8, נחם is employed in first-person speech by God, and the phrase "that he had spoken/declared to do to them" uses the variant, "I thought to do to it," חשבתי לעשות לו. Jeremiah 18:8 is especially pertinent to the tale of Jonah and Nineveh, as both authors grapple with questions about the disposition of nations. While Jeremiah applies this case to Judah, the referent in 18:7–10 potentially has more universal applicability, as the rabbis will notice in their reception of Jonah 3:10 and their midrashic juxtaposition of these two texts.

---

30 See in the Introduction a discussion of Kim, "Jonah Read Intertextually."
31 See Brown, *Jonah: The Reluctant Prophet*, 137–58.

Overview of Jonah 3:5–10, Rabbinic Reception, and Comparative Folklore

This section dealing with the Ninevites' response and God's reaction underscores important textural features and pieces of content that are critical to an appreciation of the larger work's aesthetic, its message, and its context, the world of thought it reflects and helps to shape. Stylistically, like the larger work, 3:5–10 is characterized by vocabulary that recurs throughout the narrative (e.g., forms of קרא, "to call"; forms of שוב, "to turn back"; and forms of דבר, "to speak"). The passage is also marked by formulaic patterns of speech, found elsewhere in the narrative or in other biblical passages to express an essential idea or image. Jonah 3:5–6 describes formulaically the dressing or self-covering that conveys abasement, and 3:8 expresses formulaically turning away from evil. In Jonah 3:9, the interrogative phrase "who knows?" introduces a formula expressing hope for salvation, and 3:10 includes a recurring biblical pattern of language expressing the deity's decision to relent.

The content of this section develops the theme of foreigners' capacity for repentance. Assyrians of Nineveh, great and small, young and old, are capable of humbling themselves before God, of turning away from the path of violence and evil. Their king models this kind of transformation himself. Implicit is the message that these foreigners are worth worrying about, as are their animals, who are pictured fasting and being dressed in mourning along with humans. The composer thus considers the survival and well-being of a wide ecosystem of beings. In the Israelite and wider Levantine tradition, Assyrians are iconic foreigners, invaders known to practice vicious forms of subjugation, as represented in their own propagandistic media, so that their centrality in this tale about the capacity to repent and be saved is arresting. The emphasis on the decision to change one's ways, no matter one's origins, or ancestors, or previous actions, is in tune with messages in a range of late biblical compositions, for example, Ezek 18:5–24; 33:14–16. Similarly, late biblical material increasingly emphasizes outreach to non-Yahwists, their capacity to recognize the power of God and to be accepted (e.g., Isa 56:6–8).[32] Jonah 3:5–10 is thus an important indicator of the themes of the work and of its place in a history of ideas. The book of Jonah is best understood in the setting of late biblical times.

Finally, Jonah 3:5–10 emphasizes the emotional dimensions of the characters, the regret and hope of the humans, the implicit empathy of the animals, and the capacity of the deity to take pity and relent even when dealing with corrupt subjects whose bad reputation precedes them.

Rabbinic Reception

This portion of Jonah has been elaborated in a variety of rabbinic sources, allowing these composers to consider themes concerning us versus them; sin, repentance, and forgiveness; and questions concerning changes of heart by a deity who appears unpredictable, unknowable, and perhaps even impulsive.

Exodus Rabbah, which was probably compiled into its current form as late as the eleventh or twelfth century, includes a midrash on Exod 33:12, part of a biblical scene that follows the iconic incident of the golden calf, Moses's angry smashing of the first tablets of the covenant, and the punishment of the people that follows in Exodus 32. Chapter 33 suggests that the promise of the land endures but that tensions surround the disposition of God's continued in-dwelling presence in the face of Israel's tendency to rebel (Exod 33:1–4). Exodus 33 concludes with directions for a ritual renewal of Moses's special relationship with God; and, subsequently, Exodus 34 describes the creation of new tablets and a renewal of the covenant with Israel. This portion of Scripture richly explores issues of sin, forgiveness, and the possibility of maintaining divine favor in the face of human nature. It makes sense that the rabbinic composer's act of "creative historiography"—to use a phrase coined by Yizhaq Heinemann—would turn to Jonah. Exodus Rabbah 45:1, a midrash on Exod 33:12, engages with the phrase "And say did Moses to Yahweh, 'See, you are saying to me....'" The verb "to see" employed in the imperative can simply be a command to go see something, for example, when

---

32 On Jonah's sociohistorical setting as revealed by the portrayal of foreigners see Kim, "Jonah Read Intertextually," 524–25.

Jacob asks Joseph to check on his brothers (Gen 37:14), or it may be equivalent to the common biblical introductory "behold" (הנה), which calls the attention of the person addressed to the information or message that follows (Gen 27:27). In a number of instances, however, the imperative of "to see" might be translated as "see here," followed by an implicit colon. The speaker is asking the listener for confirmation or acknowledgment of a situation, as in Gen 31:50; 41:41; 2 Sam 15:3; Jer 1:10; and Qoh 7:27, 29. In Exod 33:12, Moses is saying to God, "Now, let me get this straight," or, "If I understand you correctly." The gist of this introductory language is to point out a potential problem in or contradiction between God's promises and his actions. Does divine loyalty continue to extend at least to Moses despite Israel's wrongdoing and lack of loyalty? The first biblical text drawn into conversation with Exod 33:12 is Jer 18:7–8.

The passage from Jeremiah deals with the benefits and outcome of repentance and the possibility of God's changing his mind in respect to punishment, themes entirely relevant to the biblical context. Jeremiah, however, uses terms for "nation/people" and "kingdom" that are not ethnically specific. The passage might be seen as relevant not merely to the relationship between God and Israel but also to God's relationship with non-Israelites.[33] The rabbis thus interpret that, in the blink of an eye, God can decree death for a person, but that if the person repents, God can relent and show compassion. This, together with language shared by Jeremiah 18 and Jonah 3 (discussed above), explains the next step in the exegesis. The rabbis ask, "Who are they?" and respond, "Nineveh," invoking Jonah, his mission, and the Ninevites' response.

The midrash then focuses on clothing the animals in sackcloth, moving even more universally beyond concern for human beings to interest in living beings. After quoting Jonah 3:5 concerning the animals' being dressed for mourning, the rabbis picture the people of Nineveh asking God, "The animals do not know anything and you acquit (or benefit) them; think of us also like the beast" (Exod. Rab. 45:1). The midrashist then links this train of thought to Jonah 3:5, explaining why the behavior of mourning (not eating or drinking, dressing in sackcloth) is shared by the beasts in Nineveh. In their view, imagery of mourning is meant not to identify animals with humans but to identify humans with innocent animals and thereby move God to forgiveness. Indeed, Jonah 4:11 concludes the narrative on a similar note. The rabbis suggest that the tactic works, for they conclude, citing Jonah 3:10, "Right away, 'God was regretful (relented) about the evil that he had declared to do to them and did not do it.'"

Another rabbinic text that takes special interest in the role of the animals in Jonah is found in b. Taʿan. 16a. The portion of the Mishnah expanded in the Talmud deals with ritual behavior undertaken in community fasts (m. Taʿan. 2:1). Fasts, of course, are intimately related to matters of sin and atonement. The order of the proclaimed fast is to bring the ark into the street of the town, to cover it with ashes, and to place ashes on the head of the patriarch and on that of the head of the court. Then everyone in town places ashes on his head. Next the eldest among them performs a speech of "penitence" that makes specific reference to the atonement of the people of Nineveh in Jonah. The speaker is to point out as part of the ritual that, while the people of Nineveh wore ashes and engaged in fasting, these actions did not move God to forgive them. Rather, Jonah 3:10 says that God saw their *deeds*, that they turned away from the path of evil. A similar emphasis on changing the way one acts as the true mark of repentance is found in midrashim in Qoh. Rab. 5:1 and Gen. Rab. 54:12, featuring the description of Nineveh's change of ways in Jonah 3:10. After citing Jonah's Nineveh to exemplify the emphasis on deeds and repentance, b. Taʿan. 16a explores the indication in Jonah 3:8 that humans and animals were to be covered with sackcloth.

The image of animals in sackcloth is precisely the sort of oddity that the interpreters of Scripture, modern and ancient, seek to explain. The rabbis seem to suggest that the Ninevites practiced cruelty to animals by separating the baby animals from the parents, contrary to the ethical stance that comports with ancient Jewish law, biblical and postbiblical, that animals be treated

---

33 A second midrashic excursus on Exod. Rab. 45:1 takes a different approach, identifying the penitent nation expressly with Israel.

with consideration for their well-being and attention to their rights as sentient beings. For example, the animals also rest on the Sabbath (Exod 20:10); the donkey of Balaam is given voice when his master beats him (Num 22:28); animals are not to be muzzled while treading grain (Deut 25:4); and they may partake of the sabbatical yield as do humans (Exod 23:11). An animal may not be slaughtered the same day as its young (Lev 22:28), and the hen should be shielded from seeing its eggs taken away (Deut 22:6–7). The latter two legal traditions seem to be of a piece with the concern expressed in b. Ta'an. 16a for the treatment of animals viewed as parents and offspring. The talmudic text further suggests that the people of Nineveh are employing this tactic to blackmail God, who would be moved by his tender feelings for the animals. They picture the Ninevites saying to God, if you do not have mercy upon us, we will not have mercy upon the animals.

It is uncertain whether the next comment pertains to the treatment of the animals or explores a new matter related to God's planned punishment of Nineveh. The "calling out to God with force" (again a quotation from Jonah 3:8) is interpreted to mean that the Ninevites pose to God a philosophical and theological problem underlying their situation. They say, "One is submissive/lowly and another not submissive/lowly, one is righteous, another is evil: who yields before whom?" That is, does the lowly give way to the not lowly, the evil to the righteous, or is it the other way around? Is the composer referring here to the Ninevites' effort to force the deity's hand with the cruelty to the animals? Will God, the righteous and the nonsubmissive, yield to the lowly and cruel Ninevites for the sake of the animals and show mercy to Nineveh? Or is the message unrelated to the animals, stating that God may show people mercy even if they are lowly and unrighteous. The language of "yielding" may suggest an allusion to the previous section dealing with animal cruelty. In either case, it is the righteous and the all-powerful, that is, God, whose role it is to forgive the evil and the lowly.

A third midrashic excursus in b. Ta'an. 16a expands on the phrase "and from the violence that is in their hands" (Jonah 3:8). The midrashist emphasizes the extremes to which one must go to reverse or rectify an act of violence perpetrated by one's hands. The king of Nineveh is thus pictured telling his people that, if someone has stolen a beam that is now incorporated into his castle, he needs to tear down the castle, retrieve the beam, and return it to its owner. Only then will restitution be complete and "the violence of his hands" repaired.

Like Jonah 3:5–9 and the larger narrative of Jonah, the rabbinic texts explored above, ranging in date from late antiquity to the Middle Ages, grapple with essential questions about wrongdoing, atonement, and the possibility of forgiveness. They cite Jonah to explore these concerns. The talmudic passage, like others in the midrashic corpus, focuses on the importance of deeds that exemplify true repentance, this in contradistinction to merely assuming the trappings of the penitent, ashes or sackcloth. The midrash cited from Exodus Rabbah is especially interesting in that, like Jonah, it attends to the possibility of all people repenting and of God's granting them mercy. Nineveh of Jonah is the perfect proof case. Exodus Rabbah also emphasizes the rapidity and implicitly the unpredictability the deity's change of heart, a theme that relates well to the final scenes of Jonah in chap. 4. Both passages explored above focus on the animals of Jonah 3, the way in which mercy for animals can move the deity to pity for his least predictable and perhaps most disappointing creations, humans. The connection between the suffering of animals of human beings is also a theme of Jonah 4 and relates as well to a recurring motif in an international fund of folklore.

Animal Folklore and Jonah 3:5–10

Animals, particularly domesticated animals, are often pictured in folklore genres and popular culture to have an intimate relationship with the humans around them, reflecting perhaps the reality of ecological interdependence of living beings and the love and loyalty that household or farming animals and humans often display toward one another. The wonderful interaction between the prophet Balaam and his donkey reflects this sort of attitude in a traditional-style narrative context (Num 22:27–30). The donkey, seeing that his way is blocked by the angel of the Lord, lies down, but Balaam cannot see the angel, for special visionary or auditory capacities are often attributed to animals in folklore, sensibilities denied to humans in certain contexts. Balaam, frustrated, strikes his donkey, and the latter speaks to him, another ability of the animals of folk narrative.

His words underscore the loyalty of the donkey, the long relationship that he has had with Balaam, and his reliability and service. Balaam is moved to admit in response that the donkey has indeed been a loyal companion for many years. It is an axiom of popular culture that people and their pets come to look like one another, and so the notion of having one's animals fast along with the people and dressing them in mourning is not farcical or satirical or ironic, as many have suggested. Bengali and Tamil traditions, for example, include folk narratives that express animal empathy for or identification with human beings (Motif B299.5.2 "animal fasts to express sympathy"). A fasting bird, a fasting rat king, and other animals in a chain tale about empathetic responses react to the death of a human being and thence to one another's sadness.[34] In the case of these South Asian examples, the animals take mourning upon themselves. The image of animals in empathy is shared with Jonah, and it is this universal theme with which the author concludes the narrative.

---

34 Sarat Chandra Mithra, "Note on a Tamil Tale of the Old Dame Lousy Type," *Man in India* 5 (1925) 269–72.

4

Anger, Accusation, and Departure

4:1–5

Translation

1/ And it seemed evil to Jonah, a great evil[a]
and he was burning angry.[b]
2/ And he prayed to Yahweh and he said,
"I beseech you, Yahweh,
is this not what I said[c] when I was still on my land?
For this reason I rushed ahead to flee to Tarshish,[d]
because I know that you are a gracious God[e] and compassionate,
slow to anger, and full of loving-kindness,
and regretful about sending evil.[f]
3/ So now, Yahweh,[g] take please my life from me,
because better is my death than my life."[h]
4/ [i]And say[j] did Yahweh,
"Is it good for you to be angry?"[k]
5/ And go forth did Jonah from the city,
and he sat down east[l] of the city,
and he made for himself there a hut,
and he sat under it in the shade,
until he might see what would become of the city.[m]

Textual Notes

a G treats the image of Jonah's anger with some variation. Whereas MT Mur again employ the root רעע ("bad") which this translation is rendering as "evil," G reads καὶ ἐλυπήθη ... λύπην, "Jonah was vexed with a great vexing" or was "grieved with a great grief" (so also Vγ.). OL reads, *Et contristatus est ionas tristitia magna*, "And saddened was Jonah with a great sadness." MT continues ויחר לו, "and he was burning angry," and Vg. *iratus est*, but G reads καὶ συνεχύθη, "he was confused/troubled." OL reads "He became sorrowful" (*et maestus factus est*).
b On grammatical nuances in the expression of emotion in biblical Hebrew, see *IBHS* §22.7.b; Tucker, *Jonah*, 83.
c MT דברי, literally, "my word" (sg.). In G the translation is plural οἱ λόγοι μου, "my words." The consonantal Hebrew text can be read as singular or plural; although Ḥev translates as a singular.
d Tg. reads לימא, "to the sea," rather than "to Tarshish" as in 1:2. Mur preserves a *vacat* between the finite verb and the following infinitive.
e MT Mur read אל־חנון. G omits אל.
f Tg. reads ומתיב מימריה מלאיתאה בישא, "and turning back his Memra from bringing evil." See Cathcart and Gordon, *Targum of the Minor Prophets*, 109; É. Levine, *Aramaic Version of Jonah*, 91–92. See 2:5 and 3:5.
g יהוה, "Yhwh," in MT Mur V; G has δέσποτα κύριε, "sovereign lord."
h MT Mur מחיי טוב מותי, "better is my death than my life," is rendered by infinitive verbs in G τὸ ἀποθανεῖν με ἢ ζῆν με, "better for me to die than for me to live."
i Mur *vacat* and blank line, and MT ס paragraph marker indicate a strong gap between v. 3 and v. 4.
j In 4:4 G adds the prophet's name in the address καὶ εἶπεν ... πρὸς Ἰωνᾶν.
k As in 4:1 G renders חרה, "to be angry," with a verb that includes nuances of exceeding vexation σφόδρα λελύπησαι σύ. Tg. reads הלחדא תקוף לך, literally, "Is it especially (singularly) angering (vehement, hot) to you?"
l MT Mur מקדם usually understood directionally; in Gen 3:24, "east of the Garden of Eden" is translated in G as ἀπέναντι, "opposite" or "before."
m Tg. adds בסוף, "in the end," before the final word "in the city."

Commentary

Jonah responds with anger to God's decision to forgive and spare Nineveh and attempts to debate with the deity. These first verses are dominated by the human speaker, who insists that the deity has not acted fairly or properly. This heated "conversation" touches on qualities of covenantal lawsuit and loyalty and is akin to arguments between God and Abraham, God and Moses, God and Job, and God and various prophets when the human servant of the deity disagrees with God's actions, regarding them as unfair or insuportable, a personal affront. Not satisfied with God's peculiar and perfunctory response, Jonah sets off to watch what will happen next.

■ **1** The term for "bad" (רעה) and the verb רעע from which it derives both appear in Jonah 4:1, and, as previously, terms from the root are translated as "evil." Evil comes in the form of misfortune—the storm faced by the sailors and Jonah (1:7, 8); the evildoing committed by the Ninevites (1:2), from which they turn away (3:8); the disaster that God is about to bring upon Nineveh as punishment and from which God relents (3:10; 4:2); and the punishing heat experienced by Jonah (4:6). The doubly employed root in 4:1, as verb (וירע) and noun (רעה), endows the description of Jonah's reaction to the turn of events with a special intensity.[1] The phrasing "but it seemed evil to Jonah, a great evil" conveys the depth of negative emotion experienced by the prophet. Evil is at him or comes for him like a miasma. The phrase "to be bad/evil to" is found in 2 Sam 19:8 [7]; 20:6; Neh 2:10; and Ps 106:32. In the two instances from 2 Samuel the meaning is that trouble is on its way—to David in 2 Sam 19:8 [7] and to David and his supporters in 2 Samuel 20. Both passages deal with political issues, the aftermath of the Absalom revolt and David's reaction to Absalom's death in 1 Samuel 19 and the rebellion of Sheba in 2 Samuel 20. Nehemiah 2:10 and Ps 106:32 convey much the same emotional nuance as Jonah 4:1. The psalm recalls Moses's response to the incident at the waters of Meribah in Num 20:1–13 when the ever-complaining Israelites so disturb Moses that he hits the rock rather than commanding it verbally as God had ordered, thereby leading to his own punishment. God denies him entrance into the land of Israel. The psalmist writes that it seemed evil to Moses because of them, for they had embittered his spirit and he was rash in his speech. Nehemiah 2:10 describes the negative reaction of Sanballat and Tobiah to Nehemiah's efforts on behalf of the Judeans. Literally, "it seemed a great evil to them to seek good for the children of Israel." In other words, like Moses, they are deeply perturbed by unfolding events. The phrase רעה גדולה, "a great evil," is also found in Jonah 4:1. The word for "great" or "big" is also a common repeated term in Jonah. The storm is "great" (1:4), as are the fish (2:1), the wind (1:4), the fear of the sailors (1:10, 16), Nineveh the city (1:2; 3:2, 3; 4:11), the status of some of the Ninevites in importance or age (3:5, 7), and Jonah's joy at the shade of the planting (4:6). The emphasis on bigness or greatness further contributes to the over-the-top quality of the narrative and is a piece of its recurring, delimited vocabulary, a compositional and meaning-rich device.

Jonah is described as angered by this turn of events (ויחר לו), as the author echoes the previous phrase and anticipates references to Jonah's anger in 4:4 and 4:9. As Sasson notes, this term for being angered has the quality of heated emotion and can range in meaning from annoyance to anger to distress to depression.[2] In Jonah 3:9, I have translated the noun derived from this root (חרון) and the verb employed in 4:1 with the adjective "burning." Burning anger seems to be the nuance in many other biblical texts, including Gen 4:5–6 (Cain's anger); 31:36 (Jacob's response to his father-in-law, Laban, when the latter accuses him of theft); Num 16:15 (Moses's response to the Korah rebellion); 1 Sam 20:7 (Saul's attitude toward the young David); 2 Sam 13:21 (David's response to the rape of his daughter, Tamar); and 1 Sam 18:8 (an expression of Saul's jealousy of the growing popularity of David, his rival). The final example concerning Saul employs conventionalized language similar to that of Jonah 4:1, in which the anger phrase parallels "to be evil in his eyes," employing the verb rooted in רעע. Whereas Sasson translates mildly "he was dejected," most scholars opt for the more emotional nuance of burning anger.[3]

■ **2** The verb, פלל in the *hithpael*, usually translated as "to pray," appears earlier in Jonah 2:2. In the earlier

---

1 T. A. Perry suggests an alternate translation and interpretation: "Now Jonah [became aware that he had] committed a very great sin and he was distressed with himself" ("Changing God's Mind," 45). Diana Edelman offers the nuance that "distress distressed Jonah and he became depressed" ("Jonah among the Twelve," 156).

2 Sasson, *Jonah*, 274.

3 Ibid., 270. Compare Limburg, *Jonah*, 89; Sweeney *Twelve Prophets*, 329; and see Alter, "incensed" (*Strong as Death*, 152).

reference, Jonah, who is imprisoned in the fish, throws himself upon God's mercy and asks for rescue, a prayer of lament to which the deity affirmatively responds by leading the fish to release the prophet. In 4:2, the act of praying has the basic meaning of the root פלל, connoting intervention or interceding. Jonah makes intercession on his own behalf, finally explaining why he had fled to Tarshish upon receiving God's initial command to go to Nineveh. Implicitly, he criticizes the divine commission.[4]

Jonah's address to the deity begins with the interjection אנה found also at the opening of the sailors' words to the deity as they face having to throw their passenger Jonah overboard (1:14). Translated there as "we beseech you," the term has the nuance of "ah, now." Rather than opening a petition to change the present situation, this particle of entreaty may serve as an expression of frustration, an indicator of deep anxiety when matters over which God has ultimate control do not seem subject to judicious or easy resolution. In American English, "Please!" is sometimes employed in a similar way in the midst of difficult conversations.

The phrase employed by Jonah, הלא־זה דברי עד־היותי על־אדמתי, literally, "Was not this my word when I was still on my land?" or "Is this not what I said when I was still on my land?," is found as well in Exod 14:12. In the latter example, the people Israel, about to face the Egyptians who are coming after the escaped slaves, are filled with fear and remind their leader Moses that they had always had doubts about the whole exodus enterprise, even while still in Egypt. They say literally, "Isn't this the thing/matter that we said to you in Egypt?" The term translated "thing/matter/what is said" (דבר) literally means "word." While the Israelites repeatedly and verbally had made (and will continue to make) their concerns known to Moses, Jonah has not spoken his critique or argument. All we know until this point is that he attempted to resist his commission by fleeing. The revelation concerning motivation begins to emerge in the next phrase.

In alluding to Jonah's effort to flee to Tarshish (1:3), the author employs a *piel* form of a verb קדם rooted in the noun קֶדֶם, "front, east, aforetime." The present translation, "rushed ahead to flee," attempts to take account of Jonah's doing something quickly, ahead of time. The verb expresses Jonah's urgency, the sense of his speeding away, the impulsiveness of his action. Similarly, Alter translates "I hastened"; Limburg suggests "in the first place"; Stuart, "earlier"; and Sasson, "I planned," each seeking to capture the nuance of doing something ahead of time.[5] Sasson also points to possible interplay with phrases מקדם, "to the east of," and רוח קדים, "east wind," in Jonah 4:5 and 4:8.

Jonah continues, explaining his complaint, "because I know + a version of the formulaic pronouncement of praise for God's bountiful capacity for compassion and mercy," found in longer and shorter forms in a variety of contexts throughout the biblical tradition (Exod 34:6; Num 14:18; Ps 86:15; 103:8; 145:8; Neh 9:17, 31; Joel 2:13; Nah 1:2-3).[6] The formula and its variants are built on a variety of components, terms for divine traits including compassion, mercy, slowness to anger, capacity for abounding love, and the ability to change one's mind. The pairing of חנון, "compassionate" or "gracious," with רחום, "merciful" or "compassionate," is particularly common in biblical descriptions of the deity, as seen in the formula pattern employed by the author of Jonah and the parallels listed above.[7] Limburg relates the latter term to רחם, meaning "womb," and equates this sort of

---

4   On prayer and the root פלל as "seeking a judgment for oneself," see Greenberg, *Biblical Prose Prayer*, 22. Israel Drazin makes a case for the introspective nuance of the language here and in 2:2, 8, and explores the way in which it expresses anguish in these contexts (*Unusual Bible Interpretations*, 62–63). On the relationship between prayer and juridical language and settings, see Holtz, *Praying Legally*, 63–92.

5   Alter, *Strong as Death*, 152; Limburg, *Jonah*, 89; Stuart, *Hosea–Jonah*, 498; Sasson, *Jonah*, 270.

6   For a chart that maps and compares language shared by Jonah's version of this formula and those of other biblical texts, see Sasson, *Jonah*, 280. Thomas B. Dozeman offers a comparative study of Jonah 4:2 and Joel 2:13a*b*-b with interests in inner-biblical interpretation ("Inner-Biblical Interpretation of Yahweh's Gracious and Compassionate Character," *JBL* 108 [1989] 207–23). Similarly, see Conroy, "Jonah and Nahum," 8–13.

7   Athalya Brenner suggests that the order of words in the formula as it appears in Jonah 4:2, חנון ורחום, suggests a late biblical date ("Linguistic Criteria," 396–405), but compare Elisha Qimron, "The Language of Jonah" [in Hebrew], *BetM* 81 [1980] 181–82).

merciful orientation with "motherly love."[8] Being slow to anger (ארך אפים) literally means "long of anger," or taking a long time or extreme motivation to become angry.[9] The disposition is contrasted in the wisdom tradition with having a hot or quick temper (Prov 14:29; 15:18). Some variants include references to divine strength (Nah 1:3; see another variant in Jer 32:18-19) or truth (Exod 34:6). The term חסד, here translated as "loving-kindness," often describes an intimate and caring kind of reciprocity of action, as in the description of marriage in Jer 2:2 and Hos 2:21 [19], or an honest agreement with nuances of covenant or contract, as in the servant of Abraham's exchange with Laban concerning Rebecca's proposed marriage to Isaac (Gen 24:49); the interaction between a local man and reconnaissance spies seeking to conquer Bethel (Judg 1:24); and the Israelites' promise to spare Rahab and her family in recompense for her help (Josh 2:12). The term frequently appears in the Hebrew Bible to describe the bond between God and Israel, as in Ps 106:45.

On the phrase ונחם על־הרעה, "regretful about (sending) evil," shared only with Joel 2:13 among the passages containing variants of the divine-attributes formula, see the discussion at 3:9 and 3:10.

Versions of this confessional, prayerful formula pattern employing key terms concerning mercy, patience, and kindness thus describe the way in which Israelite authors and the culture that their writings reflect reinforce deeply the desire to think of their deity, ultimately, as loving and compassionate. The implication in Jonah is that divine loving-kindness can extend to the people of Nineveh.

As discussed in the Introduction, the presence of this formula in Jonah 4:2, Joel 2:13, and in an abbreviated variation in Nah 1:3 is cited by scholars to support an argument for intertextuality, as variously defined, within the Book of the Twelve. It seems much more likely that this formulaic collection of divine traits expressed in recurring language is a traditional formula pattern that can be lengthened or shortened, in which synonymous terms can be substituted. This sort of typological speech is used in a variety of contexts in which the qualities of the deity are cited: in prophetic oracles (Joel 2:13; Nah 1:3); in prayers or liturgy (Ps 86:15; 103:8); in the rendition of Israel's history, a historiographic typology, in which the relationship between the people and God is critical (Neh 9:17, 31); in the deity's own self-description in Exod 34:6, when the deity descends on the cloud after the preparation of the second set of tablets, made necessary by events surrounding the incident of the golden calf; and in Num 14:18 after the people's apostasy, a fearful and faithless response following the report of the spies about the strength of the indigenous population of the promised land. In this last case, Moses seeks to save the people by reminding the deity of his own self-description as merciful. In all these cases, the merciful qualities of the deity are presented as positive and hopeful, and Israelites invoke them in the hopes of God's salvific intervention, despite their propensity, like all human beings, to sin. It is striking that, in Jonah, a version of this formula pattern is placed in the mouth of the prophet as a critique of the deity![10]

■ 3 The terminology ועתה, literally, "and now," as Limburg notes, often indicates that a "practical conclusion" is to be drawn from a foregoing comment.[11] Tucker observes that the temporal adverb עתה joined with the conjunction ו "functions as a discourse marker, frequently indicating a logical conclusion."[12] Jonah 4:2 leads to the conclusion in 4:3. The formulaic evocation of divine compassion and mercy, uttered by Jonah to explain why he ran away to sea and sought to avoid the mission to Nineveh (4:2), thus connects to his expressed

---

8   Limburg, *Jonah*, 91.
9   Among the texts in which the formula appears ארך אפים is the only phrase shared by all of the instances of the divine-attributes formula (including Nahum, but excluding Neh 9:31, which presumes 9:17). Its complement, רב חסד always follows, except in Nahum.
10 Focusing on the term נחם, Thorir Thordarson points to the tension between the "logic" of covenantal expectations and promises and Yahweh's capacity to forgive humans their inevitable frailties ("Notes on the Semiotic Context of the Verb *niḥam* in the Book of Jonah," *SEÅ* 54 [1989] 226-35).
11 Limburg, *Jonah*, 92.
12 Tucker, *Jonah* (2006), 89. See also H. A. Brongers, "Bemerkungen zum Gebrauch des adverbialen *weʿattāh* im Alten Testament (Ein Lexikologischer Beitrag)," *VT* 15 (1965) 289-99, here 296-97.

desire to die (4:3). Stuart points out further that this terminology introduces the "central point" in various types of biblical composition including prayers, letters, and speeches.[13] A number of these examples have the qualities of performance acts, for example, the speech in Gen 44:33, where Judah begs Joseph to allow the lad Benjamin to return to his father, and Isa 5:3 a key point in an oracle that both evokes and reverses the mood and meaning of the "song" (Isa 5:1). In this way, Jonah's expression of his desire to die significantly directs the reader to the meaning and message of what precedes, both its immediate context and the larger narrative. Divine mercy to the Ninevites motivates Jonah to want to die, but why? Questions concerning Jonah's motivation to ask to die are placed in relief by reflections on other biblical characters who express the desire to die and on the language in which this death wish is communicated. Then one may return to matters of narrative context and character development within the book itself.

Wishing to die or never to have been born is expressed by biblical or Jewish postbiblical characters whose contexts and motivations vary.[14] Evoking the content and mood of biblical laments, the blind Tobit, cut off from the world and his community, suffers the taunts of people who do not support him in his handicapped condition. Even his wife chides him (Tob 2:14). He is utterly alienated and says, "For it is better for me to die than to live" (Tob 3:6). Similarly, Job curses the day he was born (Job 3). His children have died, and he is terribly ill. His body is wracked with sores, but his "friends" visit him with pious theological remonstrances rooted in conventional assumptions about suffering and sin. Jeremiah too curses the day of his birth (Jer 20:14–18), for he suffers derision at the hands of those who do not believe his prophecies and who denigrate him. 1 Kings 19:4, like Tob 3:6, offers a partial linguistic parallel to Jonah 4:3 in the words of Elijah. "Take my life, for I am not better than my ancestors." Elijah is persecuted by the royal court. Jezebel seeks his life and he seems to be giving up. Everyone dies. He may as well join them now.

In Num 11:10–15 Moses essentially tells Yahweh that he cannot bear the burden of the people any longer. They are now demanding meat to eat during the wilderness trek, and Moses feels as if the deity has not appreciated everything he has done as leader of the people Israel, God's people.

All these figures have in common a special intimacy with the deity. Each of the characters feels deeply about his relationship with God, and so, to some degree, Tobit, Job, Jeremiah, Elijah, and Moses all feel betrayed. In a lament, Jeremiah calls God "a disappointing stream / waters that do not flow true" (Jer 15:18). Moses virtually chastises the deity, "Why have you treated your servant so badly?" (Num 11:11). Throughout the book, Job calls Yahweh to account in an innocent sufferer's self-defense. In many ways, therefore, Jonah takes his place among these other figures who feel that the deity has deserted them, mistreated them, or betrayed them. In Jonah's case, the source of grievance is not illness or taunting or lack of divine support in bearing the burden of leadership. The mercy that God has extended to Nineveh is perceived by Jonah to be a personal betrayal and an affront. That is where the language of "and now" leads, but what exactly is the nature of the betrayal?

Scholars have approached in different ways the significance of Jonah 4:2–3 for an understanding of Jonah's characterization and for the message of the work's author. Marvin Sweeney suggests that Jonah is "questioning God's character and capacity for justice."[15] Similarly Alter points out that God "enables despised Ninevites to survive."[16] Implicitly both scholars point to a theology of blessings and curses that clearly demarcates between the blessed and the cursed, the followers of covenant versus evildoers. To be sure, this theology is problematic, as the authors of Job and Qoheleth so astutely insist, but the author of Jonah may be asking through his protagonist's reaction whether covenantal assumptions about good and evil are still operative. Can any wrongdoing be forgiven? Nineveh is a metonymic symbol of Assyria, a quintessential representative of the capacity to behave in

---

13 Stuart, *Hosea–Jonah*, 503.
14 For a beautifully articulated and psychoanalytically informed comparison of "death wishes" expressed by Jonah, Elijah, Jeremiah, and Job, see Devora K. Wohlgelernter, "Death Wish in the Bible," *Tradition* 19 (1981) 131–40. See also David Daube, "Death as a Release in the Bible," *NovT* 5 (1962) 82–104.
15 Sweeney, *Twelve Prophets*, 1:329.
16 Alter, *Strong as Death*, 15.

a vicious inhumane way, and yet the inhabitants, who are not even Yahwists, need only repent and all is forgiven. Wolff points to God's "incalculable vacillation" and suggests that Jonah implicitly asks, "What is the point of his service?," if there are no clear parameters. Wolff also emphasizes what he perceives to be Jonah's self-tormenting obsession with his own ego.[17] Leslie C. Allen's response to Jonah 4:3 is rather disturbing but represents an interpretive thread that it is well to expose. Allen concludes that Jonah is "peevishly disappointed," as he "contemplates others enjoying honey from the Jewish hive. This nationalistic prophet is running odiously close to type."[18] Reminiscent of some scholarship on Esther that condemns the Jews for their supposed ethnocentrism as well as their capacity for violence,[19] this description not only offends modern sensibilities but oversimplifies Jonah.[20]

Interpretive possibilities offered thus range from Jonah's resentment of being turned into a false prophet,[21] a matter of ego; to his protectiveness of the sanctity of the covenantal pact that makes sense of the world, and without which there is a kind of moral chaos; to his overprotectiveness of the Israelites, who have suffered mightily from Assyria's cruelty and who feel unquenchable resentment for this archetypal oppressor. Jonah's response is perhaps to be understood as drenched in an ambivalent disquiet informed by all of the above. The role of the prophet is complicated and, as Jeremiah and others insist, to declare doom or call for repentance is often a seemingly thankless task. The prophet frequently does not comprehend the true divine plan. The deity is capable of placing a lying spirit in the mouths of prophets who assume they are conveying the truth, as seen in the vision of Micaiah (1 Kgs 22:22-23). He leaves his loyal servant unsure as to whether the last orders received from the deity still apply, as seen in the tale of the wandering prophet from Judah killed by a lion, when he mistakenly believes a later prophecy allowing him to accept another prophet's hospitality in the north (1 Kings 13). The covenantal theology promising blessings or curses depending on the believer's fealty is equally complicated and uncertain, for as Jeremiah and Ezekiel have implicitly to admit, the good do suffer and the bad prosper, themes elaborated in Job and Qoheleth. It is because of this uncertainty that the people quote the proverb "The parents have eaten sour grapes, and the teeth of the children twinge" (Ezek 18:2; Jer 31:29). They are seeking in this old proverbial wisdom some explanation for suffering. Sins of those long gone explain the current suffering of those who may be innocent. Both Jeremiah and Ezekiel insist, rather, that the covenantal blessings and curses are valid; humans, however, are incapable of choosing the good, and so each looks to a time when the deity will place a new heart in human beings, allowing them to always choose the right path. The prophets thereby hope to see the terrible ambivalence and uncertainty erased (cf. Ezek 18; 36:25-38; Jer 31:27-33). Implicit also in Jonah's reaction in 4:4 are questions about the possibility of forgiveness and about its possible duration, no matter how extreme the acts of wrongdoing are, and also uncertainty concerning the special relationship of God with Israel versus his role as the deity of all mankind. How much bad-doing can be forgiven, for the Assyrians are identified with inflicting acts of gross evil in the interests of their empire? Are all human beings, all groups of people, on some level alike in the eyes of God in regard to matters of forgiveness, compassion, and mercy?[22] God's next words to Jonah only reinforce the ambivalence and uncertainty concern-

---

17 Wolff, *Obadiah and Jonah*, 168.
18 Allen, *Joel, Obadiah, Jonah, and Micah*, 229.
19 See, e.g., Bernhard W. Anderson, "Esther," *IDB* 3:821-74, here 828, 830.
20 For a critique of similarly misguided orientations to Jonah, see Muldoon, *In Defense of Divine Justice*, 8-15.
21 See the discussion of Robert R. Wilson, "Jonah in the Biblical Tradition," 7-8. Rashi already seems to have recognized this implication: ואהיה שקרן בעיניהם, ". . . then I will be a liar in their eyes."
22 For observations on Jonah's possible perspectives concerning some of these complex questions about the tension between justice and mercy, see Bruckner, *Jonah, Nahum*, 121; Procksch, *Die kleinen prophetischen Schriften*, 97; see also Terence E. Fretheim, *Reading Hosea–Micah: A Literary and Theological Commentary* (Macon, GA: Smyth & Helwys, 2013) 170-75.

ing the deity's actions in the world and the stability of the moral universe itself.

■ **4** God's response to Jonah, ההיטב חרה לך, is a rhetorical question that commences with the interrogative and a *hiphil* infinitive absolute of the verb טוב, "to be pleasing, good." One might translate the phrase thus begun, "Is it right for you to be angry?"[23] Similarly, Bewer suggests "Are you justified . . . ?" and considers God's response to be a reproof, "but a gentle one."[24] Allen emphasizes God's prerogatives: "Have you any right to be angry?"[25] Chr. H. W. Brekelmans, following GKC §113k, suggests that the infinitive absolute היטב functions as an adverb in Jonah 4:4 and translates "It seems you are really angry."[26] Employing a less than likely translation of חרה in this context, meaning "dejected," Sasson suggests that Jonah is in "a melancholic state" and that "God sympathizes with Jonah's despair, perhaps even wishes to relieve his pain."[27] Combining suggestions by Brekelmans and Sasson, Bolin suggests "Are you deeply grieved?"[28] This emphasis on despair and grief does not seem to comport with the characterization of the hero in the rest of the book. He is alienated and depressed, to be sure, but that state of mind frequently manifests itself in impulsive behavior and anger, alternating with a lamenting realization that he is in God's power (Jonah 2), followed at the beginning of chap. 3 by a grudging acceptance of divine wishes. And we will soon see in Jonah 4:5-11 where his mood stands at the end of the narrative.

Better are translations that allow the opening term ההיטב its basic meaning rooted in "to be good": "Does it do good," or "Is it good/better/of benefit?" Thus, Stuart suggests, "Does it do any good for you" + "to be angry."[29] Similarly, Sweeney notes that God is not asking about whether Jonah is right to be angry but rather whether it will do him any good.[30] Capturing the deity's possible sarcasm, Alter translates, "Are you good and angry?," noting that this is "scarcely a response, only a provocation that leaves Jonah simmering."[31]

Alter perhaps best captures the nuance of the question. It is almost as if the deity asks, "Are you happy now with being angry?" Relevant are the conundrums mentioned above concerning the state of Jonah's ego and his self-respect as a prophet; a covenantal theology that promises a particular correspondence between human responsibility and the good or bad outcomes in life; and God's treatment of Nineveh in the face of his supposedly special devotion to Israel. Does Jonah's anger address, clarify, or ameliorate any of these nagging areas of concern? For Jonah, the answer seems to be in the negative, or perhaps there simply is no answer so that once again he absents himself.[32]

■ **5** In the previous verses God and Jonah have been talking past one another, posing questions that are somewhat ambiguous, rhetorical, and unanswered by either participant in the conversation. Jonah asks, "Is this not what I said?," and the deity responds with a question that seems to comment on Jonah's state of mind. Ultimately God's plans are never fully decipherable by human beings. The message that the prophet delivered in Nineveh is somewhat ambiguous, for the root הפך employed in the *niphal* ultimately hedges bets. Would Nineveh be overturned or turn over a new leaf? For his part, Jonah is portrayed as at a loss, uncertain about or unable to accept a resolution of this crisis that takes Nineveh off the hook. He leaves the city, sits under a hut, and waits.[33]

---

23 So NRSV; Wolff, *Obadiah and Jonah*; Limburg adds "so angry" (*Jonah*, 94). Yitzhak Berger draws intertextual links to Cain's anger (Gen 4:5), God's admonition to Cain (Gen 4:6-7), and Cain's exile east of Eden (Gen 4:16) (*Jonah in the Shadows of Eden*, 13).
24 Bewer, "Jonah," 57.
25 Allen, *Joel, Obadiah, Jonah, and Micah*, 230.
26 Chr. H. W. Brekelmans, "Some Translation Problems," *OtSt* 15 (1969) 170-76, here 175-76.
27 Sasson, *Jonah*, 286-87. Similarly, see Yoo-ki Kim, "The Function of היטב in Jonah 4 and Its Translation," *Bib* 90 (2009) 389-93.
28 Bolin, *Freedom beyond Forgiveness*, 152.
29 Stuart, *Hosea-Jonah*, 499 n. 4a.
30 Sweeney, *Twelve Prophets*, 1:329.
31 Alter, *Strong as Death*, 153; see also Joüon §161b.
32 In a postcolonial reading, Chesung Justin Ryu views Jonah's anger in the context of "the power differential between the Israelites and the Ninevites," indeed an act of resistance ("Silence as Resistance: A Postcolonial Reading of the Silence of Jonah in Jonah 4.1-11," *JSOT* 34 [2009] 198-218, here 198, 200, 209).
33 For comparisons with Gen 19:27-28 picturing

Jonah 4:5 is characterized by traditional adding style, a series of brief self-contained phrases in which the thought or image is complete at the end of the line although the sentence continues. Sasson describes the author's style at this point as "belabored,"[34] but this is to fail to appreciate the purposefully deliberate way in which the narrator underscores Jonah's actions and allows the reader to take in his movements from the city, mentioned three times in the verse, to a secluded area where, isolated, he builds a hut, sits in its shade, and watches. The thrice-mentioned city is where the action will take place, and Jonah has clearly absented himself in what Norbert Lohfink and others have described as a parallel to his flight at the opening of the story.[35]

The importance of the repeated city is emphasized nicely by Sasson, for the city of Nineveh is a metonym for the Assyrians who in turn represent quintessential enemies of Israel and exemplars for the biblical writers of evil, politically abusive international citizens. Key terms in this verse also include the reference to the east, where Jonah heads, and the סכה, "hut," where Jonah sits.

The term מקדם, "east of," may well suggest not only going in an easterly direction, as is frequent in the travel descriptions of the Hebrew Bible (e.g., Gen 11:2; 13:11; Judg 8:11) or being located in a certain direction (e.g., Num 34:11; Josh 7:2), but may evoke a deliberate exile, whether self-imposed or imposed by others. The first couple's exit from Eden (Gen 3:24) takes them east of the garden (with their route back definitively blocked), and the deity removes his glory from Jerusalem so that it comes to rest on a mountain east of the city. In these cases, as in Jonah 4:5, the movement east marks alienation, separation, anxiety, and uncertainty.

The סכה, "hut," that Jonah makes similarly evokes a temporary, fragile situation. As Sasson notes, the סכה is "any shelter that is temporary"[36]—hence the iconic imagery of Israel's dwelling in huts during the wilderness trek. The hut may provide temporary housing for cattle (Gen 33:17) or for soldiers (1 Kgs 20:12, 16) as noted by Limburg (see also Neh 8:15).[37] Isaiah 1:8 describes Zion's precarious position, surrounded by the Assyrian enemy, as being like a "hut in a vineyard" (see also Job 27:18). Ackerman suggests astutely that Jonah is a character in constant "search for shelter."[38]

Jonah 4:5 as a whole has raised a number of questions for commentators concerning how best to translate the verse, in particular the tense of the verbs ויצא and וישב, in the phrases translated "go forth did Jonah" and "he sat down," respectively, and how to understand the placement of the verse's content in the narrative. These two issues both center on what scholars have seen as confusion in the plot. Several ask why Jonah is said to await what will happen when the deity has made it clear that all is forgiven and the edict of doom is lifted. Jonah is angry for this very reason. In addition, scholars ask why the plant is needed to shade Jonah when he already has his hut. A thoughtful discussion of all the opinions and options is provided by Trible.[39]

Some read the verbs as pluperfects to suggest that the actions described in 4:5 had actually taken place after Jonah's delivery of the message to Nineveh, their repentance, and God's reversal. Jonah *had been watching* from afar and is unhappy with the results. Wolff's treatment is a good example of interpretative translations that move in this direction.[40] As Tucker notes, however, given the rarity of the use of a *wayyiqtol* form as a pluperfect in the Hebrew Bible, it seems much more likely that 4:5 moves the plot along rather than indicating a "flashback."[41] Others suggest that 4:5 rightly belongs between 3:4 and 3:5, an idea to which Trible is sympathetic.[42] In this way, scholars argue, the end of the matter is as yet unknown and there are two separate instances of needing shade.

Abraham looking down upon Sodom and Gomorrah, see Ackerman, "Satire and Symbolism," 241.

34 Sasson, *Jonah*, 287.
35 N. Lohfink, "Jona ging zur Stadt hinaus (Jon 4, 5)," *BZ* 5 (1961) 155–203; Magonet, *Form and Meaning*, 58.
36 Sasson, *Jonah*, 290.
37 Limburg, *Jonah*, 95.
38 Ackerman, "Satire and Symbolism," 240. For a study that focuses on the spatial dimensions of Jonah, see Nel, "Symbolism and Function," 215–24.
39 Trible, "Studies in the Book of Jonah," 92–102. See also Sasson, *Jonah*, 287–90.
40 Wolff, *Obadiah and Jonah*, 159, 163, 169.
41 Tucker, *Jonah*, 92.
42 Trible, "Studies in the Book of Jonah," 102; for a succinct overview of various scholarly suggestions, see Salters, *Jonah and Lamentations*, 34–37.

It does seem as if many of these suggestions reflect a solution looking for a problem.[43] Jonah has fled previously in this tale, trying to avoid the prophetic mission assigned him at the opening of the narrative. That he absents himself at this point is not surprising, given the characterization drawn by the author of the book. He is a man who withdraws. Is his reaction to the situation in which he finds himself so different from Elijah's response to Jezebel's persecution? Moreover, as noted above, the language of his prophecy is purposefully ambiguous, allowing for two possibilities. The reader need not be utterly convinced as to the final outcome or as to Jonah's expectations. Nor is the double reference to shade an indication of incongruity. The makeshift hut provides some shade in the heat, but the planting provided by God offers a kind of relief that brings sheer delight. That relief, however, will be only temporary, as a divinely constructed parable begins.

Overview and Folk Motif

This little section of the book provides a critical transition from the Ninevites' repentant reaction to the deity's final pronouncement about the events in which Jonah has been involved. Like Elijah's stay on the mountain in 1 Kings 19, this removal of the prophet should prepare for a major pronouncement, a message, a key to the theme of the larger series of events that precedes it.

One rather nice detail in this section evocative of folklore and appropriate to the traditional style of the Jonah narrative is the role of the hut. In an international fund of folk narrative, a variety of heroes, holy people, hermits, and philosophers are said to take themselves to or dwell in a small hut. Thompson Motif F147.2 is "hermit's hut at a border of the other world." The Russian Baba Yaga, who serves as a magically endowed helper to the hero Ivan in his journey to seek the frog princess, lives in a small hut in the woods, in a world apart. Jonah's stay in a hut captures the nuances of holy person and borderland. Jonah is a marginal figure of sorts who is at odds with his deity, uncomfortable in his mission, meant to link human beings with the message of God. He is appropriately pictured sitting in a temporary shelter, between places and events, uncertain and liminal.

---

43 See Simon's thoughtful reflection on narrative "gaps" and the "normal conventions of biblical narrative" (*Jonah*, 39).

4

Mollification, Destruction, Anger, and Stasis

4:6–11

Translation

6/ And assign did Yahweh God[a] a *qiqayon* plant[b]
and it rose up above Jonah[c]
to be shade upon his head
to save[d] him from his evil situation.[e]
And rejoice did Jonah over the *qiqayon* plant, a great rejoicing.

7/ But assign did God a worm[f] at the rising up of the dawn on the next day,[g]
and it struck the *qiqayon*,
and it dried up.[h]

8/ And it was at the rising of the sun,
and God assigned a cutting east wind,[i]
and the sun struck down on the head of Jonah,
and he grew faint[j]
and asked that his life-force just die.[k]
And he said "better is my death than my life."[l]

9/ And say did God to Jonah,
"Is it good for you to be angry about the *qiqayon*?"[m]
And he said, "It is good for me to be angry unto death."

10/ And said Yahweh, "You, you take pity on the planting,
for which you did not labor
and which you did not grow,
that over one night came to be
and over the next night was lost.

11/ But I, should I not take pity on Nineveh the great city
that has within it more than twelve myriad human beings
who cannot distinguish between their right and their left,
and many animals?

Textual Notes

a MT Mur G Vg. S Tg. have the epithet for the deity: יי אלהים. 4QXII^g has the variant יי אדוני, "my Lord Yhwh."

b G translates the difficult to identify plant קיקיון as κολοκύνθη, "a round gourd."

c MT Mur 4QXII^g read ליונה, "above Jonah." G Vg. read ὑπὲρ κεφαλῆς τοῦ Ἰωνᾶ "over the head of Jonah." S expands ויעל (MT Mur) "and it sprouted up and rose" wy° wslq.

d MT Mur להציל, "to save," is taken by 4QXII^g G Vg. Tg. to be from the Hebrew root צלל meaning "shade": σκιάζειν αὐτῷ, "to shade him."

e Vg. omits מרעתו and has *laboraverat enim*, "for he had labored."

f One manuscript of Tg. offers a marginal variant for "worm": חזל, "crawling locust." See Cathcart and Gordon, *Targum of the Minor Prophets*, 109 n. 8. S reads "Lord God" mrʾ ʾlhʾ as in 4:6.

g MT Mur read למחרת, "on the next day." 4QXII^g expands to למחרת היום possibly to be translated "on the very next day" perhaps assimilating to 1 Chr 29:21 (so BHQ).

h MT Mur וייבש, "and it dried up" (so also G Vg. Tg.), is rendered in S wqtmth, "and cut it off."

i G renders רוח קדים חרישית (MT Mur), lit., "a cutting east wind," as πνεύματι καύσωνος συγκαίοντι, "a burning wind of the summer." Tg. reads רוח קידומא שתיקתא, "a quiet east wind." S reads "a wind of sultry heat" and adds "and it dried up the gourd," lrwḥʾ dšwbʾ wʾwbšth lqrʾ (see v. 7).

j ויתעלף, translated here "and he grew faint" from the root meaning "to wrap," is rendered by G as καὶ ὠλιγοψύχησε, "he became faint," and by Vg. as *et aestuabat*, "and he became agitated"; OL translates as *et interestuabat*, "he became extremely hot."

k MT וישאל את נפשו למות, lit., "and he asked that his life-force die" (so Vg.), is rendered by G as καὶ ἀπελέγετο τὴν ψυχὴν αὐτοῦ, "and he gave up his soul," that is, rejected his life or lost heart, and by OL as *deficiebat anima eius*, "and his soul gave out." S reads literally "he asked death for his soul," that is, sought to die: wšʾl mwtʾ lnpšh.

l MT Mur טוב מותי מחיי, "better is my death than my life," is rendered in G as in 4:3. Some Greek manuscripts add μὴ κρείττων ἐγώ εἰμι ὑπὲρ τοὺς πατέρας μου, "I am no better than my fathers"; cf. 1 Kgs 19:4. S reads mṭʿ bʾydyk mryʾ lmhb npšy mny mṭl dlʾ hwyt ṭb ʾnʾ mn ʾbhy, "It is (lit., comes/reaches) in your hands, Lord, to take my life from me, for I have been no better than my fathers."

m MT Mur ההיטב חרה, "is it good for you to be angry?," in G is rendered as Εἰ σφόδρα λελύπησαι, "are you exceedingly vexed/grieved?," employing a word choice found in 4:1, 4. See comment on Tg. 4:4.

Commentary

The finale of Jonah revolves around a shade plant, a *qiqayon*, that lives for only a day. The withering of the plant leads to a curious and oblique conversation between God and Jonah concerning anger, compassion, a death wish, and survival. Implicitly, the discourse involves deep questions about human nature, divine prerogatives, and the relatedness of living beings.

■ **6** The texture of this verse is characteristic of Jonah's traditional-style Israelite narrative literature with its delimited vocabulary, its adding style, and its sound-play. The opening verb of 4:6, מנה, in the *piel* meaning "assign" or "appoint" applied to the planting, is also employed in regard to the deity's assignment of the fish in 2:1; in 4:7, in relation to the worm that will destroy the *qiqayon*; and in 4:8 in relation to the punishing, hot wind. An important thread in Jonah emphasizes the deity's power over and sympathy for nature's living things, the fish, the sea, the planting, the wind, the animals, and human beings. This theme concludes the final section of Jonah, pointing to its underlying message and thoughtful ambiguities, its purposeful challenges to features of the conventional theological outlook expressed elsewhere in the biblical tradition.

Some scholars have suggested that the epithet for the deity found in 4:6, יהוה אלהים, marks some sort of redactional activity, sources, or additions. More likely, the epithet reflects more typical variation,[1] although Wolff suggests that the narrator may be using the epithet to pull together the work in which the deity is generally called יהוה or אלהים.[2]

Various suggestions have been offered regarding the genus of the plant, called קיקיון and mentioned only in Jonah. One candidate is the castor oil plant (*Ricinus communis*), a quick-growing, leafy planting, common in North Africa and the Middle East.[3] Another is the bottle gourd (*Cucurbita*), pictured shading Jonah in some of the visual representations of late antiquity such as the late third-century sarcophagus portraying Jonah in the Endymion pose, discussed above.[4] As Nogalski notes, the important point is that the planting is a leafy one, capable of providing shade.[5] Given the uncertainty of these identifications, the present translation retains the Hebrew term in transliteration, as do Alter and Sasson.[6]

The terminology of saving and shade create alliteration: *lĕhaṣṣîl lô* (להציל לו), "to save him," and *ṣēl* (צל), "shade."

As noted above, a thread in scholarship expresses concern about the reference to shade in this verse and in 4:5. Why is the planting necessary for shade if Jonah has the hut? Wolff, Stuart, Sasson, and Alter point to the inadequacy of the flimsy booth fully to shade the prophet.[7] Wolff also writes that perhaps the two references reflect a conflation of different traditions.[8] More important to emphasize is Jonah's rapturous joy at experiencing relief from the unrelenting heat. Language of greatness or largesse, employing the adjective from the root גדל, that is so common in Jonah here describes Jonah's great joy at experiencing relief from the beating sun. Some commentators point to Jonah's extreme reversals in mood as indicating a kind of pathology.[9] The mood swings are essential to the structure of the

---

1 See the discussion by F. D. Kidner, "The Distribution of Divine Names in Jonah," *TynBul* 21 (1970) 126–28.
2 Wolff, *Obadiah and Jonah*, 164–65. See also Sasson, *Jonah*, 291, and the thoughtful discussion by Trible, "Studies in the Book of Jonah," 82–87.
3 E.g., Wolff, *Obadiah and Jonah*, 170–71. See also the brief discussion of a possible etymology by Karl Ahrens, "Was ist *qiqājōn* Jona 4, 6.7?," *ZS* 4 (1926) 256. Muldoon, *In Defense of Divine Justice*, 135 n. 56.
4 See notes 127 and 128 to Jonah 2:1-11 above and the surrounding discussion of Jonah in mosaics and other art forms.
5 Nogalski, *Book of the Twelve*, 448. Muldoon regards the imagery here as connected to other biblical and prophetic instances in which plants symbolize the growth and downfall of civilizations (*In Defense of Divine Justice*, 134–43).
6 Alter, *Strong as Death*, 153; Sasson, *Jonah*, 292. See also Limburg, *Jonah*, 95, who translates simply "plant." For a full discussion of ancient and modern translation choices, see B. P. Robinson, "Jonah's Qiqayon Plant," *ZAW* 97 (1985) 390–403. Strawn suggests that קיקיון is an invented term that plays on the root for "to vomit" (קיא) and Jonah's name (יונה) ("On Vomiting," 455–56).
7 Wolff, *Obadiah and Jonah*, 171; Stuart, *Hosea–Jonah*, 504; Sasson, *Jonah*, 291; Alter, *Strong as Death*, 153.
8 Wolff, *Obadiah and Jonah*, 171.
9 See, e.g., Limburg, *Jonah*, 95; and Sweeney, *Twelve Prophets*, 1:330.

narrative. Repeatedly Jonah moves from a negative situation akin to death to relief or rebirth: from the deep sleep in the recesses of the ship to awakening; from the watery burial to emergence from the fish onto dry land; from the excruciating heat to the welcome shade of the planting. Repeatedly he asks for death only to be denied death and, in some cases, to reach a degree of resignation: he asks the sailors to take his life but then prays for salvation in the fish, is restored, and undertakes his mission; he asks God for death after the repentance of the Ninevites and then goes off to see what might happen next. His last request for death (4:9) is followed by greater ambiguity, as we will see.

Jonah's characterization, however, is rather consistent throughout the narrative. He is self-absorbed, even narcissistic. His efforts on behalf of the deity are grudging at best. And he is rigid. He cannot accept that life is complicated and unpredictable, including God's will. Jonah longs for simple answers and results. Consequently, he does take great pleasure in the shade at that moment and with the same passion resents its disappearance in the following verse. God's staged scene in 4:6–8 is a sign act, a dramatic parable,[10] and its message is that Jonah somehow has it all wrong. The קיקיון is said to save Jonah מרעתו, here translated "from his evil situation." What is meant is calamity or misfortune, a bad situation, but Sweeney suggests that the word for "bad" or "evil," again a frequently deployed term in Jonah, is meant to be a pun. The experienced evil is the bitter heat, but Jonah himself is guilty of wrong or, as Sweeney writes, "what Jonah is doing is not necessarily the right thing to do, at least from YHWH's or the narrator's perspective!"[11]

■ **7–8** God's demonstration continues with the repeated use of the verb מנה. Now with Jonah momentarily at his ease, physically shaded by the tree,[12] the deity creates a reversal, appointing a worm to destroy this source of cooling relief from the beating sun. At the appearance of dawn on the next day, the worm strikes the planting so that it dies, and when the sun rises, the deity appoints a brutal east wind so that the beating sun strikes Jonah's head. In a fainting condition, Jonah again asks to die. As the deity directs the fish and the ocean, he once again employs forces of nature, cosmic and minute, to control the action, Jonah, and the message.[13]

The "worm" (תולעת), possibly related to a root תלע, meaning "to gnaw"—hence מתלעת meaning "teeth," in Late Biblical Hebrew—is a pest that devours the fruit of the vine in Deut 28:39, one of the many curses to expect for faithlessness to the covenant with God. The "worm" is also pictured consuming the bodies of the dead in Isa 14:11 and 66:24. The term is thus sometimes translated "maggot" and is used in poetic parallelism with רמה ("worm") in Isa 14:11 to describe the disposition of corpses. The dead king lies on a bed of maggots, covered by worms, an unenviable but inevitable final sleep. The תולעת of some species is also associated with a crimson dye derived from its body. This color, scarlet or crimson, is mentioned in numerous priestly descriptions of materials to be employed in the tabernacle and its cult (e.g., Lev 14:4, 6; Num 4:8; 19:6). A third connotation is to smallness or insignificance, as in Job 25:6, in which human beings are compared to worms, and Ps 22:7 [6], in which the speaker of a lament thus describes himself, mocked and despised by his tormentors. In Isa 41:14, the deity addresses Israel as "you worm Jacob," perhaps an epithet of endearment, an indication that, although his people may be powerless, the deity will protect and empower them. The first and third connotations are in play here. The worm does destroy the planting, which is described as drying up or withering, but it also serves to emphasize how God can employ the most modest of creatures to do his bidding, in this case, to enact a parable meant to instruct the prophet.[14]

---

10 Gunn and Fewell suggest that the message of the parable is profoundly ambivalent (*Narrative in the Hebrew Bible*, 143).

11 Sweeney, *Twelve Prophets*, 1:330.

12 Within the Book of the Twelve, one thinks of the famous statement of Mic 4:4: וישבו איש תחת גפנו ותחת תאנתו ואין מחריד, "they will dwell, each one, beneath his own vine and beneath his own fig, with none to bring terror."

13 See Sweeney, *Twelve Prophets*, 1:330–31; Alter, *Strong as Death*, 153. Drawing parallels between Jonah and Joel, Moshe Pelli juxtaposes the imagery of the devouring worm with that of the locust ("Literary Art of Jonah," 23–24).

14 For one view of the instructional purpose of the dialogue, see Tzvi Abusch, "Jonah and God: Plants, Beasts, and Humans in the Book of Jonah (An Essay in Interpretation)," *JANER* 13 (2013) 146–52,

The worm appears at dawn on the next day. Sasson suggests that the author implies encountering trouble at awakening in a parallel to 1:5–6.[15] The arrival of dawn marks a transition, a key passage point in time and narrative events. In sound the term for dawn evokes the root meaning black, and thus suggests a time just before things are truly or fully visible, a time of murkiness, when Ruth is able discreetly to depart from Boaz's threshing floor (Ruth 3:14) and when the demonic figure, a manifestation of the deity who had wrestled with Jacob at the River Jabbok, must take his leave (Gen 32:25 [24]).

The verb translated "strike" or "attack" or "kill," from the root נכה in the *hiphil*, is often used in biblical military or other agonistic contexts (e.g., Exod 2:11, 13; 21:26; Deut 13:16; 20:13; Judg 1:8; 1 Kgs 22:34). Here the worm attacks the planting, making Jonah's life miserable in the heat; the sun will strike Jonah's head directly in v. 8, so that he wilts like the planting that had protected him. Wolff draws comparisons with Ps 121:6 and Isa 49:10, in which the punishing sun is also the subject of the verb, and suggests that the authors describe the effects of sunstroke.[16]

The author's love of wordplay and sound-play emerges in the various ע, ל, ת, and ח, ר letter combinations found in words in 4:6–9.[17]

■ **8** The precise meaning of חרישית, here translated as "cutting," is not certain, and the term is used only in Jonah. Its root appears to be חרש, "to cut in, engrave, plough," rather than the root חרש associated with silence. The east wind might be associated in the author's mind with the *scirocco*, the scorching eastern wind alluded to in the Hebrew Bible (e.g., Gen 41:6, 23, 27; Jer 18:17; Ezek 17:10). As noted by Almbladh, the reference to debilitating eastern winds makes less sense in a Mesopotamian setting, where the eastern winds are not malevolent, but one doubts that the author aims for accuracy in the local color of climate.[18] Trible discusses the difficulties in detail, sympathetic to leaving this adjective modifying east wind untranslated, as many scholars do with קיקיון (4:6).[19] The reader is probably meant to imagine a wind capable of cutting or ploughing right through a person.[20] The east wind frequently marks divine power that has a negative ecological impact. The east wind conveys the locust plague to Egypt in Exod 10:13; it destroys the transplanted vine in the parable of Ezek 17:10 (see also 19:12); and it riles the sea and wrecks ships of Tarshish in Ezek 27:26. Once again, nature does divine bidding.

The term קדם offers another example of the author's predilection for repeated roots and terminology (see 4:2, 5).

Creatively, the medieval Jewish exegete Mahari Kara suggests that the wind carries away Jonah's fragile, protective hut![21]

The verb ויתעלף, translated as "he grew faint," is related to words that mean "to cover" or "enwrap." So Tamar wraps herself in veiled disguise. Here and in Amos 8:13, where swooning or fainting seem implicit, it is as if one's life wraps around oneself or one feels the world closing in, a smothering sensation.

The term נפש, sometimes translated as "soul," refers to the living force within a person, that which animates a person. Tucker notes that nouns referring to aspects of the body such as נפש and לבב, "heart," when employed with the pronominal suffix may express a reflexive relationship, for example, "myself," "himself."[22] Jonah here asks that the life be taken away from him. Echoing 4:3 and evoking Elijah and other biblical figures who request death at God's hands, Jonah again states that he prefers death to life (see the discussion above at 4:3). The grueling unremitting heat of the day is the last straw. Jonah feels abandoned and sees no point in continuing

---

here 148. Walton describes the events surrounding the plant as an "object lesson" that ultimately expresses the message "deliverance belongs to the Lord" ("Object Lesson," 50–52).

15 Sasson, *Jonah*, 301.
16 Wolff, *Obadiah and Jonah*, 172.
17 See further Sasson, *Jonah*, 301.
18 See the discussion in Almbladh, *Studies in the Book of Jonah*, 39–40.
19 Trible, "Studies in the Book of Jonah," 53–55.
20 See also Alter, *Strong as Death*, 154. Sasson notes that the word *ḥărîšît* (חרישית) occurs only in Jonah, and he translates it as "fierce" (*Jonah*, 302–4).
21 See Meir Zlotowitz, and Nosson Scherman, *Sefer Yonah/Jonah: A New Translation with a Commentary Anthologized from Talmudic, Midrashic and Rabbinic Sources* (Brooklyn, NY: Mesorah Publications, 1978) 138–39.
22 Tucker, *Jonah* (2006), 99.

with life. As with Job, the physicality of the protagonist's experience is emphasized; emotional disease is interwoven with concretely described aspects of embodiment.[23] The deity addresses Jonah's situation, but Yahweh and the prophet are talking past one another. Neither comprehends or allows for the other's position.

The language טוב מותי מחיי, "better is my death than my life," echoes that of 4:3. A parallel is thus established between Jonah's reaction to the repentance of the Ninevites followed by the deity's apparent acceptance of their self-abasing demonstration and his reaction to the withering of the shade-providing planting. Almbladh suggests that the juxtaposition of a reference to Jonah's purported care for the plant with God's concern for the people of Nineveh in 4:11, 12 evokes the sort of *qal vahomer* (*a minore ad maius*) line of argumentation found in rabbinic exegesis.[24] Emphasis is created by comparing the less important to the more significant. The same might be said of the repetition of language in 4:3 and 4:9. At the very least, Jonah is just as upset about the life and death of the planting as he is about the life of human beings. He is upset, however, not that the Ninevites are destroyed but that they are spared!

■ **9** Echoing Jonah 4:4, God asks Jonah if it is good for him to be angry about the קיקיון, that is, about its death (see the full discussion of this phrase and its language at 4:4). We discussed above the ironic or sarcastic nuance that may be intended, and this time Jonah answers the deity in a similar tone, stating that it is good for him to be angry unto death; he is so perturbed that he wants to die. S. D. Goitein thoughtfully compares Jonah's "discontent with his prophetic office" and the resulting interaction with God to that of Baruch, the disciple of Jeremiah (Jeremiah 45).[25] Alter notes that the phrase added to the deity's question, "unto death" or "to the point of death," evidences incremental repetition.[26]

■ **10-11** Almbladh, Sasson, and others have nicely laid out the antithetic parallelism of these verses.[27] The pronouns are provided as self-standing words—אתה, "you," and אני, "I"—rather than merely being a prefixed or suffixed part of the conjugated verb, as is much more typical. The personhood of each figure is thereby emphasized–you and I. Each parallel clause employs a verb from the root חוס, "to pity" (discussed below), and each clause uses a descriptive subordinate phrase introduced by the relative pronoun אשר. Finally, the descriptions of the plant and the people may be a clue to what the author wishes to emphasize at the conclusion concerning the planting, the Ninevites, and Jonah and God's relationship to them. Before examining some of the details of texture, text, and message, it is important also to mention Sasson's astute observation that Jonah's lengthy monologue at 4:2-3 is equaled in length by God's monologue in vv. 10-11 in comparison to the brief lines of exchange in between.[28] These two speech acts, like the parallelism within the deity's monologue, should lead to message and meaning.

The root חוס can connote caring about something, for example, Joseph's brothers caring about their possessions left behind (Gen 45:20). More commonly, however, the verb means "to pity" or "to have compassion upon" or "to spare." Nehemiah asks that God remember his well-meaning actions on behalf of keeping the Sabbath and have compassion on him (Neh 13:22). In Joel 2:17, the priests are pictured as begging the deity, "Pity (or "spare") your people," who are dealing with an ecological disaster. The deity's resolve to punish is expressed with this verb and the negative particle, "will not spare," as in Jer 13:14 and Ezek 24:14 (see also Jer 21:7). Simon notes that the verb can have the nuance of "avoiding destruction because of appreciation and esteem," as in Gen 45:20, where Pharaoh essentially tells the brothers

---

23 See also Simon, *Jonah*, 41. Johan H. Coetzee notes that Jonah is rich in metaphors for bodily containment (in the ship, in the fish), and he sees such "bodily based metaphors" as critical to the messages of the book ("Where Humans and Animals Meet, Folly Can Be Sweet: Jonah's Bodily Experience of Containment the Major Drive Behind His Conduct," *OTE* 20 [2007] 320-32).

24 For another discussion of the *qal vahomer* argument as it relates to an understanding of the end of Jonah, see Rob Barrett, "Meaning More than They Say: The Conflict between Yhwh and Jonah," *JSOT* 37 (2012) 237-57, here 252-53.

25 S. D. Goitein, "Some Observations on Jonah," *JPOS* 17 (1937) 63-77, here 70-71.

26 Alter, *Strong as Death*, 154.

27 Almbladh, *Studies in the Book of Jonah*, 39; Sasson, *Jonah*, 308; Simon, *Jonah*, 45.

28 Sasson, *Jonah*, 317.

not to let devotion to what they are leaving behind in their homeland interfere with a wise decision to move to Egypt.[29] In this way, the deity may be accusing Jonah of overrating the planting even while he underrates the lives of the people of Nineveh.

Jonah did not labor or grow the plant. The root for grow, גדל, one of the frequently employed words in the book, is also found in v. 11 in reference to Nineveh, the great city.[30]

The fragility of the planting is emphasized in the imagery of existing and perishing between one night and another, and, as Sasson notes, this perhaps points more widely to the fragility and fleeting nature of life on earth (cf. Pss 90:5–6; 144:3–4; Isa 40:6–8).[31] As scholars note, the construction שֶׁבִּן לילה . . . ובן לילה is unusual and difficult to translate literally.[32] As GKC suggests, the literal construct meaning ("son of a night") may be "used poetically of things without life."[33] Thus, in Jonah the phrase seems to mean "grown in a night." The idiom captures the ephemeral nature of the plant.[34] Thus, Alter translates "which overnight came and overnight was gone."[35] Sasson offers "that came up one night and perished the next."[36] Common contemporary idioms in English that are comparable in nuance might be "here today, gone tomorrow" or "now you see it, now you don't," or "easy come, easy go."

Jonah 4:11 is a rhetorical question that has the deity ask, should he not take pity on Nineveh.[37] Part of the

---

29 Simon, *Jonah*, 44. For a reflection on חוס and חסד, see Thayer S. Warshaw, "The Book of Jonah," in Kenneth R. R. Gros Louis, ed., with James S. Ackerman and Thayer S. Warshaw, *Literary Interpretations of Biblical Narratives* (Bible in Literature Courses; Nashville: Abingdon, 1974) 191–207, here 193–98; see also Terence E. Fretheim, who relates the term to the right of the divine sovereign and the relationship between a "superior" and a "subordinate" ("Jonah and Theodicy," *ZAW* 90 [1978] 227–37, here 236–37). G. M. Butterworth suggests the translation "You are sorry to lose the plant, and should I not be sorry to lose Nineveh . . . ?" ("You Pity the Plant: A Misunderstanding," *IJT* 27 [1978] 32–34, here 32). *HALOT*, s.v. "חוס": "to be troubled about." See also the discussion of possibilities in Bolin, *Freedom beyond Forgiveness*, 160–62; and S. Wagner, "חוס," *TDOT* 4:271–77, here 271–72. Drawing comparisons with biblical portrayals of Jeremiah, Baruch, and Job, Sheldon H. Blank approaches this interchange between Jonah and God as revealing of the latter's capacity for grief or distress, related in turn to "the personhood of God" ("'Doest Thou Well to Be Angry?' A Study in Self-Pity," *HUCA* 26 [1955] 29–41, here 41). With a close analysis of key language in Jonah, Irmtraud Fischer reflects on the complex nature and significance of representations of divine mercy in Jonah ("'. . . und mir sollte nicht leid sein . . . ?' Über die Facetten von Gottes Mitleid im Jonabuch," *JBTh* 30 [2015] 89–107).
30 On the use of the word connected with growing plants, see Sasson, *Jonah*, 310; Muldoon, *In Defense of Divine Justice*, 143.
31 Sasson, *Jonah*, 318.
32 See the discussion by Simon, *Jonah*, 301.
33 GKC §128v.
34 See a similar emphasis in the felicitous reflection on French translations of Jonah by B. F. Price, E. A. Nida, and R. Péter-Contesse (*Le livre de Jonas: Un commentaire exégétique et linguistique* [Villiers-le-Bel: Alliance Biblique Universelle, 1997] 98).
35 Alter, *Strong as Death*, 154.
36 Sasson, *Jonah*, 301; see also Stuart, *Hosea–Jonah*, 499.
37 On the role of this question at the conclusion of Jonah and the importance of questions in the larger book, see Struppe, *Die Bücher Obadja, Jonah*, 144. T. Francis Glasson draws the reader's attention to Nah 3:19, a different rhetorical question concerning Assyria that ends the work, suggesting a basis for comparison and contrast between Nahum and Jonah ("The Final Question in Jonah and Nahum," *ExpTim* 81 [1969] 54–55). Like Alan Cooper ("In Praise of Divine Caprice," 144–63), Philippe Guillaume does not read the final words of Jonah as rhetorical but takes them "at face value": "You had pity over the plant . . . but I will not pity Nineveh" ("The End of Jonah Is the Beginning of Wisdom," *Bib* 87 [2006] 243–50, here 250); also his "Rhetorical Reading Redundant: A Response to Ehud ben Zvi," *JHebS* 9 (2009) 1–9. See also Muldoon, *In Defense of Divine Justice*, 140–41. Ehud Ben Zvi argues that there is no linguistic reason to deny that the syntax of the final words of Jonah can be read rhetorically. On the other hand, he suggests that Persian-period receivers of the text would recognize the rhetorical potential of the words while taking account of the actual, historical destruction of Nineveh, so that ultimately the final words of Jonah leave these readers with purposeful ambiguity and the potential to consider a double meaning ("Jonah 4:11 and the Meaning of the

reason for care is the fact that so many human beings live in this metropolis,[38] but the final two lines, as I have laid out the text, describe the Ninevites as intellectually immature, ignorant. The inability to distinguish right from left might be compared to idiomatic descriptions of children who do not know the difference between right and wrong, as in Deut 1:39 and Isa 7:15–16.[39] On the one hand, such a description of the Assyrians seems condescending and judgmental, especially in the light of the final phrase of the narrative, which might be taken to equate their worth to that of animals who are also receivers of divine mercy.[40] On the other hand, ultimately the tale ends with a message of divine care for all living beings, a sweeping and universal inclusion in God's big tent.[41]

The concern for the animals of Nineveh marks the final phrase of the narrative. This phrase has often been seen as comic, translated by the Jerusalem Bible as "to say nothing about the animals!" As discussed at 3:7–8 above, the end of Jonah 4:11 can also be seen as one of many biblical passages in which the fate of animals is bound up with that of humans. War and peace, divinely sent destruction and salvation, are experienced by both (see, e.g., Jer 12:4; Hos 2:20 [18]; 4:3; Hab 3:17). In addition, in various passages, the deity is said explicitly to care for animal life (Ps 104:14).[42] Jonah 4:11 understandably finds its place in contemporary discussions of ecology and the Bible, as it can be read as a scriptural affirmation of God's care for a panoply of the earth's inhabitants.[43]

What to make of this finale about the planting and the people and animals of Nineveh as it relates to Jonah as a whole and the messages and meanings the work conveys?

Metaprophetic Character of the Book of Jonah," *JHebS* 9 (2009) 1–13). See also Étan Levine, "Justice in Judaism: The Case of Jonah," *RRJ* 5 (2002) 170–97, here 181. A linguistic analysis of the rhetorical question in Biblical Hebrew, a limited corpus, leads Guillaume to conclude that Jonah 4:11 is not a rhetorical question at all but rather a straightforward statement predicting doom for Nineveh ("Caution: Rhetorical Questions!," *BN* 103 [2000] 11–17).

38 Sasson reads the phrase about not distinguishing between their right and their left as referring to the population density of Nineveh where people do not know their neighbors (*Jonah*, 315).

39 Carl Friedrich Keil suggests that the phrase does indeed refer to the innocent children of Nineveh (C. F. Keil and F. Delitzsch, *The Twelve Minor Prophets* [trans. James Martin; BCOT 1; Edinburgh: T&T Clark, 1837] 1:416–17).

40 See Sweeney, *Twelve Prophets*, 1:332; Lanchester, *Obadiah and Jonah*, 71.

41 Offering a unique interpretation of Jonah 4:11 that links the mention of the animals to sacrifice, Thomas M. Bolin suggests that the animals are to be understood as sacrificial, an indication of the Ninevites' submission to God ("Jonah 4, 11 and the Problem of Exegetical Anachronism," *SJOT* 24 [2010] 99–109).

42 Philip Peter Jenson suggests that concern for the animals might be viewed as a wisdom component of the work (*Obadiah, Jonah, Micah*, 38–39).

43 Drawing comparisons between Jonah and biblical psalms, Tova Forti points to the way in which the author employs animal motifs to develop the theme of God's universal providence ("Of Ships and Seas, Fish and Beasts: Viewing the Concept of Universal Providence in the Book of Jonah through the Prism of Psalms," *JSOT* 35 (2011) 359–74. See also Shemesh, "'And Many Beasts,'" 2–26. For a different take on the animals' motif, see Frank Moore Cross, "A Homily on the Book of Jonah," in Kathryn F. Kravitz and Diane M. Sharon, eds., *Bringing the Hidden to Light: The Process of Interpretation; Studies in Honor of Stephen A. Geller* (Winona Lake, IN: Eisenbrauns, 2007) 45–49, here 49. Thomas M. Bolin suggests that the mention of numerous animals might relate to divine expectations that the Ninevites, like the sailors, will offer sacrifices in thanks for their being spared ("Eternal Delight and Deliciousness: The Book of Jonah after Ten Years," *JHebS* 9 (2009) 1–11). For a scholarly debate concerning the relevance of Jonah 4:6–11 to an ecological interpretation, see Schalk Willem van Heerden, "Shades of Green—or Grey? Towards an Ecological Interpretation of Jonah 4:6–11," *OTE* 30 (2017) 459–77. For an ecological reading of Jonah, see Alexander Izuchukwu Abasili, "The Role of Non-Human Creatures in the Book of Jonah: The Implications for Eco-Justice," *SJOT* 31 (2017) 236–53. See also Strawn "On Vomiting," 457; and Trible, "Book of Jonah" 482–83.

Overview of 4:6–11: Message and Meaning in the Narrative of Jonah

Wolff suggests that the final encounter in Jonah presents a practical joke. Jonah thinks he has found a little physical relief only for it to be swept away in a divinely authored trick. Wolff is certainly correct to take note of Jonah's "comic side,"[44] but the genre of the encounter seems more like a parable or sign act than a joke. The deity creates a scenario that has implications for the person with whom it is shared, who is indeed made to be a part of the performance. If this is so, what is the message? How do the situation of the inhabitants of Nineveh and their interactions with God relate to the planting, Jonah's response to it, and God's actions? How does this scene comment on God's relationship with Jonah and both characters' relationship to the inhabitants of Nineveh?

One thread in scholarship, discussed in the Introduction, places this final scene in the context of the tension between nationalist and more universal threads in Israelite thought and literature. God's concern for the inhabitants of Nineveh, emphasized in the last few lines, places this scene and the larger narrative in the company of works such as Ruth, whose author is sympathetic to the Moabite widow, and apart from Ezra, whose priestly scribe hero is portrayed as sending away non-Judean wives and children, excluding them from Israel. Jonah cannot empathize with the Ninevites. At its worst, views of this orientation in Jonah intermingle with a crass and simplistic anti-Judaism, for example, the views of contributor to the early twentieth-century *International Critical Commentary*, Julius A. Bewer. He writes with quite a bit of animus about the "narrow, blind, prejudiced, fanatic Jews of which Jonah is but the type."[45]

A more literarily sensitive approach to this final scene asks whether Jonah is best understood as caring at all for the planting, placing concern for it above the people of Nineveh, as the deity seems to claim.[46] Alter captures the nuances of the prophet's character as drawn throughout the tale when he suggests, "Jonah does not pity the plant for withering; rather he is furious that it has been stripped of its vitally necessary shade."[47]

Ultimately, God reveals that he does not understand (or purposefully misrepresents) Jonah when he accuses him of caring more for a planting than mammals, human and animal. One might include as relevant here the deity's unsuccessful initial effort to find the first human a helpmate in Genesis 2. Does the author of the creation account imply that to God all living beings belong to the same category, one utterly different from the world of divinity? To God, is there much less difference between a human being and a cat than between mortal beings and divine? As Isa 40:22 asserts, for the being who sits above the circle of the earth, all mortal inhabitants are like grasshoppers. From Jonah's perspective, God is a deeply frustrating, inscrutable taskmaster. As Sweeney notes, God "merely demonstrates (his) capriciousness" in destroying the planting; "Yhwh is simply unreliable."[48] The deity is unknowable, his ways beyond human ken. He makes the rules but the rules are not always decipherable, fair, or applied consistently. The message of God's parable is a benevolent one, namely, that all living things matter and are valuable; and this ecological care includes plants, animals, and human beings, regardless of whether they are under the canopy of the covenant. The parable has universalistic implications, and care for life is at the center of God's orientation as ruler of the universe, which leads Craig

---

44 Wolff, *Obadiah and Jonah*, 177.

45 Bewer, "Jonah," 64; similarly Wade, *Books of the Prophets*, lxxx; Smart "Book of Jonah," 873. For a nineteenth-century version of this assessment, see C. F. Keil, who writes of a "pharisaical reliance upon an outward connection with the chosen nation" (*Twelve Minor Prophets*, 380); for a critique of such approaches, see van Wijk-Bos, "No Small Thing," 219; also Tigay, "Days of Awe," 70; and Achtemeier, *Minor Prophets 1*, 258.

46 See the argument concerning care for the planting by Abusch, "Jonah and God," 150-51.

47 Alter, *Strong as Death*, 154; see also Good, *Irony in the Old Testament*, 53; Bickerman, "Les deux erreurs," 238; Nogalski, *Book of the Twelve*, 450; James E. Sargent, *Hosea, Joel, Amos, Obadiah, and Jonah* (Basic Bible Commentary; Nashville: Abingdon, 1988) 151.

48 Sweeney, *Twelve Prophets*, 1:331. See also Cooper, "In Praise of Divine Caprice," 144–63; Bolin, *Freedom beyond Forgiveness*, 96, 177; and Daniel J. Simundson, *Hosea, Joel, Amos, Obadiah, Jonah, Micah* (AOTC; Nashville: Abingdon, 2005) 284–85.

to suggest that Jonah is ultimately about "the mystery of divine compassion."[49] Yet a deeper message intended by the author of Jonah, if not by God as presented in character, is that Jonah as human and Yahweh as deity are on completely different planes, which makes the role of prophet, God's human emissary, so difficult. God's utter autonomy and unpredictability make the deity, in Jonah's view, impossible to work for, frustrating to death. Jonah does not understand God and God does not understand him.[50] God's understanding of why Jonah initially sought to avoid the divine charge and is angered by God's forgiveness of the Ninevites is that the prophet lacks empathy. Such is the message of the plant parable. Jonah, however, cannot deal with God's capacity to change his mind. Jonah as prophet feels that he has been made to play the fool and that his mission has been a waste of time, as he had initially feared. Jonah, a mere human being, wants clear boundaries, definite consequences.[51] There the tale ends.

Jonah's lack of response to Yahweh after 4:11 is significant.[52] Taking stock of the silence at the end of the narrative, Abusch suggests that "the lack of an answer on the part of Jonah is meant to give the audience space to decide how Jonah might have responded to God's challenge and to provide its own answer to the central question of the book."[53] Simon finds that Jonah's silence is comparable to Job's response to God's monologue from the whirlwind, which Simon translates as, "I recant and I relent" (Job 42:6). Simon writes about the portrayal of Jonah, "He adopts the mute language of which the Psalmist wrote, To you silence is praise (Ps 65:2)."[54] While the comparison to Job is valid, and I would add

---

49   Craig, *Poetics of Jonah*, 180. Reflecting on the reading of Jonah in the liturgy for the Day of Atonement, Baruch A. Levine suggests that "the lesson of the gourd" has to do with "conversion to a belief in repentance" and human beings' capacity for "inner development" ("Place of Jonah," 210–11). For a theologically framed and somewhat psychoanalytical analysis of Jonah's personal journey, his self-discovery, and realizations about divine mercy, see Peter Weimar, *Eine Geschichte voller Überraschungen: Annäherungen an die Jonaerzählung* (SBS 217; Stuttgart: Katholisches Bibelwerk, 2009).

50   In a thoughtful discussion of "othering" in Jonah, Susanne Gillmayr-Bucher suggests that Yahweh is the consummate "Other" in the work ("Jonah and the Other: A Discourse on Interpretive Competence," in Ehud Ben Zvi and Diana V. Edelman, eds., *Imagining the Other and Constructing Israelite Identity in the Early Second Temple Period* [LHBOTS 456; London: Bloomsbury T&T Clark, 2014] 201–18, here 213-16). Whereas Jonah "assumes he knows God's intentions" in the context of Israelite tradition, he fails to appreciate the ways in which "power is left exclusively to YHWH." In an important thread of thought exemplified by the Jonah narrative, relationships with the deity involve individuals and groups in particular settings rather than a grand Deuteronomistic view of history. Gillmayr-Bucher suggests that the prophet is portrayed as "not willing or able to accept this new point of view." On the deity as utterly other, see also Alfons Deissler, *Zwölf Propheten II: Obadja, Jona, Micha, Nahum, Habakuk* (NEBAT 8; Würzburg: Echter-Verlag, 1984) 164. Walter Crouch suggests that the "primary, central conflict has been from the beginning, unknown to the reader, between the world-view of Yahweh and the world-view of the other main character—Jonah" ("To Question an End," 106; see esp. 110, on the work's lack of closure). See also David Lillegard, "Narrative and Paradox in Jonah," *Kerux* 8 (1993) 19–30. On God's absolute power, see van Hoonacker, *Les douze Petits Prophètes*, 327, 334. For a nuanced view of the way in which the author of Jonah juxtaposes an exaggerated view of the deity and his power with implicit challenges to the nature of divine power, see Terence E. Fretheim, "The Exaggerated God of Jonah," *WW* 27 (2007) 125–34, here 129–33.

51   In a similar vein, see Ackerman, "Satire and Symbolism," 245; and Étan Levine, "Jonah as a Philosophical Book," *ZAW* 96 (1984) 235–45, here 242–44. See also Freedman, "Did God Play a Dirty Trick?"

52   For a discussion of the role of "incomplete dialogue between Jonah and the Lord" in the narrative of Jonah, see Person, *In Conversation with Jonah*, 78; Rosenberg, "Jonah and the Prophetic Vocation," 26; Gunn and Fewell, *Narrative in the Hebrew Bible*, 143.

53   Abusch, "Jonah and God," 152. Similarly, see the conclusion of Irene Nowell, *Jonah, Tobit, Judith* (NCBC; Collegeville, MN: Liturgical Press, 2014) 17. See also the discussion by Jonathan Kaplan, "Jonah and Moral Agency," 159–61.

54   Simon, *Jonah*, 48. For a discussion of Jonah in the context of Job and Qohelet also, see Bolin, *Freedom beyond Forgiveness*, 185–86, and Guillaume, "End of Jonah," 243–50. In a somewhat similar vein, Artur

Qoheleth to the discussion, Simon's translation of Job's response and his interpretation of Jonah's silence are not quite right.

> Job's words close a longer speech:
> I know that you enable all
> and no purpose is withheld from you.
> Who is this bringing up advice without knowledge?
> Therefore, I have expounded and not understood.
> Matters are too wondrous for me,
> and I do not comprehend.
> Hear, please, and I will speak
> I will ask you and you inform me.
> With hearing by ear, I heard you
> But now my eye has seen you. (Job 42:2–5)

The final words of Job 42:6 might be translated, "For this reason I am in a state of rejection, and I am consoling myself on dust and ashes." In the previous verses Job makes confession concerning God's insurmountable power and his own lack of capacity to fully comprehend God; he is cowed, for he has experienced God with his own eyes. He accepts that God is god and he is a mere human, but he is not comforted. The abyss between mortal and immortal only seems the wider by the end of the book. There is no apotheosis in Job's self-realization, only dejected and necessary acceptance that the incomprehensible deity controls all.[55]

Qoheleth shares this sad acknowledgment, for all the conventional rules are mere "vanity," "absurdity," or "vapor" (1:1–11; 2:17, 26; 4:7, 16; 7:15; 8:14). Hard work, following the covenant, and righteousness all lead to the same place, death (5:12–16; 9:1–6). Instead of sitting in ashes in self-abasement, however, the author suggests enjoying life to the best of one's abilities until the inevitable end (5:17–19; 9:7–10), fully aware that only God controls what happens and that God's choices are not fully comprehensible (3:14–15).

In this way, Jonah takes its place among the complex reflections of late biblical writers upon heavy matters of life and death, good and evil, human and divine. Of the three works—Job, Qoheleth, and Jonah—Jonah is the most cohesive from a storytelling perspective in its texture and content. Informed by a variety of internationally shared folk motifs, it feels to the reader lighter in tone than Job and Qoheleth. In contrast to these works, however, it deals not only with issues of personal identity and the individual's relationship to a demanding deity, but also with vexing cultural issues of "us versus them" and the role of Israel's God in a universal and international context. The book of Jonah prods us to contemplate these fundamental issues concerning group- and self-definition.

Jonah beneath the Vine: Appropriation in Late Antiquity

In Christian art of late antiquity, Jonah is frequently depicted in fresco, sculpture, and mosaic, lounging sensuously beneath some sort of planting, usually naked, arm stretched out in a lugubrious pose. The pose is often identified with depictions of Endymion, the quintessentially handsome young shepherd or hunter, beloved by the moon goddess Selene. Selene asks her father, Zeus, to grant the hero eternal youth, a condition Endymion assumes in idyllic sleep, and in which the goddess visits him to make love, becoming pregnant by him to produce forty children. The image of Jonah basking happily in the shade of the planting provided by God (Jonah 4:6) creates in the biblical narrative a brief pause in Jonah's emotional and physical withdrawal, as he awaits the final disposition of the Nineveh matter.

Weiser sees the book's message, reinforced by this final scene, as thoroughly theocentric (*Das Buch der zwölf kleinen Propheten* (ATD 24; Göttingen: Vandenhoeck & Ruprecht, 1967] 227).

55   Grace I. Emmerson points to the "theme of Yahweh's ineluctable freedom of action" ("Another Look at the Book of Jonah," *ExpTim* 88 [1976] 86–88, here 87). Similarly, T. Desmond Alexander emphasizes "God's right to destroy or deliver" ("Jonah," 144); also Craghan, *Esther, Judith, Tobit, Jonah, Ruth*, 169–70; and Vawter, *Job & Jonah*, 86. Vawter writes that "Jonah is an antic prophet, but he is also the prophet of an antic God" (110). See also Nowack, *Die kleinen Propheten*, 195. Comparing Job and Jonah, Leon Roth emphasizes themes of divine compassion and prophetic self-doubt ("Job and Jonah," in Nahum N. Glatzer, ed., *The Dimensions of Job: A Study and Selected Readings*" [New York: Schocken, 1969] 71–74).

An examination of a few of the many portrayals of this scene in various media provides a window on this lively thread in reception history.

As noted in relation to images of Jonah's being swallowed and expelled, a number of these representations offer a series or cycle of episodes,[56] with the image of Jonah beneath the planting serving as the third scene. In the early fourth-century mosaic at Aquileia, Jonah rests under a vine that appears to grow on a trellis. The Jonah figure and the planting appear to rest right in the water along with the images of Jonah and the fish, surrounded by a variety of maritime creatures and fishermen in boats.[57] Similarly, the imagery on the late third-century sarcophagus in Santa Maria Antiqua combines scenes of fishermen, Jonah thrown overboard from the ship, and Jonah reclining under a vine. Jensen notes how the image of water depicted on the carving unites the various Jonah images with "the water of Jesus' baptism" and allusions to the Jordan River.[58]

A late-third-century Roman sarcophagus, now housed in the Vatican Museum, also offers a beautifully sculpted set of scenes from Jonah, each of which leads to the next: Jonah is thrown from the boat, and an open-mouthed undulating sea creature awaits him and then spews him forth. Above this narrative thread to the right is the figure representing Jonah, lounging under a planting heavy in leaves and gourds.[59] In the upper register above the sea creatures is also a line of New Testament figures and motifs, including Jesus and the disciples at Lazarus's tomb, linking the scenes from Jonah to Christian themes of baptism, resurrection, and salvation.[60]

Jonah is drawn in the same reclining pose in a set of the three archetypal scenes from Jonah in a fresco from the Catacomb of Callixtus, located in an ancient Christian cemetery on the Via Appia, southeast of Rome. Images of Jonah being offered up to the dragon-like sea creature, disgorged, and posing under the planting appear from right to left.[61]

The image of the reclining prophet in various media that strike art historians as particularly evocative of depictions of the Endymion tale point to a fascinating thread in reception history and raise questions about the role of traditional artistic conventions of late antiquity in the transformation of the biblical Jonah. Jonah thus depicted conveys religious meanings and messages that help to shape and reflect the beliefs of postbiblical Christian communities. On the one hand, as Raffaela Fazio Smith notes, Jonah of the Hebrew Bible can be read to underscore the themes of universalism and the power of the deity over nature, themes that might appeal to Christians as well as Jews.[62] On the other hand, this particular image of a sensuous young man in repose seems at first consideration an odd evocation for viewers who might correctly think of Jonah as a crusty, grouchy man, burdened with theological challenges to his beliefs and angry with his God.

Scholars point to the artists' use of ready-made images so that the "Endymion" figure may be a stock representation of a man resting. Thomas H. Mathews writes of the way in which "the pre-existing supply of images at the sculptor's disposal restricted his flexibility," but he also takes note of the way in which context and worldview can invest such figures with new meaning. With reference to the sarcophagus of Santa Maria Antiqua mentioned above, Mathews writes, "When the figure of Endymion was re-employed to tell the Jonah story an interesting transformation took place." The sculptor "makes the prophet's rest into a metaphor of the repose of the blessed. Suddenly the story of Jonah's frustration was turned into a story of full physical satisfaction, not necessarily implying that Christians should expect sex after death, but clearly implying the Christian belief in the resurrection of the body and its incorrupt beatitude after death."[63]

The work of a third-century sculptor whose marble statuettes were discovered in Asia Minor points further

---

56 Jensen, *Understanding Early Christian Art*, 172.
57 See Spier, *Picturing the Bible*, 120 fig. 87.
58 Jensen, *Understanding Early Christian Art*, 48–49, figs. 13a, 13b, and 13c.
59 See Spier, *Picturing the Bible*, 207, fig. 39.
60 Ibid., 207.
61 Ibid., 173, fig. 3A; Jensen, *Understanding Early Christian Art*, 69, fig. 20.
62 Raffaela Fazio Smith, *Face of Faith: A Short Guide to Early Christian Images* (Lulu.com, 2011) 58.
63 Thomas F. Mathews, *The Clash of Gods: A Reinterpretation of Early Christian Art* (Princeton, NJ: Princeton University Press, 1993) 31–33.

to links between Jonah and Endymion and the process of transformation. One piece portrays Jonah being swallowed whole by a large sea creature, a second depicts his being spewed forth, and a third pictures his resting under the vine.[64] The visual adaptation in this case, however, differs from previous examples in that the figure of the reposing Jonah in the Endymion pose, arm raised encircling his head, is now modestly clothed and wearing a beard. Presumably the artist sought to use the conventional template and does convey qualities of the happy, carefree rest deserved by the saved, as seen in other examples. Jonah's hands in particular are beautifully articulated in a pose of complete relaxation, but the figure has been made to look more like a prophet than a lover, thus artfully tying together the character of the Hebrew Bible and a warm Christian message about the experience of blessed salvation.

Jonah and Judaism: Yom Kippur

I conclude this commentary with some comments on the role of the book of Jonah in the liturgy of the Day of Atonement and the broader implications of this link for an understanding of the narrative's reception in Judaism.[65] Several critical themes inform the reception and interpretation of Jonah and explain its place in a communal setting that marks the process of atonement. One involves the efficacy of repentance, another God's capacious capacity to grant forgiveness, and the third the rehabilitation of Jonah and the transformation of his worldview via the interpretative process so that the story and the character of the prophet comport with the themes of repentance and forgiveness.

Jeffrey H. Tigay notes that the recitation of God's attributes in the context of Rosh Hashanah and Yom Kippur purposely omits those features associated with "strict justice," providing only those associated with mercy and forgiveness, in contrast to the formulaic list in Exod 34:6–7. The key to an appreciation of Jonah in the context of the Day of Atonement, for Tigay, is found in a number of postexilic texts such as Jer 18:7–10, which, in Tigay's view, suggests that "even categorical divine decrees are subject to modification in the light of human behavior."[66] Thus, repentance makes a difference in the outcome. Forgiveness is possible if we genuinely repent. The Ninevites of Jonah can be seen as exemplars of and for this realization. Joel Rosenberg observes in this context that, for Yehezkel Kaufman, the book of Jonah is not about the historical relationship with the Ninevites. Whatever our interpretation of the messages of the biblical book in its author's own sociohistorical context, Kaufman's view has particular resonance in exploring reasons for the reading of Jonah at Yom Kippur, a time when each Jew atones and asks God for forgiveness. Repentance in this setting is personal and individual, within the grasp of each person gathered for solemn assembly. As Rosenberg implicitly notes, the high holidays emphasize both the private and the public aspects of our religious identities and aspirations; the liturgy for Yom Kippur is a matter of personal religion and community expression, an arena in which the petitioner safely addresses God supported by and reinforced with the voices of fellow petitioners and a place of self-contemplation. Rosenberg describes the synagogue as a "secure place of retreat and an anguishing arena of self-confrontation."[67]

---

64 See Spier, *Picturing the Bible*, 192–93, figs. 1, 2, and 3.

65 For a personal reflection on some of these connections by a great scholar of Judaism, see David Daube, "Jonah: A Reminiscence," *JJS* 35 (1984) 36–43. See also the wide-ranging discussion by Gaines, *Forgiveness in a Wounded World*, 146–51. Within the framework of a theoretical approach inspired by the work of René Girard, Sandor Goodhart explores connections between the parable of the קיקיון, sacrifice, and repentance as integral to Jewish receptions of Jonah ("Prophecy, Sacrifice and Repentance in the Story of Jonah," *Semeia* 33 [1985] 43–63). For a thoughtful overview that is particularly attuned to recurring key language and leitmotifs in Jonah as they relate to biblical tradition and postbiblical Judaism, see Paul Kahn, "An Analysis of the Book of Jonah," *Judaism* 43 (1994) 87–100.

66 Tigay, "Days of Awe," 73–74. See also the brief reflection by Nahum Sarna, "Why the Book of Jonah Is Read on Yom Kippur," *BRev* 6 (1990) 24.

67 Rosenberg, "Jonah and the Prophetic Vocation," 26.

Several postbiblical interpretations of Jonah help to explain its place at Yom Kippur. These midrashic revisions of the prophet's experiences and the gloss they place upon his actions relate to the holiday's central themes. I have already noted the ways in which Pirqe de-Rabbi Eliezer rehabilitates the curmudgeonly portrait of Jonah with various heroic and mystical emphases. The *Biblical Antiquities* (*Liber Antiquitatum Biblicarum*) of the anonymous author known as Pseudo-Philo, a Hellenistic work dating from the second–fourth centuries; the medieval Midrash Jona; and the commentary of a twelfth-century French exegete, Rabbi Eliezer of Beaugency, also alter our impression of the biblical prophet, which helps to make more sense of the recitation of Jonah's story at Yom Kippur. Rabbi Eliezer reads 4:1 concerning Jonah's negative response to God's sparing Nineveh to suggest that Jonah did not in fact know that the Ninevites had repented, for he had gone out of the city. The French rabbi reads the verb in 4:5 as a pluperfect, as do some modern exegetes. He writes, "Now Jonah had—already—gone out from the city. . . ." For Rabbi Eliezer, this lack of knowledge due to his absence from the city somewhat helps to explain Jonah's negative response to God's not destroying the Ninevites. Had Jonah known that the Ninevites had indeed repented of their evil, he would have reacted differently. The rabbi explains, "Jonah was of the opinion that God had forgiven the evil of the Ninevites without repentance."[68] For Rabbi Eliezer, in 4:11 God reveals to Jonah that the Ninevites had repented: "On account of (their) repentance I had compassion on them. And here (God) told him of their repentance." The emphasis is on the efficacy of repentance and its connection to divine forgiveness, a critical theme for Yom Kippur. As suggested by Robert C. Gregg, "Perhaps many early hearers of Jonah on Yom Kippur so registered its force as scripture telling of a pardoning God that they did not suffer undue cognitive dissonance about Jonah's characterization in the text; they may have found his aggravated behavior overshadowed by the interaction between God and Nineveh—penitence rewarded by forgiveness."[69] As Gregg notes, an excerpt from Pseudo-Philo, preserved only in an Armenian translation, places special emphasis on the genuineness of the Ninevites' repentance, having them model "what devout atonement and the celebration of the forgiveness of sins is like."[70] Moreover, as Harris points out, Rabbi Eliezer suggests that Jonah does "learn his lesson" from the experience with the קיקיון,[71] a much more ambiguous matter subject to interpretation in the biblical text itself. Jonah himself is presented as a penitent by other Jewish commentators.

Pseudo-Philo's imagining of the essence of Jonah's prayer in the fish portrays the prophet as a sinner who supplicates God for forgiveness.[72] In a similar vein the medieval Midrash Jonah, like the commentary of Rabbi Eliezer of Beaugency, has Jonah learn from the life and death of the קיקיון. Instead of responding to the deity with silence, Jonah falls upon his face and petitions God to conduct his world with a measure of compassion, for, as it is written, the Lord is a God of compassion and forgiveness.[73] Similarly, the lament of Jonah is treated as a petitionary prayer.[74] Thus, the interpretative tradition suggests that Jonah himself asks God for forgiveness, emphasizing God's capacity to forgive compassionately and allowing Jonah to become a positive exemplar on the Day of Atonement. In this way, both the Ninevites and Jonah himself become models of and models for the behavior of Jews, who can petition a compassionate God in hopes of forgiveness if they genuinely repent of the evil they have done. This message not only informs the liturgy of Yom Kippur itself but has traditionally reflected and shaped the worldview of Jews throughout the year.

---

68 See Robert A. Harris, "Contextual Reading: Rabbi Eliezer of Beaugency's Commentary on Jonah," in Kravitz and Sharon, *Bringing the Hidden to Light*, 89–92. The translations of Rabbi Eliezer's commentary as quoted are by Harris. See also, more recently, Robert A. Harris, *Rabbi Eliezer of Beaugency: Commentaries on Amos and Jonah; Introduction, Translation, and Commentary (with Selections from Isaiah and Ezekiel)* (MIP; Kalamazoo: Western Michigan University, 2018).

69 Gregg, *Shared Stories*, 356.
70 Ibid., 354.
71 Harris, "Contextual Reading," 91.
72 See the translation of the Armenian text in Gregg, *Shared Stories*, 356.
73 See Jellinek, *Bet ha-Midrasch*, 1:102.
74 Ibid., 1:99.

Bibliography

1. Commentaries

Achtemeier, Elizabeth
Minor Prophets 1 (NIBC; Peabody, MA: Hendrickson, 1996).

Alexander, T. Desmond
"Jonah: An Introduction and Commentary," in David W. Baker, T. Desmond Alexander, and Bruce K. Waltke, *Obadiah, Jonah and Micah: An Introduction and Commentary* (TOTC 26; Downers Grove, IL: InterVarsity Press, 1988) 49–144.

Allen, Leslie C.
The Books of Joel, Obadiah, Jonah and Micah (NICOT; Grand Rapids: Eerdmans, 1976).

Alter, Robert
Strong as Death Is Love: The Song of Songs, Ruth, Esther, Jonah, and Daniel; A Translation with Commentary (New York: Norton, 2015).

Bewer, Julius A.
"Jonah," in Hinckley G. T. Mitchell, John Merlin Powis Smith, and Julius A. Bewer, *A Critical and Exegetical Commentary on Haggai, Zechariah, Malachi and Jonah* (ICC 23; New York: Scribner, 1912).

Brown, William P.
Obadiah through Malachi (WeBC; Louisville: Westminster John Knox, 1996.

Bruckner, James K.
Jonah, Nahum, Habakkuk, Zephaniah (NIVAC; Grand Rapids: Zondervan, 2004).

Craghan, John F.
Esther, Judith, Tobit, Jonah, Ruth (OTM 16; Wilmington, DE: Glazier, 1982).

Craigie, Peter C.
Twelve Prophets, vol. 1: *Hosea, Joel, Amos, Obadiah, and Jonah* (DSB; Philadelphia: Westminster, 1984).

Croy, N. Clayton
3 Maccabees (SCS; Leiden: Brill, 2006).

Deissler, Alfons
Zwölf Propheten II: *Obadja, Jona, Micha, Nahum, Habakuk* (NEBAT 8; Würzburg: Echter-Verlag, 1986).

Duhm, Bernhard
The Twelve Prophets: A Version in the Various Poetical Measures of the Original Writings (trans. Archibald Duff; London: Adam & Charles Black, 1912).

Fretheim, Terence E.
Reading Hosea–Micah: A Literary and Theological Commentary (Macon, GA: Smyth & Helwys, 2013).

Goldman, S.
"Jonah," in A. Cohen, ed., *The Twelve Prophets* (London: Soncino Press, 1948) 136–50.

Golka, F. W., and George A. F. Knight
Revelation of God: A Commentary on the Books of The Song of Songs and Jonah (ITC; Grand Rapids: Eerdmans, 1988).

Hennessy, T. H.
Joel, Obadiah, Jonah and Malachi (Cambridge: Cambridge University Press, 1919).

Jenson, Philip Peter
Obadiah, Jonah, Micah: A Theological Commentary (LHBOTS 496; London: T&T Clark, 2008).

Jeremias, Jörg
Die Propheten Joel, Obadja, Jona, Micha (ATD 24.3; Göttingen: Vandenhoeck & Ruprecht, 2007).

Keil, C. F., and F. Delitzsch
The Twelve Minor Prophets (trans. James Martin; BCOT 1; Edinburgh: T&T Clark, 1874).

Knight, George A. F.
Ruth and Jonah: Introduction and Commentary (Torch Bible Commentaries; London: SCM Press, 1950).

Kravitz, Leonard S., and Kerry M. Olitzky
Jonah: A Modern Commentary (New York: URJ Press, 2006).

Lanchester, H. C. O.
Obadiah and Jonah (CBSC; Cambridge: Cambridge University Press, 1918).

Limburg, James
Jonah: A Commentary (OTL; Louisville: Westminster John Knox, 1993).

Marti, Karl
Das Dodekapropheton (KHC 13; Tübingen: Mohr Siebeck, 1904).

Myers, Jacob M.
The Book of Hosea, the Book of Joel, the Book of Amos, the Book of Jonah (LBC 14; Richmond, VA: John Knox, 1959).

Nogalski, James D.
The Book of the Twelve: Hosea–Jonah (SHBC; Macon, GA: Smyth & Helwys, 2011).

Nötscher, Friedrich
Zwölfprophetenbuch oder Kleine Propheten (Würzburg: Echter-Verlag, 1948).

Nowack, Wilhelm
Die kleinen Propheten (GHAT; Göttingen: Vandenhoeck & Ruprecht, 1922).

Nowell, Irene
Jonah, Tobit, Judith (NCBC; Collegeville, MN: Liturgical Press, 2014).

Price, B. F., E. A. Nida, and R. Péter-Contesse
Le livre de Jonas: Un commentaire exégétique et linguistique (Villiers-le-Bel: Alliance Biblique Universelle, 1997).

Procksch, O.
Die kleinen prophetischen Schriften nach dem Exil (Stuttgart: Verlag der Vereinsbuchhandlung, 1916).

Renner, J. T. Erich
In Times of Crisis: Commentaries on Joel, Jonah, and Habakkuk (CRC; Adelaide: Openbook, 1995).

Robinson, Theodore H.
Die zwölf kleinen Propheten: Hosea bis Micha (HAT 1/14; Tübingen: Mohr Siebeck, 1954).

Rudolph, Wilhelm
Joel, Amos, Obadja, Jona: Mit einer Zeittafel von Alfred Jepsen (KAT 13.2; Gütersloh: Mohn, 1971).

Sargent, James E.
Hosea, Joel, Amos, Obadiah, and Jonah (Basic Bible Commentary; Nashville: Abingdon, 1988).

Sasson, Jack M.
Jonah: A New Translation with Introduction, Commentary, and Interpretations (AB 24B; Garden City, NY: Doubleday, 1990; repr., AYB 24B; New Haven: Yale University Press, 2010).

Sellin, Ernst
Das Zwölfprophetenbuch: Übersetzt und Erklärt (Leipzig: Deichert, 1922).

Simon, Uriel
Jonah יונה: *The Traditional Hebrew Text with the New JPS Translation* (JPSBC; Philadelphia: Jewish Publication Society of America, 1999).

Simundson, Daniel J.
Joel, Amos, Obadiah, Jonah, Micah (AOTC; Nashville: Abingdon, 2005).

Smart, James D.
"The Book of Jonah," *IB* 6:875–94.

Smith, George Adam
"Jonah," in *The Book of the Twelve Prophets Commonly Called the Minor* (2 vols.; EB; New York: Armstrong & Son, 1898) 2:491–541.

Snaith, Norman H.
Notes on the Hebrew Text of Jonah (London: Epworth Press, 1945).

Struppe, Ursula
Die Bücher Obadja, Jona (NSKAT 24.1; Stuttgart: Katholisches Bibelwerk, 1996).

Stuart, Douglas
Hosea–Jonah (WBC 31; Waco, TX: Word Books, 1987).

Sweeney, Marvin A.
The Twelve Prophets (2 vols.; Berit Olam; Collegeville, MN: Liturgical Press, 2000).

Trible, Phyllis Lou
"The Book of Jonah: Introduction, Commentary, and Reflections," *NIB* 7:463–529.

Eadem
"Studies in the Book of Jonah" (PhD diss., Columbia University, 1963).

Tucker, W. Dennis, Jr.
Jonah: A Handbook on the Hebrew Text (Waco, TX: Baylor University Press, 2006).

Idem
Jonah. A Handbook on the Hebrew Text (rev. and expanded ed.; Waco, TX: Baylor University Press, 2017).

Van Hoonacker, A.
Les douze Petits Prophètes (EBib; Paris: Gabalda, 1908).

Van Wikj-Bos, Johanna W. H.
Ruth, Esther, Jonah (Atlanta: John Knox, 1986).

Wade, G. W.
The Books of the Prophets Micah, Obadiah, Joel and Jonah (London: Methuen, 1925).

Walton, John H.
"Jonah," in Bryan Beyer and John H. Walton, *Obadiah, Jonah* (BSC; Grand Rapids: Zondervan, 1982) 11–81.

Watts, John D. W.
The Books of Joel, Obadiah, Jonah, Nahum, Habakkuk, and Zephaniah (Cambridge: Cambridge University Press, 1975).

Weimar, Peter
Jona (HThKAT; Freiburg im Breisgau: Herder, 1917).

Weiser, Artur
Das Buch der zwölf kleinen Propheten (ATD 24; Göttingen: Vandenhoeck & Ruprecht, 1967).

Wellhausen, Julius
Die Kleinen Propheten übersetz, mit Noten (SV 5; Berlin: Georg Reimer, 1892).

Wolff, Hans Walter
Obadiah and Jonah: A Commentary (trans. Margaret Kohl; Minneapolis: Ausgburg, 1986).

Youngblood, Kevin J.
Jonah: God's Scandalous Mercy (Grand Rapids: Zondervan, 2013).

Zlotowitz, Meir, and Nosson Scherman
Sefer Yonah/Jonah: A New Translation with a Commentary Anthologized from Talmudic, Midrashic and Rabbinic Sources (Brooklyn, NY: Mesorah, 1978).

2. Text Editions

Benoit, P., J. T. Milik, and R. de Vaux
Les Grottes de Murabba'at (DJD 2; Oxford: Clarendon, 1961).

Cathcart, Kevin J., and Robert P. Gordon
The Targum of the Minor Prophets: Translated with a Critical Introduction, Apparatus, and Notes (ArBib 14; Wilmington, DE: Glazier, 1989).

Friedlander, Gerald
Pirke de Rabbi Eliezer (The Chapters of Rabbi Eliezer the Great) according to the Text of the Manuscript Belonging to Abraham Epstein of Vienna: Translated and Annotated with Introduction and Indices (New York: Benjamin Blom, 1971).

Gelston, Anthony, ed.
The Twelve Minor Prophets (BHQ 13; Stuttgart: Deutsche Bibelgesellschaft, 2010).

Jellinek, Adolph, ed.
Bet ha-Midrasch: Sammlung kleiner Midraschim und vermischter Abhandlungen aus der ältern jüdischen Literatur (6 vols.; Leipzig, 1853–1877; repr., Jerusalem: Bamberger & Wahrmann, 1938).

Kiraz, George A., and Joseph Bale, eds.
The Syriac Peshitta Bible with English Translation: The Twelve Prophets (trans. Donald M. Walter and Gillian Greenberg; Piscataway, NJ: Gorgias Press, 2012).

Levine, Étan
The Aramaic Version of Jonah (Jerusalem: Jerusalem Academic Press, 1975).

Oesterley, W. O. E.
"The Old Latin Texts of the Minor Prophets. III," *JTS* 5 (1904) 378–86.

Sperber, Alexander
The Bible in Aramaic: Based on Old Manuscripts and Printed Texts, vol. 3: *The Latter Prophets according to Targum Jonathan* (Leiden: Brill, 1992).

Tov, Emanuel
The Greek Minor Prophets Scroll from Naḥal Ḥever (8ḤevXIIgr) (DJD 8; Oxford: Clarendon, 1990).

Ulrich, Eugene, Frank Moore Cross, and Russell E. Fuller
Qumran Cave 4.X: The Prophets (DJD 15; Oxford: Clarendon, 1997).

Ziegler, Joseph, ed.
Duodecim prophetae (GS 13; Göttingen: Vandenhoeck & Ruprecht, 1967).

3. General Studies

Abasili, Alexander Izuchukwu
"The Role of Non-Human Creatures in the Book of Jonah: The Implications for Eco-Justice," *SJOT* 31 (2017) 236–53.

Abela, A. A.
"When the Agenda of an Artistic Composition Is Hidden: Jonah and Intertextual Dialogue with Isaiah 6, the 'Confessions of Jeremiah' and Other Texts," in Johannes C. de Moor, ed., *The Elusive Prophet: The Prophet as Historical Person, Literary Character and Anonymous Artist; Papers Read at the 11th Joint Meeting of the Society for Old Testament Study and Het Oudtestamentisch Werkgezelschap in Nederland en België Held at Soesterberg 2000* (Leiden: Brill, 2001) 1–30.

Abramson, Glenda
"The Book of Jonah as a Literary and Dramatic Work," *Semitics* 5 (1977) 36–47.

Abusch, Tzvi
"Jonah and God: Plants, Beasts, and Humans in the Book of Jonah (An Essay in Interpretation)," *JANER* 13 (2013) 146–52.

Ackerman, James S.
"Jonah," in Robert Alter and Frank Kermode, eds., *The Literary Guide to the Bible* (Cambridge, MA: Belknap Press of Harvard University Press, 1987) 234–43.

Idem
"Satire and Symbolism in the Song of Jonah," in Baruch Halpern and Jon D. Levenson, eds., *Traditions in Transformation: Turning Points in Biblical Faith; A Festschrift Honoring Frank Moore Cross* (Winona Lake, IN: Eisenbrauns, 1982) 213–46.

Adelman, Rachel
"Through the Looking Glass: Pirqe de-Rabbi Eliezer's Portrait of an Apocalyptic Prophet," *The Journal of the Faculty of Religious Studies, McGill University* 39 (2011) 79–92.

Eadem
The Return of the Repressed: Pirqe de-Rabbi Eliezer and the Pseudepigrapha (Leiden: Brill, 2009).

Ahrens, Karl
"Was ist *qīqājōn* Jona 4, 6.7?," *ZS* 4 (1926) 256.

Albertz, Rainer, James D. Nogalski, and Jakob Wöhrle, eds.
Perspectives on the Formation of the Book of the Twelve: Methodological Foundations–Redactional Processes–Historical Insights (BZAW 433; Berlin: de Gruyter, 2012).

Alexander, T. Desmond
"Jonah and Genre," *TynBul* 36 (1985) 35–59.

Almbladh, Karin
Studies in the Book of Jonah (SSU 7; Uppsala: Coronet Books, 1986).

Alter, Robert
The Five Books of Moses: A Translation with Commentary (New York: Norton, 2004).

Amit, Yaira
"'There was a man . . . and his name was . . .': Editorial Variations and Their Tendenz" [in Hebrew], *BetM* 30 (1984–1985) 388–99.

Amzallag, Nissim
"Praise or Antiphonal Singing? The Meaning of להודות Revisited," *HS* 56 (2015) 115–28.

Anderson, Bernhard W., and Arthur C. Lichtenberger
"The Book of Esther," *IDB* 3:821–74.

Anderson, Joel Edmund
"Jonah's Peculiar Re-Creation," *BTB* 41 (2011) 179–88.

Andrew, M. E.
"*Gattung* and Intention in the Book of Jonah," *Orita* 1 (1967) 13–18, 78–85.

Antwi, Emmanuel Kojo Ennin
The Book of Jonah in the Context of Post-Exilic Theology of Israel: An Exegetical Study (ATSAT 95; St. Ottilien: Eos, 2013).

Avi, M.
"Jonah, Perseus and Andromeda at Joppa" [in Hebrew], *Yediot* 31 (1967) 203–10.

Ballard, Robert, Lawrence Stager, et al.
"Iron Age Shipwrecks in Deep Water off Ashkelon, Israel," *AJA* 106 (2002) 151–68.

Band, Arnold J.
"Swallowing Jonah: The Eclipse of Parody," *Prooftexts* 10 (1990) 177–95.

Barbeau, C. Marius
"Contes Populaires Canadiens," *JAF* 29 (1916) 1–136.

Barré, Michael
"Jonah 2, 9 and the Structure of Jonah's Prayer," *Bib* 72 (1991) 237–48.

Barrett, Rob
"Meaning More than They Say: The Conflict between Yhwh and Jonah," *JSOT* 37 (2012) 237–57.

Barton, John, and David J. Reimer, eds.
After the Exile: Essays in Honour of Rex Mason (Macon, GA: Mercer University Press, 1966).

Bass, George F.
A History of Seafaring Based on Underwater Archaeology (London: Thames & Hudson, 1972).

Batto, Bernard
"The Reed Sea: Requiescat in Pace," *JBL* 102 (1983) 27–35.

Bauer, Johannes B.
"Drei Tage," *Bib* 39 (1958) 354–58.

Baughman, Ernest W.
"A Comparative Study of the Folktales of England and North America" (2 vols.; PhD diss., Indiana University, 1953).

Idem
Type and Motif Index of the Folktales of England and North America (IUFS 20; Bloomington: Indiana University Press, 1966).

Beck, Mordechai
"Dreaming of Jonah/Living in Tarshish: Two Images of Jonah," *Tikkun* 10 (1995) 73–74.

Beckwith, Martha
  Hawaiian Mythology (New Haven: Yale University Press, 1940).
Begg, C. T.
  "Jeroboam II and Jonah," *BETL* 145 (2000) 251–72.
Ben-Amos, Dan
  "Analytical Categories and Ethnic Genres," in Dan Ben-Amos, ed., *Folklore Genres* (PAFSBSS 26; Austin: University of Texas Press, 1976) 215–42.
Ben Josef, I. A.
  "Jonah and the Fish as Folk Motif," *Semitics* 7 (1980) 102–17.
Ben Zvi, Ehud
  "Jonah 4:11 and the Meaning of the Metaprophetic Character of the book of Jonah," *JHebS* 9 (2009) 1–13.
Idem
  Signs of Jonah: Reading and Rereading in Ancient Yehud (JSOTSup 367; London: Sheffield Academic Press, 2003).
Idem
  "Twelve Prophetic Books or 'The Twelve?': A Few Preliminary Considerations," in James W. Watts and Paul R. House, eds., *Forming Prophetic Literature: Essays on Isaiah and the Twelve in Honor of John D. W. Watts* (JSOTSup 235; Sheffield: Sheffield Academic Press, 1996) 125–56.
Ben Zvi, Ehud, and James D. Nogalski
  Two Sides of a Coin: Juxtaposing Views on Interpreting the Book of the Twelve/the Twelve Prophetic Books (Analecta Gorgiana 201; Piscataway, NJ: Gorgias Press, 2009).
Berger, Benjamin Lyle
  "Picturing the Prophet: Focalization in the Book of Jonah," *SR* 29 (2000) 58–68.
Berger, Yitzhak
  Jonah in the Shadows of Eden (Indiana Studies in Biblical Literature; Bloomington: Indiana University Press, 2016).
Bickerman, Elias
  "Les deux erreurs du prophète Jonas," *RHPR* 45 (1965) 232–64.
Idem
  Four Strange Books of the Bible: Jonah, Daniel, Koheleth, Esther (New York: Schocken, 1967).
Biddle, Mark E.
  "Obadiah-Jonah-Micah in Canonical Context: The Nature of Prophetic Literature and Hermeneutics," *Int* 61 (2007) 154–66.
Blank, Sheldon H.
  "'Doest Thou Well to Be Angry?' A Study in Self-Pity," *HUCA* 26 (1955) 29–41.
Idem
  "The Prophet as Paradigm," in James L. Crenshaw and John T. Willis, eds., *Essays in Old Testament Ethics: J. Philip Hyatt, In Memoriam* (New York: Ktav, 1974) 111–30.
Bledsoe, Seth A.
  "Ahiqar and Other Legendary Sages," in Samuel L. Adams and Matthew Goff, eds., *Wiley Blackwell Companion to Wisdom Literature* (Wiley-Blackwell Companions to Religion; Hoboken, NJ: John Wiley & Sons, 2020) 287–309.
Bob, Steven M.
  Go to Nineveh: Medieval Jewish Commentaries on the Book of Jonah Translated and Explained (Eugene, OR: Pickwick, 2013).
Bolin, Thomas M.
  "Eternal Delight and Deliciousness: The Book of Jonah after Ten Years," *JHebS* 9 (2009) 1–11.
Idem
  Freedom beyond Forgiveness: The Book of Jonah Re-Examined (JSOTSup 236; Sheffield: Sheffield Academic Press, 1997).
Idem
  "Jonah 4, 11 and the Problem of Exegetical Anachronism," *SJOT* 24 (2010) 99–109.
Idem
  "'Should I Not Also Pity Nineveh?' Divine Freedom in the Book of Jonah," *JSOT* 67 (1995) 109–20.
Bosma, Carl J.
  "Jonah 1:9: An Example of Elenctic Testimony," *CTJ* 48 (2013) 65–90.
Botkin, B. A., ed.
  A Treasury of American Folklore (New York: Crown, 1944).
Bouillon, David
  "Bibliographie sur le livre de Jonas," Academia.edu, https://www.academia.edu/31144882/Bibliography_on_the_Book_of_Jonah_1800-2014_.
Bowers, R. H.
  The Legend of Jonah (The Hague: Martinus Nijhoff, 1971).

Bredin, Mark
"The Significance of Jonah in Vaticanus (B) Tobit 14:4 and 8," in Mark Bredin, ed., *Studies in the Book of Tobit: A Multidisciplinary Approach* (London: T&T Clark, 2006) 43–58.

Brekelmans, Chr. H. W.
"Some Translation Problems," *OtSt* 15 (1969) 170–76.

Brenner, Athalya
"Jonah's Poem out and within Its Context," in Philip R. Davies and David J. A. Clines, eds., *Among the Prophets: Language, Image and Structure in the Prophetic Writings* (JSOTSup 144; Sheffield: Sheffield Academic Press, 1993) 183–92.

Eadem
"Linguistic Criteria for Dating the Book of Jonah" [in Hebrew], *BetM* 79 (1979) 396–405.

Brody, Aaron J.
"Each Man Cried Out to His God:" The Specialized Religion of Canaanite and Phoenician Seafarers (HSM 58; Atlanta: Scholars Press, 1998).

Brongers, H. A.
"Bemerkungen zum Gebrauch des adverbialen *we'attāh* im Alten Testament (Ein Lexikologischer Beitrag)," *VT* 15 (1965) 289–99.

Brown, Erica
Jonah: The Reluctant Prophet (New Milford, CT: Maggid Books, 2017).

Budde, Karl
"Vermutungen zum 'Midrasch' des Buches der Könige," *ZAW* 12 (1892) 37–51.

Bührer, Walter
"Der Gott Jonas und der Gott des Himmels: Untersuchungen zur Theologie des Jona-Buches," *BN* 167 (2015) 65–78.

Idem
"Untersuchungen zur literarischen Gestaltung des Jona-Buches," *BN* 166 (2015) 29–50.

Burke, Aaron A., Katherine Strange Burke, and Martin Peilstöker, eds.
The History and Archaeology of Jaffa, 2 (Monumenta Archaeologica 41; Los Angeles: Costen Institute of Archaeology Press, 2017.

Burrows, Millar
"The Literary Category of the Book of Jonah," in Harry Thomas Frank and William L. Reed, eds., *Translating and Understanding the Old Testament: Essays in Honor of Herbert Gordon May* (Nashville: Abingdon, 1970) 80–107.

Buss, Martin J.
"An Anthropological Perspective on Prophetic Call Narratives," *Semeia* 21 (1981) 9–30.

Butterworth, G. M.
"You Pity the Plant: A Misunderstanding, " *IJT* 27 (1978) 32–34.

Bynum, Caroline Walker
The Resurrection of the Body in Western Christianity, 200–1336 (New York: Columbia University Press, 1995).

Carroll, Robert P.
"Jonah as a Book of Ritual Responses," in Klaus-Dietrich Schunck and Matthias Augustin, eds., *"'Lasset uns Brücken bauen . . .': Collected Communications to the XVth Congress of the International Organization for the Study of the Old Testament, Cambridge 1995* (BEATAJ 42; Frankfurt am Main: Peter Lang, 1995) 261–68.

Cartledge, Tony
Vows in the Hebrew Bible and the Ancient Near East (JSOTSup 147; Sheffield: Sheffield Academic Press, 1992).

Casson, Lionel
Ships and Seamanship in the Ancient World (Princeton, NJ: Princeton University Press, 1971).

Castillo, Arcadio del
"Tarshish in the Book of Jonah," *RB* 114 (2007) 481–98.

Child, Francis James
The English and Scottish Popular Ballads in Five Volumes (Boston: Houghton, Mifflin, 1885).

Childs, Brevard S.
"The Canonical Shape of the Book of Jonah," in Gary A. Tuttle, ed., *Biblical and Near Eastern Studies: Essays in Honor of William Sanford LaSor* (Grand Rapids: Eerdmans, 1970) 122–28.

Christensen, Duane L.
"Anticipatory Paronomasia in Jonah 3:7–8 and Genesis 37:2," *RB* 90 (1983) 261–63.

Idem
"Jonah and the Sabbath Rest in the Pentateuch," in Georg Braulik, Walter Gross, and Sean McEvenue, eds., *Biblische Theologie und gesellschaftlicher Wandel: Für Norbert Lohfink SJ* (Freiburg: Herder, 1993) 48–60.

Idem
"Narrative Poetics and the Interpretation of the Book of Jonah," in Elaine R. Follis, ed., *Directions in Biblical Hebrew Poetry* (JSOTSup 40; Sheffield: JSOT Press, 1987) 29–48.
Idem
"The Song of Jonah: A Metrical Analysis," *JBL* 104 (1985) 217–31.
Claassens, L. Juliana M.
"Rethinking Humour in the Book of Jonah: Tragic Laughter as Resistance in the Context of Trauma," *OTE* 28 (2015) 655–73.
Clark, Gordon R.
The Word "Hesed" in the Hebrew Bible (JSOTSup 157; Sheffield: Sheffield Academic Press, 1993).
Clements, R. E.
The Prayers of the Bible (London: SCM Press, 1986).
Idem
"The Purpose of the Book of Jonah," in J. A. Emerton, ed., *Congress Volume: Edinburgh, 1974* (VTSup 28; Leiden: Brill, 1975) 16–28.
Coetzee, Johan H.
"And Jonah Swam and Swam and Swam: Jonah's Body in Deep Waters," *OTE* 17 (2004) 521–30.
Idem
"Jonah from the Perspective of Jonah: Embodied Theology Illustrated," *Scrip* 90 (2005) 850–58.
Idem
"Where Humans and Animals Meet, Folly Can Be Sweet: Jonah's Bodily Experience of Containment the Major Drive behind his Conduct," *OTE* 20 (2007) 320–32.
Cohen, Abraham D.
"The Tragedy of Jonah," *Judaism* 21 (1972) 164–75.
Collins, Clifford John
"From Literary Analysis to Theological Exposition: The Book of Jonah," *JOTT* 7 (1995) 28–44.
Conrad, Edgar W.
"Forming the Twelve and Forming Canon," in Paul L. Redditt and Aaron Schart, eds., *Thematic Threads in the Book of the Twelve* (BZAW 325; Berlin: de Gruyter, 2003) 90–103.
Conroy, Charles
"Jonah and Nahum in the Book of the Twelve: Who Has the Last Word?," *PIBA* 32 (2009) 1–23.
Cooper, Alan
"In Praise of Divine Caprice: The Significance of the Book of Jonah," in Philip R. Davies and David J. A. Clines, eds., *Among the Prophets: Language, Image and Structure in the Prophetic Writings* (JSOTSup 144; Sheffield: JSOT Press, 1993) 144–63.
Craig, Kenneth M., Jr.
A Poetics of Jonah: Art in the Service of Ideology (2nd ed.; Macon, GA: Mercer University Press, 1999).
Idem
"Jonah and the Reading Process," *JSOT* 47 (1990) 103–14.
Crenshaw, James L.
"The Expression *mî yôdēaʿ* in the Hebrew Bible," *VT* 36 (1986) 274–88.
Idem
"Theodicy in the Book of the Twelve," in Paul L. Redditt and Aaron Schart, eds., *Thematic Threads in the Book of the Twelve* (BZAW 325; Berlin: de Gruyter, 2003) 175–91.
Cross, Frank Moore
"A Homily on the Book of Jonah," in Kathryn F. Kravitz and Diane M. Sharon, eds., *Bringing the Hidden to Light: The Process of Interpretation: Studies in Honor of Stephen A. Geller* (Winona Lake, IN: Eisenbrauns, 2007) 45–49.
Idem
"Studies in the Structure of Hebrew Verse: The Prosody of the Psalm of Jonah," in H. B. Huffmon, F. A. Spina, and A. R. W. Green, eds., *The Quest for the Kingdom of God: Studies in Honor of George E. Mendenhall* (Winona Lake, IN: Eisenbrauns, 1983) 159–67.
Crouch, Walter B.
"To Question an End, to End a Question: Opening the Closure of the Book of Jonah," *JSOT* 62 (1994) 101–12.
Cryer, Frederick H.
Divination in Ancient Israel and Its Near Eastern Environment: A Socio-Historical Investigation (JSOTSup 142; Sheffield: JSOT Press, 1994).
Daube, David
"Death as a Release in the Bible," *NovT* 5 (1962) 82–104.
Idem
"Jonah: A Reminiscence," *JJS* 35 (1984) 36–43.
Davies, G. I.
"The Uses of *rʿ* Qal and the Meaning of Jonah IV 1," *VT* 27 (1977) 105–11.

Davies, Philip R., and David J. A. Clines, eds.
Among the Prophets: Language, Image and Structure in the Prophetic Writings (JSOTSup 144; Sheffield: JSOT Press, 1993).

Day, John
"Problems in the Interpretation of the Book of Jonah," in A. S. van der Woude, ed., *In Quest of the Past: Studies on Israelite Religion, Literature and Prophetism; Papers Read at the Joint British-Dutch Old Testament Conference, Held at Elspeet, 1988* (OtSt 26; Leiden: Brill, 1990) 32–47.

Dell, Katharine J.
"Reinventing the Wheel: The Shaping of the Book of Jonah," in John Barton and David J. Reimer, eds., *After the Exile: Essays in Honour of Rex Mason* (Macon, GA: Mercer University Press, 1966) 85–101.

De Troyer, Kristin
"The Freer Twelve Minor Prophets Codex—A Case Study: The Old Greek Text of Jonah, Its Revisions, and Its Corrections," in Larry W. Hurtado, ed., *The Freer Biblical Manuscripts: Fresh Studies of an American Treasure Trove* (SBLTCS 6; Atlanta: Society of Biblical Literature, 2006) 75–85.

Deutsch, Yosef
Let My Nation Be Warned: The Story of Yonah, a Reluctant Prophet on a Mission of Repentance (Nanuet, NY: Feldheim, 2014).

Dietrich, Walter
"Three Minor Prophets and the Major Empires: Synchronic and Diachronic Perspectives on Nahum, Habakkuk, and Zephaniah," in Rainer Albertz, James D. Nogalski, and Jakob Wöhrle, eds., *Perspectives on the Formation of the Book of the Twelve: Methodological Foundations–Redactional Processes–Historical Insights* (BZAW 433; Berlin: de Gruyter, 2012) 147–56.

Dines, Jennifer
"Verbal and Thematic Links between the Books of the Twelve in Greek and Their Relevance to the Differing Manuscript Sequences," in Rainer Albertz, James D. Nogalski, and Jakob Wöhrle, eds., *Perspectives on the Formation of the Book of the Twelve: Methodological Foundations–Redactional Processes–Historical Insights* (BZAW 433; Berlin: de Gruyter, 2012) 355–70.

Döhling, Jan-Dirk
"Jona und des Meeres Wellen: Zum problemgeschichtlichen Horizont und zum traditionsgeschichtlichen Hintergrund der Schöpfungsdynamik in Jona 1 und 2," *BN* 158 (2013) 17–37.

Doran, Robert
2 Maccabees: A Critical Commentary (Hermeneia; Minneapolis: Fortress Press, 2012).

Idem
Stewards of the Poor: The Man of God, Rabbula, and Hiba in the Fifth-Century Edessa (Cistercian Studies 208; Kalamazoo, MI: Cistercian Publications, 2006).

Dorsey, David A.
"Literary Architecture and Meaning in the Book of Jonah," in David Merling, ed., *To Understand the Scriptures: Essays in Honor of William H. Shea* (Berrien Springs, MI: Institute of Archaeology, Siegfried H. Horn Archaeological Museum, Andrews University, 1997) 57–69.

Dorson, Richard
"Yorker Yarns of Yore," *NYFQ* 3 (1947) 5–27.

Downs, David J.
"The Specter of Exile in the Story of Jonah," *HBT* 31 (2009) 27–44.

Dozeman, Thomas B.
"Inner-Biblical Interpretation of Yahweh's Gracious and Compassionate Character," *JBL* 108 (1989) 207–23.

Drazin, Israel
Unusual Bible Interpretations: Jonah and Amos (Jerusalem: Gefen, 2016).

Dreier, Vjatscheslav
"JHWHs Grenzenlose Liebe: JHWH und seine Schöpfung im Jonabuch," in Manfred Oeming, ed., *Ahavah: Die Liebe Gottes im Alten Testament* (ABG 55; Leipzig: Evangelische Verlagsanstalt, 2018) 233–56.

Duval, Yves-Marie
Le livre de Jonas dans la littérature chrétienne grecque et latine: Sources et influence du commentaire sur Jonas de saint Jérôme (2 vols.; Paris: Études Augustiniennes, 1973).

Edelman, Diana V.
"Jonah among the Twelve in the MT: The Triumph of Torah over Prophecy," in Diana V. Edelman and

Ehud Ben Zvi, eds., *The Production of Prophecy. Constructing Prophecy and Prophets in Yehud* (BibleWorld; London: Equinox, 2009) 150–67.

Ego, Beate
"The Repentance of Nineveh in the Story of Jonah and Nahum's Prophecy of the City's Destruction: A Coherent Reading of the Book of the Twelve as Reflected in the Aggada," in Paul L. Redditt and Aaron Schart, eds., *Thematic Threads in the Book of the Twelve* (BZAW 325; Berlin: de Gruyter, 2003) 155–74.

Elata-Alster, Gerda, and Rachel Salmon
"The Deconstruction of Genre in the Book of Jonah: Towards a Theological Discourse," *LitTheo* 3 (1989) 40–60.

Emmerson, Grace I.
"Another Look at the Book of Jonah," *ExpTim* 88 (1976) 86–88.

Ephros, Abraham Z.
"The Book of Jonah as Allegory," *JBQ* 27 (1999) 141–54.

Eynikel, Erik
"One Day, Three Days, and Forty Days in the Book of Jonah," in Patrick Chatelion Counet and Ulrich Berges, eds., *One Text, A Thousand Methods: Studies in Memory of Sjef van Tilborg* (BibInt 71; Leiden: Brill, 2005) 65–76.

Feldman, Louis H.
"Josephus' Interpretation of Jonah," *AJSR* 17 (1992) 1–29.

Ferber, Stanley
"Micrography: A Jewish Art Form," *JJA* 3–4 (1977) 12–24.

Ferreira, Johan
"A Note on Jonah 2:8: Idolatry and Inhumanity in Israel," *BT* 63 (2012) 28–38.

Feuillet, A.
"Le sens du livre de Jonas," *RB* 54 (1947) 340–61.

Idem
"Les sources du livre de Jonas," *RB* 54 (1947) 161–86.

Fincke, Jeannette C.
"Divination im Alten Orient: Ein Überblick," in Jeannette C. Fincke, ed., *Divination in the Ancient Near East: A Workshop on Divination Conducted during the 54th Rencontre Assyriologique Internationale at Würzburg, 20–25 July 2008* (Winona Lake, IN: Eisenbrauns, 2014) 1–20.

Fischel, Henry
"Martyr and Prophet," *JQR* 37 (1947) 265–80, 363–86.

Fischer, Irmtraud
"'. . . und mir sollte nicht leid sein . . .?' Über die Facetten von Gottes Mitleid im Jonabuch," *JBTh* 30 (2015) 89–107.

Foley, John Miles
Immanent Art: From Structure to Meaning in Traditional Oral Epic (Bloomington: Indiana University Press, 1991).

Forti, Tova
"Of Ships and Seas, Fish and Beasts: Viewing the Concept of Universal Providence in the Book of Jonah through the Prism of Psalms," *JSOT* 35 (2011) 359–74.

Fox, Everett
The Five Books of Moses: Genesis, Exodus, Leviticus, Numbers, Deuteronomy: A New Translation with Introductions, Commentary, and Notes (Schocken Bible 1; New York: Schocken, 1995).

Frahm, Eckart
"Of Doves, Fish, and Goddesses: Reflections on the Literary, Religious, and Historical Background of the Book of Jonah," in Joel Baden, Hindy Najman, and Eibert Tigchelaar, eds., *Sibyls, Scriptures, and Scrolls: John Collins at Seventy* (2 vols.; JSJSup 175; Leiden: Brill, 2016) 1:432–50.

Frazer, James George
Folklore in the Old Testament (3 vols.; London: Macmillan, 1918).

Fredricksen, Paula
"Christians in the Roman Empire," in David S. Potter, ed., *A Companion to the Roman Empire* (Blackwell Companions to the Ancient World: Ancient History; Chichester: Wiley Blackwell, 2010) 587–606.

Freedman, David Noel.
"Did God Play a Dirty Trick on Jonah at the End?," *BRev* 6 (1990) 26–31.

Idem
"Jonah 1:4b," *JBL* 77 (1958) 161–62.

Fretheim, Terence E.
"The Exaggerated God of Jonah," *WW* 27 (2007) 125–34.

Idem
Jonah and Theodicy," *ZAW* 90 (1978) 227–37.

Idem
The Message of Jonah: A Theological Commentary (Minneapolis: Augsburg, 1977).

Idem
"The Repentance of God: A Key to Evaluating Old Testament God-Talk," *HBT* 10 (1988) 47–70.

Frolov, Serge
"Returning the Ticket: God and His Prophet in the Book of Jonah," *JSOT* 86 (1999) 85–105.

Fuller, Russell
"The Form and Formation of the Book of the Twelve: The Evidence from the Judean Desert," in James W. Watts and Paul R. House, eds., *Forming Prophetic Literature: Essays on Isaiah and the Twelve in Honor of John D. W. Watts* (JSOTSup 235; Sheffield: Sheffield Academic Press, 1996) 86–101.

Gaines, Janet Howe
Forgiveness in a Wounded World: Jonah's Dilemma (SBLStBL 5; Atlanta: Society of Biblical Literature, 2003).

Galpaz-Feller, Pnina
Jonah–A Journey to Freedom: A New Reading of the Book of Jonah (Jerusalem: Carmel, 2009).

Garber, Zev, and Bruce Zuckerman
"The Odd Prophet Out and In," in Frederick E. Greenspahn and Gary A. Rendsburg, eds., *Le-ma'an Ziony: Essays in Honor of Ziony Zevit* (Eugene, OR: Cascade, 2017) 175–202.

Gaster, Moses
The Exempla of the Rabbis: Being a Collection of Exempla, Apologues and Tales Culled from Hebrew Manuscripts and Rare Hebrew Books (London: Asia Publishing, 1924; repr., New York: Ktav, 1968).

Gaster, Theodor H.
Myth, Legend, and Custom in the Old Testament: A Comparative Study with Chapters from Sir James G. Frazer's Folklore in the Old Testament (2 vols.; 1969; repr., Gloucester, MA: Peter Smith, 1981).

Idem
The Oldest Stories in the World (Boston: Beacon Press, 1952).

Gerstenberger, Erhard S.
"Psalms in the Book of the Twelve: How Misplaced Are They?," in Paul L. Redditt and Aaron Schart, eds., *Thematic Threads in the Book of the Twelve* (BZAW 325; Berlin: de Gruyter, 2003) 72–89.

Gese, Hartmut
Alttestamentliche Studien (Tübingen: Mohr Siebeck, 1991).

Gevaryahu, Haim
"The Universality of the Book of Jonah," *DD* 10 (1981) 20–27.

Gillmayr-Bucher, Susanne
"Jonah and the Other: A Discourse on Interpretive Competence," in *Imagining the Other and Constructing Israelite Identity in the Early Second Temple Period* (LHBOTS 456; London: Bloomsbury, 2014) 201–18.

Ginsberg, H. L.
The Five Megilloth and Jonah: A New Translation (Philadelphia: Jewish Publication Society of America, 1969).

Idem
"Lexicographical Note," in Benedikt Hartmann et al., eds., *Hebräische Wortforschung: Festschrift zum 80. Geburtstag von Walter Baumgartner* (VTSup 16; Leiden: Brill, 1967) 71–82.

Gitay, Yehoshua
"Jonah: The Prophecy of Antirhetoric," in Astrid B. Beck et al., eds., *Fortunate the Eyes That See: Essays in Honor of David Noel Freedman in Celebration of His Seventieth Birthday* (Grand Rapids: Eerdmans, 1995) 197–206.

Glasson, T. Francis
"The Final Question in Jonah and Nahum," *ExpTim* 81 (1969) 54–55.

Goitein, S. D.
"Some Observations on Jonah," *JPOS* 17 (1937) 63–77.

Goldstein, Elizabeth
"On the Use of the Name of God in the Book of Jonah," in Sara Malena and David Miano, eds., *Milk and Honey: Essays on Ancient Israel and the Bible in Appreciation of the Judaic Studies Program at the University of California, San Diego* (Winona Lake, IN: Eisenbrauns, 2007) 77–83.

Good, Edwin M.
Irony in the Old Testament (Sheffield: Almond Press, 1981).

Goodhart, Sandor
"Prophecy, Sacrifice and Repentance in the Story of Jonah," *Semeia* 33 (1985) 43–63.

Goswell, Gregory
"Jonah among the Twelve Prophets," *JBL* 135 (2016) 283-90.

Grabar, André
The Beginnings of Christian Art, 200-395 (trans. Stuart Gilbert and James Emmons; Arts of Mankind 9; New York: Thames & Hudson, 1967).

Green, Barbara
"Beyond Messages: How Meaning Emerges from Our Reading of Jonah," *WW* 27 (2007) 149-56.

Greenberg, Moshe
Biblical Prose Prayer as a Window to the Popular Religion of Ancient Israel (TLJS 6; Berkeley: University of California Press, 1983).

Greenfield, Noah
"Jonah's Ark and Noah's Fish," *AJBI* 33 (2007) 37-72.

Gregg, Robert C.
Shared Stories, Rival Tellings: Early Encounters of Jews, Christians, and Muslims (Oxford: Oxford University Press, 2015).

Guillaume, Philippe
"Caution: Rhetorical Questions!," *BN* 103 [2000] 11-17.

Idem
"The End of Jonah Is the Beginning of Wisdom," *Bib* 87 (2006) 243-50.

Idem
"Rhetorical Reading Redundant: A Response to Ehud Ben Zvi," *JHebS* 9 (2009) 1-9.

Idem
"The Unlikely Malachi-Jonah Sequence (4QXII^a)," *JHebS* 7 (2007) 2-10.

Gunn, David M., and Danna Nolan Fewell
Narrative in the Hebrew Bible (Oxford: Oxford University Press, 1993).

Habel, N.
"The Form and Significance of the Call Narrative," *ZAW* 77 (1965) 297-323.

Hacham, Noah
"3 Maccabees and Esther: Parallels, Intertextuality, and Diaspora Identity," *JBL* 126 (2007) 765-85.

Hachlili, Rachel
Ancient Mosaic Pavements: Themes, Issues, and Trends; Selected Studies (Leiden: Brill, 2009).

Hallo, William W.
"Jonah and the Uses of Parody," in John J. Ahn and Stephen L. Cook, eds., *Thus Says the Lord: Essays on the Former and Latter Prophets in Honor of Robert R. Wilson* (LHBOTS 502; London: T&T Clark, 2009) 285-91.

Halpern, Baruch, and Richard Elliott Friedman
"Composition and Paronomasia in the Book of Jonah," *HAR* 4 (1980) 79-92.

Halpert, Herbert
"Three Tales from Gwent," *JAF* 58 (1945) 51-52.

Hamel, Gildas
"Taking the Argo to Nineveh: Jonah and Jason in a Mediterranean Context," *Judaism* 44 (1995) 341-59.

Handy, Lowell K.
Jonah's World: Social Science and the Reading of Prophetic Story (London: Equinox, 2007).

Hanson, Paul D.
The Dawn of Apocalyptic (Philadelphia: Fortress Press, 1975).

Harris, Robert A.
"Contextual Reading: Rabbi Eliezer of Beaugency's Commentary on Jonah," in Kathryn F. Kravitz and Diane M. Sharon, eds., *Bringing the Hidden to Light: The Process of Interpretation; Studies in Honor of Stephen A. Geller* (Winona Lake, IN: Eisenbrauns, 2007) 79-101.

Idem
Rabbi Eliezer of Beaugency Commentaries on Amos and Jonah. Introduction, translation, and commentary (With Selections from Isaiah and Ezekiel) (MIP; Kalamazoo: Western Michigan University, 2018).

Harvey, Graham
The True Israel: Uses of the Names Jew, Hebrew, and Israel in Ancient Jewish and Early Christian Literature (Leiden: Brill, 2001).

Hasel, Michael G.
"Assyrian Military Practices and Deuteronomy's Laws of Warfare," in Brad E. Kelle and Frank Ritchel Ames, eds., *Writing and Reading War: Rhetoric, Gender, and Ethics in Biblical and Modern Contexts* (SBLSymS 42; Atlanta: Society of Biblical Literature, 2008) 67-81.

Haupt, Paul
"Jonah's Whale," *PAPHS* 46 (1907) 151-64.

Hauser, Alan Jon
"Jonah: In Pursuit of the Dove," *JBL* 104 (1985) 21-37.

Hays, Christopher B.
Death in the Iron Age II and in First Isaiah (FAT 79; Tübingen: Mohr Siebeck, 2011).

Hesse, E. W., and I. M. Kikawada
"Jonah and Genesis 1–11," *AJBI* 10 (1984) 3–19.

Himmelfarb, Martha
Ascent to Heaven in Jewish and Christian Apocalypses (New York: Oxford University Press, 1993).

Eadem
Tours of Hell: An Apocalyptic Form in Jewish and Christian Literature (Philadelphia: Fortress Press, 1983).

Holbert, John C.
"'Deliverance Belongs to Yahweh!': Satire in the Book of Jonah," *JSOT* 21 (1981) 59–81.

Holmstedt, Robert D., and Alexander T. Kirk
"Subversive Boundary Drawing in Jonah: The Variation of אשר and ש as Literary Code-Switching," *VT* 66 (2016) 542–55.

Holtz, Shalom
Praying Legally (BJS 364; Providence, RI: Brown Judaic Studies, 2019).

Hoop, Raymond de
"The Book of Jonah as Poetry: An Analysis of Jonah 1:1–16," in Willem van der Meer and Johannes C. de Moor, eds., *The Structural Analysis of Biblical and Canaanite Poetry* (JSOTSup 74; Sheffield: Sheffield Academic Press, 1988) 156–71.

Horwitz, William J.
"Another Interpretation of Jonah 1 12," *VT* 23 (1973) 370–72.

Houk, Cornelius B.
"Linguistic Patterns in Jonah," *JSOT* 77 (1998) 81–102.

House, Paul R.
"Endings as New Beginnings: Returning to the Lord, the Day of the Lord, and Renewal in the Book of the Twelve," in Paul L. Redditt and Aaron Schart, eds., *Thematic Threads in the Book of the Twelve* (BZAW 325; Berlin: de Gruyter, 2003) 313–38.

Hull, Vernam
"Conall Corc and the Corco Luigde," *PMLA* 62.4 (1947) 887–909.

Hunter, Alastair
"Jonah from the Whale: Exodus Motifs in Jonah 2," in Johannes C. de Moor, ed., *The Elusive Prophet: The Prophet as Historical Person, Literary Character and Anonymous Artist* (OTS 45; Leiden: Brill, 2001) 142–58.

Hurvitz, Avi
"The History of a Legal Formula: *kōl 'ašer-ḥāpēṣ 'āśāh* (Psalms CXV 3, CXXXV 6)," *VT* 32 (1982) 257–67.

Ingram, Virginia
"Satire and Cognitive Dissonance in the Book of Jonah, in the Light of Ellens' Laws of Psychological Hermeneutics," in J. Harold Ellens, ed., *Psychological Hermeneutics for Biblical Themes and Texts: A Festschrift for Wayne G. Rollins* (London: T&T Clark, 2012) 140–55.

In-Sob, Zong
Folk Tales from Korea (London: Routledge & Kegan Paul, 1952).

Jensen, Robin Margaret
Understanding Early Christian Art (London: Routledge, 2000).

Jenson, Philip Peter
"Interpreting Jonah's God: Canon and Criticism," in Robert P. Gordon, ed., *The God of Israel* (Cambridge: Cambridge University Press, 2007) 229–45.

Jepsen, Alfred
"אמן," *TDOT* 1:292–23.

Jeremias, Jörg
"Das Jonabuch in der Forschung seit Hans Walter Wolff," in Hans Walter Wolff, *Studien zum Jonabuch: Mit einem Anhang von Jörg Jeremias* (Neukirchen-Vluyn: Neukirchener Verlag, 2003) 93–128. Original without appendix by Jeremias, 1965.

Johnson, A. R.
"Jonah II. 3–10: A Study in Cultic Phantasy," in H. H. Rowley, ed., *Studies in Old Testament Prophecy: Presented to Theodore H. Robinson by the Society for Old Testament Study on His Sixty-fifth Birthday, August 9th, 1946* (Edinburgh: T&T Clark, 1957) 82–102.

Joüon, Paul
"Notes philologiques sur le texte *hébreu* de Osée 2, 7, 11; Joël 1, 7; 1, 15 (=1S. 13, 6); Jonas 1, 8; Habacuc 2, 2; Aggée 2, 11-14; Zacharie 1, 5; 3, 9; Malachie 1, 14," *Bib* 10 (1929) 417–20.

Kadari, Tamar
"Aggadic Motifs in the Story of Jonah: A Study of Interaction between Religions," in Alberdina Houtman et al., eds., *Religious Stories*

in Transformation: Conflict, Revision and Reception (Jewish and Christian Perspectives 31; Leiden: Brill, 2016) 107–25.

Kahn, Paul
"An Analysis of the Book of Jonah," *Judaism* 43 (1994) 87–100.

Kaiser, Barbara B.
"Five Scholars in the Underbelly of the *Dag Gadol*: An Aqua-Fantasy," *WW* 27 (2007) 135–48.

Kaplan, Jacob
"The Archaeology and History of Tel Aviv-Jaffa," *BA* 35 (1972) 66–95.

Kaplan, Jonathan
"Jonah and Moral Agency," *JSOT* 43 (2019) 146–62.

Keller, Carl A.
"Jonas, le portrait d'un prophète," *TZ* 21 (1965) 329–40.

Kidner, F. D.
"The Distribution of Divine Names in Jonah," *TynBul* 21 (1970) 126–28.

Kim, Hyun Chul Paul
"Jonah Read Intertextually," *VT* 126 (2007) 497–528.

Kim, Yoo-ki
"The Function of היטב in Jonah 4 and Its Translation," *Bib* 90 (2009) 389–93.

Knapp, Andrew.
"The Murder of Sennacherib, Yet Again," *JAOS* 140 (2020) 165–81.

Komlós, Ottó
"Jonah Legends," in Ottó Komlós, ed., *Etudes orientales à la mémoire de Paul Hirschler* (Budapest: Allamositott, 1950) 41–61.

Kraeling, Emil G.
"The Evolution of the Story of Jonah," in *Hommages à André Dupont-Sommer* (Paris: Adrien-Maisonneuve, 1971) 305–18.

Krantz, Eva Strömberg
Des Schiffes Weg Mitten im Meer: Beiträge zur Erforschung der nautischen Terminologie des Alten Testaments (ConBOT 19; Lund: Gleerup, 1984).

Kristeva, Julia
Desire in Language: A Semiotic Approach to Literature and Art (ed. L. S. Roudiez; trans. Thomas Gora et al.; European Perspectives; New York: Columbia University Press, 1980).

Kugel, James
The Bible as It Was (Cambridge, MA: Belknap Press of Harvard University Press, 1997).

Idem
How to Read the Bible: A Guide to Scripture, Then and Now (New York: Free Press, 2007).

Idem
The Idea of Biblical Poetry: Parallelism and Its History (New Haven: Yale University Press, 1981).

Idem
"Two Introductions to Midrash," *Prooftexts* 3 (1983) 131–55.

Kurichianil, John
"Jonah, A Disobedient Prophet," *ITS* 52 (2015) 163–76.

LaCocque, André, and Pierre-Emmanuel LaCocque
Jonah: A Psycho-Religious Approach to the Prophet (Studies on Personalities of the Old Testament; Columbia: University of South Carolina Press, 1990).

Landes, George M.
"A Case for the Sixth-Century BCE Dating of the Book of Jonah," in Prescott H. Williams Jr. and Theodore Hiebert, eds., *Realia Dei: Essays in Archaeology and Biblical Interpretation in Honor of Edward F. Campbell, Jr. at His Retirement* (Scholars Press Homage Series 23; Atlanta: Scholars Press, 1999) 100–116.

Idem
"Jonah: A *Māšāl*?," in John G. Gammie et al., eds., *Israelite Wisdom: Theological and Literary Essays in Honor of Samuel Terrien* (Scholars Press Homage Series 3; Missoula, MT: Scholars Press, 1978) 137–58.

Idem
"The Kerygma of the Book of Jonah: The Contextual Interpretation of the Jonah Psalm," *Int* 12 (1967) 3–31.

Idem
"Linguistic Criteria and the Date of the Book of Jonah," *ErIsr* 16 (1982) 147–70.

Idem
"Textual 'Information Gaps' and 'Dissonances' in the Interpretation of the Book of Jonah," in Robert Chazan, William W. Hallo, and Lawrence H. Schiffman, eds., *Ki Baruch Hu: Ancient Near Eastern, Biblical and Judaic Studies in Honor of Baruch A. Levine* (Winona Lake, IN: Eisenbrauns, 1999) 273–93.

Idem
"The 'Three Days and Three Nights' Motif in Jonah 2:1," *JBL* 86 (1967) 446–50.

Lasine, Stuart
"Jonah's Complexes and Our Own: Psychology and the Interpretation of Jonah," *JSOT* 41 (2017) 237–60.

Lauterbach, Jacob Z.
Mekilta de-Rabbi Ishmael (3 vols.; 1933–1935; repr., Philadelphia: Jewish Publication Society of America, 1976).

Lazarus, Benjamin M.
Humanist Comic Elements in Aristophanes and the Old Testament (Piscataway, NJ: Gorgias Press, 1914).

Levine, Baruch A.
"The Place of Jonah in the History of Biblical Ideas," in Stephen L. Cook and S. C. Winter, eds., *On the Way to Nineveh: Studies in Honor of George M. Landes* (ASOR Books 4; Atlanta: Scholars Press, 1999) 201–17.

Levine, Étan
The Aramaic Version of the Bible: Contents and Context (BZAW 174; Berlin: de Gruyter, 1988).

Idem
Heaven and Earth, Law and Love. Studies in Biblical Thought (BZAW 303; Berlin: de Gruyter, 2000).

Idem
"Jonah as a Philosophical Book," *ZAW* 96 (1984) 235–45.

Idem
"Justice in Judaism: The Case of Jonah," *RRJ* 5 (2002) 170–97.

Lichtert, Claude
"Entre rappels et reversements: Les particularités littéraires et théologiques du récit de Jonas," in Elena Di Pede and Donatella Scaiola, eds., *The Book of the Twelve–One Book or Many? Metz Conference Proceedings, 5–7 November 2015* (FAT 2.91; Tübingen: Mohr Siebeck, 2016) 134–44.

Idem
"Un siècle de recherche à propos de 'Jonas': (1re partie)," *RB* 112 (2005) 192–214.

Idem
"Un siècle de recherche à propos de 'Jonas': (2e partie)," *RB* 112 (2005) 330–54.

Lillegard, David
"Narrative and Paradox in Jonah," *Kerux* 8 (1993) 19–30.

Limburg, James
"Jonah and the Whale through the Eyes of Artists," *BRev* 6 (1990) 18–25.

Lindblom, Johannes
"Lot-Casting in the Old Testament," *VT* 12 (1962) 164–78.

Lindenberger, J. M.
"Ahiqar: A New Translation and Introduction," in James H. Charlesworth, ed., *The Old Testament Pseudepigrapha* (2 vols.; Garden City, NY: Doubleday, 1983–1985) 2:479–507.

Ling, Roger
Ancient Mosaics (Princeton, NJ: Princeton University Press, 1998).

Liptzin, Sol
"The Literary Impact of Jonah," *DD* 7 (1978) 9–20.

Liverani, Mario
Assyria: The Imperial Mission (trans. Andrea Trameri and Jonathan Valk; Mesopotamian Civilizations 20; Winona Lake, IN: Eisenbrauns, 2017).

Loader, James A.
"Jonah's Commission," *OTE* 22 (2009) 589–604.

Lohfink, Norbert
"Die Gattung der 'Historischen Kurzgeschichte' in den letzten Jahren von Juda und in der Zeit des Babylonischen Exils," *ZAW* 90 (1978) 319–47.

Idem
"Jona ging zur Stadt hinaus (Jon 4, 5)," *BZ* 5 (1961) 185–203.

Long, Burke O.
"The Effect of Divination upon Israelite Literature," *JBL* 92 (1973) 489–97.

Lord, Albert B.
The Singer of Tales (HSCL 24; Cambridge, MA: Harvard University Press, 1960; repr., Cambridge, MA: Harvard University Press, 1988).

Loretz, Otto
"Herkunft und Sinn der Jona-Erzählung," *BZ* 5 (1961) 18–29.

Love, Nathan Patrick
"Translating Jonah 2:9: Looking for a Breath of Fresh Air," *BT* 64 (2013) 266–83.

Machinist, Peter
"The Fall of Assyria in Comparative Ancient Perspective," in Simo Parpola and R. M. Whiting, eds., *Assyria 1995: Proceedings of the 10th Anniversary Symposium of Neo-Assyrian Text Corpus Project, Helsinki, September*

7-11, 1995 (Helsinki: Neo-Assyrian Text Corpus Project, 1997) 179–95.

Idem
"Nahum as Prophet and as Prophetic Book: Some Reconsiderations," in Heinz-Josef Fabry, ed., *The Books of the Twelve Prophets: Minor Prophets, Major Theologies* (BETL 295; Leuven: Peeters, 2018) 103–29.

Magness, Jodi, et al.
"The Huqoq Excavation Project: 2014–2017 Interim Report," *BASOR* 380 (2018) 61–131.

Magonet, Jonathan
Form and Meaning: Studies in Literary Techniques in the Book of Jonah (Bible and Literature 8; Sheffield: Almond, 1983).

Malinowski, Bronislaw
Magic, Science, and Religion and Other Essays (Garden City, NY: Doubleday, 1954).

Mankowski, Paul V.
Akkadian Loanwords in Biblical Hebrew (HSS 47; Winona Lake, IN: Eisenbrauns, 2000).

Mann, Steven T.
"Performance Prayers of a Prophet: Investigating the Prayers of Jonah as Speech Acts," *CBQ* 79 (2017) 20–40.

Marcus, David
From Balaam to Jonah: Anti-prophetic Satire in the Hebrew Bible (BJS 301; Atlanta: Scholars Press, 1995).

Idem
"Nineveh's 'Three Days' Walk' (Jonah 3:3): Another Interpretation," in Stephen L. Cook and S. C. Winter, eds., *On the Way to Nineveh: Studies in Honor of George M. Landes* (ASOR Books 4; Atlanta: Scholars Press, 1999) 42–53.

Mather, Judson
"The Comic Art of the Book of Jonah," *Soundings* 65 (1982) 280–91.

Mathews, Thomas F.
The Clash of Gods: A Reinterpretation of Early Christian Art (Princeton, NJ: Princeton University Press, 1993).

McCarter, P. Kyle
"The River Ordeal in Israelite Literature," *HTR* 66 (1973) 403–12.

McKenzie, Steven L.
"The Genre of Jonah," in Mark A. O'Brien and Howard N. Wallace, eds., *Seeing Signals, Reading Signs: The Art of Exegesis; Studies in Honour of Antony F. Campbell, SJ for his Seventieth Birthday* (JSOTSup 415; London: T&T Clark, 2004) 159–71.

Menn, Esther
"No Ordinary Lament: Relecture and the Identity of the Distressed in Psalm 22," *HTR* 93 (2000) 301–41.

Meredith, Christopher
"The Conundrum of *ḥtr* in Jonah 1:13," *VT* 64 (2014) 147–52.

Miles, John R., Jr.
"Laughing at the Bible: Jonah as Parody," *JQR* 65 (1975) 168–81.

Millar, Fergus
"Transformations of Judaism under Greco-Roman Rule: Responses to Seth Schwartz's 'Imperialism and Jewish Society,'" *JJS* 57 (2006) 139–58.

Miller, Cynthia, ed.
The Verbless Clause in Biblical Hebrew (Winona Lake, IN: Eisenbrauns, 1999) 196

Miller, Patrick D.
They Cried to the Lord: The Form and Theology of Biblical Prayer (Minneapolis: Fortress Press, 1994).

Idem
"Trouble and Woe: Interpreting Biblical Laments," *Int* 37 (1983) 32–45.

Mithra, Sarat Chandra
"Note on a Tamil Tale of the Old Dame Lousy Type," *Man in India* 5 (1925) 269–72.

Moberly, R. W. L.
"Preaching for a Response? Jonah's Message to the Ninevites Reconsidered," *VT* 53 (2003) 156–68.

Mowinckel, Sigmund
"Hat es ein israelitisches Nationalepos gegeben?," *ZAW* 53 (1953) 130–52.

Muldoon, Catherine L.
In Defense of Divine Justice. An Intertextual Approach to the Book of Jonah (CBQMS 47; Washington, DC: Catholic Biblical Association of America, 2010).

Mulzer, Martin
"Die Datierung des Jonabuches: Eine Prüfung der Argumente," *BZ* 61 (2007) 230–48.

Idem
"Satzgrenzen im Jonabuch im Vergleich von hebräischer und griechischer Texttradition," *BN* 113 (2002) 61–68.

Idem
"ספינה (Jon 1, 5) (gedeckter) Laderaum," *BN* 104 (2000) 83–94.

Muraoka, Takamitsu
"A Case of Diglossia in the Book of Jonah," *VT* 62 (2012) 129–31.

Narkiss, Bezalel
Hebrew Illuminated Manuscripts (Jerusalem: Keter, 1969).

Idem
"The Sign of Jonah," *Gesta* 18 (1979) 63–76.

Nel, Philip J.
"The Symbolism and Function of Epic Space in Jonah," *JNSL* 25 (1999) 215–24.

Neusner, Jacob
Eliezer ben Hyrcanus: The Tradition and the Man (2 vols.; SJLA 3–4; Leiden: Brill, 1973).

Niccacci, Alviero
"Syntactic Analysis of Jonah," *LASBF* 46 (1996) 9–32.

Niditch, Susan
"The Challenge of Israelite Epic," in John Miles Foley, ed., *A Companion to Ancient Epic* (Blackwell Companions to the Ancient World: Literature and Culture; Oxford: Blackwell, 2005) 277–87.

Eadem
"The Composition of Isaiah 1," *Bib* 61 (1980) 509–29.

Eadem
"Fish Swallows Man: The Tale of Jonah and Its Reception History in Folkloristic Perspective," in Peter Machinist et al., eds., *Ve'Ed Ya'leh (Gen 2:6): Essays in Biblical and Ancient Near Eastern Studies Presented to Edward L. Greenstein* (2 vols.; WAWsup 5–6; Atlanta, GA: SBL Press, 2021) 2:1079–95.

Eadem
Judges: A Commentary (OTL; Louisville: Westminster John Knox, 2008).

Eadem
The Responsive Self: Personal Religion in Biblical Literature of the Neo-Babylonian and Persian Periods (AYBRL; New Haven: Yale University Press, 2015).

Eadem
The Symbolic Vision in Biblical Tradition (HSM 30; Chico, CA: Scholars Press, 1980).

Nielsen, E.
"Le message primitif du livre de Jonas," *RHPR* 59 (1979) 499–507.

Nixon, Rosemary A.
The Message of Jonah: Presence in the Storm (Bible Speaks Today; Downers Grove, IL: InterVarsity Press, 2003).

Nogalski, James D.
"Intertextuality and the Twelve," in James W. Watts and Paul R. House, eds., *Forming Prophetic Literature: Essays on Isaiah and the Twelve in Honor of John D. W. Watts* (JSOTSup 235; Sheffield: Sheffield Academic Press, 1996) 102–24.

Nogalski, James D., and Marvin A. Sweeney, eds.
Reading and Hearing the Book of the Twelve (SBLSymS 15; Atlanta: Society of Biblical Literature, 2000).

Olyan, Saul
"The Literary Dynamic of Loyalty and Betrayal in the Aramaic Ahiqar Narrative," *JNES* 79 (2020) 261–69.

Oppenheim, A. Leo
"Perspectives on Mesopotamian Divination," in *La divination en Mésopotamie ancienne et dans les régions voisines: 14th Rencontre assyriologiques internationale (Strasbourg, 2–6 juillet 1965)* (Paris: Presses universitaires de France, 1966) 35–43.

Orlinsky, Harry
"Nationalism, Universalism and Internationalism in Ancient Israel," in Harry Thomas Frank and William L. Reed, eds., *Translating and Understanding the Old Testament: Essays in Honor of Herbert Gordon May* (Nashville: Abingdon, 1970) 206–37.

Orth, Michael
"Genre in Jonah: The Effects of Parody in the Book of Jonah," in William W. Hallo, Bruce William Jones, and Gerald L. Mattingly, eds., *The Bible in the Light of Cuneiform Literature* (Scripture in Context 3; ANETS 8; Lewiston, NY: Mellen, 1990) 257–81.

Pajunen, Mika S., and Hanne von Weissenberg
"The Book of Malachi, Manuscript 4Q76 (4QXII^a), and the Formation of the 'Book of the Twelve,'" *JBL* 134 (2015) 731–51.

Parpola, Simo
"The Murder of Sennacherib," in Bendt Alster, ed., *Death in Mesopotamia: Papers Read at the XXVIe Rencontre Assyriologique Internationale* (Mesopotamia 8; Copenhagen: Akedemisk, 1980) 171–82.

Parsons, Elsie Clews
"Spirituals and Other Folklore from the Bahamas," *JAF* 41 (1928) 453–524.

Patai, Raphael
"Jewish Seafaring in Ancient Times," *JQR* 32 (1941) 1–26.

Paul, Shalom M.
"Jonah 2:7: The Descent to the Netherworld and Its Mesopotamian Congeners," in Marilyn J. Lundberg, Steven Fine, and Wayne T. Pitard, eds., *Puzzling Out the Past: Studies in Northwest Semitic Languages and Literatures in Honor of Bruce Zuckerman* (CHANE 55; Leiden: Brill, 2012) 131–34.

Payne, David F.
"Jonah from the Perspective of Its Audience," *JSOT* 13 (1979) 3–12.

Payne, Robin
"The Prophet Jonah: Reluctant Messenger and Intercessor," *ExpTim* 100 (1989) 131–34.

Peilstöker, Martin, and Aaron A. Burke, eds.
The History and Archaeology of Jaffa, 1 (Monumenta Archaeologica 25; Los Angeles: Cotsen Institute of Archaeology Press, University of California Los Angeles, 2011).

Peleg, Yitzhak
"'Yet Forty Days and Nineveh Shall Be Overthrown' (Jonah 3.4): Two Readings (Shtei Krie'ot) of the Book of Jonah," in J. Harold Ellens et al., eds., *God's Word for Our World*, vol. 1: *Biblical Studies in Honor of Simon John De Vries* (JSOTSup 388; London: T&T Clark, 2004) 262–74.

Pelli, Moshe
"The Literary Art of Jonah," *HS* 20/21 (1979–1980) 18–28.

Perkins, Larry
"The Septuagint of Jonah: Aspects of Literary Analysis Applied to Biblical Translation," *BIOSCS* 20 (1987) 43–53.

Perry, T. A.
"Changing God's Mind: Abraham versus Jonah," in Diana Lipton, ed., *Universalism and Particularism at Sodom and Gomorrah: Essays in Memory of Ron Pirson* (AIL 11; Atlanta: Society of Biblical Literature, 2012) 43–52.

Idem
The Honeymoon Is Over: Jonah's Argument with God (Peabody, MA: Hendrickson, 2006).

Person, Raymond F., Jr.
In Conversation with Jonah: Conversation Analysis, Literary Criticism, and the Book of Jonah (JSOTSup 220; Sheffield: Sheffield Academic Press, 1996).

Idem
"The Role of Nonhuman Characters in Jonah," in Norman C. Habel and Peter Trudinger, eds., *Exploring Ecological Hermeneutics* (SBLSymS 46; Atlanta: Society of Biblical Literature, 2008) 85–90.

Pesch, Rudolf
"Zur konzentrischen Struktur von Jona 1," *Bib* 47 (1966) 577–81.

Peters, Kurtis
"Jonah 1 and the Battle with the Sea: Myth and Irony," *SJOT* 32 (2018) 157–65.

Petersen, David L.
"A Book of the Twelve?," in James D. Nogalski and Marvin A. Sweeney, eds., *Reading and Hearing the Book of the Twelve* (SBLSymS 15; Atlanta: Society of Biblical Literature, 2000) 1–10.

Pilpović, Sanja, and Ljubomir Milanović
"The Jonah Sarcophagus from *Singidunum*: A Contribution to the Study of Early Christian Art in the Balkans," *Classica et Christiana* 11 (2016) 219–45.

Porten, Bezazel
"Baalshamen and the Date of the Book of Jonah," in Maurice Carrez, Joseph Doré, and Pierre Grelot, eds. *De la Tôrah au Messie: Études d'éxégèse et d'herméneutiques bibliques offertes à Henri Cazelles pour ses 25 années d'enseignement à l'Institut Catholique de Paris (Octobre 1979)* (Paris: Desclée, 1981) 237–44.

Pope, Marvin H.
"The Word שחת in Job 9:31," *JBL* 83 (1964) 269–78.

Propp, Vladimir
Morphology of the Folktale (2nd ed.; rev. and ed. Louis A. Wagner; Publications of the American Folklore Society, Bibliographical and Special Series 9; Austin: University of Texas Press, 1968; Russian original, 1928).

Pyper, Hugh S.
"Swallowed by a Song: Jonah and the Jonah-Psalm through the Looking-Glass," in Robert Rezetko, Timothy H. Lim, and W. Brian Aucker, eds., *Reflection and Refraction: Studies in Biblical Historiography in Honour of A. Graeme Auld* (VTSup 113; Leiden: Brill, 2007) 337–58.

Qimron, Elisha
"The Language of Jonah," *BetM* 81 (1980) 181–82.

Rad, Gerhard von
: *God at Work in Israel* (trans. John H. Marks; Nashville: Abingdon, 1980).

Idem
: "The Prophet Jonah," in *God at Work in Israel* (trans. John H. Marks; Nashville: Abingdon Press, 1980 [essay originally published in 1950]) 58-70.

Ratner, Robert J.
: "*Derek*: Morpho-Syntactical Considerations," *JAOS* 107 (1987) 471-73.

Idem
: "Jonah: Toward the Re-education of the Prophets," *DD* 17 (1988-1989) 10-18.

Idem
: "Jonah, the Runaway Servant," *Maarav* 5-6 (1990) 281-305.

Redditt, Paul L.
: "The Formation of the Book of the Twelve: A Review of Research," in Paul L. Redditt and Aaron Schart, eds., *Thematic Threads in the Book of the Twelve* (BZAW 325; Berlin: de Gruyter, 2003) 1-26.

Redditt, Paul L., and Aaron Schart, eds.
: *Thematic Threads in the Book of the Twelve* (BZAW 325; Berlin: de Gruyter, 2003).

Robinson, B. P.
: "Jonah's Qiqayon Plant," *ZAW* 97 (1985) 390-403.

Robson, James E.
: "Undercurrents in Jonah," *TynBul* 64 (2013) 189-215.

Rofé, Alexander
: *The Prophetical Stories: The Narratives about the Prophets in the Hebrew Bible, Their Literary Types and Their History* (Publications of the Perry Foundation for Biblical Research in the Hebrew University of Jerusalem; Jerusalem: Magnes Press, 1988).

Roffey, John W.
: "God's Truth, Jonah's Fish: Structure and Existence in the Book of Jonah," *ABR* 36 (1988) 1-18.

Römer, Thomas
: "Introduction: The Book of the Twelve—Fact or Fiction?," in Ehud Ben Zvi and James D. Nogalski, eds., *Two Sides of a Coin: Juxtaposing Views on Interpreting the Book of the Twelve/the Twelve Prophetic Books* (Analecta Gorgiana 201; Piscataway, NJ: Gorgias Press, 2009) 3-7.

Rosenberg, Joel
: "Jonah and the Prophetic Vocation," *Response* 22 (1974) 23-26.

Roth, Leon
: "Job and Jonah," in Nahum M. Glatzer, ed., *The Dimensions of Job: A Study and Selected Readings* (New York: Schocken, 1969) 71-74.

Rudolph, Wilhelm
: "Jona," in Arnulf Kuschke and Ernst Kutsch, eds., *Archäologie und Altes Testament: Festschrift für Kurt Galling zum 8. Jan. 1970* (Tübingen: Mohr Siebeck, 1970) 233-39.

Russell, John Malcolm
: "Sennacherib's Lachish Narratives," in Peter J. Holliday, ed., *Narrative and Event in Ancient Art* (Cambridge Studies in New Art History and Criticism; Cambridge: Cambridge University Press, 1993) 55-73.

Idem
: *Sennacherib's Palace without Rival at Nineveh* (Chicago: University of Chicago Press, 1991).

Ryu, Chesung Justin
: "Silence as Resistance: A Postcolonial Reading of the Silence of Jonah in Jonah 4.1-11," *JSOT* 34 (2009) 198-218.

Sakenfeld, Katharine Doob
: *The Meaning of Hesed in the Hebrew Bible: A New Inquiry* (HSM 17; Missoula, MT: Scholars Press, 1978).

Salters, Robert B.
: *Jonah and Lamentations* (OTG 29; Sheffield: JSOT Press, 1994).

Sarna, Nahum
: "Why the Book of Jonah Is Read on Yom Kippur," *BRev* 6 (1990) 24.

Sauter, Gerhard
: "Jonah 2: A Prayer out of the Deep," in Brent A. Strawn and Nancy R. Bowers, eds., *A God So Near: Essays on Old Testament Theology in Honor of Patrick D. Miller* (Winona Lake, IN: Eisenbrauns, 2003) 145-52.

Schart, Aaron
: "The Jonah-Narrative within the Book of the Twelve," in Rainer Albertz, James D. Nogalski, and Jakob Wöhrle, eds., *Perspectives on the Formation of the Book of the Twelve: Methodological Foundations–Redactional Processes–Historical Insights* (BZAW 433; Berlin: de Gruyter, 2012).

Schellenberg, Annette
: "An Anti-Prophet among the Prophets? On the Relationship of Jonah to Prophecy," *JSOT* 39 (2015) 353-71.

Schmidt, Hans
Jona: Eine Untersuchung zur vergleichenden Religionsgeschichte (FRLANT 9; Göttingen: Vandenhoeck & Ruprecht, 1907).

Scholem, Gershom, and Eric J. Schwab
"On Jonah and the Concept of Justice," *CritInq* 25 (1999) 353–61.

Schöpflin, Karin
"Notschrei, Dank und Disput: Beten im Jonasbuch," *Bib* 78 (1997) 389–404.

Schultz, Richard L.
"The Ties That Bind: Intertextuality, the Identification of Verbal Parallels, and Reading Strategies in the Book of the Twelve," in Paul L. Redditt and Aaron Schart, eds., *Thematic Threads in the Book of the Twelve* (BZAW 325; Berlin: de Gruyter, 2003) 27–45.

Schwartzbaum, Haim
Studies in Jewish and World Folklore (Fabula Supplement B.3; Berlin: de Gruyter, 1968).

Scialabba, Daniela
"The LXX Translation of Jonah 1:6: Text-critical and Exegetical Considerations," in Siegfried Kreuzer, Martin Meiser, and Marcus Sigismund, eds., *Die Septuaginta – Orte und Intentionen, 5: Internationale Fachtagung veranstaltet von Septuaginta Deutsch, Wuppertal 24.–27. Juli 2014* (WUNT 361; Tübingen: Mohr Siebeck, 2016) 645–54.

Scott, R. B. Y.
"The Sign of Jonah," *Int* 19 (1965) 16–25.

Segert, Stanislav
"Syntax and Style in the Book of Jonah: Six Simple Approaches to Their Analysis," in J. A. Emerton, ed., *Prophecy: Essays Presented to Georg Fohrer on His Sixty-fifth Birthday, 6. September 1980* (BZAW 150; Berlin: de Gruyter, 2011) 121–30.

Seidler, Ayelet
"'Fasting,' 'Sackcloth,' and 'Ashes': from Nineveh to Shushan," *VT* 69 (2019) 117–34.

Shazar, Zalman
"Jonah: Transition from Seer to Prophet," *DD* 7 (1978) 1–8.

Shemesh, Yael
"'And Many Beasts' (Jonah 4:11): The Function and Status of Animals in the Book of Jonah," *JHebS* 10 (2010) 2–26.

Sherwood, Yvonne
A Biblical Text and Its Afterlives: The Survival of Jonah in Western Culture (Cambridge: Cambridge University Press, 2000).

Eadem
"Cross-Currents in the Book of Jonah: Some Jewish and Cultural Midrashim on a Traditional Text," *BibInt* 6 (1998) 49–79.

Shuchat, Raphael
"Jonah the Rebellious Prophet: A Look at the Man behind the Prophecy Based on Biblical and Rabbinic Sources," *JBQ* 37 (2009) 45–52.

Smelik, K. A. D.
"The Literary Function of Poetical Passages in Biblical Narrative: The Case of Jonah 2:3–10," in Janet Dyk, ed., *Give Ear to My Words: Psalms and Other Poetry in and around the Hebrew Bible: Essays in Honor of Professor N. A. van Uchelen* (Amsterdam: Societas Hebraica Amstelodamensis, 1996) 147–59.

Smith, Morton
Palestinian Parties and Politics That Shaped the Old Testament (Lectures on the History of Religions n.s. 9; New York: Columbia University Press, 1971).

Smith, Raffaela Fazio
Face of Faith: A Short Guide to Early Christian Images, Lulu.com, 2011.

Snaith, N. H.
"The Sea of Reeds: The Red Sea," *VT* 15 (1965) 395–98.

Spiegel, Shalom
The Last Trial: On the Legends and Lore of the Command to Abraham to Offer Isaac as a Sacrifice; The Akedah (New York: Schocken, 1969).

Spier, Jeffrey, ed.
Picturing the Bible: The Earliest Christian Art (Fort Worth, TX: Kimbell Art Museum, 2007).

Steffen, Uwe
Die Jona-Geschichte: Ihre Auslegung und Darstellung im Judentum, Christentum und Islam (Neukirchen-Vlyun: Neukirchener Verlag, 1994).

Idem
Das Mysterium von Tod und Auferstehung: Formen und Wandlungen des Jona-Motivs (Göttingen: Vandenhoeck & Ruprecht, 1963).

Steiger, Johann A., and Wilhelm Kühlmann, eds.
Der problematische Prophet: Die biblische Jona-Figur in Exegese, Theologie, Literatur und Bildender Kunst. Berlin: de Gruyter, 2011.

Sternberg, Meir
The Poetics of Biblical Narrative: Ideological Literature and the Drama of Reading (Indiana Literary Biblical Series; Bloomington: Indiana University Press, 1985).

Stone, Ken
Reading the Hebrew Bible with Animal Studies (Stanford, CA: Stanford University Press, 2018).

Strack, H. L., and Günter Stemberger
Introduction to the Talmud and Midrash (trans. and ed. Markus Bockmuehl; Minneapolis: Fortress Press, 1992).

Strawn, Brent A.
"Jonah's Sailors and Their Lot Casting: A Rhetorical-Critical Observation," *Bib* 91 (2010) 66–76.

Idem
"On Vomiting: Leviticus, Jonah, Ea(a)rth," *CBQ* 74 (2012) 445–64.

Stuart, Douglas K.
"'The Great City of Nineveh' (Jon. 1:2)," *BibSac* 171 (2014) 387–400.

Suriano, Matthew.
A History of Death in the Hebrew Bible (New York: Oxford University Press, 2018).

Sweeney, Marvin A.
"Synchronic and Diachronic Concerns in Reading the Book of the Twelve Prophets," in Rainer Albertz, James D. Nogalski, and Jakob Wöhrle, eds., *Perspectives on the Formation of the Book of the Twelve: Methodological Foundations–Redactional Processes–Historical Insights* (BZAW 433; Berlin: de Gruyter, 2012) 21–34.

Swetnam, James
"No Sign of Jonah," *Bib* 66 (1985) 126–30.

Syrén, Roger
"The Book of Jonah—a Reversed Diasporanovella?," *SEÅ* 58 (1993) 7–14.

Talmon, Shemaryahu
"A Unique Depiction of a Scene from the Book of Jonah in a 13th Century Illuminated Hebrew Manuscript," in Jan Heller, Shemaryahu Talmon, and Hana Hlavackova, eds., *The Old Testament as Inspiration in Culture: International Academic Symposium Prague, September 1995* (Trebenice: Mlýn, 2001) 72–95.

Thomas, Lowell.
Tall Stories: The Rise and Triumph of the Great American Whopper (New York: Funk & Wagnalls, 1931).

Thompson, Stith
The Motif-Index of Folk Literature (6 vols.; Bloomington: Indiana University Press, 1955–1958).

Idem
The Types of the Folktale: A Classification and Bibliography (FFC 184; Helsinki: Suomalainen Tiedeakatemia, 1973.

Thordarson, Thorir
"Notes on the Semiotic Context of the Verb *niḥam* in the Book of Jonah," *SEÅ* 54 (1989) 226–35.

Tiemeyer, Lena-Sofia
"Attitudes to the Cult in Jonah: In the Book of Jonah, the Book of the Twelve, and Beyond," in Lena-Sofia Tiemeyer, ed., *Priests and Cults in the Book of the Twelve* (ANEM 14; Atlanta: SBL Press, 2016) 115–29.

Eadem
"Jonah the Eternal Fugitive: Exploring the Intertextuality of Jonah's Flight in the Bible and Its Later Reception," in Jesper Høgenhaven, Frederik Poulsen, and Cian Power, eds., *Images of Exile in the Prophetic Literature: Copenhagen Conference Proceedings, 7–10 May 2017* (FAT 2/103; Tübingen: Mohr Siebeck, 2019) 255–68.

Eadem
"A New Look at the Biological Sex/Grammatical Gender of Jonah's Fish," *VT* 67 (2017) 317–23.

Tigay, Jeffrey
"The Book of Jonah and the Days of Awe," *CJ* 38 (1985–1986) 67–76.

Trépanier, Benoit
"The Story of Jonas," *CBQ* 13 (1951) 8–16.

Trible, Phyllis
"Divine Incongruities in the Book of Jonah," in Tod Linafelt and Timothy K. Beal, eds., *God in the Fray: A Tribute to Walter Brueggemann* (Minneapolis: Fortress Press, 1998) 198–208.

Eadem
: *Rhetorical Criticism: Context, Method, and the Book of Jonah* (Guides to Biblical Scholarship: Old Testament; Minneapolis: Fortress Press, 1994).

Eadem
: "A Tempest in a Text: Ecological Soundings in the Book of Jonah," in Stephen L. Cook and S. C. Winter, eds., *On the Way to Nineveh: Studies in Honor of George M. Landes* (ASPR Books 4; Atlanta: Scholars Press, 1999) 187–200.

Ussishkin, David
: *The Conquest of Lachish by Sennacherib* (Publications of the Institute of Archaeology 6; Tel Aviv: Tel Aviv University, Institute of Archaeology, 1982).

Uther, Hans-Jörg
: *The Types of International Folktales: A Classification and Bibliography, Based on the System of Antti Aarne and Stith Thompson* (3 vols.; FFC 284; Helsinki: Suomalainen Tiedeakatemia, 2004).

Vanderhooft, David S.
: "Biblical Perspectives on Nineveh and Babylon: Views from the Endangered Periphery," *JCSMS* 3 (2008) 83–92.

van Heerden, Schalk Willem
: "Shades of Green—or Grey? Towards an Ecological Interpretation of Jonah 4:6–11," *OTE* 30 (2017) 459–477.

van Heerden, Willie
: "Humour and the Interpretation of the Book of Jonah," *OTE* 5 (1992) 375–88.

Vanoni, Gottfried
: "Elija, Jona und das Dodekapropheton: Grade der Intertextualität," in Erich Zenger, ed., *'Wort Jhwhs das Geschah . . .' (Hos 1, 1): Studien zum Zwölfprophetenbuch* (Freiburg: Herder, 2002) 113–21.

van Wijk-Bos, Johanna W. H.
: "No Small Thing: 'The Overturning' of Nineveh in the Third Chapter of Jonah," in Stephen L. Cook and S. C. Winter, eds., *On the Way to Nineveh: Studies in Honor of George M. Landes* (ASOR Books 4; Atlanta: Scholars Press, 1999) 218–38.

Vawter, Bruce
: *Job & Jonah: Questioning the Hidden God* (New York: Paulist Press, 1983).

Vermeylen, Jacques
: "Le livre de Jonas: Un écrit politico-religieuse?," *ScEs* 54 (2002) 287–97.

Wagner, S.
: "חוס," *TDOT* 4:271–77.

Walsh, Carey
: "Between Text and Sermon: Jonah 3," *Int* 69 (2015) 338–40.

Walsh, J. T.
: "Jonah 2, 3–10: A Rhetorical Critical Study," *Bib* 63 (1982) 219–29.

Walton, John H.
: "The Object Lesson of Jonah 4:5–7 and the Purpose of the Book of Jonah," *BBR* 2 (1992) 47–57.

Warshaw, Thayer S.
: "The Book of Jonah," in Kenneth R. R. Gros Louis et al., eds., with James S. Ackerman and Thayer S. Warshaw, *Literary Interpretations of Biblical Narratives* (Bible in Literature Courses; Nashville: Abingdon, 1974) 191–207.

Watts, James W., and Paul R. House, eds.
: *Forming Prophetic Literature: Essays on Isaiah and the Twelve in Honor of John D. W. Watts* (JSOTSup 235; Sheffield: Sheffield Academic Press, 1996).

Weber, Beat
: *Jona: Der widerspenstige Prophet und der gnädige Gott* (BG 27; Leipzig: Evangelische Verlagsanstalt, 2016).

Weimar, Peter
: *Eine Geschichte voller Überraschungen: Annäherungen an die Jonaerzählung* (SBS 217; Stuttgart: Katholisches Bibelwerk, 2009).

Weitzman, Steven
: *Song and Story in Biblical Narrative: The History of a Literary Convention in Ancient Israel* (Indiana Studies in Biblical Literature; Bloomington: Indiana University Press, 1997).

Wendland, Ernst
: "Recursion and Variation in the 'Prophecy' of Jonah: On the Rhetorical Impact of Stylistic Technique in Hebrew Narrative Discourse with Special Reference to Irony and Enigma (Part Three)," *AUSS* 36 (1998) 81–110.

West, Mona
: "Irony in the Book of Jonah: Audience Identification with the Hero," *PRSt* 11 (1984) 233–42.

Wilson, Robert D.
　"The Authenticity of Jonah," *PTR* 16 (1918) 280–98, 430–56.

Wilson, Robert R.
　"Jonah in the Biblical Tradition," *Reflection* 76 (1978) 6–8.

Wilt, Timothy L.
　"Jonah: A Battle of Shifting Alliances," in Philip R. Davies and David J. A. Clines, eds., *Among the Prophets: Language, Image and Structure in the Prophetic Writings* (JSOTSup 144; Sheffield: JSOT Press, 1993) 164–82.

Idem
　"Lexical Repetition in Jonah," *JOTT* 5 (1992) 252–64.

Winter, Irene
　"Royal Rhetoric and the Development of Historical Narratives in Neo-Assyrian Reliefs," *SVC* 7.2 (1981) 2–38.

Wiseman, D. J.
　"Jonah's Nineveh," *TynBul* 30 (1979) 29–51.

Wohlgelernter, Devora K.
　"Death Wish in the Bible," *Tradition* 19 (1981) 131–40.

Wöhrle, Jakob
　"A Prophetic Reflection on Divine Forgiveness: The Integration of the Book of Jonah into the Twelve," *JHebS* 9 (2009) 2–17.

Idem
　"So Many Cross-References! Methodological Reflections on the Problem of Intertextual Relationships and Their Significance for Redactional Analysis," in Rainer Albertz, James D. Nogalski, and Jakob Wöhrle, eds., *Perspectives on the Formation of the Book of the Twelve: Methodological Foundations–Redactional Processes–Historical Insights* (BZAW 433; Berlin: de Gruyter, 2012) 3–20.

Wolff, Hans Walter
　Studien zum Jonabuch: Mit einem Anhang von Jörg Jeremias (Neukirchen-Vluyn: Neukirchener Verlag, 2003).

Woude, A. S. van der
　"Nachholende Erzählung im Buch Jona," in Alexander Rofé and Yair Zakovitch, eds., *Isac Leo Seeligmann Volume: Essays on the Bible and the Ancient World* (Jerusalem: Rubenstein's Publishing House, 1983) 263–72.

Yates, Gary
　"The 'Weeping Prophet' and 'Pouting Prophet' in Dialogue: Intertextual Connections between Jeremiah and Jonah," *JETS* 59 (2016) 223–39.

Zakovitch, Yair
　"Did Jonah Proclaim What God Told Him?," in Y. Hoffman and F. H. Polak, eds., *A Light for Jacob: Studies in the Bible and the Dead Sea Scrolls: In Memory of Jacob Shalom Licht* (Jerusalem: Bialik Institute, 1997) 55–60.

Zapff, Burkard M.
　"The Perspective on the Nations in the Book of Micah as a 'Systematization' of the Nations' Role in Joel, Jonah and Nahum? Reflections on a Context-Oriented Exegesis in the Book of the Twelve," in Paul L. Redditt and Aaron Schart, eds., *Thematic Threads in the Book of the Twelve* (BZAW 325; Berlin: de Gruyter, 2003) 292–312.

Zimmerman, Frank
　"Problems and Solutions in the Book of Jonah," *Judaism* 40 (1991) 580–89.

Indexes

1. Passages

This index lists major citations of ancient literature except those from Jonah.

a/ Hebrew Bible/Old Testament

Genesis
1	62, 71
1:9	46, 71
2	118
2:21	42
3:24	102, 109
4:5–6	103, 108
4:6–7	108
4:8	54
4:9	27
4:10	32
4:16	108
5	16
6:4	32
6:6	97
6:7	97
6:11	96, 97
6:13	96, 97
7:12	88
7:17	88
8:21	97
11:2	109
12:10–20	47
13:11	109
14:8	94
14:13	47
15:6	92
15:12	42
16:5	96
18:21	32
19:21	88
19:25	88
19:29	88
19:27–28	108
20:1–18	47
20:2	94
21:17	43
22:4	74
22:15	87
24:3	46
24:7	46
24:23–24	6, 46
24:49	105
25:23	55
26:1–16	47
27:27	99
28:2	32
29:4	6
30:36	87
31:36	103
31:50	99
32:25 [24]	114
33:17	99
37:14	99
37:34	93
39:14	47
41:5	87
41:6	114
41:23	114
41:27	114
41:37	92
41:41	99
41:46	33
42:7	6, 46
42:18	74
43:32	47
44:33	106
45:20	115
49:5	96
50:17	49
50:20	40

Exodus
1:16	47
1:19	47
2:11	114
2:13	114
2:23	33
3:18	56, 87
5:3	56
10:7	92
10:13	114
10:17–20	92
12:1	36
14:11	47
14:12	104
14:16	46
14:22	46
14:31	92
15	76
15:13	64
15:22	56
19:9	92
19:16	74
20:10	100
21:26	114
22:22	32
23:11	100
28:20	33
32	98
32:14	97
32:31	49
32:32	37
33	98
33:1–4	98
33:12	98
34	98
34:6–7	13, 122
34:6	6, 10, 12, 104, 105
39:13	33

Leviticus
12:6	29
12:8	29
13:6–7	87
14:4	113
14:6	113
15:14, 29	29
15:29	28
18:28	65
20:22	65
22:28	100

Numbers
4:8	113
6:10	29
10:33	87
11:10–15	106
11:11	106
11:15	37
14:11	92
14:18	104, 105
14:33	88
16:15	103

Numbers (*cont.*)		10:3	94	19	103
16:30–34	55	10:5	94	20:7	103
16:30	60	10:23	94	25:33	94
19:6	113	12:11	94	26:12	42
20:1–13	103	12:12	94	27:12	92
20:12	92	15:1	45	28	60
21:25	94	15:18	43	30:12	55
21:27	94	18:6	45	31:4	48
22:27–30	100	18:8	45		
22:28	100	19:10–13	15	2 Samuel	
23:11	47			3:31	93
34:11	109	Judges		7:4	27
		1:8	114	12:22	96
Deuteronomy		1:18	43	13:21	103
1:32	92	1:24	105	14:5	43
1:39	117	3:11	88	15:3	99
2:26	94	4:3	95	19:8 [7]	103
9:18	88	4:17	50	20	103
9:25	88	4:21	42	20:6	103
11:6	55	8:1	47	20:10	55
13:16	114	8:11	109	22:5	62
15:9	31	9:24	96	22:7	59, 63
15:12	47	9:54	48		
18:15–22	73	11:19	94	1 Kings	
18:19–22	14 n. 68	11:26	94	1:16	43
19:10	49	15:11	47	6:11	27
19:13	49	18:23	43	6:25	62
20:13	114	19:17	46	7:3	42
21:8	49			7:7	42
22:6–7	100	Ruth		7:37	62
25:4	100	3:14	114	8	63, 64
27:15–26	96			8:29	61
27:25	49	1 Samuel		8:30	60
28:12	96	2	58	8:35	63
28:20	96	2:5	58	8:36	60
28:39	113	2:16	95	8:38	63
29:22	88	4:1	27	8:39	60
32:21	64	4:6	47	8:41–43	64
32:22	62	4:9	47	8:42	61
		5:12	32	8:45	60
Joshua		7:6	93	8:46–51	63
2	50, 92	10:6–10	88	8:49	60
2:3	94	10:20–21	45	9:2	87
2:12	105	13:19	47	10:22	33
5:2	87	14:21	47	10:23	33
6–7	45	14:41–42	45	12:22	27
7:2	109	14:42–43	44	13	107
7:14	45	15:10	27	13:20	27
9	50	18:8	103	16:1	28
10:1	94	18:25	40	17:2	28

17:8	28	8:21–23	93	18:7–8 [6–7]	59
17:9	29			18:7 [6]	59, 61, 63
19	13 n. 61, 106, 110	Nehemiah		18:42 [41]	59
19:1–5	15	1:5	49	22:7 [6]	113
19:4–12	13 n. 61	2:6	88	22:30 [29]	63
19:4	106, 111 n. 1	2:10	103	24:2	62
19:8	56, 88	8:15	109	26:12	65
20:12	109	9:17	104	28:1	63
20:16	109	9:31	104, 105	30:3 [2]	59
21:17	28	11:1	45	30:4 [3]	60, 63
21:27–29	93	13:22	115	30:10 [9]	62
21:27	93			31:7 [6]	64
21:28	28	Esther		31:23 [22]	59, 60
22:22–23	107	3:7	45	34:9 [8]	94
22:34	114	4:1–3	93	38:20 [19]	64
22:49	33	4:1	93	41:5–6 [4–5]	64
		4:14	96 n. 28	41:6 [7]	64
2 Kings		4:16	55	41:7 [6]	64
1:3	29	9:24	45	42:8 [7]	58, 60, 62
5:27	33			42:9–10 [8–9]	64
6:16	43	Job		42:10–11 [9–10]	64
14:25	15, 28, 29	3	106	48:3 [2]	42
14:26–27	29	9:29–31	62	48:8 [7]	33, 41
17:14	92	10:22	60	49:10 [9]	62
18:11	93	10:26	60	54:8 [6]	50, 65
18:19	93	12:20	94	55:7	29
19:1–2	93	16:17	96	55:16 [15]	63
19:1	93	24:16	49	58:3 [2]	96
19:36	31, 94 n. 12	25:6	113	65:2	119
20:3	49	26:6	60	65:14 [13]	63
		27:18	109	66:13–14	65
1 Chronicles		28:9	62	68:23 [22]	60
12:18 [17]	96	34:13 [12]	55	69:2–3 [1–2]	58
24:5	45	37:12	55	69:3 [2]	60
24:31	45	38:17	63	69:16 [15]	60
25:8	45	40:13	62	70:3 [2]	58 n. 29
26:13	45	40:25 [41:1]	72	71:20	63
29:21	111 n. g	42:6	119, 120	72:10	33
				73:27	64
2 Chronicles		Psalms		77:4 [3]	63
2:15	34	3:9 [8]	65	79:1	61
19:2–3	28	5:3 [2]	59	86:15	104, 105
19:7–10	28	5:8 [7]	61	88:3 [2]	32, 63
20:20	92	9:14 [13]	63	88:4–5 [3–4]	59, 60
30:27	63	12:3 [2]	64	88:7–8 [6–7]	58
36:23	46	13:6 [5]	65	88:7 [6]	60
		16:10	63	88:18 [17]	58
Ezra		17:9	58 n. 29	89:9 [8]	46
1:2	46	18:6–7 [5–6]	59	89:31–32 [30–31]	64
3:7	34	18:6 [5]	60	90:5–6	116

Psalms (cont.)		21:16	95	23:14	27 n. d, 33
97	72	22:29	46	25:6–8	55
97:11	71	30:8	64	26:19	63
102:3	32	31:18	94	32:6	43
103:4	62, 63			34:17	45
103:8	104, 105	Ecclesiastes/Qohelet		36:15	93
104:4	63	1:1–11	120	36:16	93
104:14	117	1:2	64	36:18	93
106:17	55	2:17	120	37:8	93
106:32	103	2:26	120	37:10	93
106:45	105	4:7	120	37:37	31
107:10	63	4:16	120	38:3	49
107:18	63	5:12–16	120	38:10	63
107:23	46	5:17–19	120	38:14	29
107:24	60	7:15	120	38:17	62
107:30	48	7:27	99	40–55	16
115:3	50	7:29	99	40:6–8	116
115:17	63	8:14	120	40:22	118
116:3	62	9:1–6	120	41:9	31
116:4	49	9:7–10	120	41:14	113
116:16	49			42:6	31
116:17–18	65	Song of Songs		45:2	63
118:25	49	1:15	29	49:1	31
119:66	94	2:14	29	49:10	114
119:87–88	64	4:1	29	56:6–7	18
119:147	59	5:2	29	59:6	96
120:1	59	5:14	33	59:11	29
121:6	114	6:9	29	60:8	29
124:3	55			60:9	27 n. d, 33
135:6	50	Isaiah		61:5	94
136:26	46	1:8	109	63:7–64:11	59
138:2	61	1:10–15	59 n. 34	66:19	27 n. d, 33
139:15	63	1:15	96	66:24	113
142:4 [3]	63	1:21–31	59 n. 34		
143:3–4	63	2:16	27 n. d, 33	Jeremiah	
143:4–5	63	5:1	106	1:4	28
143:7	63	5:3	106	1:10	99
144:3–4	116	5:17	94	1:11	28
145:8	104	6:1	61	1:13	28, 87
146:4	43	7:15–16	117	2:1	28
147:13	63	7:17	93	2:2	105
		7:20	93	5:28	43
Proverbs		8:7	93	8:19	64
1:12	55	14:9	59	10:9	33
2:12	95	14:11	113	12:4	117
10:5	42	14:13	42	13:3	28, 87
14:29	105	14:15	42, 59	13:4	29
15:18	105	22:20	31	13:6	29
18:9	46	23:1	27 n. d, 33	13:8	28
19:15	42	23:6	33	13:14	115

15:15–18	14	4:6	88	Hosea	
15:18	106			2	46
15:19	14	Ezekiel		2:20 [18]	117
16:1	28	1:16	33	2:21 [19]	105
18:5	28	3:16	28	4:3	117
18:7–10	97, 122	3:18	95	6:2	73, 74
18:7–8	99	3:19	95	7:11	29
18:8	97	3:22	29	11:8	88
18:10	97	6:1	28		
18:11	95	7:16	29	Joel	
18:17	114	8:2	107	1	96
20:8–10	14	10:9	33	1:13	93,
20:13–18	14	12:8	28	1:14	93
20:14–18	106	13:22	95	1:18	95
20:16	88	17:10	114	1:20	95
21:7	115	18	107	2:12–14	6
23:19	40	18:2	107	2:12	93
23:20	40	18:5–24	96	2:13	104, 105
23:22	95	18:25–32	96	2:14	92 n. j, 96
24:4	28	19:12	114	2:17	115
25:5	95	24:1	28		
25:29	31	24:6–13	77 n. 121	Amos	
26:3	95	24:14	115	7:10–17	16
26:15	49	27:5–7	35	8:13	114
28:12	28	27:8	43		
29	28	27:9	41	Micah	
31:27–33	107	27:12	27 n. d	7:14	94
32:18–19	105	27:25	27 n. d	7:18–20	6, 10, 12
33:1	28, 87	27:26	114		
33:19	28	27:27	41	Nahum	
34:9	47 n. 42	27:28	43	1:1	31, 93
34:12	28	27:29	41	1:2	6, 10, 12, 104
35:15	95	28:13	33	1:3	6, 10, 12, 13, 104, 105
36:3	95	32:23	42		
36:7	95	33:14–16	98	1:4	46
36:9	93	36:25–38	107	1:5	13
36:27	28	38:6	42	1:14	13
37:6	28	38:13	27 n. d, 33	2	13
42:7	28	38:21	31	2:8	31
43:8	28			2:9	31
45	115	Daniel		3	13
49:18	88	1–6	21, 69	3:4	13
49:29	31	1:5	54	3:7	31
51:35	96	1:10	54	3:18	93
		1:11	54	3:19	116 n. 37
Lamentations		6:4	43		
2:12	63	6:7	69	Habakkuk	
2:19	63	9:4	49	1:2–4	59
3:54	60	10:6	33	2:17	95
3:55–56	59	12:2	60	3:8	46

Habakkuk (*cont.*)
3:17   117

Zephaniah
2:13   31
2:15   31

Haggai
1:1   28 n. 1
1:3   28
2:6   46
2:20   28

Zechariah
1:1   28
4:8   28
6:9   28
7:4   28
7:7   31
7:8   28
7:13   31
8:1   28
8:20–23   18

Malachi
1:9   6

b/New Testament

Matthew
12   73
12:36–37   73
12:38–42   73
12:40   73
12:41   73

1 Corinthians
15:4   73

c/Apocrypha and Pseudepigrapha

Tobit
2:14   106
14   12 n. 60
14:3–4   20 n. 91

1 Maccabees
10:76   34

2 Maccabees
7:31   47

3 Maccabees
6:5   69

d/Dead Sea Scrolls

1QH^a
11 I, 18   68

4QXII^a 4, 10, 27, 39 n. k, m

4QXII^f 4, 39 n. f

4QXII^g 4, 27 n. a, b, 39 n. g, 53 n. j, 111 n. c

8ḤevXIIgr   4–5

e/Rabbinic Literature and Other Later Jewish Texts

MISHNAH
m. Taʿanit
2:1   99

BABYLONIAN TALMUD
b. Baba Batra
74b   70
b. Berakot
54b   54 n. n
55b-56a   89
b. Sanhedrin
89b   89
b. Šabbat
152a   77 n. 121
b. Taʿanit
16a   99

Genesis Rabbah
5:5   71
24:2   71
54:2   99
56:1   74
91:7   74

Exodus Rabbah
23:6   74
45:1   99

Qohelet Rabbah
5:1   99

Mekilta Pisha
1   37
1:84–87   36 n. 57

f/Greek and Roman Texts

Homer
Odyssey
5:291–96   40

Herodotus
Histories
9.24   95

Virgil
Aeneid
1:81–91   40

2. Authors

Abasili, Alexander Izuchukwu
    117
Abela, A. A.
    13
Abramson, Glenda
    21
Abusch, Tzvi
    113 n. 14, 118 n. 46, 119
Achtemeier, Elizabeth
    17 n. 79, 43 n. 24, 118 n. 45
Ackerman, James S.
    22 n. 110, 116 n. 29, 119
Adelman, Rachel
    71 n. 87
Ahrens, Karl
    112 n. 3
Alexander, T. Desmond
    2 n. 4, 120 n. 55
Allen, Leslie C.
    21 n. 101, 29, 35, 93, 107, 108
Almbladh, Karin
    5, 8, 41, 114, 115
Alter, Robert
    29, 34, 48, 65, 86, 92, 94–95, 104, 106, 108, 112, 115–16, 118
Amit, Yaira
    28 n. 2
Amzallag, Nissim
    65 n. 66
Anderson, Bernhard W.
    107 n. 19

Anderson, Joel Edmund
    12 n. 57
Andrew, M. E.
    21 n. 101
Antwi, Emmanuel Kojo Ennin
    6 n. 23, 7 n. 27
Avi, M.
    34 n. 43

Bakhtin, Mikhail
    22 n. 110
Band, Arnold J.
    22 n. 110
Barbeau, C. Marius
    68
Barré, Michael
    59 n. 32, 64 n. 62
Barrett, Rob
    115 n. 24
Bass, George F.
    35 n. 47
Batto, Bernard
    49 n. 62
Bauer, Johannes B.
    55 n. 8
Baughman, Ernest W.
    67
Beck, Astrid B.
    16 n. 74
Beck, Mordechai
    23 n. 112
Beckwith, Martha
    68
Begg, C. T.
    24 n. 112
Ben-Amos, Dan
    22
Ben Josef, I. A.
    67
Ben Zvi, Ehud
    6 n. 24, 11, 28 n. 1, 116 n. 37
Benoit, P.
    4 n. 11, 14 n. 64
Berger, Benjamin L.
    40 n. 2
Berger, Yitzhak
    11 n. 57, 108 n. 23
Bewer, Julius A.
    16 n. 74, 48 n. 55, 108, 118

Bickerman, Elias J.
    23 n. 112, 32 n. 29, 58 n. 23
Biddle, Mark E.
    12 n. 59
Blank, Sheldon H.
    13 n. 61, 116 n. 29
Bob, Steven M.
    23 n. 112
Bolin, Thomas M.
    31 n. 23, 32, 108, 117
Bosma, Carl J.
    46 n. 40
Botkin, B. A.
    68 n. 79
Bowers, R. H.
    23 n. 112
Bredin, Mark
    20 n. 91
Brekelmans, Chr. H. W.
    108
Brenner, Athalya
    8 n. 33, 57 n. 19
Brody, Aaron J.
    19 n. 89, 41 n. 4, 43 n. 25,
    44 n. 32
Brongers, H. A.
    105 n. 12
Brown, Erica
    14 n. 67, 112 n. 23, 97 n. 31
Brown, William P.
    56 n. 10
Bruckner, James
    18 n. 86, 107 n. 22
Budde, Karl
    16 n. 75
Bührer, Walter
    13 n. 61, 57 n. 20
Burke, Aaron
    34 n. 44, 44 n. 30
Burrows, Millar
    22 n. 110
Buss, Martin J.
    30 n. 16
Butterworth, G. M.
    116 n. 29
Bynum, Caroline Walker
    74 n. 95

Carroll, Robert P.
    41 n. 8

Cartledge, Tony
    65 n. 66
Casson, Lionel
    35 n. 47, 39 n. g
Castillo, Arcadio del
    33 n. 36
Cathcart, Kevin J.
    5, 39 n. d, 40 n. u, 54 n. r
Child, Francis J.
    51
Childs, Brevard
    21 n. 101
Christensen, Duane L.
    3 n. 4, 8 n. 30, 94 n. 17
Claassens, Juliana M.
    17 n. 78
Clark, Gordon R.
    64 n. 61
Clements, R. E.
    17 n. 78, 56 n. 14
Coetzee, Johan H.
    20 n. 90, 115 n. 23
Cohen, Abraham D.
    42 n. 19
Collins, Clifford John
    15 n. 71
Conroy, Charles
    13 n. 63
Cooper, Alan
    32, 116 n. 37, 118 n. 48
Craghan, John F.
    6 n. 23, 14 n. 64, 120 n. 55
Craig, Kenneth M.
    6 n. 23, 58 n. 24, 118
Craigie, Peter C.
    34 n. 41, 64 n. 64
Crenshaw, James L.
    11, 13 n. 61, 96 n. 28
Cross, Frank M.
    4 n. 12, 57, 59–60, 117 n. 43
Crouch, Walter B.
    2 n. 4, 119 n. 50
Croy, N. Clayton
    69 n. 84
Cryer, Frederick H.
    44

Daube, David
    106 n. 14, 122 n. 65

Davies, G. I.
    6 n. 22
Day, John
    8, 16
De Troyer, Kristin
    88 n. 11
Deissler, Alfons
    119 n. 50
Dell, Katherine J.
    6 n. 24, 13 n. 62
Deutsch, Yosef
    23 n. 112
Dietrich, Walter
    10 n. 43
Döhling, Jan-Dirk
    55 n. 3
Doran, Robert
    35 n. 51, 47 n. 44
Dorsey, David A.
    2 n. 4
Dorson, Richard
    68 n. 78
Downs, David J.
    3 n. 5
Dozeman, Thomas B.
    104 n. 6
Drazin, Israel
    23 n. 112, 46 n. 38, 104 n. 4
Dreier, Vjatscheslav
    2 n. 4, 17 n. 79
Duhm, Bernhard
    22 n. 108
Duval, Yves-Marie
    23 n. 112

Edelman, Diana V.
    28 n. 1, 103 n. 1, 119 n. 50
Ego, Beate
    12 n. 60
Elata-Alster, Gerda
    36 n. 57
Emmerson, Grace I.
    120 n. 55
Ephros, Abraham Z.
    22 n. 108
Eynikel, Erik
    56 n. 9, 88 n. 14

Feldman, Louis H.
    24 n. 112

Ferreira, Johan
    18 n. 86, 64 n. 61
Feuillet, A.
    14 n. 64, 18 n. 86
Fewell, Danna
    55 n. 7, 113 n. 10, 119 n. 52
Fincke, Jeannette C.
    40 n. 30
Fischel, Henry
    37
Fischer, Irmtraud
    116 n. 29
Foley, John Miles
    10 n. 48, 80 n. 134
Forti, Tova
    117 n. 43
Frahm, Eckhart
    22 n. 111
Fredriksen, Paula
    47
Freedman, David N.
    41 n. 3, 119 n. 51
Fretheim, Terence E.
    2 n. 4, 6 n. 22, 17 n. 78, 96 n. 27,
    107 n. 22, 116 n. 29, 119 n. 50
Friedlander, Gerald
    52 n. 67, 71 n. 88, 77 n. 118
Friedman, Richard Elliott
    6 n. 23, 88 n. 12
Fuller, Russell
    4 n. 12, 10

Gaines, Janet Howe
    2 n. 4, 3 n. 7, 122 n. 65
Galpaz-Feller, Pnina
    12 n. 57
Garber, Zev
    22 n. 110
Gaster, Moses
    89
Gaster, Theodore H.
    66, 89
Gelston, Anthony
    5
Gese, Hartmut
    58 n. 23
Gevaryahu, Haim
    15 n. 70
Gillmayr-Bucher, Susanne
    119 n. 50

Ginsberg, H. L.
    32 n. 32, 43
Gitay, Yehoshua
    16, 18, 19, 21 n. 96, 30 n. 22,
    88 n. 12
Glasson, T. Francis
    116 n. 37
Goitein, S. D.
    115
Goldman, S.
    23 n. 112
Goldstein, Elizabeth
    34
Golka, Friedemann W.
    6 n. 22, 20 n. 94
Good, Edwin M.
    21 n. 108
Goodhart, Sandor
    122 n. 65
Gordon, Robert P.
    5 n. 19, 13 n. 62, 39 n. d, 40 n. u,
    92 n. j
Goswell, Gregory
    11 n. 53
Grabar, André
    75 n. 110
Green, Barbara
    21 n. 98
Greenberg, Moshe
    56 n. 114, 104 n. 4
Greenfield, Noah
    12 n. 58
Gregg, Robert C.
    23 n. 112, 36 n. 57, 72 n. 91,
    73 n. 93, 76 n. 114, 79 n. 131,
    95 n. 24, 123
Guillaume, Philippe
    10 n. 45, 116 n. 37, 119 n. 54
Gunn, David
    55 n. 7, 119 n. 52

Habel, N.
    30 n. 16
Hacham, Noah
    69 n. 83
Hachlili, Rachel
    75, 78 n. 124
Hallo, William W.
    21 n. 108
Halpern, Baruch
    6 n. 23, 22 n. 110, 88 n. 12

Halpert, Herbert
  68 n. 78
Hamel, Gildas
  4 n. 8, 67 n. 76
Handy, Lowell K.
  4 n. 9, 17, 21, 32 n. 28, 34 n. 44, 41 n. 6, 55 n. 4
Hanson, Paul D.
  59 n. 34
Harris, Robert A.
  123
Hasel, Michael G.
  30 n. 21
Haupt, Paul
  55 n. 4
Heerden, Schalk Willem van
  117 n. 43
Heerden, Willie van
  22 n. 108
Hennessy, T. H.
  18 n. 86
Hesse, E. W.
  3 n. 4, 12 n. 58
Himmelfarb, Martha
  71 n. 90
Holmstedt, Robert D.
  8 n. 33
Hoonacker, A. van
  8 n. 33, 14 n. 64
Hoop, Raymond de
  8 n. 30
Horwitz, William J.
  48 n. 52
Houk, Cornelius B.
  7 n. 26
House, Paul R.
  10 n. 45, 11
Hulbert, John C.
  22 n. 110
Hull, Vernam
  89 n. 16
Hunter, Alastair
  12 n. 57
Hurwitz, Avi
  49

In-Sob, Zong
  89 n. 15
Ingram, Virginia
  22 n. 108

Jellinek, Adolf
  77 n. 121
Jensen, Robin Margaret
  74 n. 98, 75 n. 105, 78, 79 n. 131, 79, 121,
Jenson, Philip P.
  13 n. 62, 16 n. 72, 22 n. 109, 117 n. 42
Jepsen, A.
  92 n. 1
Jeremias, Jörg
  1 n. 2
Johnson, A.R.
  60 n. 36
Joüon, Paul
  39 n. k, 59 n. 30, 108 n. 31

Kadari, Tamar
  23 n. 112, 77 n. 120-21
Kahn, Paul
  122 n. 65
Kaiser, Barbara Bakke
  22 n. 110
Kaplan, Jacob
  34
Kaplan, Jonathan
  21 n. 106, 119 n. 53
Kaufmann, Yehezkel
  15 n. 70
Keil, Carl Friedrich
  117 n. 39, 118 n. 45
Keller, C. A.
  2 n. 4, 14 n. 69
Kidner, F. D.
  112 n. 1
Kikawada, I. M.
  3 n. 4, 12 n. 58
Kim, Hyun Chul Paul
  11-12, 98 n. 32
Kim, Yoo-ki
  108 n. 27
Kiraz, George A.
  5
Kirk, Alexander T.
  8 n. 33
Knight, George A. F.
  6 n. 22, 16 n. 75, 29
Komlós, O.
  23 n. 112, 66 n. 73

Kraeling, Emil G.
  17 n. 84, 20 n. 91
Krantz, E. S.
  41 n. 5
Kravitz, Leonard S.
  23 n. 112
Kristeva, Julia
  10 n. 47
Kugel, James L.
  52, 57 n. 21, 77 n. 119
Kühlmann, Wilhelm
  23 n. 112
Kurichianil, John
  35 n. 54

LaCocque, André
  13 n. 61, 18 n. 86, 22 n. 110, 42 n. 19
LaCocque, Pierre-Emmanuel
  13 n. 61, 18 n. 86, 22 n. 110, 42 n. 19
Lanchester, H. C. O.
  14 n. 68, 117 n. 40
Landes, George M.
  8 n. 36, 21, 56 n. 9, 58, 88 n. 14
Lasine, Stuart
  42 n. 13, 61 n. 44
Lauterbach, Jacob Z.
  37 n. 58
Levine, Baruch A.
  14 n. 65, 119 n. 49
Levine, Étan
  5, 17 n. 78, 92 n. j, 117 n. 37, 119 n. 51
Lichtert, Claude
  1 n. 2, 11 n. 54
Lillegard, David
  119 n. 50
Limburg, James
  2 n. 4, 21, 23 n. 112, 30 n. 22, 35, 44, 60 n. 39, 95-96, 104-5, 109
Lindblom, Johannes
  44 n. 31
Ling, Roger
  74, 75
Liptzin, Sol
  23 n. 112
Liverani, Mario
  30 n. 20

Loader, James A.
    87 n. 4
Lohfink, Norbert
    17, 109
Long, Burke O.
    44 n. 30
Lord, Albert B.
    7
Loretz, Otto
    8 n. 38
Love, Nathan Patrick
    64 n. 63

Machinist, Peter
    66 n. 70, 93 n. 11
Magness, Jodi
    76 n. 13
Magonet, Jonathan
    6 n. 23, 34
Malinowski, Bronislaw
    44
Mann, Steven T.
    56 n. 11
Marcus, David
    87–88, 22 n. 110
Marti, Karl
    8 n. 33
Mather, Judson
    22 n. 110
Mathews, Thomas F.
    121
McCarter, P. Kyle
    58 n. 25
McKenzie, Steven L.
    2 n. 4
Menn, Esther
    57
Meredith, Christopher
    49 n. 56
Milanović, Ljubomir
    79 n. 131
Miles, John R. Jr
    10 n. 48, 22 n. 110, 28 n. 2
Milik, J. T.
    4 n. 11
Millar, Fergus
    37
Miller, Cynthia
    65, 94
Miller, Patrick D.
    33 n. 33, 56 n. 12

Mithra, Sarat Chandra
    101 n. 34
Moberly, R. W. L.
    88 n. 11
Muldoon, Catherine L.
    9 n. 37, 58 n. 26, 112 n. 5,
    116 n. 30
Mulzer, Martin
    9 n. 39, 42 n. 18, 53 n. h, 54 n. n,
Muraoka, Takamitsu
    46 n. 36,
Myers, Jacob M.
    18 n. 86, 21

Narkiss, Bezalel
    73 n. 92, 77 n. 121, 79 n. 131,
    80–81
Nel, Philip J.
    20 n. 90, 109 n. 38
Neusner, Jacob
    70
Niccacci, Alviero
    7 n. 27
Nida, E. A
    116 n. 34
Niditch, Susan
    6 n. 24, 28 n. 2, 44 n. 30,
    59 n. 34, 66 n. 70
Nielsen, E.
    16 n. 76
Nixon, Rosemary A.
    23 n. 112
Nogalski, James D.
    6 n. 22, 9 n. 42, 10 n. 43, 46,
    11 n. 56, 24 n. 112.
Nötscher, Friedrich
    18 n. 86
Nowack, W.
    67 n. 77, 120 n. 55

Oesterley, W. O. E.
    5
Olitzky, Kerry M.
    23 n. 112
Oppenheim, A. Leo
    44 n. 30
Orlinsky, Harry
    32 n. 32
Orth, Michael
    21 n. 108

Parsons, Elsie Clews
    68 n. 78
Patai, Raphael
    41 n. 6
Paul, Shalom M.
    62 n. 53
Payne, David F.
    19 n. 87
Payne, Robin
    35 n. 53
Peleg, Yitzhak
    88 n. 12
Pelli, Moshe
    29 n. 15
Perkins, Larry
    4 n. 10
Perry, T. A.
    88 n. 12, 103 n. 1
Person, Raymond L., Jr
    2 n. 4
Pesch, Rudolf
    8 n. 30
Péter-Contesse, R.
    116 n. 34
Peters, Kurtis
    40 n. 1
Petersen, David L.
    11
Pilpović, Sanja
    79 n. 131
Pope, Marvin H.
    62
Porten, Bezazel
    47 n. 41
Price, B. F.
    116 n. 34
Procksch, O.
    8 n. 33, 107 n. 22
Propp, Vladimir
    2
Pyper, Hugh S.
    57 n. 21

Qimron, Elisha
    104 n. 7

Ratner, Robert J.
    21 n. 102, 36 n. 54, 95 n. 23
Redditt, Paul A.
    9 n. 40, 11 n. 56

Renner, Erich
    18 n. 86
Richter, Wolfgang
    6 n. 23
Robinson, B. P.
    112 n. 61
Robinson, Theodore H.
    18 n. 86, 56 n. 12
Robson, James E.
    6 n. 21
Rofé, Alexander
    8 n. 32, 18 n. 86, 21
Roffey, John W.
    2 n. 4
Römer, Thomas
    11 n. 56
Rosenberg, Joel
    18 n. 86, 119 n. 52, 122
Roth, Leon
    120 n. 55
Rudolph, Wilhelm
    18 n. 86, 28
Russell, John M.
    1 n. 1, 30
Ryu, Chesung Justin
    108 n. 32

Sakenfeld, Katharine
    64 n. 59
Salmon, Rachel
    36 n. 57
Salters, R. B.
    56 n. 13, 58, 109 n. 42
Sargent, James E.
    118 n. 47
Sarna, Nahum
    122 n. 66
Sasson, Jack M.
    2 n. 4, 8–9, 22 n. 110, 28–29, 33, 35, 40–43, 54, 60–61, 63, 87–88, 93–94, 103–4, 108–9, 112, 114–16
Sauter, Gerhard
    65 n. 68
Schart, Aaron
    9 n. 40, 10
Schellenberg, Annette
    17 n. 80, 20, 88 n. 14
Scherman, Nosson
    23 n. 112, 77 n. 120, 114 n. 21

Schmidt, Hans
    60 n. 73, 66, 67 n. 76
Scholem, Gershom
    14 n. 64, 21 n. 104
Schöpflin, Karin
    17 n. 77, 19 n. 88
Schultz, Richard L.
    10 n. 51
Schwab, Eric J.
    14 n. 64, 21 n. 104
Schwartzbaum, Haim
    89 n. 19
Scialabba, Daniela
    39 n. i
Scott, R. B. Y.
    12 n. 60, 73 n. 93
Segert, Stanislav
    7 n. 26
Seidler, Ayelet
    12 n. 57, 93 n. 2
Sellin, Ernst
    66 n. 73
Shazar, Zalman
    19 n. 87
Shemesh, Yael
    12 n. 58, 95 n. 20
Sherwood, Yvonne
    22 n. 110, 23 n. 112, 36 n. 57, 88 n. 14
Shuchat, Raphael
    23 n. 112
Simon, Uriel
    2 n. 4, 21, 42, 48, 87
Simundson, Daniel J.
    118
Smart, James D.
    18 n. 86, 118 n. 45
Smelik, K. A. D.
    57 n. 17
Smith, George Adam
    16 n. 75
Smith, Morton
    17
Smith, Raffaela Fazio
    121
Snaith, Norman H.
    34 n. 45, 41, 62
Sperber, Alexander
    5
Spiegel, Shalom
    74 n. 97

Spier, Jeffrey
    74 n. 98, 79 n. 131, 121 n. 57, 122 n. 64
Stager, Lawrence
    34 n. 46, 41 n. 7
Steffen, Uwe
    23 n. 112, 67 n. 75
Steiger, Johann Anselm
    23 n. 112
Stemberger, Günter
    71 n. 87, 74 n. 96
Sternberg, Meir
    35 n. 53
Stone, Ken
    95 n. 21
Strack, H.L.
    71, 74 n. 96
Strawn, Brent A.
    2 n. 4, 44 n. 32, 65 n. 68, 112 n. 6
Struppe, Ursala
    7 n. 27, 116 n. 37
Stuart, Douglas K.
    21, 28–29, 31 n. 27, 42, 58, 87–88, 92, 104, 106, 108, 112
Sweeney, Marvin A.
    10 n. 43, 47, 88, 106, 113, 118
Swetnam, James
    73 n. 93
Syrén, Roger
    21

Talmon, Shemaryahu
    77 n. 120
Thomas, Lowell
    68 n. 78
Thompson, Stith
    36, 51, 66–68, 110
Thordarson, Thorir
    105 n. 10
Tiemeyer, Lena-Sofia
    12 n. 57, 19 n. 88, 55
Tigay, Jeffrey H.
    19 n. 87, 32 n. 32, 122
Tov, Emanuel
    5 n. 13
Trépanier, Benoit
    14 n. 64, 21 n. 104
Trible, Phyllis Lou
    5 n. 15, 7, 9 n. 39, 16 n. 75, 21, 22 n. 110, 34, 46, 87, 95 n. 21, 96, 109, 114

Tucker, W. Dennis, Jr.
  8 n. 33, 29, 41, 47, 49, 63, 65,
  94–95, 105, 109, 114

Ulrich, Eugene
  4 n. 12
Ussishkin, David
  1 n. 1
Uther, Hans-Jörg
  66

Vanderhooft, David
  93 n. 9
Vanoni, Gottfried
  13 n. 61
Vaux, Roland de
  4 n. 11
Vawter, Bruce
  13 n. 61
Vermeylen, Jacques
  18 n. 86

Wagner, S.
  116 n. 29
Walsh, Carey
  31 n. 23, 95 n. 21
Walsh, J.T.
  57 n. 16
Walter, Donald M.
  5 n. 20
Walton, John H.
  33, 43, 92, 114 n. 14
Warshaw, Thayer S.
  116 n. 29
Watts, John D. W.
  2 n. 4, 67 n. 75
Weber, Beat
  2 n. 4, 58 n. 27
Weimar, Peter
  2 n. 4, 7, 18 n. 86, 119 n. 49
Weiser, Artur
  120 n. 54
Wellhausen, Julius
  16 n. 75
Wendland, Ernst
  32 n. 28
West, Mona
  21 n. 95
Wilson, Robert D.
  14, 55 n. 4, 56 n. 13, 107 n. 21

Wilt, Timothy L.
  6 n. 21, 35 n. 52
Winter, Irene
  30
Wiseman, D. J.
  88
Wohlgelernter, Devora K.
  106 n. 14
Wöhrle, Jakob
  10, 11 n. 55
Wolff, Hans Walter
  1 n. 2, 21 n. 108
Woude, A. S. van der
  8 n. 32, 18 n. 86
Wuk-Bos, Johanna W. H.
  21 n. 108, 87 n. 7

Yates, Gary
  14 n. 69
Youngblood, Kevin J.
  2 n. 4

Zakovitch, Yair
  88 n. 14
Zapff, Burkard M.
  11
Ziegler, Joseph
  5 n. 16
Zlotowitz, Meir
  23 n. 112, 77 n. 120, 114 n. 21
Zuckerman, Bruce
  22 n. 110

3. Subjects

Aaron, 36, 55, 75
Abraham, 13, 47, 64, 72, 74, 75, 92, 102, 105
Achan, 45
Adding style, 7, 57, 59, 109, 112
Ahiqar, 36
Alexis, 35
Amos, 17, 28
Animals, 54, 66, 94–95, 98, 99, 100–101, 117
Anti-Judaism, 107, 118
Appropriations, 23 n. 112, 69, 73 n. 92
Aquileia, 75, 76 n. 115, 78, 79, 121
Aramaic, 42, 43, 46–47, 49

Aramaism, 42, 43, 94 n. 16
Ashurbanipal, 30
Authorship, 15, 17

Baal, 46, 55
Balaam, 47, 100–101
Beit-Guvrin, 75, 76 n. 115, 78

Canaanite epic, 55
Comedy, 22, n. 110, 69

Daniel, 21, 71, 75
David, 37, 41, 42, 92, 96, 103
Death, 42, 48, 52, 55, 59–60, 113–15
Debates with deity, 102–5, 115
Deep, 60
Deities, 6, 19, 40, 43 n. 25, 50
Deuteronomistic History (DtrH), 15–16, 27, 29, 119 n. 50
Divination, 44–45
Dove, 29

Ecology, 62, 100, 114–15, 117–18
Eleazar, 69
East, 3 n. 5, 30, 41, 102 n. 1, 104, 108 n. 23, 109, 111 n. i, 113–14
Elephantine, 47
Eliezer of Beaugency, Rabbi, 123
Elijah, 13, 15, 28–29, 35, 48, 70–71, 106, 114
Emotions of the Deity
  Anger, 13, 95–96, 104–5
  Compassion, 6, 12, 19 n. 87, 90, 99, 104–5, 107, 112, 115, 119, 120, 123
  Favor, 12, 64, 98
  Forgiveness, 1, 3–4, 16, 17, 19 n. 87, 37, 59, 81, 96, 98–99, 107, 119, 122–23
  Loving-kindness, 64, 105, 116
  Mercy, 12 n. 59, 21 n. 101, 64, 100, 104
  Pity, 98, 100, 115–16, 118
  Repentance, 1, 3, 10–11, 17 n. 78, 19 n. 87, 44 n. 32, 73–74, 77 nn. 120–22, 90, 92–93, 95, 97–100, 107, 109, 113, 119 n. 49, 122–23
  Wrath, 6, 30, 44, 47, 49–50, 95
Endymion, 79, 112, 120–22

Enuma Elish, 62
Esarhaddon, 30
Esther, 12 n. 57, 21, 31 n. 23, 45, 69, 93 n. 2, 107
Evil, 6, 27 n. b, 31–33, 44, 45, 90, 92, 94 n. 17, 95–100, 103, 105–7, 113, 123

Fasting, 12 n. 57, 70, 93, 98–99, 101
Fear, 6, 14, 19, 41, 46–47, 49, 50, 66, 68, 87, 92, 103, 104
Fish, 3 n. 5, 22 n. 110, 34, 54–56, 58, 60, 65–81, 87–88, 112–13, 115 n. 23, 121, 123
Folklore
  Animal folklore, 14 n. 64, 66, 68, 71, 100–101
  Comparative folklore, 27, 36, 50, 51, 66, 68, 89–90, 110
Format, 7, 59

Genre, 1, 4 n. 9, 5, 15, 16, 17 n. 84, 20–22, 27, 56, 64, 71, 78, 118
Gideon, 47

Habakkuk, 14, 28
Hades, 53 n. g, 59
Haggai, 28
Heracles, 56
Herodotus, 95
Hezekiah, 27, 49
Hosea, 28
Ḥuqoq, 76–78, 82
Hut, 108–10

Idols, 39 n. d, 64
Inanna, 56
Irony, 43 n. 24, 65 n. 68, 90, 94 n. 16
Isaiah, 9, 16, 27, 32
Ishmael, Rabbi, 36

Jaffa/Joppa, 34, 70
Jeremiah, 9, 13 n. 61, 14, 15, 17 n. 84, 29–30, 35, 37, 97, 99, 106, 107, 115, 116 n. 29
Jeroboam II, 15, 24 n. 112, 28–29
Jerusalem, 10, 17, 34, 40 n. u, 61, 63, 70, 89, 94, 95, 109
Jesus, 73, 75–76, 78–79, 121

Jewish medieval illustrations, 80–85
Jewish/Rabbinic interpretations of Jonah, 23, 36–37, 41 n. 6, 51–52, 55 n. 5, 69–73, 98–100, 122–23
Joel, 10, 12 n. 59, 13, 14, 28, 113 n. 13
Job, 13, 32, 72, 80, 90, 102, 106, 107, 115, 119, 120
Johanan ben Zakkai, Rabbi, 51, 70
Jonah and Judaism, 17, 23 n. 112, 71–72, 122–23

King of Nineveh, 32, 93, 100
Korah, 72, 103

Lachish, 1, 94, 95
Lament, 1, 3–4, 6, 7, 13, 14, 20, 34, 49–50, 54–57, 60–66, 106, 108, 123
Leviathan, 55, 66, 70, 72–73, 79 n. 130
Linguistic register, 5, 7 n. 26, 7–8, 46 n. 36, 54, 56–57, 59, 60, 65
Literary forms, 13, 20, 21, 22 n. 110, 49, 56
Lots, 19, 44–45, 51,

Malachi, 10
Micah, 10, 12 n. 59, 28
Midrash, 12 n. 59, 16, 36–37, 52, 55 n. 5, 71–73, 77, 99–100, 123
Mosaics, 74–79, 82–83, 120–21
Moses, 13, 14, 16, 30, 35, 37, 47, 55, 75, 92, 97–99, 102, 103, 104, 105, 106
Mosul, 30
Mot, 55
Mourning customs, 12 n. 59, 57, 93, 95, 98–99, 101

Nahum, 10, 12 n. 60, 13–14, 21 n. 108, 28, 30 n. 22, 93, 105 n. 9, 116 n. 37
Natural imagery, 40, 50, 69, 95, 112–13, 114, 116,
Nineveh, 30–31, 33, 79 n. 131, 87–89, 109, 116–17, 123
Ninevites, 92, 98–100, 106, 108 n. 32, 115–17, 122

Phalanthus, 67

Phoenician, 34, 41, 46
Pirqe de-Rabbi Eliezer, 51–52, 70–73, 76–77, 123
Poetry and prose, 7–9, 50, 56, 58, 59, 64
Poseidon, 40
Prayer, 6 n. 23, 9, 20, 32, 39 n. d, 49, 51, 56–58, 63–64, 72–73, 81, 104, 123
Primeval Ocean, 50, 56, 58, 60–62
Prophecy, 14 n. 68, 19 n. 87, 21 n. 108, 88–90, 93, 110
Prophet, 2, 4, 9–10, 12–16, 20, 28–29, 37, 61, 74, 87, 88 n. 14, 89, 105, 107–8, 118–19
Pseudo-Philo, 123

Qînâ, 57, 60
Qiqayon, 112, 112 n. 6

Recurring vocabulary, 6, 87
Red Sea, 33 n. 36, 54 n. m, 76
River, 53 n. j, 58 n. 25, 60, 66,
Runaway servant, 3–4, 35–36

Sackcloth, 91 n. g, 93–95, 99–100
Sacrifice, 37, 40 n. u, 48, 50–51, 65, 67, 69, 77, 117 n. 43, 122 n. 65
Samson, 47, 48
Saul, 41, 42, 45, 48, 60, 88, 103
Sea, 6, 27 n. d, 34–35, 37, 40–41, 43 n. 25, 46, 48–52, 54–58, 60, 66–69, 105
Seafaring
  Captain, 39 n. g, 42–43, 77
  Cargo, 34, 41
  Ship, 34–35, 39 n. c, 41–43
    Sailors, 40–41, 43 n. 25, 44 n. 32, 45–46, 47, 48 n. 55, 49, 64, 67, 70, 77–80
Sennacherib, 1, 30, 31, 69
Sheol, 34, 42, 53 n. g, 55–56, 58–60, 63, 72
Sleep, 6, 19, 39 n. e, 42–43, 68, 120
Storm, 13, 34, 40–41, 45, 48, 50–51
Structural approaches, 2–7
Synagogue, 71, 76, 82, 122

Tarentum, 67
Tarshish, 27 n. d, 33–34, 41, 104, 114

Telemachus, 35
Temple, 12 n. 57, 17, 54 n. k, 61, 63, 72, 73
Text-critical considerations, 4–5, 27, 39–40, 53–54, 86, 91–92, 102, 111
Thompson Motifs, 36, 51, 66–68, 110
Tiamat, 62
The Twelve, 9–12, 13 n. 63, 105

Typological language, 62, 64, 69, 105

Underworld, 42, 55–56, 59–60, 62–63, 66, 72

Violence, 32, 91 n. h, 95, 96–97, 100
Visual art, 76–85
Vow, 49, 50, 65, 73

Worldview, 62, 119 n. 50

Wind, 13, 39 n. a, 40, 45, 104, 111 n. i, 114
Worm, 111 n. f, 113–14

Yom Kippur (Day of Atonement), 122–23

Zephaniah, 14, 28, 30 n. 22
Zeus, 120

Designer's Notes

In the design of the visual aspects of *Hermeneia*, consideration has been given to relating the form to the content by symbolic means.

The letters of the logotype *Hermeneia* are a fusion of forms alluding simultaneously to Hebrew (dotted vowel markings) and Greek (geometric round shapes) letter forms. In their modern treatment they remind us of the electronic age as well, the vantage point from which this investigation of the past begins. The Lion of Judah used as visual identification for the series is based on the Seal of Shema. The version for *Hermeneia* is again a fusion of Hebrew calligraphic forms, especially the legs of the lion, and Greek elements characterized by the geometric. In the sequence of arcs, which can be understood as scroll-like images, the first is the lion's mouth. It is reasserted and accelerated in the whorl and returns in the aggressively arched tail: tradition is passed from one age to the next, rediscovered and re-formed.

> "Who is worthy to open the scroll and break its seals. . . ."

Then one of the elders said to me

> "Weep not; lo, the Lion of the tribe of David,
> the Root of David, has conquered,
> so that he can open the scroll and its seven seals."
> Rev. 5:2, 5

To celebrate the signal achievement in biblical scholarship which *Hermeneia* represents, the entire series will by its color constitute a signal on the theologian's bookshelf: the Old Testament will be bound in yellow and the New Testament in red, traceable to a commonly used color coding for synagogue and church in medieval painting; in pure color terms, varying degrees of intensity of the warm segment of the color spectrum. The colors interpenetrate when the binding color for the Old Testament is used to imprint volumes from the New and vice versa.

Wherever possible, a photograph of the oldest extant manuscript, or a historically significant document pertaining to the biblical sources, will be displayed on the end papers of each volume to give a feel for the tangible reality and beauty of the source material.

The title-page motifs are expressive derivations from the *Hermeneia* logotype, repeated seven times to form a matrix and debossed on the cover of each volume. These sifted-out elements will be seen to be in their exact positions within the parent matrix.

Horizontal markings at gradated levels on the spine will assist in grouping the volumes according to these conventional categories.

The type has been set with unjustified right margins so as to preserve the internal consistency of word spacing. This is a major factor in both legibility and aesthetic quality; the resultant uneven line endings are only slight impairments to legibility by comparison. In this respect the type resembles the handwritten manuscripts where the quality of the calligraphic writing is dependent on establishing and holding to integral spacing patterns.

All of the typefaces in common use today have been designed between AD 1500 and the present. For the biblical text a face was chosen which does not arbitrarily date the text, but rather one which is uncompromisingly modern and unembellished so that its feel is of the universal. The type style is Univers 65 by Adrian Frutiger.

The expository texts and footnotes are set in Baskerville, chosen for its compatibility with the many brief Greek and Hebrew insertions. The double-column format and the shorter line length facilitate speed reading and the wide margins to the left of footnotes provide for the scholar's own notations.

Kenneth Hiebert

Category of biblical writing, key symbolic characteristic, and volumes so identified.

1
Law
(boundaries described)
  Genesis
  Exodus
  Leviticus
  Numbers
  Deuteronomy

2
History
(trek through time and space)
  Joshua
  Judges
  Ruth
  1 Samuel
  2 Samuel
  1 Kings
  2 Kings
  1 Chronicles
  2 Chronicles
  Ezra
  Nehemiah
  Esther

3
Poetry
(lyric emotional expression)
  Job
  Psalms
  Proverbs
  Ecclesiastes
  Song of Songs

4
Prophets
(inspired seers)
  Isaiah
  Jeremiah
  Lamentations
  Ezekiel
  Daniel
  Hosea
  Joel
  Amos
  Obadiah
  Jonah
  Micah
  Nahum
  Habakkuk
  Zephaniah
  Haggai
  Zechariah
  Malachi

5
New Testament Narrative
(focus on One)
  Matthew
  Mark
  Luke
  John
  Acts

6
Epistles
(directed instruction)
  Romans
  1 Corinthians
  2 Corinthians
  Galatians
  Ephesians
  Philippians
  Colossians
  1 Thessalonians
  2 Thessalonians
  1 Timothy
  2 Timothy
  Titus
  Philemon
  Hebrews
  James
  1 Peter
  2 Peter
  1 John
  2 John
  3 John
  Jude

7
Apocalypse
(vision of the future)
  Revelation

8
Extracanonical Writings
(peripheral records)

אל תפרד
די להוה
אנה נתן לך ברי
די אנתתך ואנון
יהבו לי כסף
די אנה יהבת לה
ואף על ספר
אנתתא די לקחת
ברתי אחתך